D1219093

ESENIN: A LIFE

Esenin, 1923.

ESENIN
A Life

by
GORDON MCVAY

ardis/ann arbor

ISBN: 0-88233-182-5

For my mother and my father

ACKNOWLEDGEMENTS

I wish to record my special gratitude to the friends and acquaintances of Sergei Esenin, who talked to me about the poet: †Petr Chagin, Alexandra Esenina, Ryurik Ivnev, †Sergei Konenkov, †Alexei Kruchenykh, Avgusta Miklashevskaya, †Lev Povitsky, Ilya Shneider, and Nikolai Stor (in Moscow); Anna Nikritina and Vsevolod Rozhdestvensky (in Leningrad); †Georgy Leonidze (in Tbilisi); and Alexander Kusikov (in Paris).

I am indebted to several Soviet archives and manuscript departments: the Central State Archive of Literature and Art, Moscow; the Institute of Russian Literature, Leningrad; the Institute of World Literature, Moscow; the Manuscript Department of the State Saltykov-Shchedrin Public Library, Leningrad; and the State Literary Museum, Moscow.

I am also grateful to Professor R. H. Freeborn and Professor P. F. Yushin for their advice, and to Anne Charvet, Douglas McVay, and my wife, for their helpful suggestions.

All the translations in the text are my own, unless otherwise indicated. Selected source notes for each chapter are given at the back of the book, together with a general bibliography.

G. McV., Norwich

INTRODUCTION

"Sergei Esenin is the most popular and most widely read poet in Russia."
(Alla Marchenko, *The Poetic World of Esenin,* Moscow 1972)

Sergei Esenin led a short and turbulent life, which quickly passed into legend and myth. Dylan Thomas, who resembled him so much, once wrote: "No-one can deny that the most attractive figures in literature are always those around whom a world of lies and legends has been woven, those half mythical artists whose real characters become cloaked forever under a veil of the bizarre.

"They become known not as creatures of flesh and blood, living day by day as prosaically as the rest of us, but as men stepping on clouds, snaring a world of beauty from the trees and sky, half wild, half human..."

Esenin has been compared with Robert Burns and with Rimbaud, and most of all, with François Villon; yet such is his complexity that he has also been characterised as the "Don Quixote of the village and the birch-tree," and even likened to St. Francis of Assisi. He has been called a poet of death, and a poet of eternal youth.

Sergei Esenin lived in an extraordinary historical period, during the years before and after the October Revolution. Yet, although he should undoubtedly be seen within the framework of his times, his individual psychology seems at least as influential in the development of his life.

His biography is mirrored, too, in his poetry, which has intense emotional power and apparent sincerity. Esenin's poetry appeals to millions. He poses and solves no great questions; he tells about his life and land, at times cheerfully, more often elegaically.

This book seeks to understand some aspects of his elusive personality, as seen in his life and poetry.

CONTENTS

ESENIN: A LIFE

Chapter One: Childhood and Schooldays (1895-1912)

Sergei Esenin was born on October 3, 1895 (September 21, according to the pre-Revolutionary calendar). He described himself thus: "The son of a peasant of the Ryazan province, Ryazan district, from the village of Konstantinovo. My childhood was spent amidst the fields and steppes."[1]

In his various brief autobiographies, written mainly from 1922-25 (V, 7-24), Esenin always began with a reference to his peasant origin. The first fifteen years of his life—until his initial visit to Moscow in 1911—passed in the seclusion of central Russia, and it was from the rural landscape and way of life that he drew inspiration throughout his short poetic career.

The wooden huts of the ancient village of Konstantinovo sprawled out along a wide straight track above the steep hilly right bank of the river Oka.There were six or seven hundred huts, with about two thousand people, and the village stretched on and on. In summer the peasant women milked the cows, tended the sheep and pigs and lit the stoves, whilst the men and boys looked after the horses and gathered the harvest in the fields. There was the beauty of the meadows and the wide Oka, but also the misery of heavy labour and poverty. The peasants' land was divided into small strips, the soil was not rich, and many peasants had to seek extra work in Moscow or Petersburg. By contrast the estate of the local landowner, with its large garden of lilac and jasmin bushes surrounded by a high wooden fence, seemed like a fairy-tale to the youngsters of the village.

The Esenins had lived in Konstantinovo for several generations. On December 15, 1871, Nikita Osipovich Esenin, the grandfather of the poet, bought some land which was made out to his lifelong possession and that of his heirs, and built there a hut and cattle-shed. Nikita Osipovich was nicknamed "Monk" because of his piety. In his youth he had intended to enter a monastery, but at the age of twenty-eight he married a sixteen-year-old girl, Agrafena Pankratievna. The nickname "Monk" stuck, however, to the Esenin family—the poet's sisters recall that right up to Sergei's death they were hardly ever called "Esenin."[2]

Nikita Osipovich was literate, sober, and respected in the village where for many years he was the village elder and the owner of a small grocer's shop. He died in his early forties (about 1887), leaving his wife with several young children, one of whom, Alexander (b.1873), was to be the father of the poet. Agrafena Pankratievna tried to look after her children by taking in lodgers—artists working in the eighteenth-century village church which stood opposite the Esenins' hut, and itinerant monks. But her life was hard, and when Alexander finished the village-school, he was sent to work in Moscow. At the age of about eighteen he married Tatyana Fyodorovna Titova, a local village girl who was only sixteen, and returned to Moscow almost immediately, leaving his wife with her mother-in-law. Sergei, the future poet, was born a few years later. It appears that from the beginning his parents did not live in harmony. When Sergei was born, and then baptised, his father remained in Moscow.

Some mystery surrounds the early marital strife between Sergei Esenin's parents. One explanation is that Tatyana and her mother-in-law got on badly—Tatyana had to work for Agrafena's lodgers, Alexander Esenin sent money to his mother but not to his wife, and when Alexander's brother married, this new daughter-in-law became Agrafena's favourite. Moreover, the Titovs, led by Tatyana's father, Fyodor, shunned the Esenins. "Grandfather quarrelled with the Esenin family before my mother's marriage," remarks Ekaterina, the elder of the poet's sisters. It has been suggested that perhaps the Titovs wanted their daughter to marry a richer man.

Undoubtedly Tatyana Fyodorovna remained on bad terms with her mother-in-law for many years. "As a result," writes Ekaterina, "Sergei felt out of place at the Esenins' and was always drawn to his other grandmother—Natalya Evteevna Titova." During this period, maintains the poet's younger sister Alexandra, "our mother gave birth to two children:Sergei and another child, who soon died. When Sergei was about four, my mother took him with her and returned to her father's house," at Matovo at the other end of the village.

Esenin mentions the move in his autobiographies, but very

briefly, and claims he was only two when he went to live with his mother's parents (V, 7, 20). Only once does he offer an explanation for this event, in his first fullish autobiography of May 1922: "From the age of two, because of my father's poverty and the large size of our family, I was given to my rather rich maternal grandfather to be brought up" (V,7). Since the tone of the 1922 autobiography tends elsewhere to be tongue-in-cheek, the expression "because of ...the large size of our family" might contain a veiled reference to some occurrence. I. G. Atyunin, who in 1926 collected biographical information about Esenin from the villagers of Konstantinovo, writes: "For four years Sergei grew in peace and quiet, the pet and general favourite of the family, when suddenly the happy family home was destroyed. His mother gave birth to a second son (who soon died)–his father did not recognise this son as his own and separated from Tatyana, or rather cast her and Sergei to the mercy of fate, and stopped sending money from Moscow." A second cousin of the poet, N. I. Titov, claims that soon after her marriage Tatyana Fyodorovna secretly gave birth to a *daughter*, who was promptly sent elsewhere. According to N. I. Titov, Sergei was born some time *after* the birth of this daughter. Some scandal of this kind evidently lay behind Tatyana's departure from the Esenin household. It would also explain why she was not given a warm welcome home by her father, who took in Sergei, but sent his daughter to town to earn bread for herself and her son.

Tatyana Fyodorovna Esenina, born Titova (1875-1955), Esenin's mother, was clearly a woman of strong personality. Esenin was to write tenderly of her in several of his poems, perhaps partly because she came to symbolise for him his lost village childhood. Alexandra describes her as "graceful, beautiful, the best singer in the village; she played the accordion, and knew how to organise merry games." Her beauty no doubt attracted the village lads–there is a photograph of her in old age, apparently with a son (not Sergei) in uniform; perhaps this was a further illegitimate son?[3] Alexandra pictures thus her mother, who must have been about forty at the time: "She wasn't strict, though she never caressed us like other mothers: she wouldn't stroke us on the head or kiss us as she considered this would make us spoilt. When I had children of my own, she often said: 'Don't kiss the baby, don't pamper him. If you want to kiss him, then do so when he's asleep.' She wouldn't give a beggar more than ten copecks, but if a man suffered a real misfortune she was one of the first to help him... She was full of pity for orphans. For years and years she lived only with little children and she had fallen into the habit of talking aloud. This amused our father and sometimes he said to me jokingly: 'Go and listen to mother talking to the devil.' Our mother was illiterate. If we read a work of fiction she used to say: 'So you're looking at rubbish again! You should read a worthwhile book, not that nonsense'." Yet Tatyana Fyodorovna, for all her illiteracy, told fairy stories and sang songs which included some set to the words of Pushkin, Lermontov and other poets. Even when an adult, Sergei used to love the heartfelt, simple singing of his mother. Tatyana Fyodorovna knew a wide range of Russian folk songs and romances, and on the eve of church festivals she sang all kinds of melodies from the church service. Esenin was fortunate to grow up in an atmosphere of song, and at the end of his life, when he dedicated a poem to his younger sister, it came as no surprise that he began it with the lines: "Sister, sing me the song that old mother / Used to sing us in days long ago..." (III, 184). Esenin's mother was very much a peasant woman, superstitious (she once said she had seen a magician all in white), and full of religious exclamations when she spoke in her simple Ryazan dialect. She believed that by praying she would persuade God to forgive all her sins, but that God would not forgive the sins of those who had insulted her. She gave birth to many children, who nearly all died in infancy, and she looked on in bewilderment as her son became a famous Russian poet.

Her husband, Sergei's father, was absent almost all the time in Moscow. In his childhood Alexander Nikitich Esenin (1873-1931) had a fine treble voice, and when he was eleven or twelve was even offered a place in the choir of Ryazan Cathedral; but instead he was sent off to Moscow as an apprentice in a butcher's shop, where he spent more than thirty years of his life right up to the Revolution. Only when meat was scarce during the Civil War and the shop closed, did he return to live in Konstantinovo, a man sick with asthma and pathetically ignorant of peasant labour. Alexander Nikitich seems at first sight a sad, unhappy figure. Certainly, after the Revolution, he felt out of place in the village.

The young Esenin does not appear to have been very fond of his parents. In childhood he took his mother for a stranger when she visited her father where Esenin lived. "For five years," writes Ekaterina, "our mother did not live with our father, and all this time Sergei was brought up by his grandfather and grandmother Natalya Evteevna. Not seeing his mother and father, Sergei became used to thinking of himself as an orphan, and at times it was more hurtful and painful for him than for a real orphan." Nikolai Sardanovsky, who knew Esenin well as a child, writes: "Sergei didn't show particular love for his family and was continually arguing with his father and mother, despite the fact that his parents were higher than the usual peasantry and could of course direct him only for the better... We all as outsiders formed the opinion that Esenin was unfriendly towards his family..." Sardanovsky's only qualification of this statement is that Esenin always spoke well of Alexander Nikitich. Though never close to his father, he appears to have respected him. Whereas his mother was shrewd and firm, Esenin's father seemed more of a wistful and dreamy nature.

Esenin's sisters, Ekaterina and Alexandra, were not born until 1905 and 1911, and so it was as a lone child that he grew up in the house of his maternal grandparents. These grandparents inevitably played a more significant role in his upbringing than did his parents.

Esenin's grandfather, Fyodor Andreevich Titov (1846-1927) was a "character." Ekaterina Esenina describes him as "clever in conversation, merry in festivities and cruel in wrath." He was "handsome, of good height, with grey pensive eyes and fair hair... He was one of four sons of a Konstantinovo peasant... In our region which has little land, many people took on seasonal work... Early in spring grandfather used to journey to Petersburg and sail on his barges till late in autumn." At the peak of his prosperity Fyodor Andreevich possessed no fewer than four barges of his own. On returning home the peasants thanked God by buying icons for the church, and then the merry-making would begin. "Barrels of ale and wine were rolled up to our house and drunken guests fell asleep in the grass near grandfather's house... Grandfather sang well and appreciated good singing. The festivities lasted a week or even longer, then became rarer, on market days, and by the end of winter ceased completely for lack of money. Then dark days descended upon the Titov house." Grandfather became niggardly, economising on salt, matches and kerosene. At times he acted cruelly: "He made his youngest son miserable for life. This youngest son, Pyotr, was frightened by a cow when a child and as a result was very nervy. Once, when he was eight or so, he was naughty and, fearing grandfather's wrath, didn't go to apologise but hid in the attic. Grandfather flew into a rage at such impertinence. He himself went up into the attic, found his son cringing there in a dark corner, took him by the collar and hurled him downstairs." This son was the epileptic uncle Esenin mentions with affection (V, 16) in one of his autobiographies. At the age of thirty, during an epileptic fit, Pyotr dropped a samovar of boiling water on himself, and died a few days later from these burns.

Grandfather Fyodor was a man of contrasting moods. He could also be extremely gentle. "Few women know how to handle children as he did," writes Ekaterina. "He adored tucking a child up in bed, telling fairy-tales and singing."

There seems to be some confusion about how rich Fyodor Titov was. In his autobiographies Esenin referred to his grandfather as "rather well-to-do" (V, 7, 20) or "well-to-do" (V, 23), and after his death the poet was frequently reviled as of kulak origin, far removed from ordinary peasantry. Yet Ekaterina now claims that their grandfather was a poor man when Sergei went to live with him: "At that time, as far as Petersburg was concerned, everything was finished for grandfather. Two barges had been destroyed by fire, and the rest sank during floods. Grandfather was ruined as his barges were not insured."

Whether or not he was wealthy–and at all events he was one of the richer peasants–Fyodor Andreevich stood out by his erudition in biblical matters. He was evidently an Old Believer, a schismatic. Esenin recalls: "Grandfather used to sing old songs to me, such protracted and mournful songs. On Saturdays and Sundays he told me the Bible and the Holy Story" (V, 16). In 1924 Esenin wrote: "In my early verse one can see the very strong influence of my grandfather. From the age of three he drummed into my head the ancient patriarchal Church culture" (IV, 225-226). Thanks to his grandfather, Esenin learnt to read at a very early age, and grew up surrounded by an atmosphere of books, chiefly religious. Moreover, apart from the Bible, it appears that young Sergei became acquainted with Russian religious paintings. The critic Lvov-Rogachevsky comments that "not for nothing did he copy Novgorod icons from childhood," and Esenin's last wife, S. A. Tolstaya, explaining some primitive drawings of animals and noses which Esenin made towards the end of his life, says: "He told me that he was sent to study at some icon-painter's and this man made him draw noses. This was so boring that Sergei left him and thus learnt to draw nothing but noses." Esenin's words to the critic Ivan Rozanov are frequently cited: "Looking back on all my past life I have to say that no one had such significance for me as my grandfather. I owe him the most of all...He was a remarkable man. A vivid personality, a broad nature...My grandfather had a fine memory and knew by heart a great number of folk songs, but chiefly oral religious poems *(dukhovnye stikhi)."*

"Intelligent, industrious and, above all, very kind and sensitive," writes Atyunin, "he loved and pampered Sergei, evoking the child's fervent love and affection." Visiting the village in 1926, the poet Nasedkin was struck by the "unusually rich language, not devoid of the powers of imagery," of Esenin's grandfather, then a man eighty years old. Assiduous reader of the Bible, and a man who had known wealth, Fyodor not surprisingly grumbled when the Communists came to power: "The godless ones, it's because of them that the Lord is punishing men." With kindly humour Esenin depicts him in one poem as lamenting the closing of the village church—his grandfather says that now he goes furtively into the forest and prays to the aspen trees, for "maybe that will do" (III, 15).

While his grandfather's role should not be exaggerated, it does appear that he greatly influenced the young Esenin, and that many of Fyodor's traits are seen in the poet's character. Esenin wrote of his grandfather: "He was a great one for drinking and living it up. . ."

Esenin's maternal grandmother, Natalya Evteevna Titova, was a complement to her husband—together they are reminiscent of the grandparents in Gorky's *Childhood.* She is portrayed as all softness, piety and superstition. "My grandmother loved me with all her might, and her tenderness knew no bounds" (V, 21). "At home she gathered all the cripples who in Russian villages sing religious poems from 'Lazarus' to 'St. Nicholas' " (V, 11). The poet repeatedly recalls being "dragged around from one monastery to another" by his grandmother (V, 11, 22; IV, 226).

She used to send little Sergei to church, and wash his hair—neither of which he enjoyed, so he later claimed. She also told him fairy tales, and Esenin states that this first aroused in him his creative instinct: "I began to write poetry early in life. My grannie was the cause of this: she used to tell me fairy tales. Some stories with poor endings didn't satisfy me, and I revised them in my own way" (V, 11). He says he began to write verse at the age of eight or nine, although this verse was as yet imitative of the folk works he had heard.

The young poet was clearly spoilt, and he recalled: "I grew up mischievous and disobedient. I was a fighter" (V, 11). In manhood he remembered in a poem "the feelings of childish years"—the peasant hut, the smell of tar, the icon-lamp and the white snowstorm: "... I'm nine years old./ My grannie, couch and cat.../ And grannie sings/ A sad song of the steppes,/ And over her yawning mouth/ She makes the sign of the cross" (III, 130-131).

Esenin's second cousin, N. I. Titov, maintains that Natalya became addicted to vodka: "His grandmother's habit of drinking vodka turned into alcoholism. . . Vodka brought grandmother to an untimely grave." Natalya Evteevna died in about 1911.

Thus Sergei Esenin, child of a temporarily broken marriage (his mother even asked for a divorce, but her husband refused her request) grew up in his grandparents' home. Yet his brief autobiographical accounts, and even more his poetic evocation of that period, do not indicate an unhappy childhood. His grandparents had three grown-up sons, and Sergei grew up in their company. In his autobiographies he recalls many a lively escapade he had with them:

> My uncles were mischievous wild lads. When I was three and a half they put me on a horse without a saddle and at once set it off in a gallop. I remember being mad with fear and holding on tight to its mane. Then they taught me to swim. One uncle (uncle Sasha) took me in the boat, pushed off from the bank, divested me of my clothes and threw me into the water like a pup. I splashed about clumsily and afraid, and whilst I was nearly choking he just shouted: "Heh, you swine! What good will you be?" "Swine" *(sterva)* was for him a term of affection. Later, when I was eight, I often served another uncle as a retriever, swimming in lakes to fetch ducks they had shot. I was very well schooled in climbing trees. None of the boys could compete with me. . . (V, 7-8; see also V, 20).

On a more academic level, Esenin says that when he was five one uncle taught him to read (V, 24), although his grandfather presumably played a major role in this, teaching him to read the scriptures.

Sergei was proud of being a ring-leader—he stresses this latter distinction in several autobiographies (V, 8, 20) and recollects it in a later poem (II, 107). His seems to have been a healthy, rough early life—"My childhood was like that of all village lads" (V, 23).

Only at times can the embryonic poet be sensed—as when he recalls the following detail of watering horses in the Oka: "At night when it is calm weather the moon stands still in the water. When the horses drank I thought they would drink up the moon at any moment, and I was glad when it sailed away from their mouths with the ripples of water" (V, 16). This detail later recurred to him in a poem: "Today the horses have drunk/ The moon from the water" (II, 66).

■

From 1904 until 1909, Sergei Esenin—like his father before him—attended the Konstantinovo Primary School, a one-storeyed wooden building in the centre of the village. In about 1904 he returned with his mother to the Esenin household, but he was evidently unhappy there. Ekaterina writes that, whereas "the laughter and jokes of young people" reigned in the Titov household, the Esenins kept a "strict and gloomy home."

In his autobiographies Esenin is silent about his primary school days. His classmate Klavdy Vorontsov–an orphan brought up in the house of the village priest–recalls that Sergei was one of the ablest pupils, the best fighter, and an enthusiast for all kinds of games, such as checkers, hide-and-seek and skittles. Vorontsov continues in his unsophisticated style: "Whilst liking various games and fights at the same time he liked books even more, already by the last class of village school there was a mass of books he had read and if he saw someone with a book he had not read he would not be parted from it, he cheated or offered sweets for it, and he got it in the end." Atyunin observes: "His only fault at school was that he was spoilt and mischievous. In all the pranks of the pupils Sergei was the instigator and leader; his comrades jokingly called him 'the general' *(voevoda)*. Despite the fact that Sergei grew up weak and puny, no one dared to insult him and he used to engage everyone in violent fistfights." Atyunin also says that Sergei was a religious fanatic for a brief while, but at the age of ten or eleven he already used to abscond from church and go to play instead. (Such episodes are related with pride in Esenin's autobiographies, V, 8, 11-12.) Instead of buying communion bread at the church, he bought tobacco.

Esenin's misbehaviour at primary school was such that in the third form he was kept down for a second year for "naughtiness." In May 1909 he finished the school, with excellent in all subjects: Scripture, Russian reading, Church Slavonic reading, History, Geography, Arithmetic, Written exercises in Russian, and Calligraphy. To mark his completion of the four-year village school he was given a certificate, which hung for many years in a glass frame on the wall of the Esenins' hut.

In a poem written in 1918 he was to claim:

I only finished
    The parish school,
I only know the Bible and fairy tales,

I only know that oats sing in the wind...
And on holidays
How to play
The accordion. (II, 46)

But in fact Esenin—unlike most of the children in Konstantinovo—did not merely "finish the parish school." One of the teachers there had been the local priest, Ivan (Ioann) Smirnov, a man widely respected by the villagers. Whilst at school, Esenin and several classmates had frequented Father Ivan's house, and Esenin had borrowed books from him. Smirnov insisted that he should continue his studies, as did Sergei's grandfather, Fyodor Titov—although Klavdy Vorontsov asserts that Esenin's "father and mother were vehement opponents of this good cause." Nonetheless, after a family meeting for which Esenin's father came to Konstantinovo for a few days before returning to Moscow, it was decided that he should study at the Church boarding school at Spas-Klepiki.

Spas-Klepiki, then a good-sized trading village, lay some twenty miles to the north-east of Konstantinovo, amidst the Meshchera forests, a region of peat bogs and lakes. A. Kan, special correspondent of the local newspaper *Ryazan Life (Riazanskaia Zhizn')*, painted a gloomy picture of life there in August 1912. The village was fairly wealthy, but its inhabitants tolerated dirt and drunkenness. A. Kan described the village fair: "The inns were literally besieged. . . At times it was difficult to meet a sober person. . . It was more like a congress of alcoholics than a fair. Dreadful." After the revels, stagnation returned: "The holidays have passed. Boredom reigns. There is no cause for jollity. . . 'Here one could take to drink,' say some people. . . Here there is quiet and calm." There was also a second-grade boarding school, opened in 1896, which trained teachers for parish schools. As the fees were moderate, the Esenins could afford to send their son there. In his autobiographies Esenin passes over this stage in his life, apart from a few brief comments. "When I grew up they very much wanted to make a village teacher of me, and so they sent me to a closed church-teachers' school, on completing which, at the age of sixteen, I was to enter the Moscow Teachers' Institute. Fortunately this did not happen.

Methodology and didactics had so sickened me that I would have nothing of it" (V, 8). "At home they wanted me to be a village teacher. When they took me off to school, I felt terribly homesick for my grandmother and once ran home all the hundred or more versts.[4] At home they gave me a good scolding and took me back" (V, 12).

The school at Spas-Klepiki—which Esenin attended from 1909 till 1912, spending his holidays at home—was directed by church authorities and had a bias towards religious education, but it provided also for a traditional range of secular subjects. An exercise-book of a fellow-pupil of Esenin's, Ivan Smirnov (no relation, presumably, of the Konstantinovo priest), contains a timetable which shows that there was no teaching of foreign languages, but there were four hours of Church Slavonic, the language used in the Holy Scriptures and Church Services.[5] Esenin, indeed, singles out these lessons in an autobiography: "My studies left no trace in me apart from a sound knowledge of the Church Slavonic language. That is all that I retained" (V, 16). Scripture comprised a thorough study of all aspects of the Church. Smirnov's notebook lists some twenty-three items, including the Catechism, Church Service, Holy history of the Old and New Testaments, brief information about Church history, prayers, rites, officiates at the Church Service, sacred vestments, the Liturgy, Eucharist, Church festivals, the all-night Vigil, baptism and anointment, penitence and matrimony. The extracts of Russian literature copied out by Smirnov include Lermontov's "Angel," the letters of Tatyana and Onegin from Pushkin's *Eugene Onegin,* and some verse by Nikitin. The literature teacher at Spas-Klepiki was especially fond of Pushkin, and recalls reading the whole of *Eugene Onegin* and *Boris Godunov* to his pupils.

The daily regimen at Spas-Klepiki could be dispiriting. There were lessons all day and there was homework in the evening; there were prayers at morning and night; and permission was required to go outside the school, for instance to the weekly market. Smirnov jotted down in his notebook: "I am in my final year at the Spas-Klepiki second-grade school. Dirt, dust, meagre food contribute to nothing but various illnesses." As for Esenin, Atyunin writes: "The supervision of his educators weighed oppressively on this child of Nature and in 1911 he wrote to Klavdy Vorontsov: 'Soon it will be June, yet I'm still languishing in this prison and can't wait to be let out'." In a poem of about 1912, entitled "My Stay at School" ("Prebyvanie v shkole"), the poet lamented: "I am suffocating within these cold walls,/ Dampness and dark without a gleam of hope,/ There is a smell of mould in the sad corners–/ That is the fate of a poet..." (V, 206).

Yet there was some consolation. Esenin made a very close friend in Grigory (Grisha) Panfilov, a boy two years his senior to whom he wrote many frank letters, chiefly after leaving school (V, 27-50). There seems to have been a kind of informal "Panfilov circle," where the boys discussed literary and other matters.

The teacher of Russian language and literature at the school, Evgeny Mikhailovich Khitrov, has left the following schoolmasterly description of Esenin:

> His outstanding characteristic was his joie de vivre, gaiety and even a certain tendency towards excessive laughter and frivolity. He wasn't noted for assiduousness and dependability in the execution of his schoolwork, and by his continual conversations and laughter during lessons he frequently provoked dissatisfaction and rebukes. But one couldn't be angry with him. His jokes were harmless, and moreover he disarmed all reproaches by his candid repentance and the general softness and tenderness of his character. In addition, to atone for his misdemeanour, he would go and bring you one of his poems to read through.

Although Khitrov professes that "one couldn't be angry" with Esenin, his classmates scarcely shared this view. They often complained that Esenin would not let them concentrate on their work, and fistfights usually ensued. For his part, Esenin was not exactly enamoured of some of his classmates. "Yakovlev's a real idiot," he wrote. "And Kalabukhov's the height of rottenness and nastiness" (V, 28). The schoolmaster wrily recalls that "there is no photograph of the finishing pupils of 1912. The class was not united in friendship."

Young Sergei was happy to spend his summer holidays in the open. He was brave at catching crayfish with his bare hands, and he also liked catching ducklings. "In summer he was hardly ever at home," writes Vorontsov. "As soon as he had eaten he was off." He was fond of swimming and playing at cards; in winter he liked skating. One of his childhood friends, Nikolai Sardanovsky, attempts to describe Sergei's appearance at this time:

> Outwardly he did not produce the impression of a sick person, although in his youth he had had trouble with his lungs. His face was of a pleasant, even, white colour. His eyes were light-blue and beautiful. He always looked you straight in the eyes. His mouth was very mobile and expressive. His hair was soft and perfectly fair. . . He was continually gesticulating with his hands, in a peculiar, angular way. . . He always dressed neatly and even with some pretension at dandyism. Being a thoroughly good-looking boy, he used to tell me that he attached no importance to his outer appearance. . . Somewhat later he admitted that a person's appearance is of no small importance.

Sardanovsky alludes to some early lung-infection Esenin had suffered.[6] Yet ill-health did not prevent the handsome peasant lad from having an eager eye for the village girls. Sardanovsky writes: "As far back as I can remember him he was extremely amorous and fond of women." Atyunin relates:

> He used to love listening to the accordion and because of this often attended the so-called *ulitsy* and *posidelki* [parties for village youth in autumn and winter]. In his escapades he didn't favour any particular girl, he liked chasing the women but usually without discriminating. Only later did he take a strong fancy to a friend's sister, Anna Sardanovskaya, and there was an occasion when one summer evening Anna and Sergei, both very red, ran into the priest's house holding hands and asked a nun there to part them, saying: "We love one another and give our word to marry in the future. Part us, and may whoever betrays his word and marries first be beaten with brushwood by the other."

Atyunin continues that Anna was the first to break this vow, and upon hearing of her marriage, Esenin sent her a letter via the nun, requesting the nun to beat Anna with all her might. In the poem "My Life" ("Moi put' "), written several years later, Esenin was to recall how he fell madly in love at the age of fifteen, and had

"sweet thoughts" of marrying "this best of girls" when he became old enough (III, 132).[7]

As for his early verse of 1910-12, it is difficult to determine which love poems are spontaneously felt, and which are in emulation of folk poetry. At all events, they show a healthy sensuousness, and tell of how, for instance, the poet will kiss the girl until he is drunk, and crumple her like a flower, whilst she will throw back the silk of her bridal veil and let him carry her drunk into the bushes till morning (I, 68).

In all this Esenin would have been little different from many other peasant boys—but there was one thing which distinguished him from others. He was a poet.

He himself connects his first conscious efforts at writing poetry with his last year or so at Spas-Klepiki: "I began to write early, when I was about nine, but I link my conscious creativity with the age of sixteen or seventeen" (V, 9, 21). Sardanovsky remembers that Esenin began to show him his verse in 1910: "To my complete surprise he had quite a lot of poems." But Sardanovsky was not awestruck at this: "His aspiration and ability to write verse in no way raised him in our eyes, whilst his arrogance in evaluating his talent and his continual conversations about his poetry bored us." Sardanovsky adds in extenuation that "all this was a result of his extreme desire to receive as quickly as possible a great deal of information about literature in general, and opinions about his own verse in particular." Nor did Esenin receive encouragement for his poetic endeavours when he was on holiday at home. When he read by lamplight at night and wrote, his mother, illiterate and superstitious, warned him of the dire consequences of such folly—he would go mad, she said.

It was his literature teacher at Spas-Klepiki, E. M. Khitrov, who acted as the main judge and supporter of his poetry. At Khitrov's request Esenin wrote out ten of his best poems in two small notebooks and gave them to his teacher. Khitrov recalls that, especially in Esenin's final year at school, he began to show signs of greater profundity. However, Sergei was not alone among the schoolboys as a would-be poet. His chief rival was a certain Egor Tiranov, whom Esenin clearly resented as a challenger to

his crown. In a letter to Panfilov he inveighs, in an unspecified context, against Tiranov's "stupid pranks" which "I regard as madness. He often raves" (V, 28). Throughout his life Esenin was to resent all poets who rivalled his fame—and Tiranov, though modest in talent, may be regarded as the first thus to arouse his wrath.

What themes inspired the young Esenin, what aspects of life? Nikolai Sardanovsky declares:

> I think that Esenin did not particularly like peasant labour. . . One summer we were cutting his grandfather's hay on the public meadows. For a peasant boy he worked poorly and we ate wild strawberries more than we mowed. It was very noticeable that during the harvesting Seryozha fell into special rapture at the charms of the rural landscape. The beauty of the sunsets on the meadow, the grandeur and languor of nights in the fields, and especially the strenuous work and exuberance of the peasants working in the meadow. . .—all this attracted him so much that he always spent this time in field-huts with the peasants, although he himself did not need to work there.

Esenin had the leisure to read and dream, to write and play—he wrote in a letter in July 1911, "They've all gone hay-making. I'm at home. There's nothing to read, so I play croquet" (V, 27).

When Sergei began to show his verse to his friend in 1910, Sardanovsky recalls: "His poems were chiefly descriptive and partly lyrical in content. Descriptions of rural Nature comprised the main theme of his poems." Meanwhile, Khitrov viewed his pupil's first efforts with the solemn eye of a schoolmaster: "His poems were short, at first all on the theme of love. This did not particularly please me."

In his last months in Spas-Klepiki Esenin wrote a cycle of poems, entitled "Sick Thoughts" ("Bol'nye dumy," V, 202-210). Here there is very little about Nature or love, but a vast amount of misery, gloom, boredom and tears. Feeling sure that "there is no happiness in life," the young poet "repents" of his "sins before God" and longs for oblivion "in the cold grave." These poems are immature and imitative, but they demonstrate that the sixteen-year-old Esenin was very unhappy, at least in his poetic posture.

The weak cycle of "Sick Thoughts" was written by 1912. Clearly Esenin's poetic gifts were undeveloped at that time, and it is extremely unlikely that his quatrain "There where the cabbage-patches..." ("Tam, gde kapustnye griadki...," I, 64), was really written in 1910. Esenin himself made this claim in 1925, but there is evidence to suggest that the quatrain may date from 1919-20. In the draft version of his poem "The Hooligan" ("Khuligan," II, 97-98), written in 1919-20, after line 12 Esenin has crossed out the following stanza: "Then you see how a maple, without looking round,/ Comes out to the glass of the swamps/ And a dear little maple sucks/ The wooden udder of its mother." ("Togda vidish' kak klen bez ogliadki/ Vykhodit k steklu bolot/ I klenenochek malen'kii matke/ Dereviannoe vymia soset.")

In May 1912 Esenin completed his stay at the Spas-Klepiki school and was given the title of "elementary school teacher." Academically, he finished rather above average. His final marks show that he was awarded "excellent" (5) in four subjects—Russian language, Russian history, Geography and Handwriting—and "very good" (4) in Scripture, Church history, Church singing, Arithmetic, Geometrical drawing, Didactics, and elementary practical knowledge of Hygiene. Surprisingly, his only less distinguished mark was a "good" (3) in Church Slavonic language—the very subject of which he later claimed a "sound knowledge" from school.

The teachers turned a blind eye on his mischief and awarded the future "hooligan" an "excellent" for behaviour.

Esenin, c. 1913.

Chapter Two: A Peasant Youth in Moscow (1912-15)

Upon leaving Spas-Klepiki, Esenin felt no desire to become a teacher. He spent some weeks in the village of Konstantinovo, fishing, reading and writing. Then, at about the end of July 1912, he took up permanent residence in Moscow, working at first in the same butcher's shop as his father. Until March 1915 he lived, with few interruptions, in Moscow, experiencing a succession of jobs—the only time in his life that he was to earn money by means not connected with his poetry. These years may seem the most prosaic in the poet's life, years of routine labour and membership of minor organisations. He soon left Krylov's butcher's shop in Shchipok Street—he is said to have opposed the insistence of the owner's wife that he should stand up whenever she entered the room. It seems that Sergei then went to work at a bookshop, a natural choice for a sixteen-year-old interested in poetry. For several months he worked at this bookshop, until its liquidation early in 1913 left him unemployed and caused him to return for a while to Konstantinovo. In March he was back in Moscow, where he became a worker at Sytin's printing works. The factory of I. D. Sytin published a quarter of all the books produced in Russia, and Esenin worked, first in the dispatch office, and then as a copy holder *(podchitchik,* a proof reader's assistant). His work there could "considerably satisfy his thirst for verse," writes Sardanovsky—here he saw the very process of how a book is made and admired in particular the elegance of Balmont's manuscripts. In addition, he was thrown into contact with industrial workers for the first time in his life—the workers at Sytin's printing house took an active part in several strikes. Although it has been claimed that Esenin greatly enjoyed working at Sytin's factory, it is perhaps more probable that the peasant lad felt confined there. In about May 1914 he made an abortive effort to flee from Moscow to Yalta in the south, telling his father "I find conditions oppressive where I am treated as a thing, I don't want to be dependent on anyone." Nonetheless, as his father had forewarned, he soon found himself penniless and had to return to Moscow, and thence to Konstantinovo. In September 1914 Sergei became a proofreader *(korrektor)* at the printing house of Chernyshev-Kobelkov. In December of the same year he left the printing house and from that time dedicated himself completely to the writing of poetry.

For an understanding of Esenin's emotional and mental state during his first years in Moscow–especially during 1913–the group of letters he wrote to his Spas-Klepiki friend, Grisha Panfilov, are of particular value (V, 27-50). The bustle of Moscow, with its grimy merchant quarters, was bound to shock a peasant lad, raised in placid idleness and educated amidst rural solitude. The monotony of mercenary routine repelled him at once; if at Spas-Klepiki he had read Tolstoy, then his latent idealism could blossom here in the city. His first letter from Moscow (V, 29) is full of such terms as "to feel oneself," "to awaken," not to be like a soulless animal. He decided to write a declarative work, an inextant verse drama entitled *The Prophet,* expressing his disdain for the "blind crowd, steeped in vice." He vowed to Grisha: "I shall be firm as my prophet, draining the poison-filled glass for the sake of sacred truth, in consciousness of the noble feat" (V, 32).

Panfilov was evidently surprised at his friend's new awakening. Early in 1913 Esenin admitted: "Yes, I have changed. I have changed in my views, but my convictions are the same and have taken even firmer root in the depths of my soul" (V, 32). He describes some of these changes, and although he does not mention Tolstoy, the influence is unmistakable: "On personal conviction I have stopped eating meat and fish; fanciful things such as chocolate, cocoa and coffee I no longer use and I don't smoke tobacco. This has been going on for nearly four months. I have also begun to regard people differently. Genius for me is a man of word and deed, such as Christ. All the others, apart from Buddha, are merely sinners who have fallen into the abyss of debauchery" (V, 32). Judging Man by this moral criterion, Esenin expressed "sympathy" for such people as Belinsky and Nadson: "But I don't recognise the likes of Pushkin, Lermontov, Koltsov, and Nekrasov. You are of course aware of the cynicism of A. P(ushkin), the coarseness and ignorance of M. L(ermontov), the falsehood and cunning of A. K(oltsov), the hypocrisy, excitability, gambling and oppression of his serfs of N. N(ekrasov), whilst Gogol is the very apostle of ignorance, as Belinsky called him in his famous letter" (V, 32-33).[1]

Alone in a strange milieu, and scarcely on speaking terms with his father, Esenin took consolation in the Bible and the figure of Christ:

> Grisha, at present I'm reading the Gospels and finding a great deal that's new for me. . . Christ for me is perfection. But I don't believe in Him as others do. They believe through fear of what shall be after death. But I believe in Him purely and holily as in a man endowed with a bright mind and noble soul, as a model of the practice of love for one's neighbour.
>
> Life. . . I cannot understand its meaning, and yet nor did Christ reveal the purpose of life. He showed only how to live, but no one knows what one can achieve by this. . . Yet all the same, we must know why we are living. I know you won't say: in order to die. You yourself said once: "Nonetheless I think that there is another life after death." Yes, I think so too, but why do we have this life? Why do we live? (V, 35).

A letter dated April 23, 1913 shows a further development in Esenin's ideas during this period. He propounds a belief in moral Man and in universal brotherhood: ". . . *I am you. I am in you, and you are in me.* . . People, look at yourselves, did not Christs emerge from you, and can you not be Christs? Can I with will-power not be a Christ...? Oh, Grisha! How absurd all our life is. It distorts us from the cradle, and instead of truly real people some kind of monster emerges" (V, 39). Not surprisingly, others failed to share his new idealism: "People think me a madman and were going to take me to a psychiatrist, but I sent them all to the devil and go on living, although some people fear to come near me"(V, 40). With his new philosophy of sympathy and understanding for all men, Esenin forgave his detractors and advised Panfilov: "Yes, Grisha, love and pity people, be they criminals and villains and liars, or martyrs and righteous men. . . And love your oppressors and do not put them to shame, but lay bare with kindness the diseases in people's lives. . . *All people are one soul. . .*" (V, 40). No man should envy another, for "I am you and all things accessible to you are accessible to me. . . So that is the enigma of men's lives. . . For all there is one truth: *I am you.* If people understood this, and especially the learned ones, then there would be no bloodshed on earth and brothers would not be the slaves of brothers. . ." (V, 41).

Esenin's philosophising is rare in his writing—at almost no other time did he propound such a general "philosophy of life," however vague and derivative from Tolstoy and the Bible. (The only comparable period in his life is perhaps his religious Utopian reaction to the Revolution, especially in 1918—in, for instance, "The Keys of Mary" ["Kliuchi Marii," IV, 173-201]). The adult Esenin was not an abstract thinker: he felt rather than thought, and when he thought, it was in concrete terms. Only in his adolescence was he so open to the seductive power of the abstract word—and this commitment to an idea was characteristically shortlived. Ivan Rozanov quotes him as saying: "I was soon visited by religious doubts. In my childhood there were sharp transitions: sometimes a prayerful period, then a period of extreme mischievousness right up to the wish to blaspheme and commit sacrilege." This changeability was also to typify his adolescence and manhood.

Esenin's idealism was not confined to theorising and personal morality. Early in 1913 he informed Grisha: "Not long ago I carried out some agitation among the workers with letters. I distributed among them the monthly journal *Flames (Ogni)* which has a democratic tendency. It's a very good journal. . . You must take out a subscription for it. After Easter I will publish some of my things there" (V, 33).

The journal *Flames* which Esenin distributed was a small, poorly printed work, and at the end of its third number in January 1913 its financial position was so shaky that it had to appeal to its readers to attract new subscribers: "Reader friends, propagate the journal *Flames.*" (This may indeed have led Esenin to urge Panfilov to subscribe). However, it ceased publication in March 1913 after its fifth number, and thus Esenin was unable to publish any of his poems in it. The intentions of the editors were serious and honourable—they aimed to satisfy the growing spiritual needs of the new democratic workers by providing them with a varied, readily understandable range of material on literary and social themes. In practice, *Flames* adopted a materialist, anti-mystical, at times pro-Marxist attitude, unmasking poverty and oppression, although of course unable to make any specific call to revolution or the overthrow of the Tsar. Esenin's own views at the time were scarcely "materialistic," but it is significant that he recommended its "democratic tendency."

Later in the year, he became caught up in even more dangerous activity than distributing the journal *Flames.* In September many Moscow workers took part in a one-day protest strike, and shortly afterwards Esenin wrote to Panfilov that "8 comrades have been arrested for recent movements in solidarity with the tramworkers. There is much fuss and one has to bustle about" (V, 43). A long letter to his friend (V, 43-46) shows Esenin's trepidation and distress, although he evidently enjoyed the element of espionage and adventure:

> Dark clouds have gathered over my head, all about there is falsehood and deceit. My sweet dreams are dashed, and all has been borne away by the rushing whirlwind in its nightmarish spiral. . . Fate plays with me. . . I wrote to you: alter your envelopes and handwriting. I am being followed, and the other day my flat was searched. I won't explain everything in a letter, for you can't hide even a pin-head from these pashas and their all-seeing eye. One has to keep silent. Someone is reading my letters, but very neatly, without tearing open the envelope. I ask you once more to avoid all sharp comments in your letters, otherwise it will all end sadly both for me and for you (V, 44).

Esenin's father was clearly anxious for his son's safety, for he also wrote a letter of rebuke to Panfilov (V, 44). Esenin felt depressed and discouraged. Moscow was too cold, soulless and mercenary for the romantic youth. "I am expecting something, I believe and disbelieve in something. The dreams of a holy cause have not been realised" (V, 46). He passes veiled, almost conspiratorial criticism about despotism and the Tsar (V, 47)— Klavdy Vorontsov once made a rather confused comment about Esenin that "the system of the power of the 'Monarchy' did not please him, and so in disputes he always spoke out against religion and in political matters and, to tell the truth, he was always considered irrefutable." Nevertheless, Esenin cannot be called truly politically conscious during this period. His objections to the bourgeoisie and despotism were mainly inspired by idealism and a youthful love of adventure and revolt–he seems to have viewed his cause as a crusade against the forces of darkness. In a letter to Panfilov he resorts to allegory, consoling himself that "the dawn is not far off, and after it the bright day. We shall sit by the sea and await fine weather, some time the stormy waves will abate and we shall be able to sail without fear in a flat-bottomed boat" (V, 47).

Some Soviet critics have exaggerated Esenin's links with the "revolutionary workers." True, in March 1913 a letter fell into police hands, protesting against the policy of the "liquidators," a Social-Democratic faction, in the newspaper *The Ray (Luch),* and supporting the Bolsheviks. This letter was signed by fifty workers of the Zamoskvorech'e region, including Esenin, and the police subsequently investigated the backgrounds of these fifty. On September 23, 1913 there was a large strike in Moscow, in which the workers of Sytin's printing house, including–perhaps–Esenin, took part. In early November 1913 Esenin was systematically followed by spies who in their secret reports referred to him by the code-name "Typesetting" ("Nabor"). Nevertheless, the fact remains that the police found no evidence whatsoever against him. The most that can be said is that Esenin sympathised genuinely, if vaguely, with the oppressed workers. That the secret police should investigate him might well flatter and alarm the young poet, but it tells more about police suspiciousness than about his revolutionary daring. The Russian secret police has always been noted for its enthusiasm.

His links with the workers *might* have proved an event of lasting importance in his life, but in reality the period of his "revolutionary" ardour was clearly as transient as that of his Tolstoyan fervour–hence the almost total absence of social themes in his poetry at this time, and his failure even to mention any early revolutionary involvement in his autobiographies.

When Esenin left Spas-Klepiki at the age of sixteen, his education was inevitably superficial, and in Moscow he sought to put this right. In October 1913 he wrote to Panfilov that, although short of money, he had enrolled in the historico-philosophical section of Shanyavsky University (V, 45-46). The poet regarded this as a biographical fact of great significance, for in his autobiographies he singled out this one event to the exclusion of virtually everything else in his 1912-15 Moscow period (V, 12, 17, 21, 24): "In 1913 I joined Shanyavsky University as an external student. After spending one and a half years there I had to return to the village owing to material circumstances" (V, 17).

Shanyavsky University was a "university for the people," open to anyone over sixteen, without discrimination of sex, nationality or religion. It opened in 1908, and from 1911 was permanently housed in a three-storeyed stone building on Miussky Square. In 1912-13 there were 129 teachers and 3669 students, mainly young people, schoolteachers, office and factory workers. Lectures took place in the evening, between 5 and 10 p.m., in order that people who had to work during the day could be present. Along with other workers at Sytin's printing house, Esenin began to attend, although, it would appear, infrequently. The university's historico-philosophical section provided courses of lectures on such subjects as political economy, medieval history, the history of 18th century France and of 19th century Russia, but Esenin's chief interest lay in the literary courses. In 1913-14 a well known professor, P. N. Sakulin, lectured on the history of mid-19th century Russian literature. His themes included the ideas current in the 1840s; Belinsky's critical works; the "accusatory" ("oblichitel'naia") literature of the 1860s; Nihilism; Chernyshevsky and his novel, *What is to Be Done? (Chto delat'?);* the poetry of the 1860s, including Nekrasov, Nikitin, Maikov, Fet and Polonsky; and the works of Dostoevsky and Tolstoy in the 1860s. Esenin sought out Professor Sakulin, and recited his verse to him. For the second-year students Professor Yu. I. Aikhenvald lectured on Russian literature of the second half of the 19th century, including on the aesthetic and philosophical aspects of Lev Tolstoy's works, and on "populism" in literature, as seen in the works of Nekrasov and Gleb Uspensky. Sardanovsky writes: "While studying at Shanyavsky University, Sergei concentrated his attention exclusively on literature, and he had Aikhenvald's book, *Silhouettes of Russian Writers,* continually at hand."

Esenin's desire to study was evidently great and long-lived. Even as late as mid-1915, after his poetic debut in Petrograd, he intended to "study seriously" at Shanyavsky University (V, 60), although nothing came of his wish. Perhaps he was thinking of the whole of his education, including his irregular attendance at Shanyavsky University, when he later recalled: "I studied a lot, but finished nothing" (V, 24).

His attendance at the University was useful in two ways. Firstly, it gave him a more systematic knowledge of 19th century Russian literature and encouraged him to continue reading a great deal; secondly, it introduced him to some poets of his own age, Semenovsky, Nasedkin, Kolokolov and Filipchenko (V, 21). Of these poets, Nasedkin was to become a close friend, especially towards the end of Esenin's life, when he married Esenin's sister, Ekaterina. The young poets used to meet and discuss, sometimes heatedly, general literary matters and the merits of their own verse. At times Esenin went to the Tretyakov Art Gallery and to the Moscow Arts Theatre (where he saw *The Cherry Orchard)*—although throughout his life he was to remain notably indifferent to all branches of art apart from poetry and folk songs.

At some date, probably between 1912 and 1914, he joined the Surikov Literary and Musical Society, which consisted of "writers from the people." According to a leading member of the Society, Deev-Khomyakovsky, Esenin "arrived from the village with no money whatsoever and came to the poet S. N. Koshkarov-Zarevoy," who was then president of the Surikov group. For a while Esenin lived at Koshkarov's and attended meetings of the Society, which in 1912 was a "most mighty organisation of proletarian-peasant writers," comprising many people close to the Socialist Revolutionaries and Social-Democrats. "The activity of the society was directed not only at discovering writers of natural talent, but also at political work." There were conspiratorial meetings beneath an age-old oak at

Kuntsevo, and:

> . . . There, under the guise of writers' excursions, we first introduced Esenin to the circle of social and political life. There the young poet first recited his verse in public. . . It seemed to us that Esenin would make not only a poet, but also a good public worker *(obshchestvennik).* In the years 1913-14 he was extremely close to the Society's public work, occupying the position of secretary of the Society. He often appeared together with us at evening meetings in workers' auditoria, and carried out tasks which were fraught with considerable risk.

Deev-Khomyakovsky makes the excursions to Kuntsevo sound portentously earnest, but another memoirist is probably nearer the truth, at least as far as Esenin was concerned. Vasily Gorshkov describes an outing to Kuntsevo, allegedly in the early summer of 1912, when Esenin recited his verse with great success:

> That bright and fiery midday Seryozha was especially cheerful. . . He was encircled by people. Girls vied in showering him with questions and requests. They stared at him, not trying to hide from him that he was good-looking, that they liked him for himself and his verse, both as a poet and as a youth. Seryozha was clearly flattered by this first feminine attention. His light blue eyes were aflame and shining, he laughed in unforced merriment, he whirled around and ran barefoot. . . Dear, blue-eyed, golden-haired child!

Esenin had become secretary of the Society by December 1914, at a time when the decision was taken to publish a fortnightly journal, *The People's Friend (Drug naroda).* Esenin was anxious about the publication of the journal, and perhaps recalling his earlier propagation of *Flames,* he even suggested that the Surikov members should disseminate it themselves since money was short. He had written "The Jackdaws" ("Galki") for publication in the first number, but this poem, which is said to have criticised the war, was confiscated in the press and has never been found. Nevertheless, another poem of his appeared in this first number—"Patterns" ("Uzory," I, 99), which reflects the slaughter of war, but in a stylised, ornamental way. The journal *The People's Friend* sounded at times a pan-Slavic and anti-urban note, although its chief and most consistent criticism was of the "bourgeois" intelligentsia and its culture. It advocated above all a uniting of the popular intelligentsia, who as yet exist merely as "cultural lone-wolves" ("kul'turnye odinochki")—only when these lone cells unite will Russia's problems be peacefully solved.

However well-meaning as "public workers," the members of the Surikov Society were mainly mediocre as poets. In 1915 the Petersburg *Monthly Journal (Ezhemesiachnyi zhurnal)*, reviewing their publications, dismissed their literary merits—"not one new, vivid or bold word, not one interesting or even merely independent thought." Esenin was clearly inclined to support this judgment, for in February 1915 he resigned from the editorial board on the question of the quality of the published material. He declared: "We must create a real literary journal. It is not right to print feeble works," and then took his hat and walked out of the editor's office. Arriving in Petrograd in 1915, recalls L. M. Kleinbort, he spoke mockingly and "with peasant cunning" about the Surikov members.

Deev-Khomyakovsky hoped in vain that Esenin would become a "good public worker," for the poet's heart lay elsewhere. By 1914 he was already primarily interested in literature and his own poetic career. He had always read a great deal, at home, at school, and in Moscow, and he had dabbled in verse for many years. Literature, and, in particular, poetry, increasingly became the focal point of his life. In his letters to Panfilov this tends to be obscured by his search for a philosophical and political ideal, but even here there are clues to this underlying current in his life. On his first brief visit to Moscow in 1911 he bought some twenty-five books (V, 27). In Konstantinovo in mid-1912, "I have few books, I've read them all. I took some from Mitka and I've got only eight more to read. . . Please tell me the address of some newspaper and advise me where to send my poems. . . I've destroyed some, corrected others" (V, 28). He sends Panfilov a poem he has written (V, 30-31) and tells of some inextant works he intends to write (V, 32, 36). He buys a volume of Nadson's verse early in 1913 (V, 38) and quotes from various poets—Lermontov, Nikitin, especially Nadson—in his letters. By the end of 1913 he has attempted to publish some verse in a newspaper, and longs to move to the literary centre, Petersburg (V, 48). "One evening I'm sitting, writing as usual and smoking. . ." (V, 49)–such a sentence gives a glimpse of the poet early in 1914. A factory girl recalls that "all his leisure time he used to read, and he spent his wages on books and journals, not thinking in the least how he would live."

Even at school he had held a high opinion of his own verse, and in 1913 or 1914 his desire to be published was at last satisfied. In this, as throughout his life, Esenin showed a tactical mastery of what the public required. Sardanovsky comments: "Naturally he very much wanted to see his poetry in print, but, unable to count on the editors' attention to his more serious poems, he turned quite strategically to children's verse and indeed soon–I think at the beginning of 1914–his first poem was published in a. . . children's journal. . . His delight knew no bounds."

Esenin allegedly gave to his doubting father the first three roubles he earned by his verse, as a proof that poetry also pays. Sergei himself, of course, had no doubt about the intrinsic value of poetry. In 1914, when the workers of Sytin's printing house chaired Maxim Gorky all the way to his car, Esenin was so impressed that he argued that in his opinion "writers and poets were the most famous people in the land."

However "strategically" he may have acted, the children's journals in which Esenin's poems were published in Moscow in 1914 could not fully satisfy his ambitions. Such journals as *Little World (Mirok,* an illustrated monthly for small children, published by Sytin's printing house) and *Little Thawed Patch (Protalinka,* a well-printed illustrated monthly for older children) could serve but as stepping-stones to greater glory. For a while Esenin participated in the thinnish but serious literary monthly *The Milky Way (Mlechnyi Put'),* to which his Shanyavsky University friends Kolokolov and Semenovsky also contributed, but a personal quarrel with a certain Nikolai Livkin soon led to his withdrawal from the journal.

Dissatisfied with his progress in Moscow, the young poet was contemplating a fateful step. Some time earlier he had written to Panfilov: "I am thinking of moving to Petersburg, come what may. . . Moscow is not the nerve-centre of literary development–it takes everything ready-made from Petersburg"

(V, 48). At the end of 1914 he is said to have met some writers from Petersburg, who strengthened his desire to go to the capital. In an autobiography he explained: "At the age of eighteen I was surprised, upon sending my verse to various journals, that they were not printed, and I suddenly descended upon Petersburg" (V, 9). The members of the Surikov Society viewed this move with disquiet. "We consider," writes Deev-Khomyakovsky, "that from this moment Esenin's ruin as a social poet begins. . . He went, not to our friends, but to writers who were then clearly in favour of the monarchy."

Relatively little is known about Esenin's personal relationships during his early Moscow years. By means of their correspondence, Grisha Panfilov had acted from afar as the poet's confidant throughout 1913. Lonely in Moscow, Esenin had as his closest friend a person to whom he could only write. Sergei was an irregular correspondent, and evidently so too was Grisha, yet distance and the passing of time did little to dim the closeness and candour of their friendship. None of Panfilov's letters to Esenin seems to have survived, but from Esenin's letters it is clear that the two youths had much in common–a search for an ideal; a belief in life after death (V, 35); a respect for truth and sincerity (V, 36).[2]

Perhaps Esenin never saw Grisha again after leaving Spas-Klepiki–his letters give no indication of any such meeting–and he was alarmed when Grisha fell ill. At the end of a letter in late January 1914, as if sensing the impending catastrophe, Esenin suddenly broke down in a touching address to his friend: "Somehow I feel sad, Grisha. Things are hard. I'm alone, quite alone, so alone, and there is no one to whom I can lay bare my soul, for the people here are so shallow and coarse. You are far away from me, and one can't express everything in a letter, oh, how I'd love to see you. I grieve deeply at your illness. . . Loving you, S. E." (V, 50).

Far away in Spas-Klepiki, Grisha Panfilov was slowly dying of tuberculosis. Esenin wrote once more to his friend–but on February 25, 1914 the end came. Five days later, Grisha's father wrote a moving letter to Esenin from Spas-Klepiki, telling how his son "closed his eyes, seemed to fall asleep, and passed into eternity":

> . . . It is clear, Seryozha, that you had a genuine sincere friendship. Nearly every day he remembered you, it's a pity, he said, that Seryozha is not near me and I have no one to calm my sorrowful soul. He used to read your letters several times and admire your portrait. Seryozha, he died a martyr, the illness had so dried him up that only skin and bones remained. . . Your letters are all safe, I have collected them in an envelope and sealed it with wax; indeed, all his letters. . . lie locked in a case, as a memory of dear Grisha. Seryozha, the loss of Grisha is painful and unbearable for us. . .

As for Sergei, his friend Sardanovsky witnessed his reaction: "I could see how he grieved very much for one of his friends at the Spas-Klepiki school. . . who died. . . of consumption." Esenin had written to Grisha only a few months before (V, 45): "I often envy your friend Pyrikov. Probably the gods loved him too much, so that they made him die young: how good it must be to set like a star before dawn." Pyrikov, too, had died of consumption.

Grisha Panfilov was not the only person to whom Esenin wrote from Moscow. Alone in the large city, Esenin felt the need for female companionship. Seventeen letters and postcards have recently been published addressed to Mariya Parmenovna Balzamova, a village girl Esenin had met and befriended in Konstantinovo in July 1912, shortly before his departure for Moscow. Balzamova, a few months his junior, went to work as a teacher in a village in Ryazan province, and Esenin's letters to her from Moscow indicate that, in 1912-14, they conducted a kind of long-distance adolescent romance, which was filled with candour and earnest idealism. One letter shows that he and Balzamova had never even kissed one another in Konstantinovo—and the strain of maintaining such a chaste love affair by correspondence led to numerous misunderstandings, before the relationship finally petered out.[3]

Esenin's letters to Mariya Balzamova are an important source of information about his thoughts and feelings during his early Moscow years. In many respects, they corroborate the impression conveyed by his letters to Panfilov: Esenin frequently felt lonely, depressed, even despairing. He had high ideals, including a wish to help the suffering masses *(narod),* yet he soon became bitterly disillusioned by the egoism, sensuality, lust and vulgarity of nearly everyone surrounding him in Moscow. He was extremely sensitive to any unjust or mocking words directed against him—and one letter reveals that, after being taunted in 1912, he even attempted to poison himself by drinking a small quantity of some "essence." This impetuous action resulted in a burnt mouth and aching chest—although another letter shows that this self-destructive impulse was not merely momentary: "I can't imagine what's the matter with me, but if things continue in this fashion,—I will kill myself, I'll hurl myself from my window and smash myself to pieces. . ."[4] Although in several of the letters Esenin describes himself as "pure" and "tender," when wishing to break with Balzamova he denounced himself as a "scoundrel" in a manner which strangely prefigures his late poem, "The Black Man" ("Chernyi chelovek"): "I am worn out, covered in lies and one can even say. . . that I have buried my soul or sold it to the devil—and all for my talent. . ."

Apart from his correspondence with Mariya Balzamova, there is a letter—written some time between 1912 and 1914—which Esenin sent to a certain Lidiya Mitskevich: "Lida! It's a long time since I saw you. I'd like to see you at least one last time. . . I'm completely alone at present and I'd like to talk to you. At least to sigh about the past. . . I'm feeling very depressed—probably as a result of my sickliness. If you can't [meet me] then don't be afraid to refuse. After all you'll lose nothing by it. . . S. A. E."

While working at Sytin's printing house in 1913, Esenin fell in love with a girl some four years older than he, who worked in the correctors' department. A photograph exists of a group of type correctors at the factory. In the back row, arms folded, stands Sergei Esenin, long-haired and elegantly dressed. On the floor sits a pleasant, dark-eyed young woman in a blouse. This was Anna Romanovna Izryadnova. She was entranced by Esenin, whom, as she later recalled, people at the factory had at once nicknamed the "cherub." She describes him with a love which borders on reverence: "He was so pure and bright, his soul was so untouched and good–he was quite radiant." Esenin and Izryadnova began to live together, and in December 1914 or January 1915 their son, Yury, was born. Esenin was thus a father at the tender age of nineteen, but he seems to have regarded his paternal duties very lightly. Some two months after Yury's birth he left Izryadnova, his son and Moscow, and travelled to Petersburg in search of fame and fortune. This was the first instance of how he "scattered" his children "all over the world" (as he lets his mother reproach him in a poem of 1924, III, 66). Only occasionally in 1915 and 1916 did he come to Moscow to visit Anna and his son–but when in Petrograd, recalls L. M. Kleinbort, "he did not say a single word about his wife or child."

Leaving Moscow for Petersburg–as when he had earlier come to Moscow from Konstantinovo–signified the beginning of a completely new way of life for Esenin. Yet, whereas memories of Konstantinovo were to haunt him all his life, he seems to have broken with Moscow without regret. He abruptly left his father, his family and the "public workers," and journeyed to Petersburg in pursuit of glory.

Esenin, c. 1915.

Chapter Three: First Steps to Fame (1915-16)

Esenin's arrival in Petrograd brought him into a strange and unfamiliar world. The youth who had worked in a factory and distributed pro-Marxist literature now entered the complex literary life of the capital, with its salons and its conflicting movements–Symbolism, Acmeism, Futurism. The First World War continued, and the Revolution lay but two years away.

The arrival of an unknown peasant youth might seem insignificant against such a background, but in fact sections of the Russian intelligentsia were profoundly interested in their own concept of the Russian peasantry. Feeling incomplete and cut off from the soil, they looked to rural Russia for a kind of salvation. The poets Nikolai Klyuev and Sergei Klychkov had been acclaimed a few years before, for they seemed to represent the eternal peasant, religious and yet bound to the earth, quaint in their dialect and folk world, the bearers of untold riches. It was primarily a stylised peasant, to suit the taste of the urban aesthete, and, to succeed, the conquering peasant poet was required to act out the masquerade.

The reaction of many Petersburg writers to Esenin during his first months in the capital is revealing. He is described in various memoirs as if he were ethereal. He was "blue" and "pink" and "golden," a "long-awaited miracle," a "sensation exhibited in a shop window." In Gorky's words, "the city met him with that delight with which a glutton greets a strawberry in January." Such a welcome could be most dangerous for a young poet.

In March 1915 Sergei Esenin arrived in Petersburg, or, as it was then known, Petrograd. In his autobiographies Esenin tends to stylise the circumstances of his arrival in the capital. It is nearly always Blok he mentions first (as if establishing a kind of apostolic succession with the leading poet of the day), then Gorodetsky, and finally Klyuev, and he notes with satisfaction his immediate success. ". . . I suddenly descended upon Petersburg. There I was received very warmly. The first person I saw was Blok, the second–Gorodetsky. . . Gorodetsky introduced me to Klyuev. . ." (V, 9, written in 1922; similarly V, 21, written in 1925). The identical pattern is repeated in the 1923 autobiography, and he adds: "My verses made a great impression" (V, 12). In the 1924 autobiography he singles out Gorodetsky rather than Blok as the chief person who received him (V, 17).

Esenin's autobiographies contain many errors and omissions, and the statement (V, 9, 21) implying that he was eighteen when he went to Petrograd may have led many people astray, for a disturbing number of memoirists subsequently dated his arrival in Petrograd as 1914.

Esenin's self-introductory note to Blok has survived: "Alexander Alexandrovich! I'd like to talk to you. For me this is very important. You don't know me, but perhaps you've come across my name in some journals. I'd like to call at about 4. With respect, S. Esenin" (V, 54). Blok has added at the bottom of this sheet: "A peasant of the Ryazan province. Aged 19. Verse that is fresh, pure, full-throated. Language of many words [?]. Came to me on March 9, 1915" (V, 247). Esenin was to recall: "When I looked at Blok sweat poured from me because it was the first time I had seen a living poet" (V, 9).

It seems hard to believe that, straight from the station, Esenin really did lug his suitcase down the Nevsky Prospekt and call on Blok (who gave him tea and fried eggs)—but such was the story he stood by, and there is no proof to the contrary. The urban, cultured Blok was, of course, very different from Esenin, and for much of his life Esenin was to admire Blok rather grudgingly, probably largely because he sensed in him a great rival, both close to him and alien. Throughout his life Esenin (who had a weakness for celebrities and name-dropping) used to refer to the conversations he had had with Blok. Thus in a pub in the summer of 1924 he turned to a young poet and pontificated: "Blok taught me how to write lyric verse when I got to know him in Petersburg and read him my early verse. 'A lyric poem shouldn't be excessively long,' Blok told me. The ideal length of a lyric poem is 20 lines."

Blok autographed a volume of his poetry for Esenin and gave him letters of recommendation to the writers M. P. Murashov and S. M. Gorodetskv. In the note to Murashov he wrote: "Dear

Mikhail Pavlovich! I am sending you a talented self-taught peasant poet. He will be closer to you, since you are a peasant writer, and you will understand him better than anyone. Yours, A. Blok. P. S. I have selected 6 poems and sent him with them to Sergei Mitrofanovich. Do all you can to help."

Esenin's visit to Blok was thus successful–he had met the poet, quite impressed him with his verse, and Blok had given him letters of recommendation. Yet the two poets had remained distant–it is revealing that Blok thought Esenin would be closer to Murashov than to himself. In his letter of April 22, 1915, in reply to Esenin's request for a further meeting, Blok wrote that he was tired and busy, that "we will say nothing significantly new to one another," and that "you and I are so different." However, he also expressed solicitude for Esenin's future, advising him not to hurry or be nervous in his literary career, for "we must answer sooner or later for every step we take, and it is difficult to take steps now, in literature perhaps most difficult of all."

Wearing a blue *poddevka* (a kind of Russian peasant coat) and Russian boots, Esenin went to Murashov with Blok's note, and after hearing Esenin's verse, Murashov recommended him to various journals and offered him temporary accommodation, which he accepted.

On March 11, two days after meeting Blok, Esenin went to see Gorodetsky. Sergei Mitrofanovich Gorodetsky (1884-1967) was already a celebrated poet, author of numerous books and currently an adherent of the school of Acmeism. Unlike Blok, he reacted ecstatically to Esenin's arrival, and in one autobiography Esenin stressed his role in particular: "I arrived in Petrograd and sought out Gorodetsky. He received me very cordially. Almost all the poets at that time used to meet at his flat. They began to talk about me and started to print me like mad" (V, 17).

Gorodetsky's memoirs, written in 1926, give a valuable insight into this period. He admitted that in 1915 he and others were intrigued by the village and pan-Slavism; Klyuev had already met with success; and thus: "The fact of Esenin's appearance was the realisation of a long-awaited miracle. . . He brought his verse wrapped in a rustic kerchief. . . A kind of festival of song began. We kissed one another and Sergunka again recited his verse. . . Esenin settled at my place and spent several months there. . ."

It seems that Esenin, only a few days after arriving in Petrograd, was beginning to "act the peasant." Murashov (if he is describing a meeting of March 1915) and Gorodetsky both refer to noticeably peasant features in his dress—a blue peasant coat and his verse wrapped in a country kerchief—which, whilst fully conforming to a Petersburg aesthete's conception of a peasant, were certainly not typical of Esenin's apparel during his Moscow years. On a photograph of this period, whilst Gorodetsky relaxes rather aristocratically, Esenin, wearing a simple spotted shirt and playing an accordion, smiles into the camera with beguiling candour.

In 1926, with the benefit of hindsight, Gorodetsky wrote self-critically about his role in these early months in Petrograd:

> What did I give him in this first decisive period? Only one thing of positive value: the realisation of his first success, the recognition of his mastery and his right to work, the encouragement, affection and love of a friend. But negative—much more: everything that Petersburg literature of those days cultivated in me: the aesthetics of the servile village, the beauty of decay and hopeless revolt. . . The crossing of our Petersburgian literary dreams with a voice born in the village seemed to us a justification of all our work and a festival of a kind of neo-populism. We thought *we* were triumphant, but in fact it was a victory for idealistic philosophy. . .

Like Blok, Gorodetsky inscribed a volume of his verse for Esenin on the day of their first meeting. But, whereas Blok's words were formal and restrained—"To Sergei Alexandrovich Esenin in kind memory. Alexander Blok. March 9, 1915. Petrograd"—Gorodetsky's inscription on his volume of verse *The Fourteenth Year (Chetyrnadtsatyi god*—meaning 1914) was full of endearment: "To my little spring brother Sergei Esenin with love and ardent faith. 11.III.915 Sergei Gorodetsky."[1] Gorodetsky also wrote out recommendatory notes for the "new youthful talent" to the journalist S. F. Librovich and the publisher V. S. Mirolyubov. In writing to Librovich, Gorodetsky seemed rather condescending about Esenin: "Soon I'll send you a new 'game'. . ." The next day Esenin called upon Mirolyubov, publisher of the *Monthly Journal,* and handed him his allegedly anti-war poem "The Jackdaws" (V, 222).

Towards the end of March Esenin met a new group of people, including Ryurik Ivnev, Vladimir (Volodya) Chernyavsky, Mikhail (Misha) Struve, and Konstantin (Kostya) Landau.[2] Ryurik Ivnev (the pseudonym of M. A. Kovalyov, b. 1891) was already a poet of some repute—his verse was balanced and disciplined in form, but dark and guilt-laden in content. He and his poetry-loving friends were wealthy enough to move in a world of literary salons, both as guests and hosts. Ivnev met Esenin at a poetry concert and was at once entranced by the charm of the beautiful, almost boyish poet. On March 27 he addressed a poem to Esenin, paying homage to Sergei's peasant purity. Two days later Esenin reciprocated with a poem "To Ryurik Ivnev" ("Riuriku Ivnevu," V, 188).

Esenin was achieving success and acceptance with unprecedented ease. In Kostya Landau's luxurious room, which Ivnev nicknamed "Aladdin's lamp," Esenin recited his verse. "And we," recalled Ivnev many years later, "as if under a magic spell, tirelessly listened to these poems which seemed to us a revelation leading us into a completely different world, quite unknown or known only by hearsay." Vladimir Chernyavsky, then a student, later to become an actor, explains that the "intellectuals" were instantly delighted by Esenin because "from the first minutes upon meeting him, even before they knew his verse, these 'intellectuals' felt in the new arrival that charm of freshness, that utter spontaneity he then had, that kind of primitive but not coarse healthiness, that youthfulness—half-placid, half-mischievous, that smell of the distant village which seemed to them almost a salvation."

Gorodetsky, Ivnev and others introduced Esenin with great success to their social and literary milieux. According to Ivnev, leading Symbolists such as Vyacheslav Ivanov and Blok, such strict judges as Zinaida Gippius and her husband Merezhkovsky, were "charmed and conquered by Esenin's muse," whilst only the old poet Fyodor Sologub resented the ease with which Esenin rose to fame. Ivnev's general point may be valid, although others besides Sologub were hostile towards Esenin, and there was frequently an element of condescension in people's attitude.

Some two weeks after their first meeting, Ivnev held an evening in honour of Esenin, at which the young poet again recited his verse. "Men experienced in literary battles listened avidly, with bated breath. Golden Rus looked at us with its wily Ryazan eyes. Esenin already recited in a masterly fashion." After the "official" part of the evening had finished, Esenin began to sing some *chastushki* (folk quatrains), and then, with the lights extinguished, he sang obscene verse out loud. "Such laughter, such eyes, such a smile I had never met in my life before," recalls Ivnev. "All who remember his smile know what charm it contained, what overwhelming power."

By April Esenin was already being invited to rich families and salons. Chernyavsky comments:

> Many people remember how fat ladies fixed him pathetically with their lorgnettes, and he had only to pronounce words with an emphasis on the "o" sound–"korova" ("cow") or "senokos" ("haymaking")–for them all to get into a ferment of delight. "Repeat what you said, ko-ro-va? Isn't that marvellous!" Our general sentimentality. . . took grotesque forms here, and Sergei, blinking patiently and smiling, used to ask them sometimes quite inoffensively what it was they couldn't understand. Although his remarkable yellow curls were not yet fully grown, people used to call him "the little shepherd," "Lel'," [3] "Angel."

In the weekly journal *The Voice of Life (Golos zhizni),* dated April 22, four poems by Esenin were published, preceded by an article about him by Zinaida Gippius. Here she ascribed his immediate popularity to the fact that our "refined and tired *littérateurs* know what's what and realise that the new Ryazan poet is a real poet, and many of them have even a particular attraction to the style of true 'earthy' poetry." She noted the simplicity and exactness of Esenin's cheerful verse, contrasted him with urban poets, and concluded patriotically that the phenomenon of Esenin is yet another proof of "how rich is our land, we have enough of everything."

Significantly, she linked Esenin at once with another "poet from the people," Nikolai Klyuev–and Esenin, carefully following every word that appeared about him in print, read Gippius' observations with great interest. Although Chernyavsky recalls that Esenin was dissatisfied with the article–"It's a stupid article. She feels me all over like an object"–he was probably moved by it to a fateful step, for on April 24, only a few days after the appearance of Gippius' words, he took the initiative of writing to Klyuev:

> Dear Nikolai Alexeevich! I have read your verse and talked a lot about you with Gorodetsky, and I can't help writing to you. All the more so because we two have much in common. I also am a peasant and write like you, only in my own Ryazan tongue. My poems have proved successful in Petersburg. 51 out of 60 have been accepted. . . And in *The Voice of Life* there is an article about me by Gippius, under the pseudonym Roman Arensky, where you too are mentioned. There are many things I'd like to discuss with you. . . (V, 55).

Esenin's first stay in the capital was coming to an end, for, perhaps on April 29, he left Petrograd and, after a brief visit to Moscow, returned to the village of Konstantinovo. In less than two months he had achieved astonishing success–Gorodetsky was already planning to publish a volume of his verse in the autumn (V, 55). Yet on April 30 Chernyavsky wrote to a friend: "Yesterday we saw off Sergunka Esenin. No one has debauched him, and yet no one has given him real food. We were all empty with him." As Chernyavsky comments, Esenin left Petrograd "with 'great expectations,' knowing that he would return and that he had already begun to conquer" there.

On about May 4 he arrived in Konstantinovo. It appears that he was due to be called up for military service in mid-May, and in June his Petrograd friends were alarmed to hear that he had indeed been called up. The news turned out to be a rumour, however, and, temporarily exempted, Esenin spent the summer of 1915 peacefully in Konstantinovo. He had no wish to join the army—not through cowardice, Chernyavsky explains, but because, apart from his revulsion for the war, his only aim in life was poetry and his absolute right to live, wander and act as he chose. Esenin wrote to Chernyavsky that he was exempted from military service until the autumn "because of my eyes," but "at first they were going to take me at once" (V, 58). In a footnote in his manuscript memoirs Chernyavsky adds: "I remember that, not without a certain [cunning] hint, he told me about village lads who procured by a special, not very dangerous method an artificial dislocation of their limbs by means of a carriage wheel." Nowhere else does there appear to be any indication of a deficiency in Esenin's eyesight, and his sly "hint" may seem puzzling. Nevertheless, the critic V. Vdovin dismisses quite persuasively any hypotheses about the poet's self-disfigurement. The postponement of Esenin's call-up was by no means unique, and "weak eyes" may have been the pretext for deferment given to him by the authorities.

From Konstantinovo Esenin wrote to Murashov: "It's good in Petersburg, but here is a million times better." Yet, having tasted the first pleasures of success, he clearly could not remain long in the village. In August Gorodetsky wrote effusively to him: "Dear Sergunya, my beloved friend. . . How I should like to tug at your curly hair now. I won't tell you what you mean to me, because you know that yourself. Such meetings as ours are the miracles which make life worth living. I was in Moscow. Your fame goes everywhere, everyone is delighted with you. And legends are spread too. . . That's how famous you are. Only don't let this rubbish turn your head, but work quietly and a bit more calmly."

On April 24 Esenin had written to Klyuev in the hope of corresponding with him and eventually meeting him. He had sent this postcard to Klyuev's address in the northern wilderness, to Olonets province, Vytegra district—and during the summer of 1915 Klyuev sent at least five letters to Esenin in Konstantinovo. By May 2 Klyuev assured Esenin:

> Dear little brother, I consider it a delight to know you and speak with you. . . If you have anything to say to me, then write at once. . . I

> especially need to know the words and comparisons of Gorodetsky, neither subtracting nor adding thereto. In order to be ready and to hold one's heart proudly before a dangerous temptation for such people as you and me. I felt much in your words, continue, my dear, and receive me in your heart.

Eager to establish a special literary bond with Esenin, Klyuev in a further letter emphasised the gulf separating them both from Petersburg's "bookish poets." Proud of his peasant origin, Klyuev resented the condescending praise bestowed upon him by such poets. He warned Esenin: "My white dove. . . You do know that you and I are goats in the literary orchard and are tolerated there only by grace and that there are many venomous prickly cacti in this orchard which you and I must avoid for the health both of our spirit and our body. . . For God's sake, reply promptly. I kiss you, my friend. . ." On September 6 he informed Esenin: "I shall be in Petrograd until September 20. It would be good to arrange a joint recital with you somewhere. . ." In fact, Klyuev prolonged his stay in Petrograd, and wrote to Esenin on September 23: "I am dying to see you, my dear beloved one, and if you are able to come for this, then come at once without replying to this letter. . ." Esenin later recalled: "Klyuev sent a telegram to me in my village and invited me to come to him" (V, 17). In Petrograd towards the beginning of October 1915 the two poets met for the first time.

Nikolai Alexeevich Klyuev (c. 1884-1937),[4] a peasant from the far north, with strong religious, sectarian connections, had sprung to poetic fame in Petersburg in 1911—three books of Klyuev's verse were published in the years 1911-13. In Klyuev's strange character sincerity and duplicity were intermingled—he could be an actor and hypocrite, although he was a poet of remarkable power, original and with his roots deep in the peasant religious soul. In about late 1914 Klyuev wrote to the poet Shiryaevets in that peculiar style of folk wisdom and saccharine affectionateness which is so characteristic of his letters: "Every day I go into the grove—and sit there by a little chapel—and the age-old pine trees, but an inch to the sky, I think about you. . . I kiss your eyes and your dear heart. Today such a blue-feathered dawn looks upon these lines, and the hare under my window nibbles the hay in the rick. O, mother wilderness! paradise of the spirit, paradise of thought! How hateful and black seems all the so-called Civilised world and what I would give, what cross, what Golgotha I would bear–so that America should not encroach upon the blue-feathered dawn, upon the chapel in the forest, upon the hare by the hayrick, upon the fairy tale hut. . ." This letter gives some indication of the poetic powers of Klyuev, the peasant who hated "civilisation," the monk-like poet for whom Nature was a temple.

Gorodetsky describes him as "a wonderful poet, cunning and clever, charming in his insidious humility"; Ivnev says that Klyuev, although a fine poet, was a "comedian of genius"("genial'-nyi komediant") who "believed less than an atheist"; whilst the poet Anatoly Mariengof admired the way that in 1923 Klyuev "made the sign of the cross over weak Mosselprom beer. . . and that, for the sake of the mystical mummery and great falsehood which we call art, he put on a crown of thorns and stood with palm outstretched amidst the beggars at the cathedral entrance with a heart that was cynical and blasphemous, cold to both love and faith."

Once, when accused of deceit, Klyuev answered that "lying is perhaps the only weapon which they (true men from 'the people') have against the intelligentsia." In bourgeois salons he behaved ascetically, refusing tea and meat, and Chernyavsky recalls that in 1916 Esenin complained about his hypocrisy–Klyuev, "arriving home from being a guest where he had meekly drunk nothing but hot water and eaten rusks, announced loudly that he was starving and asked his sister to give him 'ham and tea' as quickly as possible." In 1917 Esenin told a friend how Klyuev deceived the rich people of Petersburg: "Klyuev, you know, said 'I'm illiterate' ('Ia negramotnyi'). And he stressed the 'o' sound in 'negramotnyi'! That was just for the salons." Georgy Ivanov claims that Klyuev lived in a luxurious hotel room in Petersburg and read Heine in the original.

Klyuev sought to dominate his "younger brother" from the start, and Esenin's other Petrograd friends were powerless to prevent this from happening. Their memoirs form a plaintive chorus on the theme of Esenin's increasing alienation from them. Gorodetsky writes of Klyuev: "Probably he first met Esenin at my place. And he dug his claws into him. I can find no other word for the beginning of their friendship. . . Klyuev. . . took possession of the young Esenin, as in his time he had possessed each of us. . . Being stronger than all of us he took possession of Esenin more strongly than anyone. . . Klyuev drew Esenin further and further away from me." Ivnev also recalls that the "idyll" of the friendship between Esenin, himself and his friends was short-lived: "Gradually our paths began to diverge. He began to form an ever closer friendship with Klyuev." Chernyavsky notes that from November Esenin left Gorodetsky, and Klyuev became his closest friend, greatly influencing him throughout 1916. In his manuscript memoirs relating to December 1915 Chernyavsky regretted Klyuev's "spiritual domination" over Esenin–Klyuev "has taken complete command of our Sergunka: he fastens his little belt for him, strokes his hair and follows him with his eyes."

On October 17, 1915 the first meeting took place of a literary group which called itself *Strada* ("Toil" or "Hard work during harvest"). Various writers, urban as well as peasant, met at Gorodetsky's flat, including Esenin, Klyuev, Pimen Karpov, Ieronim Yasinsky and Alexei Remizov. Mikhail Murashov states that Esenin wished to be in charge of the "village" section of the journal the group hoped to publish, although in fact no journal appeared. *Toil* did manage to produce two literary anthologies, in 1916 and 1917, and Esenin contributed a poem to the first volume (I, 231-232, 382). On November 19 and December 10, 1915 he recited his verse at evenings of the group, but *Toil* proved short-lived and of little lasting consequence.

Everywhere now Klyuev and Esenin appeared together, the terrible twins of an increasingly false folkiness. Some spectators saw through their masquerade; others were suitably impressed. The writer Boris Lazarevsky reacted favourably on October 21, when he went to an evening recital at the *Monthly Journal:*

> I, who don't usually like verse. . . suddenly heard two poets–and what poets! This Nikolai Klyuev is a Great Russian Shevchenko. . .

> Then his companion Sergei Esenin recited. A 19-year-old lad, blond and curly like a cherub, and he also amazed me. In a quarter of an hour these two. . . taught me to respect the Russian people and above all to understand that which I had not understood before–the music of the people's language and the torment of the Russian people–contemplative, poisoned for centuries by vodka.

The more general reaction was one of revulsion and ridicule. A literary society known as *Beauty (Krasa)* had been formed in 1915–in April Esenin had already written to Klyuev: "I'll also be in *Beauty*" (V, 55). It consisted of many of the same people as *Toil*–the urban writers Gorodetsky and Remizov were the initiators of the group, the peasant poets Klyuev, Esenin, Klychkov and others were members. United by an extreme interest in Russian antiquity and folk poetry, the *Beauty* group held a large concert in the Tenishevsky Hall on October 25, 1915. Esenin recited his verse and sang folk quatrains to an accordion accompaniment, and together with Klyuev he sang *stradaniia* (folk laments). Gorodetsky says that this was Esenin's first public success, as opposed to his previous recitals in closed gatherings. This was also the beginning of the theatrical, stylised performances of Esenin and Klyuev, masquerading in white and silver "Russian" shirts such as they never wore in everyday life, and glorifying an idealised village and peasantry. The critic Viktor Shklovsky comments aptly on the accordion-playing of Esenin and his colleagues: "This occupation was of course wrong, for they were not accordionists. Imagine a poet-intellectual reading his verse and then playing the piano without any skill." Georgy Ivanov describes the evening vividly, noting Esenin's embarrassment–Esenin was dressed in a pink silk Russian blouse with a golden belt, and had rouge on his cheeks.

Undeterred by the unfavourable publicity which the concert provoked, the two peasant poets became inseparable in the following months. During this period, writes Ivan Rozanov, "Esenin cannot be regarded separately from Klyuev: so closely were they then linked. Klyuev undoubtedly put Esenin in the shade and exerted a terrible influence on him." Virtually all memoirists and critics are united in condemning Klyuev's influence on Esenin in the latter part of 1915 and in 1916. Esenin became almost unrecognisable: arrogance replaced his former embarrassment, he dressed up in pseudo-Russian garments sewn at first-class tailors', and his actions and words became unnatural and sly. There seemed no limit to their masquerade. They wore ancient crosses on their chests. In January 1916 Esenin and Klyuev came to Moscow and visited Anna Izryadnova, the factory girl who had borne Esenin's first son: "They had sewn themselves boyar costumes–long velvet caftans; Sergei wore a light blue silk shirt and yellow high-heeled boots." Some people had advised him to wear a "poetic velvet jacket like Byron," but instead he followed Klyuev, and looked like the leader of a gipsy choir. Talking to the Futurist poet Mayakovsky in early 1916, Esenin spoke, recalled Mayakovsky, "in the kind of voice icon-oil would probably speak in if it came to life." Esenin and Klyuev began to appear occasionally at bohemian literary taverns, "The Stray Dog" ("Brodiachaia sobaka") and "The Comedians' Halt" ("Prival komediantov"). "All the spring and summer of 1916," states the critic L. M. Kleinbort, "they appeared at salons. And in the same theatrical costumes they journeyed to towns and villages with Plevitskaya. All this began to earn them a balletic reputation." In February 1916 an article in the *Journal of Journals (Zhurnal zhurnalov)* mocked the "balletic little peasants": "One can hardly believe they are Russians, to such a degree do they strive to preserve the 'style russe' and show their 'national face'. . . It's not even ballet, but Italian opera itself." Kleinbort hints that Esenin and Klyuev even visited Rasputin's salon–if so, it would have been fascinating to witness the confrontation of Klyuev and Rasputin.

Why did Esenin imitate Klyuev so slavishly during these months? Partly, no doubt, he "jumped on the bandwagon" of Klyuev's success, realising that the shortest road to fame lay in allying himself with the interest in Russian folk poetry. But probably just as much, he was genuinely impressed by the powerful personality and views of Klyuev, a man several years his senior. Many poets and writers far more cultured and experienced than Esenin had succumbed to Klyuev's hypnotic authority. Esenin saw that the urban poets were interested in his *peasantness,* and hence it seemed opportune to develop these distinguishing features of his work and behaviour. Klyuev's theory that the future of Russia lay with literate peasants like him gave Esenin confidence and even a sense of superiority—he and Klyuev could feel themselves peasant-prophets. Whereas the Petrograd *littérateurs* tended to dabble dilettantishly in Russian archaism and folklore, Klyuev had a greater consistency, the strength of holding his beliefs as a "firm outlook on life, a way of living, a form of attitude to the world" (Gorodetsky's words)—and this despite the duplicity in Klyuev's character. His outlook, as seen in his poetry, was mystical, and steeped in a world of fairy tale, folklore and rare dialectisms—an "unreal" outlook which could only foster the religious and fairy tale elements in Esenin's previous poetry and upbringing. Klyuev influenced not only Esenin's behaviour, but also his poetry—Sakulin noted in May 1916 that at times it even seemed that Esenin was "singing under the hypnotic influence of his more mature *confrère,*" and Chernyavsky writes that "Esenin almost revered Klyuev as a poet."

There is another element in the relationship between Klyuev and Esenin which is never made explicit in Soviet publications, but which is occasionally hinted at. As Chernyavsky writes, "this relationship. . . about which it is *dangerous* to speak in a few words, will inevitably become a large *and, probably, puzzling* theme for a future researcher." After a few years Esenin grew further and further away from Klyuev and often spoke sharply about him—yet the two men continued to meet, often after long intervals, right up to Esenin's death. Soviet critics nowadays usually interpret this estrangement unconvincingly, claiming it to be a result of political differences—that Esenin disliked Klyuev's chauvinism during the First World War, or that Klyuev was hostile to the October Revolution, whereas Esenin was much more "progressive." Yet an analysis of the two poets' works before 1919 shows little difference of approach. True, they quarrelled later on literary matters such as Imaginism, but even this is insufficient to explain Esenin's words in 1922 that "Klyuev and I, for all our inner discord, formed a great friendship which continues to this day despite the fact that we have not seen one another for six years" (V, 9).

The unspoken feature was Klyuev's homosexuality. Chernyavsky's manuscript memoirs discuss this candidly, although someone has lightly crossed out these passages. Chernyavsky, having noted how Klyuev stroked Esenin's hair and followed him with his eyes, writes that in 1916 Esenin began to attack Klyuev's sanctimoniousness. Chernyavsky continues:

> Not for one moment did I think that Klyuev's erotic attitude towards him, in the sense of its external manifestation, could meet anything but a sharp rebuff from Sergei, when spiritual tenderness and peaceful gentleness entered the plane of physiology. Sergei spoke about this with totally genuine and healthy revulsion, not concealing that he had had to evade physically the persistent claims of "Nikolai" and threaten him with a huge scandal and severance of their relations, which would be disadvantageous to their poetic cause. . . On returning from his first visit to Moscow Sergei related that Klyuev was jealous of a woman with whom he [Esenin] had had his first–urban–romance. "As soon as I went for my hat, he sat down on the floor in the middle of the room and remained there, whining like a woman at the top of his voice: don't go, don't dare go to her". . . I repeat, however, that in another–deeper–sphere of consciousness Esenin's attitude to Klyuev was different. . .

The "inner discord" between Esenin and Klyuev, therefore, was in some measure due to Klyuev's homosexual attitude to Esenin. This factor helps to explain why Klyuev wrote such ingratiating letters to Esenin before ever meeting him, "dug his claws" into him at their first meeting, and then possessively guarded and strengthened his influence over him.

Esenin for his part seems to have valued their relationship, as is evident from his inscription to Klyuev beneath a photograph of himself in a fur hat: "My dear Kolya! For long years I shall carry away your love. I know that this face will make me weep (as people weep upon flowers) many years hence. But this shall be grief *(toska)* not for lost youth, but for your love, which shall be like an old friend for me. Your Seryozha 1916. March 30. Pt. [Petrograd]."

The question of Esenin and homosexuality has been seldom discussed. Chernyavsky stresses that Esenin was revolted by

Klyuev's attitude, and there are many testimonies to Esenin's attraction to the opposite sex. His sensuality towards women is reflected in his prose tales "The Steep Bank" ("Iar," IV, 7-142) and "By the White Water" ("U Beloi vody," IV, 143-153), written in mid-1915/1916. Both the men and women in these tales have a strong sexuality, and there is much rustic wrestling in the hay and emphasis on breasts, hot lips and trembling bodies (IV, 20, 79, 114, 143-4, 147, 152). In "The Steep Bank" this is incidental, but the short and rarely mentioned "By the White Water" is little more than a titillating study of female sexuality.

It seems that in the surroundings of Konstantinovo Esenin had hardly, if ever, considered that love might be other than between man and woman. Chernyavsky states that in Petrograd Sergei "once told me in a friendly talk what love is like in the village, lyrically idealising it. I recall that he made no personal confessions then, and in part love served only as a pretext for reminiscing about the girls and landscape of Ryazan."

In the rich and sometimes "decadent" literary salons of Petrograd, however, Esenin found himself in a very different milieu. "A few months after his first arrival, in a friendly conversation with me," continues Chernyavsky, "he frankly raised the new problem which had disturbed him, and about which he had formerly not thought very much: the question of what he called 'muzhelozhstvo' ('pederasty'), expressing his surprise that there was so much of it about. . . Some people said that he would be inevitably 'debauched,' but it turned out that there was no reason to fear for him. . ."

Of course, the milieu was not wholly homosexual. Rich women, bored and frustrated, pursued him eagerly. There was one poetess who sat on his lap; another walked about naked before him "and he wasn't sure what attitude to take to this"; whilst a third woman surprised him by the way she kissed—Esenin said: "I hadn't known that people kiss like that in Petersburg. She sucked so hard as if she was going to drink me all in with her lips."

Nevertheless, it was noticeable that throughout his life Esenin wrote few love poems, and numerous critics have asserted that he sacrificed love of women for other loves—love of poetry, fame, and his motherland. Ryurik Ivnev declares: "I know for certain that Seryozha never loved any woman. He didn't 'bother' long with them. They soon bored him. Never in his life did he have a 'great feeling,' a 'great love'." Ivnev also says: "He never loved anyone with a simple human love. In this lay his tragedy and, perhaps, in this lay his greatness. . . All who knew Esenin well know that he never really loved any woman."[5]

If this was so, Esenin would seem to fall into the pattern of the lonely and essentially cold artist described by Thomas Mann. In Mann's *Doctor Faustus* the Devil tells the composer Adrian Leverkühn: "Love is forbidden you, in so far as it warms. Thy life shall be cold, therefore thou shalt love no human being. . . Cold we want you to be, that the fires of creation shall be hot enough to warm yourself in. Into them you will flee out of the cold of your life." In a poem of 1918 Esenin advocated: "You who live, be as cold/ As the autumnal gold of the limes" (II, 59).

All this in itself may prove nothing, yet it is apparent that several of Esenin's poems written in the first half of 1916 express love for a man amidst a rural setting (I, 206, 207, 210). It cannot be argued that he was merely composing folk-like love poems here as seen from the viewpoint of a girl, for in the first of these poems the verbs referring to both people are masculine (I, 206, lines 11, 14, 16). In the poem "Mist has covered the horizon" ("Dal' podernulas' tumanom"), written in June 1916, he states: "On the dry straw in a sled/ Peasants' sweat is sweeter than honey" (I, 210). A manuscript variant of this last line might suggest that he is referring to a man's love: "On the dry straw in a sled/ Peasants' sweat is more beautiful than girls" ("Krashe devok pot muzhichii"). In mid-1916 Klyuev was Esenin's guest in Ryazan province.

The "new problem" of "pederasty" undoubtedly "disturbed" Esenin, as Chernyavsky noted. In 1915 he met, for instance, the openly homosexual poet Mikhail Kuzmin. Innokenty Oksenov, who saw Esenin in Petrograd in 1915, writes that perhaps in those surroundings, where Kuzmin and others were present, "lay the source of his future doom. One had to be a person with a devilishly healthy soul in order to avoid all the corrupting influences of that time and milieu."

This may all be inconclusive, but it is clear that Esenin met with the homosexual advances, not only of Klyuev, but of others. B. A. Sadovsky [Sadovskoy] relates that in Petrograd in 1916 Esenin came rushing in towards midnight "in violent hysterics. He shouted and rolled on the floor, beat his fists against his chest, tore his hair and wept." Esenin then told Sadovsky that in a tavern a certain "Vurdalak" ("Vampire"), who used to visit the notorious homosexual Prince Andronnikov, "had declared his 'love' for Esenin and, probably imagining himself to be with one of Andronnikov's 'boys,' had accompanied his 'declaration' with appropriate gestures. I took a long time convincing Esenin not to cause any fuss, as a complaint to court would only provide V. with advertisement and uselessly sully his own name." As for the Prince, Sadovsky says that Andronnikov "had, they say, two adjacent bedrooms–one with beds, the other with lecterns–and used to explain sweetly to his guests: my boys sin, and here they repent."

Thus Esenin, with his rather feminine softness and charm, was the object of men's desire. The memoirs quoted stress that he was appalled and revolted by this–but those few poems of 1916, and the testimony of friends that he never really loved any woman, might indicate a certain ambivalence in Esenin's reactions. He may have succumbed to the pressure of the milieu and discovered in himself a latent bisexuality.

Whilst Esenin's personal behaviour shows a decline throughout the period 1915-16 (he became increasingly affected, pretentious and conceited, although his charm somehow survived), the fortunes of his poetic career rose astoundingly. It was as if he was already sacrificing himself for the sake of his fame. "All the best journals of that time (1915) began to print me," he recalled (V, 12). His verse was published on the pages of *The Voice of Life,* whose contributors included many distinguished "intellectuals"–Akhmatova, Blok, Gippius, Gorodetsky, Gumilyov, Georgy Ivanov, Ivnev, Merezhkovsky, Remizov–but which claimed to aspire to a "unification of the democratic and progressive elements of Russian society." His poems were published in Mirolyubov's *Monthly Journal,* whose contributors included the peasant poets Shiryaevets, Oreshin, Klychkov, and also Gorodetsky and Blok; and in P. B. Struve's *Russian Thought (Russkaia mysl')*. He was printed in the "quality" journal *Northern Notes (Severnye zapiski)*, and in the *New Journal for Everyone (Novyi zhurnal dlia vsekh)*. Nearly all these journals claimed to be serious and progressive; many of them supported Symbolism rather than Futurism in poetry and were patriotically anti-German because of the war. To many of them Nikolai Klyuev contributed, his name hovering never far from that of Esenin.

Two journals expressed interest in the songs and fairy tales Esenin collected, and Esenin perhaps hoped to publish a volume of folk poetry he was gathering (as well as a volume of his own verse, to be entitled *Avsen')*, although nothing came of these plans. There was some competition for receiving Esenin's verse—thus Mirolyubov, of the *Monthly Journal*, plaintively asked him "not to forget our readers" by contributing to other journals which paid more handsomely: "Writers from the people shouldn't scatter their verse everywhere as our Petersburg poets do."

The peak of Esenin's literary career during these years was reached, however, in the publication of his first volume of verse, *Radunitsa*. (The title-word refers to the religious custom of remembering the dead by their graves in the week after Easter). The book was on sale by February 1916. According to Kleinbort, Esenin had first tried to publish a book under that name in 1912. Earlier in 1915 Gorodetsky had planned to publish it, but the persuasive Klyuev sought out his own publisher, M. V. Averyanov, and *Radunitsa* appeared almost simultaneously with Klyuev's *Secular Thoughts (Mirskie dumy)*.

By this time Esenin had written probably well over a hundred poems, but he selected only thirty-three for publication in *Radunitsa* Although he had spent most of the past three years in Moscow and Petrograd, his inspiration remained almost exclusively rural, for the industrial and political life of the great cities had made no deep impression on his peasant mind. Moreover, it was the decorative, traditional aspects of village life which he reflected in his verse—the landscape (seasons, trees, birds), dancing and folk songs. There were very few personal love lyrics; instead, by 1915 the image of Rus, the *rodina* (motherland) was the beloved heroine of his verse, a motherland which may be sad and impoverished, yet at the same time calm and imbued with a peasant religiousness. Jesus and the saints wandered as lowly pilgrims in the forests and along the paths of rural Rus, and the poet knelt in prayer before the temple of Nature. This religiosity may have stemmed more from the apocrypha and folk legend than from the Gospels and the Orthodox Church. Esenin remembered the religious poems he had heard in childhood, and–although there was little religious imagery, and even less religious sentiment, in his poetry of 1910-12–he intensified these elements in the years 1914-16, after his Tolstoyan fervour in Moscow in 1913 and his contact with mystical *littérateurs* in Petrograd.

His own personal mood fluctuated and was frequently contradictory; monastic and mischievous, meek and murderous, moved by both joy and grief. Rus and religion were interwoven in his consciousness, and yet, especially in 1914-16, the "monk" at times mocked the pilgrims and priests, and the patriot felt alone and destined for an early death. Violent and suicidal motifs arose unexpectedly, conflicting with the idyllic serenity and contentment of many poems. And yet perhaps they were not so unexpected–for Esenin was a lone vagrant, a lone worshipper, a lone contemplator. A greater personal sorrow, even a sense of guilt, are felt in his poems of 1915-16–his soul is sick and lost, his fall is fatal, and in his homelessness he asks for the prayers of others (I, 211, 204, 200, 209). "Sick with a warm grief" (I, 216), he longed for something elusive and irretrievably lost, and felt that soon he would leave this earth and one green evening hang himself upon his sleeve (I, 193).

By 1915-16 his poetry had become much more assured and individual in its imagery and tone than was his earlier verse, even though he continued to derive support from folk poetry and Klyuev and Blok.

Esenin's choice of thirty-three poems for *Radunitsa* reveals not only what works he himself perhaps most esteemed at the time, but also what "image" of himself he wished to impress upon his readers. Two linked leitmotivs stand out in *Radunitsa*–religious Rus and the folkloric village. The overall mood is calm, serene and religious, and, although there are rare traces of personal grief and a sorrowful village, these are far outweighed by a dreamy, fairy tale, otherworldly tonality. There is no hint of murder or suicide in *Radunitsa*—a golden beauty lies upon these pages.

When the volume was published, "it was written about a great deal" (as Esenin contentedly remembered in 1923): "Everyone said with one voice that I was talented. I knew that better than others" (V, 12). Never before had he received such attention from the critics, and he was indeed much praised, especially for the freshness, musicality and colourfulness of his verse.

It would be misleading, however, to suggest that Esenin's first book met with unqualified praise. Even those critics whose reaction was generally favourable found much to censure. Professor Sakulin felt that Esenin was as yet immature in his poetic language and under the influence of Klyuev, and another critic, signing himself "Yu-n," also noted that Esenin was "very close" to Klyuev in his attitude of mind. This probably did not worry Esenin much at the time, for he felt proud to be compared to a poet he almost revered. But other criticisms were more pointed—he must refrain from a certain "cheap and already vulgar" quality in his style (N. Vengrov); his rhythms are "somewhat monotonous" (Z. Bukharova); his vocabulary at times "cannot be understood without the use of Dal's dictionary" and his rhymes can be "annoying" (A. Polyanin). The poet was also warned to beware of the attraction of fashionable trends (Bukharova) and the urban attitude that the village is merely "interesting" (Polyanin). Deev-Khomyakovsky briefly reviewed *Radunitsa* in the Moscow journal *The People's Friend,* noting Esenin's strong reliance on folk songs and implying that Esenin and Klyuev, although "interesting," lack a sense of "civic grief."

In addition to this well-meaning advice, there were also several critics who greeted *Radunitsa* with undiluted mockery, regarding it as sheer theatricality. Thus B. Olidort called Esenin's verse "a kind of rhymed catalogue of village objects of prime importance," whilst N. O. Lerner savaged the chauvinism and "intolerable nationalistic bravado" of Esenin and Klyuev, and mocked their abuse of dialect words, which "one can recommend as exercises to anyone interested in translating from 'folk' language into Russian."

As has been apparent from Esenin's behaviour in the salons, there was indeed an element of posture in the "peasant poet." This even extended to the way he inscribed copies of *Radunitsa* to various friends in February 1916, using abstruse dialect words and dubbing himself "the hypostasis of the wooden plough-village," "the minstrel of the strawy wilds." However, the pretentiousness of these dedications contrasts sharply with his simple inscription on a copy of the book for E. M. Khitrov, his teacher at Spas-Klepiki–here Esenin wrote: "To the good old teacher Evgeny Mikhailovich Khitrov from his grateful pupil, the author of this book. . ."

Chapter Four: Military Service (1916-17)

During the year of Esenin's rise to fame, the First World War continued. The poet was eventually called up to the army in 1916, and overtaken by the February Revolution of 1917. Yet his military service is something of a mystery, and there has been much conjecture about the dates and deeds of those days.

In his autobiographies Esenin is largely silent about this period, in contrast to his accounts of his triumphant reception in literary Petrograd in 1915. In 1922 he confined himself to a list of his peregrinations during the years of war and revolution (V, 9); only in 1923 did he write at some length about his military service, and in so doing made several statements which have long been a subject of controversy:

> In 1916 I was called up for military service. Thanks to a certain patronage from Colonel Loman, the aide-de-camp of the Empress, I was presented with many privileges. I lived in Tsarskoe not far from Razumnik Ivanov. At Loman's request I once recited my verse to the Empress. After I had recited my verse she said that my poetry was beautiful, but very sad. I replied that such is the whole of Russia. I cited poverty, the climate and so on.
>
> The Revolution found me at the front in one of the disciplinary battalions which I had got into for refusing to write verse in honour of the Tsar. I refused, taking the advice and seeking the support of Ivanov-Razumnik. . . (V, 13).

In his last two fullish autobiographies Esenin reverted to his former silence. In 1924 he wrote merely that: "In the first part of my stay in Petersburg I often met Blok, Ivanov-Razumnik. Later Andrei Bely. . ." (V, 17). In 1925 he omitted all mention of 1916-early 1917.

Why did Esenin reveal only in 1923 a whole series of important events—that he served in Tsarskoe Selo, received privileges from Colonel Loman, recited his verse to the Empress, and was sent to a disciplinary battalion for not composing verse in honour of the Tsar? The reason, it would seem, was that in 1923 he had just returned from a fifteen-month trip abroad, and he was seeking here to reaffirm his loyalty to the Bolshevik regime and to explain away his undoubtedly known activity in the "Tsar's village" in 1916. His depiction of these events should be examined with caution.

In mid-1915 Esenin had been exempted from the army "because of his eyes." The following year there was no reprieve, and the young poet found himself dressed in army uniform, an attire more austere and international than his recent *style russe.* Uncertainty has shrouded the exact time and circumstances of his call-up. The 1926 memoirs of M. P. Murashov unfortunately offer no precise dates, and their accuracy has been questioned by P. Yushin. Murashov claims that Esenin was placed first of all in a reserve battalion, and then in a "Trophy Commission" consisting of writers, painters and musicians, before finally being transferred to Tsarskoe Selo. It does seem clear that until at least February 1916 Esenin was a civilian, free to act as he pleased in Petrograd. From the end of that month, and throughout March, his mood darkened. He did not wish to serve in the army—he was a poet, his fame was increasing, he did not like the war and killing, he had always resented discipline (be it at home, school, or the butcher's shop), and hence call-up was in every way undesirable. His gloomy utterances of March 1916 seem to reflect his anxiety about the call-up.

On March 15 he gave Murashov a portrait of himself on which he inscribed four lines: "My dear friend Misha,/ You're like a whirlwind, whilst I'm like a snowstorm,/ Cherish under your quiet roof/ The love and memory of me" (V, 189). Murashov, a man eleven years his senior, was surprised at this elegiac tone, but Esenin replied sadly: "No, my friend,... my life will be short, you will outlive me, you're a robust fellow, but I often shrink before dangers. You know how to struggle with life." According to Murashov, Esenin was also writing at this time the most suicidal of all his early poems, "I'm tired of life in my native land" ("Ustal ia zhit' v rodnom kraiu," I, 193-194)—and on that same day, March 15, he wrote a funereal sixteen-line poem to Murashov, ending with the lines: "Eternal distance lies before us,/ Our path is pensive and simple./ The dirt-covered graveyard/ Will give us shelter beyond the hills" (V, 190). Esenin's mood of leave-taking is also seen in his inscription to Klyuev on March 30—clearly he felt that a parting was imminent: "My dear Kolya! For long years I shall carry away your love..."

March 1916 was a month of torment. Esenin, feeling extremely vulnerable, had even considered fleeing from the capital, for in April his army life outside Petrograd was to begin.

The critics P. F. Yushin and V. A. Vdovin, often disagreeing in their interpretation of the facts, have recently published new information about Esenin's military service. They show that in April 1916 he moved to Tsarskoe Selo, where the Tsar's family lived, only a few miles from Petrograd. In mid-January 1916 Colonel Loman began to seek Esenin's transference; early in February the "imperial assent" was given; and on April 5 Loman signed a document that Esenin was to serve in Train No. 143 in Tsarskoe Selo. On April 20 his service in Tsarskoe Selo began.

In his 1923 autobiography Esenin did not specify what "privileges" he received from Colonel Loman, the "aide-de-camp" of the Empress. It is now known that Esenin served in the Tsarskoe Selo Military Sanitary Train No. 143, which bore the name and enjoyed the patronage of the Empress Alexandra Fyodorovna, and was used for transporting the sick and wounded in battle to the rear. Dmitry Nikolaevich Loman was a successful courtier: colonel of the bodyguard of the Pavlovsky regiment, *ktitor* (church warden) of the *Fyodorovsky Gosudarev Sobor* (Imperial Cathedral), head of the Tsarskoe Selo Infirmary No. 17 attached to the cathedral, and director of the Military Sanitary Train No. 143. Loman was also one of the initiators and an active member of the "Society for the Renaissance of Artistic Rus."

Yushin claims that the documents he has published "bring complete clarity to the intricate problem about the beginning of S. Esenin's military service. It was arranged by courtiers who, with the 'imperial assent,' drew the poet close to their side." He suggests that Esenin's salon appearances and the politically neutral tone of his poetry aroused the interest of the members of the pro-monarchical "Society for the Renaissance of Artistic

Rus." Indeed, as early as 1926 V. Khodasevich was hinting at much the same thing: "Esenin didn't come to Loman straight from the street. Undoubtedly there were some connecting links, and above all circumstances, on the strength of which Loman deemed it necessary to take an interest in Esenin's fate." And when Esenin recited his verse to the Empress, continues Khodasevich, this too "was arranged for Esenin by people with whom he was connected in some way or other, and who were close to the Empress."[1]

Despite these suggestions, it seems more probable–as V. A. Vdovin argues–that there was no plot by "courtiers" to bring Esenin to Tsarskoe Selo, and the "imperial assent" authorising Esenin's appointment was a mere formality, given on behalf of (but not directly by) the Tsar. Gorodetsky may have first brought Esenin to Loman's notice, and Klyuev certainly interceded on Esenin's behalf to hasten his attachment to the Train No. 143. It was Esenin's literary friends, not "courtiers," who sought to protect the young poet from the dangers of the battlefield.

At all events, Esenin began to work in the office of the Train No. 143, and also had certain duties in the Infirmary No. 17, which was named after the princesses Mariya and Anastasiya. Murashov visited him in Tsarskoe Selo–in what resembled a gloomy servants' room he found Esenin smoking cheap cigarettes and dressed in a khaki field tunic and black breeches. Murashov gave the penniless poet fifteen roubles, and Colonel Loman entered and wrote out a note permitting Esenin to obtain one bottle of wine and two bottles of beer. Evidently Esenin's drinking capacity already far exceeded this, for when Loman left, he altered the note to four bottles of wine and twelve bottles of beer. Murashov was baffled by the nature of Esenin's service: "He didn't have any clear duties. And he seldom went to the infirmary. In the office he helped the doctors' assistants and nurses to write out lists of the sick, or to fill in ration-cards, sometimes he wasn't summoned for several days and then he lay all day in his semi-prison-like room."

Murashov and others imply that Esenin's "military" duties were almost nominal, although it is now known that he made several trips with the Train No. 143, transporting wounded soldiers. His first such journey lasted from April 27-May 16, 1916. On May 31 he copied out his poem "Rus' " at Konotop in the Ukraine, during one of these excursions. A photograph exists of the poet, in army uniform, lying on the ground amidst the orderlies of the train, apparently during the trip to Konotop. Some time in the latter part of June he paid a brief visit to the village of Konstantinovo. There he saw Anna Sardanovskaya, who wrote to him by July 14, when he was already back in Tsarskoe Selo: ". . . Thank you for not having forgotten Anna yet, nor does she forget you. I am rather puzzled why it is you remember me when you are drinking beer, I don't see the connection. Perhaps you wouldn't remember me without the beer? What marvellous weather has set in since you left, and the nights are sheer magic!. . You write that you are idling around. Why did you stay for such a short time in Kon(stantinovo) then?. . . A. S."

In mid-1916 Esenin seems to have been in Petrograd several times. At Murashov's on July 3 he wrote a poem (V, 190) whose gloomy and murderous mood clearly reflects, not only the music and painting which immediately inspired it, but also his own depression at this time. If on March 15 he had referred to "the eternal distance before us" (V, 190), so on July 3 he declared defeatedly: "No, I cannot aspire/ Into the eternal putrified distance." The last lines of the poem assert that "If there is anything on earth,/ Then it is mere emptiness."

Loman instructed Esenin how to behave were he to meet the Empress. Murashov comments:

> As was later ascertained, Loman was preparing a meeting of the Empress with the poet Esenin. This soon took place. When I next visited Esenin he told me that Colonel Loman had introduced him to the Empress, and then to the princesses Mariya and Anastasiya. And two days later he was taken to recite his verse to them. . . Then Esenin was dragged along to recite his verse more often. This depressed him greatly.He again began to ask me to arrange a transfer for him some time, but I couldn't do this.

Esenin found it hard to write verse in these circumstances, and once wrote a satirical poem about Colonel Loman, in which he made it plain that poets should not have to empty bed pans. "This poem was handed over to Colonel Loman who laughed a great deal and stopped sending the poet so often to work in the infirmary."

Murashov suggests that Esenin did not recite only once to the Empress, as he had implied in his 1923 autobiography. At a concert on July 22 he recited his poem "Rus' " to the Empress and her daughters, and also declaimed a poem composed especially for that occasion, when the Empress' daughters had visited the infirmary. This poem (V, 191) was written in an ornate archaic handwriting as if for presentation. In return for his services he received a gold watch and chain "from the study of His Majesty." On this or another occasion the poet received a cotton kerchief with the imperial crown and two-headed eagles on it, which he then gave to his younger sister. Alexandra Esenina explains that Sergei had been presented at Court and was given this to contain his underwear when he went to the baths.

Only eight months remained before the Tsar's abdication—and the twenty-year-old peasant was hobnobbing with the highest in the land. Soviet critics understandably feel a certain embarrassment in discussing Esenin's activities at the Court. The easiest way out is taken by those such as E. Naumov who evade the question and merely declare that "at all events Esenin did not dance to the palace's tune, which clearly disappointed the Tsar's menials." Yet it should be appreciated that, rightly or wrongly, many people were incensed by Esenin's behaviour at the Court. This is most vividly brought out by Georgy Ivanov, who, although an anti-Communist writing in emigration, is so specific that one should not dismiss his words lightly as mere slander. Ivanov makes one particular accusation against Esenin—that he not only recited his verse to the Empress, but also, in the late autumn of 1916, "requested and obtained permission from the Empress to dedicate a whole cycle to her in his new book." Ivanov says that at first Esenin denied this, then admitted it, then retracted his admission, and finally disappeared somewhere. Sofya Chatskina, the publisher of *Northern Notes,* which had earlier printed some of Esenin's verse, was so outraged that in her flat she "hysterically tore up

Esenin's manuscripts and letters, shrieking: 'We have nursed a viper! The new Rasputin! The second Protopopov!' " Ivanov continues: "Esenin's book *Goluben'* came out after the February revolution. Esenin had managed to remove the dedication to the Empress. But some second-hand booksellers in Petersburg and Moscow were able to obtain some proof-sheets of *Goluben'* with the fateful: 'I dedicate with reverence. . .' . . . In Solovyov's shop on Liteiny one such copy, with the comment 'extremely curious,' appeared in the catalogue of rare books. V. F. Khodasevich held it in his hands. . ."

Atyunin also says that Esenin "composed and declaimed his works to the Empress," and, although no published Soviet source makes this admission, Georgy Ivanov's claim may perhaps be true.

Admittedly, Esenin was not politically minded, and he may not have felt any strong affection for the Tsar's family—Vorontsov asserts that even as a child "the system of the power of the 'Monarchy' did not please him."[2] Yet the poem he wrote in honour of the young princesses is loyally obsequious—he greets the "youthful humility in their tender hearts" (V, 191), and expresses patriotic awe at their boundless compassion. Atyunin claims that Esenin enjoyed the Court's favour until "the long poem he wrote 'about Novgorod' put an end to the 'imperial grace'." This may seem an interesting suggestion—his poem "Marfa Posadnitsa" (I, 310-314) was indeed banned by the Tsarist censor and not published until April 9, 1917, so that the imperial family could conceivably have been offended by its veiled advocacy of rebellion against the Moscow Tsar. Yet the poem met with the censor's objections by January 1916, before Esenin ever went to serve in Tsarskoe Selo, so that this can scarcely have been the reason for his "disgrace."

One touchstone by which to measure loyalty to imperial Russia was a writer's attitude to the First World War, which in the Soviet Union is described as the "imperialist" war. According to this line of thought, the more one disapproved of the war, the more progressive, democratic, and hence anti-monarchical one was. This has led some Soviet critics to endeavour at all costs to prove Esenin's opposition to the war, although Gorodetsky said as early as 1926: "Somehow the war did not touch Esenin deeply. . ." Admittedly, in 1921 Esenin claimed to Ivan Rozanov:

> A sharp difference from many Petrograd poets at that time lay in the fact that they succumbed to militant patriotism, whilst I, despite all my love for the fields of Ryazan and for my fellow countrymen, always sharply disapproved of the imperialist war and militant patriotism. This patriotism is organically utterly alien to me. I even met with unpleasantness through not writing patriotic verse on the theme of "thunder of victory, resound," but a poet can write only about that with which he is organically linked.

It should be borne in mind, however, that the poet made this assertion some years after the Revolution.

Esenin touched upon the theme of war in several poems of 1914 and 1915. It is not difficult to detect a nationalistic note at times. In "The Bogatyrs' Whistle" ("Bogatyrskii posvist," I, 91-92), published in November 1914, he showed the "good-for-nothing Germans" trembling before the Russian folk heroes, whilst "Rus celebrates its victorious holidays," and in "The Mother's Prayer" ("Molitva materi," I, 90) a mother feels joy as well as grief at her son's heroic death. In "Mikola," one of the poems he recited to the Empress, God is shown telling St. Nicholas to pray with the Russian people for victories (I, 81). It is perhaps significant that those who seek to demonstrate the poet's "hostility" to the war have to fall back on references to an inextant work he is claimed to have written: the "anti-war" poem "The Jackdaws."[3] A newly discovered article, previously thought of as "Iaroslavny", but in fact entitled "The Yaroslavnas Weep" ("Iaroslavny plachut"), was republished in October, 1975. Yet this article—originally printed in February 1915 under the name "Sergei Esetin"—can scarcely be said to express any forceful criticism of the war.

It seems fairest to say that, in his verse, Esenin neither exulted in the war, nor condemned it outright. Apart from occasional glimpses of nationalism, he generally confined himself to expressing compassion for the bereaved and anxious womenfolk. There is no need to apologise on Esenin's behalf for this—he was no Marxist, to reject the war for reasons of class or politics; he was a peasant lad, who himself had no wish to fight or be killed, and yet who, at the outbreak of war, patriotically desired his country's victory. When people discuss his reactions to various events, it is often overlooked just how young he was—eighteen when war broke out, twenty when he was introduced to the imperial court, and barely twenty-two at the time of the October Revolution. One should scarcely expect political subtlety from a young village poet who had been subjected to such bewildering influences in Petrograd in 1915 and 1916.

By September 1916 Esenin was complaining of material hardship in Tsarskoe Selo, and appealing to a literary fund for a loan of 150 roubles: ". . . For, having received old official boots, I walk in holes in the wet, am frequently forced to go hungry because of the meagre food and to wear tatters, whilst those in command order: Dress more cleanly and have a change of shirt for church—but where on earth from, for a shirt and trousers even without boots cost about 50 roubles, and boots almost as much" (V, 67-68). It is perhaps unlikely that he was inventing a complete myth about his material distress. His letter to the publisher Averyanov complains in very similar terms: "My position is wretched. I go about ragged, as hungry as a wolf, and all about everyone tells me to act more smartly" (V, 71). In a letter to Yasinsky on November 20, 1916 Esenin said he needed more money to help his family, "which, because of my father's illness, is almost starving" (V, 70). In this same letter the poet claimed that he was "completely tied down by soldier's fetters" and unable to escape (V, 69).

From all this it would appear that, for reasons unknown, Esenin's position in Tsarskoe Selo worsened in late 1916, and he was no longer free to visit Petrograd so frequently. Murashov writes:

> He was given leave to go to Petrograd seldom and reluctantly. In one of his letters he declared: "If you're free, come for a minute, we haven't met for a long time and it would do no harm to have a talk, and there is something to talk about, only this time without spirits, for otherwise I would become an inveterate drunkard *(tol'ko uzh bez spirta, a to ia spilsia bylo sovsem).*" I continued to visit him quite often, he was oppressed by his stay in Tsarskoe Selo, every day the stuffy atmosphere thickened about him.

Esenin was clearly unhappy in Tsarskoe Selo and already sought solace in alcohol. In December 1916 the poet Vsevolod

Rozhdestvensky saw him in military uniform: "I looked at Esenin and could scarcely recognise him. In his rough, oversize greatcoat, . . . his hair cropped short, hollow-cheeked and unusually fidgety, he seemed like an adolescent boy clad in a hospital dressing gown. Where had his dashing curls gone, and his somewhat haughty smile?. . ."

During these months, Nikolai Klyuev was not permanently in Tsarskoe Selo. In about July-August 1916 Esenin wrote to him: "Come, brother, in autumn at all costs. I miss you very much, and I'm very bored. The main thing is the utter loneliness. How I remember the past. . . Can it be brought back? Your Sergei Esenin" (V, 65). In mid-October Esenin and Klyuev were together in Petrograd. The critic V. A. Vdovin says that the "smooth-tongued courtier" Loman, who was "weaving a spider's web around the poet," suggested that Esenin and Klyuev should write loyal verse in praise of the Tsar, cathedral and court, but Klyuev refused on behalf of both poets in an epistle entitled "A Little Pearl from the Lips of Peasants" ("Biser malyi ot ust muzhitskikh"). At the end of the year Esenin inscribed a photograph to Klyuev: "To dear Kolya, with many memories for our bright days. Sergei Esenin. Anno 1916. December 28." For his part, Klyuev in 1916 dedicated a poem "to the most beautiful of the sons of the Christian kingdom, the peasant of Ryazan province, the poet Sergei Esenin." Here Klyuev described Esenin tenderly, as a "willow-youth" ("otrok verbnyi"), "with a voice sweeter than maidens' beads." In January 1918, feeling hostile towards Klyuev, Esenin was to write cuttingly to Ivanov-Razumnik: "I know what made him write 'to the most beautiful'. . ." (V, 77).

In 1916 and 1917 Esenin met Ivanov-Razumnik (the pseudonym of Razumnik Vasilevich Ivanov, 1878-1946), a critic, sociologist and literary historian who lived in Tsarskoe Selo. Esenin, unused to the world of philosophical abstractions, became greatly influenced by Ivanov-Razumnik's ideas. The poet mentions him in two autobiographies (V, 13, 17) and in a letter to Shiryaevets in June 1917 singles him out as the only intellectual evoking his trust and candour. Whilst rejecting Merezhkovsky and Gippius, Blok and Gorodetsky, Esenin says of Ivanov-Razumnik: "His character is deep and firm, he is illumined with thought, and before him I am myself, Sergei Esenin, and I rest and see myself and am kindled" (V, 75).

According to Esenin, it was through Ivanov-Razumnik's advice and support that he refused to write verse in honour of the Tsar (V, 13). Ivanov-Razumnik wrote an article in 1914-15 (published in Volume 1 of *The Scythians [Skify]* in 1917) in which he condemned the First World War as a product of "petty-bourgeois" or "philistine" culture. He defended the human personality, the good of the people, and the people's freedom, and was opposed to all forms of nationalism, imperialism or dogma such as Marxism. He declared that the merchants' war was alien to democracy, and socialists should not concern themselves with it—socialists should advocate neither victory nor defeat; they should help the wounded, but not the war. Although an avowed anti-nationalist, Ivanov-Razumnik was not an amorphous cosmopolitan—indeed, in this same article he declared himself a "nationalist" in the non-militant sense, a supporter of a people's right to its own art, culture and language. In this respect, he said, art is always "national" as well as international.

Soviet critics are sometimes reluctant to admit Ivanov-Razumnik's influence on Esenin, for Ivanov-Razumnik was a "liberal" and opponent of Marxism, but in fact, as Deev-Khomyakovsky wrote, Esenin met the February Revolution in Ivanov-Razumnik's embrace.

Esenin claimed to have been in a disciplinary battalion during the February Revolution, as a result of his refusal to write verse in honour of the Tsar (V, 13). Many people accept his word without examination, but there is no documentary evidence to support it. It appears that Esenin was merely indulging in a pretence of revolutionary heroism. The poet was still in Tsarskoe Selo on February 6, 1917 (V, 72), and he was free to go to Petrograd on February 11 (I, 386). On February 19 he recited his verse in Tsarskoe Selo. The poetess Malvina Maryanova states that when the February Revolution began towards the end of the month, Esenin visited her in Petrograd. There is controversy as to whether Esenin made a trip to Mogilyov towards the end of February.

At all events, Esenin remained in or near Petrograd in the

first half of March 1917. Some time in that month, after the Tsar abdicated and the sanitary trains were removed from imperial control, Esenin evidently deserted from the army. Years later he was to boast about his desertion (III, 275), but in fact his action, if prudent, was hardly heroic.

So ended the poet's military service, a period about which, in later years, he was notably reluctant to speak.

Chapter Five: Between Two Revolutions (1917)

Esenin's later autobiographies tell us little about his life during 1917. In 1922 he listed his nomadic wanderings during the "years of war and revolution," when he "travelled all over Russia, from the Arctic Ocean to the Black and Caspian Seas" (V, 9). In 1923 he wrote: "During the revolution I voluntarily left Kerensky's army and, living as a deserter, worked with the SRs [Socialist Revolutionaries], not as a party member, but as a poet. When the party split I went with the left group and in October was in their fighting squad" (V, 13). In 1924 he admitted: "I met the first period of revolution sympathetically, but spontaneously rather than consciously." He also recalled that "in 1917 my first marriage took place, to Z. N. Raikh. In 1918 I parted from her" (V, 17-18). Finally, in October 1925, the poet omitted the years 1916-18 until, towards the end, almost as an afterthought, he wrote: "In the years of revolution I was wholly on the side of October, but I regarded everything in my own way, with a peasant bias" (V, 22).

Such were his brief recollections about these troubled months, a period in his life which is little discussed.

When the February Revolution began, Esenin was apparently in Petrograd. Ryurik Ivnev describes him shortly after the outbreak of revolution. Ivnev saw four people walking arm in arm:

> I looked–Klyuev, Klychkov, Oreshin[1] and with them Esenin. They all seemed new somehow–broad-chested, tousled, all with their coats unfastened. They rushed up to me, pricked me with bitter words. "Our time has come!"–hissed the unctuous Klyuev. Esenin also tried not to lag behind: he made some meaningless caustic comments. I looked at him and could not believe my eyes. "What's come over you?," I asked. "Pack it in, it's disgusting". . .

Esenin had good reason to feel exuberant, for the February Revolution, and the Tsar's abdication on March 2, were soon to free him from the "soldier's fetters" which had bound him in Tsarskoe Selo. On March 30, shortly before Easter, the peasant poets Esenin, Klyuev, Klychkov and Pimen Karpov sent a paschal greeting to their "brother" poet Shiryaevets, who was living in Turkestan. After Klyuev's affectionate greeting, Esenin too hailed the "dear minstrel of Zhiguli and the Volga" (V, 179). The peasant poets had never before sensed so vividly that "their time had come"; they could feel their class solidarity, their superiority over the "nobles" who had previously patronised them. Esenin's hostility to the Petrograd *littérateurs,* which seems to have been overlaid with a feeling of class envy and inferiority, permitted but one exception–he continued to admire Ivanov-Razumnik.

Ivanov-Razumnik was one of the editors of the first volume of *The Scythians,* which was published in Petrograd in August 1917. The Scythians' outlook was vague, wild and somewhat pretentious–they claimed to be strong-willed, daring and close to the earth, the worshippers of Life, Beauty and Truth, implacable revolutionaries opposed to all "external order." They contrasted their "sacred folly" with the compromise-ridden greyness of the universal Philistine *(Meshchanin),* who "spoils art by aestheticism, science by scholasticism, life by vegetation, and revolution by petty reform-making." But they consoled themselves that the Scythians' arrow shall strike. The contributors to this volume included Esenin, Bely, Bryusov, Klyuev and Remizov. Ivanov-Razumnik, besides opposing the war, also wrote an article "Socialism and the Revolution" in June 1917, declaring himself in favour of a more radical revolutionary spirit than had been maintained after the February Revolution.

Esenin's "Scythian" mood, especially in the months from March to June 1917, can be judged from the series of longish poems published in the second volume of *The Scythians* in December. These poems–"The Comrade" ("Tovarishch"), "The Singing Call" ("Pevushchii zov"),"Otchar' "–are remarkably revealing of his response to revolution. They show that he was immediately drawn to the broad canvas of social themes for almost the first time in his life, but the new gamut of colours and movement dazzled his vision and confused his thought. He became increasingly vague and wild.

In "The Comrade" (I, 264-268), simple workers, dissatisfied with their poverty, sing the *Marseillaise* and die in the struggle for "freedom, equality and labour," dreaming of an "eternal free fate." They are stirred by the "February breeze" and the "iron word 'Rre-e-pu-u-ublic!' "—but there is a politically "unreal" element in Esenin's treatment of their revolt: Christ hears the sound of their "innocent speeches," descends from an icon and dies by their side, without resurrection.

A month later, in April 1917, Esenin wrote "The Singing Call" (I, 269-271), in which he saw the February Revolution not only as a Biblical event, a religious mystery, but also as peasant-based, peaceful, and nationalistic (as well as of universal significance):

In a peasant manger
　A flame is born
Bringing peace to all the world!
A new Nazareth
　Lies before you.
The shepherds already praise
　Its morning. . .

Perish, English monster. . .
Your sons shall not understand
Our northern wonder!. . .

　The Star of the East
　Is aflame! (I, 269-270).

The poem ended with the lines: "We were born for love and faith,/ Not for devastation!"

This sincerely held humane attitude was to prove unsuited to the stern revolutionary years, and from March 1917 Esenin's outlook inevitably incurred much criticism. It was all very well for his mentor, Ivanov-Razumnik, to praise these poems as "the only true manifestation in poetry of the people's spirit during the days of revolution"—but proletarian critics soon after the October Revolution began to attack Esenin for "mysticism. . . which any serious Marxist sharply condemns." Vsevolod Rozhdestvensky blames the Scythians, such as Ivanov-Razumnik, Bely and Remizov, for leading Esenin away from a true understanding of the people and its role in the revolution: "They flattered his boundless vanity and almost proclaimed him a 'prophet' of the new world."

The poem "Otchar' " (I, 273-277), written in June 1917, again shows Esenin's exultation in the storm of revolution and the grandeur of renewed peasant might, and ends with a peaceful vision which he was later to repeat, almost word for word, in a passage of "The Keys of Mary" in 1918 (IV, 190-191). Yet his idealisation of the mighty peasant led him to extremes, as in his lines: "O miracle-worker!/ Broad-cheeked and red-mouthed,/ ... Rock my soul to sleep/ On your toes!" (I, 275).

After June 24 (when he wrote to Shiryaevets), Esenin's movements are but vaguely known. In various autobiographies he mentions a journey to the "Arctic Ocean" (V, 9), and to Murmansk, Arkhangelsk and Solovki (V, 13-14, 18). This flight of Esenin to the far northern seaboard of Russia is little discussed, and poorly documented. The writer Sofya Vinogradskaya claims that Esenin himself liked reminiscing about this period of his life:

> He fled to Novaya Zemlya as a deserter at the time of Kerensky. He used to talk about his life there in a hut with an earthen floor, about the struggle for existence and his fight against big voracious birds which forced their way into his room and destroyed all his supplies of food and water. . . Most of all I remember his description of these birds–large, restless, powerful birds. And Esenin himself, like a gentle white bird, seemed to grow in height when he described them with a characteristic movement of his arms.

There is some doubt, however, whether Esenin ever visited Novaya Zemlya, a large island off the north of Russia, but it appears that he did indeed travel north, and moreover in the company of Zinaida Raikh, whom he married on August 4. Vladimir Chernyavsky writes that Esenin reminisced "about his courtship, which was connected with a trip on a steamship, and about how he had 'got spliced' in the great wide northern landscape."

Zinaida Nikolaevna Raikh, later to become a famous actress, but then working as a secretary and typist for the Petrograd newspaper *The People's Cause (Delo naroda)*, had perhaps first met Esenin in the office of that newspaper. *The People's Cause* was an SR publication, in which Esenin's works had appeared from March 1917. She was born into a middle-class family on June 21, 1894, and seems to have been of Jewish extraction.[2] Although Raikh's school leaving marks were inferior to those of her future husband, they sufficed to earn her the title of "primary school teacher with the right to give private lessons." Esenin wrote that he parted from her in 1918, but in fact the legal divorce did not follow until October 1921. During that time two children were born, a daughter Tatyana (in mid-1918) and a son Konstantin (in early 1920).[3] Atyunin, who is generally reliable, maintains that Esenin "did not recognise his son and this was the grounds for divorce."[4] Zinaida Raikh subsequently married Vsevolod Meierkhold [Meyerhold], the celebrated theatrical director.

The Imaginist poet Anatoly Mariengof, who was to become Esenin's closest friend in 1919, describes Raikh in his lengthy, largely unpublished memoirs, written in 1953-55. Mariengof did not like Raikh—"I usually called her 'this plump Jewish lady' "—and this perhaps lends greater credibility to his testimony when he continues:

> Whom did Esenin love?. . . Most of all he hated Zinaida Raikh. And this woman, with a face as white and round as a plate, this woman, whom he hated more than anyone else in life,—her—her alone did he love. Zinaida told him that he was her first man. And she lied. This—in peasant fashion. . .—Esenin could never forgive her. Tragically, fatefully, he couldn't. . . I believe that she too never loved again. If Esenin had beckoned to her with his little finger she would have run away from Meierkhold without an umbrella in rain and in hail.

It is widely supposed that the autobiographical poem "Letter to a Woman" ("Pis'mo k zhenshchine," III, 57-60), written in 1924, was addressed to Zinaida Raikh. In the last years of his life Esenin continued to see both Raikh and her new husband, and frequently thought of her, even up to the eve of his death. The importance of Zinaida Raikh in Esenin's inner life should not be overlooked—it serves perhaps as a corrective to Ivnev's assertion that Esenin never experienced a "great love."[5]

It seems that in about late July Esenin, Raikh and the poet Alexei Ganin left Petrograd and travelled northwards. They visited Vologda (Esenin and Raikh were married in a church near Vologda on August 4), and the newlyweds continued their journey to Arkhangelsk, Solovki and Murmansk, before returning to Petrograd in August or September.

In Petrograd, Ryurik Ivnev called on Esenin and Raikh in their two-room apartment on Liteiny Prospekt: "I found it strange to see Esenin 'married.' When we were sitting at the tea table, if ever Zinaida Nikolaevna went out of the room for a minute, he began to say jokingly to me, with a wink: 'There you see, now I'm married. Well, do you like my wife? Go on, tell me, don't be bashful—perhaps you don't like her, eh?' Then, with a crafty smile, 'And what about you? Aren't you going to take the plunge?' "

The first months of his marriage to Zinaida Raikh were months of calm and happiness in Esenin's life. Vladimir Chernyavsky even goes so far as to say that the end of 1917 was the most shadow-free period that remained in the poet's life. Chernyavsky often went to see the couple on Liteiny Prospekt—Raikh, he says, was young, beautiful and calm; and Esenin was a changed person: "He seemed more manly,. . . with an agitated seriousness. . ., he believed in his personal popularity and the importance of the *voice of the poet Esenin* in the thunder of events." Esenin was "gratified by the right to the simple words: 'I have a wife'."

Of the new acquaintances he made in the late autumn of 1917, the peasant poet Pyotr Oreshin (1887-1938) has left the fullest account of Esenin at this time. Oreshin was at once struck by Esenin's dandyish clothes (a new grey suit, white collar, blue tie), and his light gait: "Nobody trod as lightly as Esenin. . . Esenin looked more like an elegant gentleman than a peasant poet. . . He was only 22 years old, his graceful figure was full of confidence and physical strength, and pink youthfulness shone tenderly on his face." Esenin immediately began name-dropping, asking Oreshin in quick succession if he had met Klyuev, Gorodetsky, Blok, Klychkov and Shiryaevets—and the dazed Oreshin had to admit that he had met none of them. Then Esenin recited for about an hour, "waving his arms and standing on tiptoe. . . with his right hand on the golden crown of his head." Esenin talked a lot: "For he was a great and persistent chatterbox, and his speech at that time was flowery, allegorical, more in images than with logical arguments, easily flitting from one subject to another–entertaining, inimitable speech. He himself was amazingly young. No wonder people called him Seryozha."[6] Yet Oreshin also says that Esenin generally spoke little:

> He had that inborn gift–the ability to speak without words. In fact, he spoke very little, but to make up for this everything played a part in his conversation: a slight nod of the head, most expressive gestures of his rather long arms, a sudden knitting of his brows, or the screwing up of his blue eyes. . . He spoke, weighing every word and developing his intonation to the extreme, but a person listening to him always felt–I did, for instance–that at any set moment Esenin was expressing his inmost being, whereas in reality no one could ever dive to the very bottom of Esenin's thought!

At 4 a.m. the youthful, energetic, mischievous Esenin left Oreshin to return to Raikh–his parting words to Oreshin were: "I love my wife, brother!. . . One can't. . . live alone!"

This period of domestic calm coincided, however, with the outbreak of the October Revolution (on October 25, old style; November 7, new style). In an autobiography Esenin claimed that he was in the "fighting squad" of the left wing SRs at that time (V, 13). There is no documentary proof of this, although Blok refers to it in his diary at a later date, on February 21 (new style) 1918.

Soviet critics are conspicuously silent about Esenin's life during the months immediately before and after the October Revolution. No letter of his is published for July-December 1917,[7] and this may suggest that some evidence has been deliberately suppressed. Perhaps some Soviet scholar will discover and publish the missing evidence, and thus allay all suspicions?

Esenin, evidently on November 3, 1918.

Chapter Six: From October to Imaginism (1917-19)

Virtually everyone is agreed that Esenin welcomed the October Revolution enthusiastically, even if he did not understand its real purposes and implications. Soviet critics contentedly quote the poet's later declaration that "in the years of revolution I was wholly on the side of October, but I regarded everything in my own way, with a peasant bias" (V, 22)—and, what may be somewhat more unexpected, emigres such as Georgy Ivanov and Vladislav Khodasevich wholeheartedly concur. Even the poet's posthumous detractors inside the Soviet Union had to admit that Esenin accepted the revolution, however idiosyncratically. Thus A. Revyakin wrote: "Esenin was attracted by the cinematographic nature of the revolution, its tempestuous sounds, the roar and hubbub of upheaval, the expectation of a mystical, narrowly *kulak,* patriarchally pious future for the village," and by the excitement of "elemental," unorganised conflict.

As Russia was predominantly a peasant country, Esenin had assumed that the peasantry would play a leading role in the new society. Unstable in his political views, as in much else, he probably saw the October Revolution at first as a welcome heightening of the mood of revolutionary excitement, and a promise of peace and land for the peasants. It would be a mistake to imagine him, even in his Klyuevan period, as a meek and angelic youth enchanted by the golden calm of church bells and incense. He had also the "broad Russian soul," a rebel spirit akin to that of Vasily Buslaev, who, according to the *byliny* (folk epics), issued a challenge to God. In his poem "O Russia, spread thy wings" ("O Rus', vzmakhni krylami"), written in 1917, Esenin openly contrasted himself with Klyuev. Whereas Klyuev is "meek," "monastically wise and gentle," Esenin himself is cheerful and rebellious, "even secretly arguing with the secret of God" (I, 292). This side of Esenin would naturally welcome a revolution.

In his political views he was as contradictory and elusive as in other things, and there are somewhat conflicting pictures of his political attitudes in December 1917.[1] Ryurik Ivnev quotes

Esenin as saying of the October Revolution, in about December 1917: "Such events happen once every three hundred years, or even more rarely," and Ivnev comments: "Without doubt he was one of the few poets who were in step with the revolution." Yet it should be remembered that his "step" had a "peasant bias" (V, 22), and he was still close to the "Scythians" and the left wing Socialist Revolutionaries–significantly, his first long poems after the October Revolution were dedicated to Andrei Bely (II, 7) and Ivanov-Razumnik (II, 13). E. Lundberg was close to the Scythians when he met Esenin and Ganin at Ivanov-Razumnik's in December, and he noted in his diary: "In Esenin there is a combination of mischievousness and great refinement. Sometimes almost decadent. . . Ivanov-Razumnik is pampering Esenin. I hope he doesn't spoil him completely. . ." Some seven months later, in July 1918, Lundberg found fault with Ivanov-Razumnik's "spiritual maximalism" and expressed fears that Esenin would end in "chaos" and "crime."

Ivanov-Razumnik, Esenin's spiritual mentor in 1916-18, was never a member of the Socialist Revolutionary party, but he was close to the party as literary editor of its various organs, the newspapers *The People's Cause* and *Banner of Labour (Znamia truda)* and the journal *Our Path (Nash put')*. Towards the end of his life he claimed that his views continued the populism of Herzen, Chernyshevsky, Lavrov and Mikhailovsky, with the basic socio-philosophical criterion of "man as an end in himself," and he criticised Bolshevism for its methods of dictatorship, collectivisation, and sacrificing man to the machine, to national wealth. "Art is free and cannot be set on bayonets."

There can be little doubt that in many respects Esenin agreed with Ivanov-Razumnik–the poet soon feared that man in the new Communist society would be sacrificed to the machine, and, on the question of "cultural construction," Esenin all his life placed art above politics. (In September 1924 he was to declare: "It is absolutely impossible to write according to a given line." And he said of a Communist friend: "The only trouble is that he loves Communism more than literature.") It is very probable that in the first months after the October Revolution some of Ivanov-Razumnik's criticisms of the new regime were passed on to Esenin.

"We stood in our time," recalled Ivanov-Razumnik, "for a 'deepening' of the political revolution to the social: we–that is, our literary group, the so-called 'Scythians'. . . –Alexander Blok, Andrei Bely, Nikolai Klyuev, Sergei Esenin and a few others." Ivanov-Razumnik talks of the "beast" Marxism: "This beast, by at first pretending to be a fox, was able to swallow up everyone one at a time: in January 1918–the Constituent Assembly and the right wing SRs, in April the anarchists, in July–the left wing SRs." Russian Marxism was "coarse" and "flatly prosaic."

Many outstanding writers gathered round the ideological leader, Ivanov-Razumnik–including the Symbolists Blok and Bely, and the peasant poets Esenin, Klyuev and Oreshin. But the "Scythian" group was extremely loosely-knit, and its members were in the main politically naive. They were poets, not politicians, sharing in common a strong national consciousness, considerable admiration for the Russian peasantry, and an emotional and spiritual approval of the contemporary historical events. They believed themselves "revolutionaries," but it was a revolutionary spirit vastly different from the disciplined, materialistic outlook of the new Bolshevik government. Furthermore, the original "Scythians" covered a wide political spectrum, ranging from Alexei Remizov, who openly mourned the fall of the autocracy, to Valery Bryusov, who contributed only to the first volume of *The Scythians* and in 1920 was to join the Communist Party. Andrei Bely (1880-1934) contributed, however, to both volumes. Esenin had met him, presumably at Ivanov-Razumnik's in Tsarskoe Selo in early 1917, and had been deeply impressed by Bely's poetic practice and theory. Bely greeted the October Revolution as fire and fury, fate and folly:

> . . . And you, elemental combustion,
> Devour me, deliriously roar,
> O Russia, o Russia, my Russia,
> Messiah of moments unborn!

Although there were more pages of poems by Esenin than by Klyuev in Volume Two of *The Scythians,* Esenin was undoubtedly forced to take second place. According to Ivanov-Razumnik,

Klyuev was the first poet of the people, whereas Esenin was "much younger than Klyuev, his paths lie yet ahead." Andrei Bely added his tribute to Klyuev, whose heart "combines pastoral truth with magical wisdom; the West with the East; combines indeed the sighings of the four corners of the Earth." For a person as ambitious as Esenin, second place would no longer suffice. Shortly after this second volume appeared, he wrote to Ivanov-Razumnik, voicing his hurt pride: "Your stamping of Klyuev as the 'first profound poet of the people'. . . forces me not to appear in a third volume of *The Scythians,* for what you and Andrei Bely regard as the height of perfection, I regard as a mouse's squeaking" (V, 76-77). Esenin declared that the tone of some of Klyuev's poetry was now repellent to him, and that Klyuev had recently become his "enemy" (V, 77). In a poem of 1917 (published in 1919) Klyuev lamented that "the white flower Seryozha. . . has fallen out of love with my tale," and in other poems referred to Esenin as "my brother, fiancé and son," "my cornflower." In 1918 Esenin dedicated a poem to Klyuev, with the opening line "My love is no longer the same" ("Teper' liubov' moia ne ta," II, 72), and went on to criticise Klyuev's poetry as earthbound.

Esenin was beginning to grow away from Klyuev's influence. In time this almost coincided with the October Revolution, but it seems improbable that political reasons were the basic cause of their increasing estrangement. The most frequent Soviet explanation is indeed the political one—that Esenin was far more in favour of the October Revolution than was the conservative, religious Klyuev—although P. F. Yushin, with some justification, maintains that in fact Klyuev was the more revolutionary. Local Vytegra and Olonets newspapers in 1918 referred to "comrade Nikolai Klyuev," and even reported in May 1918 that "N. Klyuev has entered the ranks of the Bolshevik party and is taking a most active part in its work. . ."

Esenin's poetry of this period is generally too vague to deduce any definite political stance. His long poem "Advent" ("Prishestvie," II, 7-12) is dated October 1917, and, despite notes of optimism, its overall tone is one of anxiety—there is an apocalyptic feeling, with the Advent and Crucifixion implicit. In "Transfiguration" ("Preobrazhenie," II, 13-17), dedicated to Ivanov-Razumnik in November 1917, the tone is optimistic again, although the poem is full of vague religious and animal symbolism. A "new sower," a "bright guest" is coming to us, and after the hour of Transfiguration our days will be filled with milk and a rich harvest—a dream of peaceful peasant prosperity. Esenin's political naiveté continued into 1918, when, according to G. Ustinov, at a Bolshevik gathering he "smiled affably at absolutely everyone—whoever was speaking and whatever they said. Then the yellow-haired boy himself felt the urge to say his word. . . and he said:—The revolution... is a raven.... a raven which we send forth from our head... to do reconnaissance... The future is more..."

In 1917-18 Esenin couched his long revolutionary poems in terms of abstruse Christian symbolism, which may help to account for their relative "unpopularity" today. Yet they are the understandable outburst of a poet whose roots to a considerable extent were steeped in religious symbolism, and who wished to ride the wave of revolutionary fervour. They are exclamatory, wild, and clearly influenced by the more learned Scythians, Ivanov-Razumnik and Bely. In his article "Two Russias" ("Dve Rossii"), written in November 1917, Ivanov -Razumnik identified the attitude of Klyuev and Esenin with his own view, which was: "We see pillage and coercion and spiritual decline, but we also see sacrifice and heroism and spiritual burning. . . Great is our grief, our indignation—about the decline; great is our joy, our exultation—about the burning of the human soul." Ivanov-Razumnik believed that the revolution would soon be trampled upon, before being resurrected. Such views are reflected, for instance, in Esenin's poem "A Village Prayer Book" ("Sel'skii chasoslov," II, 44-48), which was published in June 1918. Vladimir Chernyavsky (to whom Esenin dedicated "A Village Prayer Book") states that Esenin regarded Ivanov-Razumnik "with great respect and love. . . The articles of R. V. Ivanov, who accepted Esenin in his entirety as a major *poet of the revolution,* fully satisfied and supported Sergei. He probably never found such 'paternal generosity,' either before or after, in any of the authoritative people writing about their contemporaries."

Nevertheless, Esenin's longer poems of 1917-18 sound somewhat false. Perhaps a certain pretentiousness is evident even in such a detail as the dedication of his famous poem "Inoniya," written in January 1918. The poem bears the lofty dedication: "To the prophet Jeremiah" (II, 33)–yet an original manuscript contains a more humble inscription: "I dedicate to Z. N. E."–that is, to Zinaida Nikolaevna Raikh-Esenina.[2] In "Inoniya" (II, 33-41) the defiant and self-hyperbolising "prophet Esenin Sergei" spits Christ's body from his mouth, and threatens to pluck God's beard and lick the faces of martyrs and saints from the icons–for "I promise you the city of Inoniya,/ Where the god of the living lives." Disdaining the old God and the old Crucifixion, he proclaims a "new Nazareth" and envisages a peasant paradise, with cornfields and huts and his aged mother. The poem, full of explosive energy, has struck some as blasphemous, others as the replacement of one religion by another.

Esenin was now generally recognised as a talented and promising poet, on the threshold of real fame. He was often mentioned in literary journals, but Ivanov-Razumnik was alone at this time in placing him at the forefront of literary Russia. Esenin himself clearly realised this. His pre-revolutionary success had been confined to the salons and Court; now he had to win the affections of a wider audience. As long as he remained closely linked with the Scythians and published his verse in the left wing Socialist Revolutionary press, he could not hope to escape the censure of Marxist and proletarian critics. His favourite books at this time were not works of Marxist doctrine, but the Bible and the Old Russian "Lay of Igor's Raid" ("Slovo o polku Igoreve").

Fortunately for Esenin, the first years after the revolution were marked by a great upsurge in his energies and literary activity. He devoted himself to his cosmic prophetic poems about the revolution, and ate and drank little. "I had never seen him before in such a continuously creative state," recalls Chernyavsky.

An expert graphologist, D. M. Zuev-Insarov, comments on Esenin's handwriting of this period: "*1918.* The letters become almost vertical. . . The links between letters almost completely disappear. –Moods coloured in ambitious tones increase. Critical evaluation of his own actions becomes blunted. Self-confidence increases. Little by little his personality becomes distorted." It was from 1917 onwards that the characteristic handwriting of the mature Esenin became fixed, with almost every letter isolated from its neighbours. Memoirists tend to romanticise about this, finding a beauty and purity in the lone, rounded letters, although the writer Yury Olesha is more incisive: "It is understandable that if every letter stands apart, then the owner of that handwriting has a high opinion of himself. Indeed, even in cursive writing such a man manages to place every letter separately, as if remembering each one, as if valuing each one very highly. A model of such handwriting is Esenin's. . . Every letter is rounded, almost a circle, each one stands separately, green on the white paper like a bush in the snow." To judge the opinion of Zuev-Insarov and Olesha, one may look at the way Esenin wrote out the poem in 1917 which contains the lines: "People say that soon I'll become/ A famous Russian poet" (photocopy on I, 295).

Esenin was beginning to seek his own poetic voice, free from the influence of Klyuev, Blok and anyone else who might impede his independence. On January 3, 1918 he spent the evening at Blok's, and Blok's detailed diary note about Esenin's conversation vividly conveys the hotchpotch of ideas in which Esenin then professed belief. Chernyavsky maintains that only once, as far as he knows, did Esenin behave provocatively towards Blok–and that was during these days, when Esenin was captivated by belief in a new peasant Russia. Chernyavsky also observes: "In the coldness which he felt towards Blok and in Blok there was, I think, an element of straightforward jealousy for the right to be the 'first Russian poet' in the October period." January 1918 was the month in which Blok composed "The Twelve" ("Dvenadtsat' "), and Esenin actually suggested one adjective of the poem to Blok.

On February 21, 1918 the Soviets published a proclamation, *Our Socialist Fatherland Is in Danger!,* and Blok noted that same day in his diary that Esenin had enrolled in a fighting squad, which was presumably to defend Soviet power. Such militant action seems uncharacteristic of Esenin, and until more details are known, perhaps Blok's diary entry should be regarded as an indication of Esenin's enthusiastic good intentions rather than a positive and actual military contribution.

For three years Esenin had been living primarily in or near Petrograd. He now took an important decision, for in the spring of 1918 he moved to Moscow, where he was to spend most of the rest of his life. In an autobiography he explained this move rather misleadingly: "Together with the Soviet government I left Petrograd" (V, 13). It is true that in March 1918, because of the military threat to Petrograd, the Soviet government transferred to Moscow. Esenin tries to give the impression that he followed because of solidarity with the Soviet regime, but in fact the political reason was simply that Esenin went along with the left wing Socialist Revolutionaries who followed the Soviet government to Moscow. For some months after arriving in Moscow Esenin continued to publish his verse in the SR newspaper *Banner of Labour,* and then in the peasant-orientated *Voice of the Peasant Workers (Golos trudovogo krest'ianstva).* On July 4, 1918 *Banner of Labour* ceased publication, when the left wing SRs broke with the Government.

Although the immediate reason for Esenin's move to Moscow is thus clear–Ivanov-Razumnik, Oreshin and others also transferred to Moscow at this time–the change of city may also have met a deeper need in Esenin. Petrograd, admittedly, had been the scene of his first major success, and his years in Moscow from 1912-15 had been dull and unhappy in comparison; but Esenin may have been feeling somewhat out of his depth in literary Petrograd. In Petrograd there were the educated intellectuals; Moscow, in contrast, was more "Russian," less European–and contained fewer rival poets. It is hard to visualise the Imaginists achieving such scandalous fame in the city that was once St. Petersburg! Bunin quotes approvingly a judgment by his fellow-emigre Georgy Adamovich: "Esenin appeared in Petersburg. . . and was received among writers with derisive surprise. . . Sologub's comment about him is unrepeatable in print, Kuzmin frowned, Gumilyov shrugged his shoulders, Gippius, looking at his *valenki* (felt boots) through her lorgnette, asked: 'What kind of *guêtres* are those?' All this forced Esenin to move to Moscow and there he quickly became popular by joining the Imaginists." Bunin's attitude is, of course, biased–it was three whole years before Esenin felt "forced" to move to Moscow, and the welcome he received from the leading Petrograd writers was by no means as universally derisive as this statement pretends. Nevertheless, Esenin was probably relieved to escape from his Petrograd past, where he was known as a disciple of Klyuev and where rumours about his activities in Tsarskoe Selo may have been an embarrassment. In a way, Moscow offered the chance of a fresh start.

Khodasevich describes Esenin shortly after his arrival in Moscow in the spring of 1918: "He was somehow physically pleasant. He was attractively harmonious; soft but assured movements; a face which was not beautiful, but pleasing. But best of all was his gaiety, light, lively, but not noisy or grating. He was very rhythmical. He looked you straight in the eyes and at once produced the impression of a man with an honest heart, no doubt a most excellent companion." Very rarely does a memoirist describe Esenin's face as "plain" or "unattractive," although on some photographs his face does have a coarsish, "unspiritual" quality. Roman Gul maintained: "Esenin was ugly. . . A Slavonic face with a slight touch of Mordovia in the cheek bones. His face was irregular, with a small forehead and petty features. Such faces are handsome in adolescence." As for his clothes, in 1918 he dressed smartly, even dandyishly, still with a preference for peasant costume, although smart town suits were beginning to replace the peasant coat in his affections.

Once he had settled down in Moscow, Esenin began to seek an outlet for his energy. Ilya Ehrenburg could see that the poet was volatile and chameleon-like: "Unlike Klyuev, Esenin was always changing roles: . . . he couldn't stop acting (or had no wish to). . . In May 1918 he told me that everything must be overthrown, the whole structure of the universe must be changed, and the peasants will set fire to the lot and the world will be burnt up." For Esenin, 1918 was "an exceptionally happy time," recalls Oreshin. "His name was much talked about in the literature of that period. Every poem of his provoked a reaction. Every poem was met by torrents of praise and abuse. Esenin worked tirelessly, his magnificent talent developed and blossomed with remarkable power."

Several memoirists assert that he did not need alcohol as a stimulus during these months, even though he began to frequent some of the literary cafes which enjoyed great popularity in the first years after the revolution. From April until June he published his verse in the SR press, but from the second part of the year his links with the SRs diminished, probably partly because the left wing SRs were now more openly in opposition to the Bolsheviks.

Esenin's daughter Tatyana was born in mid-1918, but as with the birth of his son Yury in 1915, the poet's paternal reaction was one of withdrawal. Less than a month after Tatyana's birth he was in Konstantinovo, and it was here that a further love affair developed. This time it was not a simple village girl who charmed him, but the landowner herself, Lidiya Ivanovna Kashina. Lidiya Kashina seems to have been a beautiful young woman, who had parted from her husband, a "very important general," and now lived on her estate in Konstantinovo with her two young children. Much to his mother's displeasure, Esenin had become friendly with the *barynia* (lady) in 1917, if not earlier, and during his visit in 1918 their affections clearly ripened. In August 1918 he dedicated his poem "Green Coiffure" ("Zelenaia pricheska," II, 54-55) to Kashina. Lidiya Kashina evidently made a lasting impression on Esenin—she is believed to be the prototype of the heroine of "Anna Snegina," which the poet began to write in December 1924.

Nevertheless, contrary to the popular conception of Esenin as a Don Juan figure, the enigma of his coldness towards women remains. G. Ustinov observes: "Esenin married young, and suffered some kind of profound tragedy, about which he spoke only in passing and with hints, even during intimate conversations when he used to open up, in as far as his generally secretive and often divided personality allowed. . . Esenin had a peculiar, unhealthy attitude to women and marriage. In this attitude there was something extremely painful." Perhaps Esenin was thinking of his love-hatred for Zinaida Raikh;[3] certainly, Anna Sardanovskaya (who died in 1922) seems a distant, peripheral figure. Or perhaps his allusions to some profoundly tragic early experience were merely an attempt to explain away his inability to love any woman deeply and constantly. On October 8, 1918, only a few months after Raikh had borne him their first child and he had dedicated "Green Coiffure" to Kashina, Esenin wrote a poem which begins: "I shall not caress/ Any girl./ Ah, there is but one I love,/ Forgetting earthly love,/ The Mother of God in heaven" (II, 61). In a poem of about 1918 he explained: "I want to be quiet and strict,/ I am learning silence from the stars" (II, 58).

Esenin remained in Konstantinovo during the summer of 1918, returning to Moscow by September. A period of rapid realignments began. Klyuev had now dropped out of the immediate scene, and was henceforth to play but a marginal role in Esenin's everyday life. Klyuev was evidently not tempted to move to Moscow; instead he withdrew to his northern wilderness, where he endeavoured to combine the two strands of religion and revolution into an ingratiatingly decorative pattern of verse. Esenin put out feelers towards several new groupings in the closing months of 1918, before finally settling on an alliance with the Imaginists. On the one hand, he seems to have come closer to the Bolsheviks now than at any time since the Revolution. On August 22, 1918 most of his long poem "The Dove of the Jordan" ("Iordanskaia golubitsa") was published in the literary supplement to the Bolshevik newspaper *Izvestiya VTsIK.* This was the first time since the October Revolution that his verse had been printed by this central Bolshevik organ, and the poem contained the resounding lines: "My native land is my mother,/ I am a Bolshevik" (II, 50). The Imperial family had been wiped out only a month before Esenin published this declaration. What did he feel about the murder of the Empress to whom he had recited his verse in 1916, and of the princesses he had praised in a poem? At all events, he promptly asserted: "I am a Bolshevik."

Towards the end of 1918 Esenin seemed, for a short while, to be drawing close to the proletariat. He began to take an interest in the proletarian poets and the new proletarian cultural organisations ("Proletcult"). In mid-September he attended the first all-Russian Proletcult conference in Moscow, and he befriended in particular the talented proletarian poet, Mikhail Gerasimov (1889-1939). With Gerasimov, Klychkov and the poetess Nadezhda Pavlovich, Esenin worked enthusiastically on a film scenario, *The Beckoning Dawn (Zovushchie zori,* IV, 235-250). The film was never produced, but the scenario, which Esenin neatly copied out, reflected the new collectivistic revolutionary spirit of the age, both romantic and naive. This was not the only occasion when the individualistic Esenin collaborated in a collective effort. In October-November he worked with Klychkov and Gerasimov on *Kantata,* a three-part poem in honour of those slain during the October Revolution. The element of collaboration here was heightened by the fact that the text of *Kantata* was to serve as an illustration for a memorial plaque by the distinguished sculptor Sergei Konyonkov (1874-1971), which was duly unveiled in the Kremlin by Lenin in November 1918. Esenin became a frequent visitor at Konyonkov's Moscow studio in Krasnaya Presnya, and greatly valued the boisterous companionship and artistic sensibility of the peasant-born sculptor. At various times between 1918 and 1922 Esenin planned to write a monograph about Konyonkov's work, but never managed to do so.

Nevertheless, despite these collective efforts and his friendship with Gerasimov, a member of the Communist Party since 1905, Esenin's connection with the Proletcult was tenuous and short-lived. In his whole way of thinking and feeling Esenin was poles apart from the almost Victorian self-righteousness of the Proletcult, with its zealous protection of the chastity of proletarian ideology. Proletcult journals were hostile to Esenin's mysticism, and in November 1918 the Proletcult journal *Furnace (Gorn)* refused to publish a poem by the "peasant poet" Esenin. Esenin for his part looked down from a lofty height upon the artistic shortcomings of most proletarian poets, as is clear from his 1918 article about proletarian writers (IV, 216-221). Here he singles out Gerasimov as the only outstanding proletarian poet.

Furthermore, it should be understood that he had never planned to enter the Proletcult circles "unarmed," as it were.

Although he was drifting away from Klyuev and the Scythians, he was surrounded by other peasant writers, including Oreshin and, above all, Sergei Klychkov (1889-1940). The latter was evidently the person closest to Esenin towards the end of 1918. Late in 1918 Esenin and Klychkov lived in a low-ceilinged attic-type room inside the building of the Moscow Proletcult itself, which had formerly been the mansion of the merchant Morozov. It was presumably as a result of this that Esenin first became involved with Proletcult meetings, where young proletarian poets such as Kazin, Sannikov, Obradovich, Poletaev and Alexandrovsky, and older Symbolists such as Vyacheslav Ivanov and Andrei Bely, met to discuss artistic matters. Esenin apparently considered forming a close literary alliance with Klychkov in the latter part of 1918. Klychkov had collaborated with Esenin on *Kantata* and *The Beckoning Dawn;* they joined the Writers' Trade Union together in December 1918; for a while they thought of founding a new literary school to be known as "aggelism"[4]; and in late September-early October they sought in vain to form a peasant section within the Moscow Proletcult.

Whilst the latter two ideas were stillborn, one other scheme was more successful. As Esenin and his friends had stressed in their application to the Proletcult (V, 181-182), it was now extremely difficult to get works of literature published. Alongside the increasing food famine in Moscow, there was a "paper famine"—many former "bourgeois" literary journals were closed down, and priority was given to political, "agitational" literature. Accordingly, in about September, Esenin and some other writers gathered together to form their own co-operative publishing concern. Five people attended the first organisational meeting: Esenin, Klychkov, Oreshin, Bely and the journalist Lev Povitsky. It was decided to call the publishing firm the *Moscow Labour Artel of Artists of the Word (Moskovskaia Trudovaia Artel' Khudozhnikov Slova)*—Povitsky was to manage the financial side; Esenin and Klychkov were to hold discussions with the printing works and bookshops; whilst Bely quixotically declared: "And I'll carry the paper from the warehouse to the printing works!" At the time, recalls Povitsky, all the paper in Moscow was confiscated and under state control, but Esenin devised an ingenious method of acquiring the precious commodity:

> He obtained it by the same means that he applied somewhat later in his new publishing concern "The Imaginists." This method was very simple and always achieved the desired results. He used to dress up in his long-tailed peasant coat, comb his hair in peasant fashion and set off to visit the member on duty at the Presidium of the Moscow Soviet.[5] Standing hatless before the latter, he would bow and, putting on a peasant accent, beg him "for the sake of Christ" to show "God's mercy" and provide some paper for "peasant" verse. Of course it was unthinkable to refuse such a supplicant, from whom it was hard to avert one's delighted gaze. And so we got our paper.

The publishing concern, the "Moscow Labour Artel of Artists of the Word," lasted until about April 1920, when it went into liquidation. During that time five of Esenin's books appeared under its imprint—*Transfiguration* and *A Village Prayer Book* (both late 1918), a considerably revised second edition of *Radunitsa* (late 1918/early 1919), *The Keys of Mary* and a second edition of *Goluben'* (both by early 1920). Although these books have markedly religious titles, at Esenin's suggestion the firm dated some of its publications in a "revolutionary" way—instead of "1918," the covers bore the date mark: "the second year of the first century."

1918 had been a successful year for Esenin. His work had been much discussed, even if the critical reaction had been chiefly abusive. Apart from the three above-mentioned volumes published by the "Labour Artel," two other slim books of his verse had appeared in the course of the year—*The Infant Jesus (Isus-mladenets)* and the long-delayed first edition of *Goluben'*—and he had contributed to anthologies such as *Krasnyi zvon*[6] and *The Spring Salon of Poets (Vesennii salon poetov).* Yet he was still in a transitional stage in his creative evolution, in a kind of late adolescence with his poetic voice still unsteady. He might proclaim "I'm a Bolshevik" in one poem and blaspheme against the old God in another—yet his books still bore religious titles, and he insisted upon capital letters for important religious names (such as God, and the Mother of God).[7] It was in the last months of

1918 that he worked on his remarkable and fanciful poetic tract, *The Keys of Mary* (IV, 173-201)–yet it was also about this time that he conceived his poem "The Celestial Drummer" ("Nebesnyi barabanshchik," II, 66-69), with its fervent wish for revolution "both on earth and in heaven."

Esenin subsequently dated "The Celestial Drummer" as 1918,[8] but the poem was not published until 1920. Why the delay in publication, when he had endeavoured, in his own fashion, to write a militant revolutionary work which berates the "white herd of gorillas"–that is, the opponents of Bolshevism? The reason is clear: Esenin's wild, anarchistic revolutionary spirit was unacceptable to serious Marxists. The poet at the time was full of cosmic and mystical notions, about the earth, moon and village being "feminine," whilst the sun and town are "masculine"–and the Communist leader Bukharin frankly retorted that such metaphysics are rubbish, "you should study Marx a bit more seriously." Early in 1919 Esenin was living at the hotel Luxe, where his friend Georgy Ustinov had two large rooms, and Ustinov, who worked for the newspaper *Pravda,* endeavoured to have "The Celestial Drummer" published in that Bolshevik organ. The reply must have opened Esenin's eyes–N. L. Meshcheryakov, an editor of *Pravda,* rejected the poem as "Incoherent nonsense. Unsuitable. N. M."

On the wall of Esenin's room in January 1919, recalls D. Semenovsky, an eight-pointed brocade cross hung on a piece of blue silk. Although there is no reason to portray Esenin as a conventional "believer" (no Orthodox Russian would have written "Inoniya"), such an apparently trivial detail is revealing. It seems to symbolise the gulf between Esenin and such people as Meshcheryakov and Bukharin. Hence it is no surprise that Esenin's desire to join the Communist Party at about this time came to nothing. As Georgy Ustinov writes, Esenin, with his marked individuality, alien to any kind of discipline, would never have made a Party member, and when Meshcheryakov rejected "The Celestial Drummer," Esenin finally gave up any idea of joining the Party, even though this rejection hurt his pride.

For some months Esenin had been leading a nomadic

existence in Moscow, sharing rooms with Klychkov, Ustinov and others. His happy domestic routine with Zinaida Raikh had been smashed for ever. V. Levin writes: "Sometimes he disappeared for several days, vanishing who knows where with unknown people. This was the period of his friendship with Mariengof, Shershenevich, Kusikov and other representatives of Moscow's literary bohemia of the time. Zinaida put up with these aspects of his character, but it was hard for her, very hard. . ."

Some new friends had appeared towards the end of 1918, and they were to play a major role in Esenin's life during the following years.

Chapter Seven: The Tender Hooligan (1919)

Throughout 1918 Esenin had been seeking fresh poetic allies, and his own poetic voice, and the path to national fame. He found, or so it seemed to him for a long time, all three in the new literary movement which became known as "Imaginism" ("imazhinizm"). The theory that the image is the essence of poetry was not new, nor was the practice—it can be seen in the literature of many ages. Furthermore, the "Imagist" movement had recently developed in English poetry, with Ezra Pound as one of its leading exponents. In 1915 an article about these "Imagists" appeared in a Petrograd volume, and the Russian poets who were soon to call themselves the "Imaginists" ("imazhinisty") read this article and took heed of the name and theory. Even before he first met Mariengof and Shershenevich, Esenin's poetic evolution was leading him towards "Imaginism"—his cosmic revolutionary long poems of 1917-18 were saturated with religious and animal images. It was as a young, rebellious poet, individualistic and volatile, that he first made contact with the poets who were soon to publish the Imaginist *Declaration.*

Four poets signed this *Declaration* in late January 1919: Sergei Esenin, Ryurik Ivnev, Anatoly Mariengof, and Vadim Shershenevich. Ivnev had befriended Esenin in March 1915, and now they found common ground in Imaginism. Ivnev's verse of 1912-16 was full of a dark hatred for the flesh, which must be burnt and purified in a kind of self-castigating religious ecstasy—a "decadent," death-obsessed vision which was, however, expressed with considerable poetic skill. If before the Revolution Ivnev had entertained Klyuev in his icon-filled room, so after the Revolution he listened to Lunacharsky talking of Marxism, and indeed came to Moscow in March 1918 as Lunacharsky's secretary. According to Georgy Ivanov, in 1918 Ivnev stated that "Soviet power is Christ's power." Ivnev was the least "Imaginistic" of the Imaginists, and scarcely belongs to their poetic practice or bohemian scandals. He himself admits that what attracted him mainly to Imaginism was his friendship with Esenin.

The two main "culprits," berated in the Soviet Union, were Mariengof and Shershenevich. They were the chief practitioners of Imaginist theory, and Soviet critics condemn them for their "catalogues of images," their cynicism, eroticism and inner emptiness. Nevertheless, Shershenevich in particular was undoubtedly talented. Vadim Shershenevich (1893-1942) was a literary chameleon, the ex-Futurist who became the arch-enemy of Futurism. He is something of a tragi-comic figure—intelligent, gifted, and yet, as Esenin said to Volf Erlikh, "he was unlucky. . . he never found himself." He was witty and professional. "Vadim Shershenevich wielded a verbal foil like no one else in Moscow," writes Mariengof. "Without ceremony he. . . piled up about him the semi-corpses and corpses of the enemies of our faith, of our holy and frenzied faith in the divine metaphor, which we called the 'image'!" Yet there was a profound void beneath the gaiety of the cultured Shershenevich—there is some truth in D. Vygodsky's judgment that "Shershenevich's activity was nothing but the literary charlatanism of a gifted and well-read bourgeois who felt bored. In the last analysis, Shershenevich was the only theorist of Imaginism, its great charlatan."

Esenin never became a close friend of Shershenevich, and Mariengof suggests that this was because Esenin, so sensitive to criticism, never fully forgave Shershenevich for writing an article attacking him in 1918 in a Futurist journal. As Mariengof explains, however, Esenin came across this article only in 1920 or so, so that there must have been earlier reasons too. Perhaps Esenin resented Shershenevich's erudition and his former Futurist allegiance—at all events, in the manuscript of his own article of 1918, "The Keys of Mary," Esenin listed Shershenevich as one of the Futurists he despised, although when *The Keys of Mary* was eventually published (by early 1920) he omitted the name of the man who was now his colleague. As a result, Shershenevich was able to praise *The Keys of Mary* as the "philosophy of Imaginism," probably little suspecting that but eighteen months earlier he had been branded there as one of Esenin's literary enemies!

Of the original four "front-line" Imaginists, it was Anatoly Mariengof (1897-1962) who became Esenin's closest friend. Unlike Ivnev and Shershenevich, Mariengof was virtually unknown as a poet in early 1919–he was the youngest and least cultured of the trio. His friendship with Esenin began at first sight and was profound–despite what may have happened later, Ivnev's recent statement should be respected: "I consider that the friendship of Esenin and Mariengof was so great and genuine that it continues a 'posthumous existence,' despite the severance that took place." Mariengof himself, when approaching old age, recalled the days in 1919 when he and Esenin were as one person:

> Esenin and I lived in one room. When the central heating was not working in January, we slept under one blanket. For about four years we were never seen apart. We shared our money: his was mine, mine was his, or, more simply, both his and mine were–ours. We published our poems under one cover and dedicated them to one another. Not infrequently it happened that we conversed without speaking. Simply a kind of mysticism. That is: one of us would be lying on a sofa; the other sat in silence in an armchair. And suddenly–either he would answer my silent thought, or I his. It even became uncanny. In short: it was a great, beautiful, manly, and, so it seemed, indissoluble friendship.

Elsewhere Mariengof writes: "We always spoke the truth about our verse, were strict judges of one another and believed one another firmly. Our poetic careers were different, mine lay through the city, his through the Ryazan steppe into the blue sky–and as a result we were not jealous of one another and were not at all at loggerheads (as he and Klyuev were)."

For some three years Esenin and Mariengof were inseparable friends. At a time of cold, famine and civil war, the Imaginists rejoiced in scandals and poetry. Yet few people speak well of Mariengof, and his verse sometimes betrays a cynicism which, if taken literally, is repugnant. Nevertheless, he was certainly Esenin's closest friend, and Soviet critics are unfair when they reject in its entirety Mariengof's provocative book of memoirs, *A Novel Without Lies (Roman bez vran'ia).* His book tends to be cynical and condescending, but it is also amusing, vivid and valuable in catching much of the atmosphere of the Imaginists' bohemian life.

Mariengof recalls how the Imaginists planned the first

declaration of their existence:

> Late into the night we drank tea with saccharin and talked about the image, its place in poetry, and the revival of the great verbal art of the *Song of Songs, Kalevala* and *The Lay of Igor's Raid.* Esenin already had his own classification of images. He called static ones *zastavki* [ornamental headpieces in books or manuscripts], and dynamic, mobile ones *korabel'nye* [shipborne, connected with ships], placing the second incomparably higher than the first. . . A formal school was essential for Esenin. And not only for him. With the lamentable state of our minds it never does harm to learn a bit. . .

They had met in Moscow some time towards the end of 1918, and discovered that their love of poetry had much in common. "And what we had in common," writes Shershenevich, "by dint of long arguments, took the shape of a movement which has come down to you under the name of Imaginism. . . We thought for a long time, argued even more, and on the eve of the publication of our first manifesto of Imaginism two of us refused at first to sign it."

The name "Imaginism" ("imazhinizm") had been anticipated much earlier by Shershenevich in several of his many theoretical articles, where he advocated "imazhionizm" (with an "o"). More recently, in provincial Penza, Mariengof and his friend Ivan Startsev had fallen in love with the "image" and issued a book of their "Imaginist" verse before coming to Moscow in search of fame. Thus, by different paths, three poets had recognised the supremacy of the image. For Shershenevich, the new theory was a variant of Futurism; for Mariengof, it was a youthful infatuation, which he felt was stronger than his love for any schoolgirl; and for Esenin, it was a natural development of his rich rural and religious metaphors (in the course of which the previously abundant religious metaphors virtually disappeared). It is true that in his poetry Esenin was very different from the other Imaginists, but his alliance with the group was by no means fortuitous. It has been said that Esenin's Imaginist roots can be traced back to his love of *The Lay of Igor's Raid,* the imagery of folk poetry, and even Gogol and Homer!

The Imaginist *Declaration* was published in the Voronezh

journal *Siren (Sirena)* of January 30, 1919, and the Moscow newspaper *Soviet Land (Sovetskaia strana)* of February 10. It was signed by Esenin, Ivnev, Mariengof and Shershenevich, and by the artists Boris Erdman and Georgy Yakulov. Shershenevich was evidently its chief author. Deliberately provocative and wild in tone, it hurled abuse upon literary foe and reader alike, mocking Futurism and the idea of "content" in art:

> Futurism is dead. . . We call, not back from Futurism, but over its corpse forward and ever forward, lefter and lefter. . . We find it comic when people talk about the content of art. . . We assert that the only law of art, its only and incomparable method, is the revelation of life by means of the image and the rhythm of images. . . The image, and nothing but the image. . . All content in a work of art is as stupid and senseless as newspaper collages on pictures. . . Portray whatever you wish, as long as it is in the modern rhythms of images. . . Notice how lucky we are. We have no philosophy. We propose no logic of thoughts. The logic of our certitude is more powerful than anything. We are not only convinced that we are on the right path, we know it. . . In these days of cold lodgings, only the heat of our works can warm the souls of readers and spectators. . . (IV, 251-255).

The journal *Siren* was published by the Voronezh Executive Committee of the Soviet of Workers and Red Army Deputies, and the newspaper *Soviet Land* bore on its front page the slogan "Workers of the world, unite!" In *Siren,* directly after the Imaginist *Declaration,* the reader was treated to a sample of Mariengof's verse:

> I'll make the sky, the sky, have an abortion,
> And squeeze some milk from the teats of the moon. . .

Mariengof continued with a picture of, perhaps, Soviet Moscow:

> Oh, I don't want such a city,
> Give me the alcohol of your flowers, Nice!
> One more hour and our souls will turn green,
> Like a mistress after an abortion.

In *Soviet Land* on February 10, Mariengof's poem "Magdalina" was published, dedicated "with love to Sergei Esenin." This poem of profane love contained some lines which caused great offence:

> Citizens, change
> The underclothes of your souls!
> Magdalina, today I also
> Shall come to you in clean drawers.

Lenin allegedly read this poem, and observed that its author was a "sick boy."

The Imaginists had made their noisy debut, characterising themselves–in the words of Shershenevich and Boris Erdman–as "children of the beautiful charlatan Harlequin, who always has a smile radiant with joy and May. We do not know the word 'sadness,' for even our despair is joyful and sunny." Esenin's signature headed the list of front-line Imaginists beneath the *Declaration,* although his verse as yet had almost none of the blatant cynicism of Mariengof. On February 17 Esenin's poem "Pantokrator" (II, 78-81), dedicated to Ryurik Ivnev, was published in *Soviet Land.* In part, this poem continued the mood of "Inoniya," with the poet declaring:

> You taught me, Lord,
> To swear at you, not to pray. . .
> I cry out to you: "To the devil with everything old!"
> (II, 78)

Not surprisingly, the Imaginist *Declaration* provoked controversy. On February 15 the critic V. Friche fulminated against this "prodigious poverty, both literary and intellectual, this loud and brazen self-advertisement" being published in the Soviet press, and exclaimed: "Truly, literary morals have become stultified and wild!" He thundered against the empty souls, lack of ideals, and bad taste "characteristic of the capitalist bourgeois system," of people "from bourgeois-Tsarist Russia." Unrepentant, Ryurik Ivnev retorted two days later: "The Imaginists are the only way out of the impasse of ossification in which art finds itself."

The storm grew. The Imaginists announced their own publishing firm in February—"despite the paper-famine," noted Friche angrily—and prepared to extract money from a shocked public. Proletcult poets and critics, who had earlier condemned Esenin's mysticism, now had fresh ammunition to aim at the peasant poet and his new colleagues. In the Proletcult journal *Factory Whistles (Gudki)* in March a verse-parody paraphrased the Imaginists' self-declared rejection of logic and content, and another parody ridiculed Esenin's cow-imagery:

> Esenin has given birth to a calf again,
> The most fashionable of all poets...
> Perhaps Sergei Esenin
> Will at least yield a glass of milk!

In April the same journal objected to Esenin and company being allowed to prosper—"and this at a time when the world is choking in the blood of a civil war, when the head of the much-wounded proletariat is spinning from all its efforts!"

The Imaginists were quickly achieving notoriety. As if to mock Russia's suffering, Mariengof published some poems in the volume *Reality (Iav')*, relishing the blood-letting of the Revolution. These poems are dated 1918, but their cynical exultation in the terrible bloodshed inevitably heaped more coals onto his smartly-combed head. Mariengof wrote:

> We spit blood shamefully
> At the foolish face of God...
> The wind will sweep up
> The human ham.
> In this pile of skulls
> Lies our red revenge...

He retorted to any would-be critics: "You don't like it if we guffaw blood?":

> Blood, blood, blood splashes in the world,
> Like water in a bath...
> Who cares about the dead!...
> We walk past, walk past...

A reviewer in the newspaper *Pravda* on March 12 promptly rejected this "deafening yelping" of Mariengof as alien to the proletariat.

On April 3 the Imaginists held an exhibition of verse and paintings in the Grand Hall of the Polytechnic Museum. A poster advertised the contents:

i) Shershenevich: Who We Are and How People Spit On Us
Esenin: A Stake Thrust in the Belly (of Futurism and other Old Testament stuff)
Mariengof: Revolt of Us (The Imaginists' note)
Yakulov: The Image of Colour

ii) [Verse]
Esenin: The God That Gave Birth to a Calf
Mariengof: Abortion of Despair
Shershenevich: Co-operatives of Joy

iii) Literary dispute.

A reviewer of this exhibition dismissed the Imaginists' verse as weak imitations of Futurism, but found the artists such as Yakulov more interesting. "The new group gives too few positive artistic achievements: again we have an agitational racket, grandiloquent declarations and manifestoes."

With concealed laughter and cunning, Esenin explained to the proletarian poet Kirillov why he had allied himself with a group whose theory and practice affronted the ideals of the new society: "You can't go very far on talent alone these days. A scandal, especially a beautiful scandal, is always a help to talent." He loved scandals and brawls—not only for themselves, but in order to achieve national fame. This was his "solution" to the question which had troubled him throughout 1918—how to free himself from the past influences of Klyuev and Ivanov-Razumnik, and from the inevitable limitation of being a "peasant," rather than a Russian, national poet. This was his reaction against the peasant coat and felt boots in which he had made his first steps to glory. Professor Rozanov, perceptive as so often, writes:

> It seemed to me that Esenin valued his Imaginist friends because they really were companions, adroit and enterprising, and did not crush him with their authority, as had the "Scythians." Imaginism enabled him to push away from his past. He particularly disowned that period when his name was usually mentioned after that of Klyuev. He was indignant at those critics and compilers of anthologies who numbered him among the peasant poets. . . He found the grouping of poets not according to their creative methods, but according to their parentage, absurd.

In this respect, Imaginism played a beneficial role in Esenin's development as a poet. Soviet critics today are reluctant to admit this—but many memoirists in the 1920s, and by no means only those personally sympathetic to the Imaginists, conceded that Imaginism was important in liberating Esenin's talent from its narrowly "peasant" label. Gorodetsky is particularly convincing on this point, regarding Imaginism as a kind of "university" for Esenin, which brought him a consciousness of his mastery. Elsewhere Gorodetsky declares that Esenin needed the Imaginist way of life in order to rise above Klyuev and all the other peasant poets. By copying Mariengof's dandyish dress and behaviour, Esenin became superficially European. His Imaginist life was "his revolution, his liberation."

The statement that Imaginism was Esenin's "revolution" seems very apt. In a late autobiography Esenin crossed out some words, referring to the October Revolution: "But for the revolution I might have dried up in religious symbolism which nobody needed, or my talent might have developed in a wrong and unnecessary direction." These words, which Esenin himself omitted, are sometimes quoted by Soviet critics as a tribute to the beneficial effect of the October Revolution on Esenin's work. Yet, in fact, the October Revolution had at first merely intensified his "religious symbolism which nobody needed." It was by joining the Imaginists, and implicitly rejecting or ignoring the collectivistic revolutionary construction of the new society, that Esenin freed himself from the burden of religious symbols. If in this one instance Imaginism is equated with Esenin's "revolution," a truer statement emerges: "But for *Imaginism* I might have dried up in religious symbolism which nobody needed. . ."

It would be an exaggeration to say that Esenin's "otherworldliness" was killed in him for ever, but this period certainly was the time of his most violent rejection of religion. Indeed, he went so far in his contempt for religion that even proletarian critics felt uneasy. As early as January 1918, his poem "Inoniya" had caught many people unawares. Whereas Ivanov-Razumnik found himself able to approve of the poem as a justified rejection of the historical church and the affirmation of a new word, less ingenious critics were shocked. O. Leonidov wrote that in "Inoniya" Esenin "breaks the record of undue religious familiarity," and expressed the opinion that Esenin, and not God, was the one in need of change. It seems that, after the furor created by "Inoniya," Esenin began to think of adopting a new literary pose—this time as a tender hooligan, gentle and crude, humane and cynical all at once. This polarity had always been inherent in him, and the poet was unable, and probably unwilling, to resolve his contradictions. In the draft of his 1925 autobiography, he wrote: "At the beginning of 1918 I had the firm feeling that the link with the old world was broken and I [left the group of Blok, Bely] wrote the poem 'Inoniya,' against which there were many [sharp] attacks and as a result of which the nickname 'hooligan' became attached to me" (V, 231). The concept of Esenin as a hooligan certainly seems to have been in the air since early 1918. The word "hooligan" appeared in Esenin's conversation with Blok on January 3, 1918, and Mariengof blames literary critics for first giving Esenin the idea of behaving like a hooligan in poetry and in everyday life. Mariengof writes that Esenin realised, quite soberly and coldly, that this was his path to fame, and accordingly from 1919 he gave the public what they wanted. "I don't know which Esenin transmuted the more often: his life into verse, or his verse into life. His mask became his real face, and his face became a mask. . ."

It was a dangerous "game" upon which he embarked—a game he had been playing since 1915, but never before with such furious energy: the poetic pose, the confusion of his mask and his face. Imaginism did not change him overnight, of course, and for some months, even years, the toll might not be very apparent. The Imaginists' "scandals" were not all cynical and repugnant—

there was a large measure of youthful high spirits, gaiety and mischievousness about them. For years to come Esenin would try to assure others and himself that "I'm just the same./ In my heart I am just the same" (II, 101)—but his words were not wholly convincing.

Having decided to act the part of a "hooligan," Esenin and his friends began to express this in open blasphemy. There is a well-known episode in which Esenin allegedly chopped up an icon or two for firewood in order to heat up some tea. He was so proud of this action that he later boasted about it in the manuscript of his 1922 autobiography. That episode occurred in a private gathering, but an escapade in May 1919 shocked the general public. This was the famous incident when the Imaginists daubed their verse on the walls of the Convent of the Passion ("Strastnoy monastyr'") in Moscow, a feat which the Imaginists themselves regarded with great satisfaction. Esenin tells about it in several autobiographies: "In Russia, when there was no paper available, I printed my verse, together with Kusikov and Mariengof, on the walls of the Convent of the Passion. . ." (V, 10; see also V, 13). This happened on the night from May 27 to 28, 1919, and there is a disapproving report about the incident in the newspaper *Izvestiya* on May 31, 1919. Mariengof remembers what they wrote on the convent walls—he and Esenin provocatively chose the very lines for which they had been most sharply criticised:

> I sing and appeal: Lord, give birth to a calf!
> (Esenin)
> Citizens, change the underclothes of your souls!
> Magdalina, today I also
> Shall come to you in clean drawers
> (Mariengof)

Ivan Startsev, Mariengof's schoolfriend who was close to the Imaginists, relates certain other lines that Esenin daubed on the convent walls that night:

> Look at the fat thighs
> Of this obscene wall.

Here the nuns at night
Remove Christ's trousers.

These truly "hooligan" lines were certainly composed by Esenin at about this time.[1]

The proletarian poet N. Poletaev claims that Esenin used to be arrested about twice a week, but took a childish delight in such scandals: "Who do you think you are? B......, but I... I'm Esenin! All Russia knows me!" In a way, he was "in his element" now. He had cast aside the monastic garments of Klyuev and the religious-philosophical garb of Ivanov-Razumnik—and now he sported a top hat, smart gloves, and patent-leather shoes, and posed as a raffish dandy. It was as if Imaginism helped him to "find himself" by enabling him to "lose himself." He could now let himself go—a tendency which had threatened ever since 1915. In one autobiography he called 1919 "the best time in my life" (V, 9)—a remarkable confession when one considers the plight of Russia in that year. He had fame and freedom, even if—as Lundberg had feared in July 1918—this was to lead to "chaos" and "crime." Perhaps Esenin did not care; perhaps he felt he could "beat the lot" and defy fate. His Imaginist years, from 1919 to 1922, were a kind of volcanic eruption. In the explosions, Esenin produced some brilliant works and a legend was born—but the result sooner or later had to be inner devastation. He was burning himself up, gaily and irresponsibly. In 1923 he was to offer as an explanation of his behaviour: "I indulged in obscenities and scandals/ In order to burn more bright" (II, 129).

Whilst some members of the new society might forgive the Imaginists' blasphemy, they could not condone rebelliousness in another sphere. The Imaginists were essentially anarchistic—that is, they were tacitly or openly opposed to Bolshevism. At the same time that the Proletcult critics were advocating their monopoly of proletarian, collectivistic art, a rival journal had begun its life in July 1918. It was entitled *The Life and Works of Russian Youth (Zhizn' i tvorchestvo russkoi molodezhi),* and by November 1918 its tone had become unmistakably anarchistic: "We are convinced that within a few years the younger generation will educate itself in the spirit of anarchism and stand firmly in defence of its ideals, and then in place of the Soviet system a new system will appear before the world, a system of total freedom, total joy." By early 1919 the journal had become the "Organ of the All-Russian Federation of Anarchist Youth," and it was at this point that Vadim Shershenevich made his debut on its pages. On April 13, 1919, some two months after the Imaginist *Declaration* was published, Shershenevich's article, "Art and the State" ("Iskusstvo i gosudarstvo") appeared. Here he asserted defiantly:

> . . . Art is fettered and killed by too much attention from the State. . . The State does not need an art of aspiration, but an art of propaganda. And so we see that the State supports all sorts of Demyan Bednys and so-called "proletarian poets," who produce no new achievements whatsoever either in the sphere of form, or in the sphere of ideology. They simply don't know how to write and repeat again and again in antiquated verses the ABC of socialism. . .
>
> We Imaginists—a group of anarchist art—from the very beginning. . . have not stood on our hind paws before the State.
>
> The State does not recognise us and thank God for that!
>
> We openly hurl our slogan: Down with the State! *Long live the separation of the State from art.*
>
> These are our slogans:
>
> *Long live the dictatorship of Imaginism!*
>
> *Down with critics,* these fortune-telling speculators on art. . .

Admittedly, Shershenevich made some claims in this article with which Esenin could scarcely agree (such as that poetry must be written in an urban manner, "grammar must be forgotten or reformed," and the musical, descriptive, logical and psychological elements in poetry must be rejected), but nevertheless he named Esenin as one of the original four Imaginists. On May 4, 1919 Shershenevich published a poem, some lines of which quickly achieved notoriety:

> Some people need fame and silver spoons,...
> But all I need is a morsel of love
> And a packet of twenty fags...

On May 4, in the list of those who had agreed to work for the journal, the Imaginists figured *en masse.* The list included: Alexander Kusikov, Anatoly Mariengof, Boris Erdman, Vadim Shershenevich, Grigory Shmerelson, Ivan Startsev, Nikolai Erdman, and Sergei Esenin. On June 1 a poem by Esenin was published there for the first time. True, it was not urban and realistic, as Shershenevich had advocated, but nor was it in any way akin to Bolshevism: "My soul yearns for the heavens,/ It dwells in fields not of this earth..." (II, 82). In this same number both Mariengof and Shershenevich sharply attacked Mayakovsky, and Shershenevich quarrelled with the "dubious artistic taste" of Lunacharsky, the People's Commissar of Enlightenment. Shershenevich wrote: "Does the present State really enable masters of art to create freely? Do we not know that the tables of innovators of art are breaking under the weight of manuscripts, because those upon whom the State apparatus depends say to these masters: all your seeking of new ways is a bourgeois fiction."

Such candid rebellion clearly could not be permitted much longer, and it appears that the anarchistic organ of Russian youth was closed down after this issue of June 1. Although Shershenevich (as ever) was the chief spokesman of Imaginism in the journal, Esenin did not dissociate himself from this opposition to the State, but, on the contrary, himself became a contributor to the journal.

The Imaginists were rebels, in politics as in art, and this was evidently one of the reasons Esenin felt attracted to the group. In his article "The Keys of Mary," written in late 1918 and published by early 1920, Esenin spoke out in favour of the freedom of art: "Man's soul is too complex to be chained in a set range of sounds of any one melody or sonata of life. . . That is why we find repugnant the hands of Marxist guardianship that have been raised in the ideology of the essence of the arts. It [Marxist guardianship] builds with workers' hands a monument to Marx, whereas the peasants want to build one to the cow. . . But we will defeat it. . ." (IV, 198, 199). Of course, "The Keys of Mary" is a complicated and mystical work, reflecting many influences on Esenin, but such statements, together with his hostility to Futurism and his long-standing attraction to the "image," undoubtedly paved the way for his adherence to Imaginism.

As 1919 advanced, the attacks on Imaginism in the Soviet press increased. Admittedly, for some time Esenin continued to be regarded as one of the "neo-peasant" group and was linked by critics with Klyuev—but towards the end of the year he became talked of more often as an Imaginist. "Where is the poet's true face? Surely he must find himself some day?," wondered N. Angarsky. The Imaginists' "works," wrote the venomous Friche, "are—to use their favourite word—the 'abortions' of the deteriorated brain of the dying old world." A note which was to grow louder in the next years was first sounded: the talented Esenin should leave the individualistic Imaginists. Esenin "at times has all kinds of rather distasteful Imaginistic eccentricities and boldness," observed Lunacharsky in November.[2]

The Imaginists survived unpunished for three years and more because in the early period of the Revolution Russia was slowly emerging from chaos, and weird literary groupings mushroomed amidst the cold and famine of Moscow. The Imaginists remained together longer than most, and one reason for this was the shrewd business acumen of its members. Needing an outlet for their verse, they promptly formed their own printing firm, "The Imaginists" ("Imazhinisty") in February 1919. By devious methods they contrived to obtain paper to print their books, and some forty or more Imaginist editions flooded the market in 1919-22. The peak years of their publishing activity were 1920-21—and Mariengof and Esenin also did good business when working at times in the Imaginists' bookshop on Bolshaya Nikitskaya.

On a semi-literary plane the Imaginists prospered in the various literary-bohemian cafes which sprang up in Moscow after the Revolution. Enterprising businessmen found these cafes highly profitable: they provided food and drink which were otherwise hard to obtain, and poets recited their verse as the customers ate and drank. It was in this milieu that the "tender hooligan" Esenin reigned supreme for the next three years. The pre-revolutionary darling of the salons became the post-revolutionary prince of bohemia—or as Alexei Kruchyonykh, a Futurist arch-enemy of Esenin, later wrote, the cherub became a hooligan. Mariengof tells that the Imaginists' legendary top hats—"the only ones during the revolution"—came about by accident: it was raining once in Petrograd, and top hats were the only headgear he and Esenin could acquire without coupons. Be that as it may, Esenin's top hat and patent leather shoes were dismissed by Ivanov-Razumnik as "nonsense, a fraud"—and Klyuev, beside himself with wrath, devoted a long poem in 1922 to open polemic with the Imaginist Esenin, paraphrasing Esenin's lines and declaring: "I don't want to be a famous poet/ In a top hat and lacquered shoes. . ." It was a pose, of course, on Esenin's part—yet the new clothes symbolised his psychological change, his rejection of the specifically peasant, "Klyuevan," phase of his life, in an endeavour to escape from provincialism and become the first poet of all Russia. In his Imaginist years he hardly ever visited his native village of Konstantinovo—Mariengof claims that in the course of four years Esenin spent only three days there, after which he promptly rushed back to Moscow from the boredom of village life. Even if Mariengof exaggerates Esenin's disdain for his parents and sisters during this period, and his love of city life, it is certainly true that Esenin plunged into the whirlpool of urban bohemia and neglected the village in 1919-22. He might write nostalgically about his village childhood, and lament the decline of rural Russia, but he himself was gripped by the spell of the big city.

The Imaginist pose could not remain a mere poetic device for Esenin, and his health inevitably suffered. Yet it is too facile to blame the Imaginist milieu for the poet's downfall (as do so many Soviet critics). It may have been the means, but certainly not the cause, of his fall. Imaginism enabled Esenin to achieve the heights of individualistic independence, although it also set him rolling down the slope over which he had been precariously poised for some years. Nikolai Poletaev wrote perceptively:

> The public believes that the Imaginists ruined the poet. That is not true. . . They could not influence Esenin. The twenty-year-old little-educated peasant lad, there in Petrograd, had been in the salons of the Merezhkovskys and others, had made the acquaintance of aides-de-camp and courtiers, he was exempted from the war, and introduced to the Empress, to whom he recited his poetry. How could the Imaginists influence this "experienced" person? Rather, did he not influence them? There, in Petrograd, people ruined his golden

> head. There they poured into his beautiful and tender heart the poison of stupefying mysticism and aestheticism. And he himself loved the glitter and glory and flew towards them, like a moth to a flame. . .

There is more truth in Poletaev's judgment than in the conventional choice of the Imaginists as scapegoats.

The darker sides of Imaginist life did not make themselves immediately apparent. The boisterous cafes were a source of noise, gaiety and glamour, and at first might not seem sinister and corrupting. Shershenevich writes: "Seryozha at that time loved all life. 'To give up everything, but take nothing'—these words of his were a leitmotiv of all his verse. And when he was pained, he consoled himself, like a child with a bloody nose: don't worry, mama! It'll all get better!" In 1919 Esenin did not have any excessive liking for alcohol, according to various memoirists, and was generally cheerful. "During this period," recalled the Imaginist Ivan Gruzinov, "Esenin loved conversation and philosophising. Later he began to speak less about art; and only in the last year of his life, in particular in the last months, before his death, did he again converse a great deal about art." Esenin tried to convince the proletarian poet Kirillov of the splendour of Imaginism: "Do you understand what a great thing I-magi-nism is! Words have become worn down, like old coins, they have lost their original poetic power. . . But we have found a means of reviving dead words, by enclosing them in vivid poetic images. We created this, the Imaginists. . . If you don't go along with us—then you've had it, you're lost." Kirillov remained unconvinced, but numerous other proletarian poets were impressed by Imaginism and even declared themselves adherents of "proletarian Imaginism."

It appears that Mariengof and Shershenevich, no matter how debauched and unbalanced they seemed in their poetry, were sober and hard-headed in real life. They were not alcoholic profligates, and this is generally conceded by serious critics and memoirists. However, Mariengof in particular is often blamed for having caused Esenin's addiction to alcohol. Such criticism of Mariengof seems one-sided. As with Imaginism in general, Mariengof may have been to some extent the means, but certainly not the cause, of Esenin's taking to drink. Ivnev states that Mariengof did not drink wine:

> and led a life which was as far from bohemianism as the sky is from the earth. . . As for the further accusations against Mariengof, that he "lured Esenin into the nets of Imaginism," these accusations also are totally groundless, for Esenin came to Moscow in 1918 "by no means a child," but a young poet, recognised by all Russia, not inclined to crawl into anyone's nets, as he had demonstrated in his Petersburg period when more mature and experienced "fishers of human souls" had hunted after him. All this confusion was aided in much by the circumstance that during the cult [of Stalin] such an atmosphere prevailed that, upon the slightest gesture from above, black became white and white black. . . Careerists and time-servers were willing, for the sake of one "smile from the bosses," to accuse those in disfavour of every mortal sin. . .

It is certainly absurd to portray Mariengof as Esenin's Mephistopheles—for years Esenin was to regard Mariengof as his best friend, and Esenin was not so "weak-willed" as to become anybody's stooge. He might copy Mariengof in externals—Gorodetsky claims that "in everyday life he was the shadow of the dandy Mariengof"—but there can be no doubt that Esenin willingly participated in, and often indeed initiated, many Imaginist scandals. Some inscriptions of his are revealing. In 1921 or so Esenin described himself as "the leader of the Imaginists" in a handwritten dedication on a book; on March 7, 1921 he inscribed on a book: ". . . If it weren't for Esenin, there would be no Imaginism. . ."; and in an undated inscription to Shershenevich he wrote: "To dear Dima, with love and friendship. S. Esenin. Russia shall not forget us three great brawlers."

Yet the fact remains that during his Imaginist years Esenin began to drink heavily, and this was to intensify until the end of his life. When exactly his partiality for alcohol became addictive is hard to determine, but the process would seem to have begun towards the end of 1919, although memoirists suggest dates varying from 1919 to 1922 as the beginning of his addiction.

The cafes or taverns in which Esenin recited and drank were several. One was the Poets' Cafe ("Kafe poetov") on Tverskaya Street, about which a verse-parody appeared in the Proletcult journal *Factory Whistles* in March 1919:

> The poets' cafe on Tverskaya
> Has a futuristic stage.
> Here you get all you desire,
> And bourgeois sleep away their days...
> The buffet offers beer and waters,
> Chops and chicken, new-laid eggs...
> And hopeless bards of no importance
> –Mark this well!–behave like clowns.

The editors, anticipating objections to the non-rhyme of "eggs" and "clowns," explained: "It is the profound opinion of the editors that eggs at the present time are such a rare and valuable commodity that they can rhyme with anything you like,–in particular with butter, sausage, fat and other words with such endings."

The Poets' Cafe was also known as the cafe Domino; it had two rooms, one for the public, one for poets, and did a lively trade until two o'clock every morning. "Here various kinds of speculators and people of indeterminate professions could listen to music, eat well with a 'lady' picked up from Tverskaya Street, etc. . .," writes N. Poletaev. "The speculators and their ladies, dressed like swells, were fat, red-faced, and ate and drank a great deal. Pale, badly-dressed poets sat at empty tables and waged endless arguments as to which of them was the greatest genius. . . These were the surroundings in which S. Esenin reigned in 1919." Poletaev observed Esenin from a distance, noting one characteristic detail: "His smile did not change according to whether he was speaking to a woman or to a man, and this is very rare. However courteously he spoke to everyone, it was noticeable that this 'peasant poet' regarded them as a pedestal to his future glory." That day in 1919 Esenin caused a typical scandal–he went on stage in the cafe Domino, smiling as usual, and then suddenly turned pale and addressed the public: "Do you imagine I've come out to recite my poems to you? No, I came out to tell you all to f... o...! Speculators and charlatans!" The enraged public called the police, Esenin and other poets were detained until 3 a.m.–and Esenin was well pleased. Almost the next day, continues

Poletaev, Esenin and his friends wrote their obscene verse on the walls of the Convent of the Passion.

Another incident in the cafe Domino is narrated by the poetess Malvina Maryanova. Esenin was interrupted by a poet who called out: "Esenin stole his verse from Klyuev." Esenin reacted by striking his critic twice on the face, with the words: "I have friends and literary honour." In the resultant uproar he strode from the stage, and he was excluded for a while from the VSP (All-Russian Union of Poets). In 1919 the Petrograd journal *Herald of Literature (Vestnik Literatury)* condemned the Imaginists' antics in the cafe Domino as "clownish experiments" which were bringing the writing profession into disrepute.

The chief Imaginist cafe-tavern was, however, virtually their own property: the Pegasus Stall ("Stoilo Pegasa"). This home-ground of the bohemian Imaginists inspired many virulent attacks, and seems by some accounts to have been a den of vice. An "Old Writer" in the *Herald of Literature* cast a jaundiced eye on the "new poetic stall" late in 1919:

> . . . And now there is a new cafe–the Pegasus Stall. It is led by two recent pillars of the Poets' Cafe and of Russian Imaginism: S. Esenin and Mariengof. . . In the new cafe everything is as in the previous cafes: bad coffee and dinners at high prices, a stage, mediocre verse, maxims on the walls and beneath the glass on the tables,–pearls of wisdom and inspiration from the poets in charge. And yet, aren't there too many poetic stalls in Moscow?

A couple of years later, in about 1921, Dmitry Furmanov went there to hear Mariengof recite, and he was not favourably impressed:

> The Pegasus Stall is in essence nothing more than a stall of bourgeois spoilt children. Here people congregate who play absolutely no part in the movement of society, painted, shrill and stupid young "ladies" whose tiny hands are kissed in the old style by their poet admirers; here people throw away tens of thousands of roubles for a "light breakfast," as if it were a mere copeck: that is, the public is no stranger to speculation; here you will see polished bourgeois kiddies–excellently dressed, smoothly shaved, sleek, fashionable, foppish–in short, all the

> same riff-raff who formerly revelled in obscene salon-anecdotes and ditties, and for that matter, still do. . . Mariengof himself is a typical glossy dandy. He creates the most repulsive impression, that is, by his openly bourgeois essence. . .

The Pegasus Stall (the former cafe Bim-Bom) was situated on the corner of the Maly Gnezdnikovsky Pereulok and Tverskaya Street (present-day Gorky Street), and here, whilst the customers ate and drank, a kind of orchestra played and the Imaginists recited. O. Litovsky recalls Esenin acting as waiter in the cafe, dressed in a dinner jacket and with a napkin under his arm. The Pegasus Stall remained open from 1919 until late 1924, and, unlike the cafe Domino, only the Imaginists and their guests recited there. Here a number of women were to sit, who were to play roles of varying importance in Esenin's life: Isadora Duncan, Galina Benislavskaya, Nadezhda Volpin, Avgusta Miklashevskaya. In his Imaginist years Esenin was extremely unsettled, and N. Poletaev even declares, somewhat exaggeratedly:

> The Stall became Esenin's residence. He literally lived there. At first, I think, Esenin drank little (and I never saw his friends drunk at all). Esenin's temperament was such that, if he drank but a small amount, he began to shout and act rowdily. . . And the poet's fame grew and grew. People knew and loved him. Young people were crazy about his verse. And it must be said that for Esenin fame was everything. Obscurity and insignificance were synonyms in his vocabulary. . .

The Pegasus Stall stayed open until at least 2 a.m., and it seems that the poets began to recite at about 11:30 p.m. Until the period of NEP (the New Economic Policy, introduced by Lenin in 1921), the Pegasus Stall was, in the words of Ivan Startsev, "the only place in Moscow for gatherings of bohemians and the unbridled cafe public until 2 or 3 in the morning." Even Mariengof, who revelled in the trappings of bohemianism, had to describe the milieu there as one of shrill foxtrots, and an empty-hearted, red-lipped crowd reeking of wine, powder and cheap little passions from Tverskoy Boulevard.

Esenin (left) with Anatoly Mariengof, c. 1919-1921.

Chapter Eight: Poet of the Dying Village (1920)

Zinaida Gippius had emigrated from Russia at the end of 1919, and her husband Merezhkovsky, comparing Lenin with Rasputin, consoled himself in exile that "the second Rasputin will fall, and the second revolution begin,–no, not the second, but the first." Those members of the older generation of intellectuals who found the October Revolution uncongenial, dwelled mainly in Petrograd, and were far from Esenin's horizons. In his florid, elegant, archaistic handwriting Alexei Remizov wrote to Esenin on August 17, 1919: "Dear Sergei Alexandrovich! Why have you forgotten about me–you don't send your books. I keep waiting and they don't come. If you see Nikolai Alexeevich, I send him my greetings. . ." Remizov addressed the letter to Esenin, c/o the Poets' Cafe, Tverskaya, Moscow. In fact, Esenin was unlikely to see Nikolai Alexeevich Klyuev. Mariengof relates that Klyuev wrote to Esenin, presumably late in 1919–his letter was

> smooth-tongued, compounded of treacle and unction. But in Klyuev's treacle there was venom. . . Esenin read and re-read the letter. By evening he knew every jot of it by heart. His face went yellow, he was silent, he frowned. . . Then during the next three days he wrote his reply slowly and thoughtfully like a poem. . . He dragged out of the dark recesses of his memory whatsoever would make Mikolushka turn just as yellow as had "Mikolushka's bright hawk." Esenin wanted to be the leader of Russian poetry, and there were Klyuev's admonishing and guardian-like words. . .

The Imaginist Esenin strongly resented being classified as Klyuev's "younger brother." Indeed, he had turned his back on his intellectual pretensions of recent years. Whereas Blok, Bely and Ivanov-Razumnik were leaders of the "Free Philosophical Association" which arose in Petrograd late in 1919–an association which concentrated on problems of philosophy, religion and culture–Esenin and the Imaginists had chosen the bohemian road, and in the Pegasus Stall called themselves officially the

"Association of Free Thinkers."

Yet some personal ties remained from the past. Just as Esenin continued to be well disposed towards Gorodetsky, so he retained his admiration for Ivanov-Razumnik, although from a greater distance than in 1916-18. The Imaginists in 1920 were close to the left wing Socialist Revolutionary journal *Banner (Znamia),* one of whose editors was Ivanov-Razumnik. Between May and November 1920 Shershenevich, Esenin, Mariengof and Nikolai Erdman all contributed to *Banner*—Esenin published there a few poems (II, 27, 89, 97-98), but no theoretical articles. The Imaginists and the left wing SRs were on common ground in opposing the notion of a specifically "proletarian" culture. In *Banner* in mid-1920 Shershenevich published a long article about Imaginism, proclaiming once more the primacy of the image in poetry:

> Equally alien both to the petty-bourgeois individualism of the Symbolists and the petty-bourgeois communism of the Futurists, Imaginism is the first peal of the true World Revolution, but a revolution that is not material but spiritual. . . For the Imaginist the image is an end in itself. . . Imaginism is masculine art, whereas Symbolism is feminine art, as Sergei Esenin asserts. . . Imaginism is ideologically closer to Symbolism than to Futurism. . .

1920 and 1921 were the years in which Imaginism sought to establish its theoretical bases at some length. Many theoretical and critical booklets were published by the Imaginists and their supporters, including works by Shershenevich, Mariengof, Ivan Gruzinov, the composer Arseny Avraamov, Ippolit Sokolov and Sergei Grigorev. Mariengof says that Esenin also worked on the theory of Imaginism at this time, but that his unfinished manuscript is lost. At all events, Esenin's "The Keys of Mary" was published by early 1920, to be acclaimed by Shershenevich as representing the "philosophy of Imaginism": "The book is written with great erudition and even greater lyrical temperament." Although Esenin's article was written chiefly towards the end of 1918, it certainly was congenial to Imaginism in many of its points. "The Keys of Mary" (IV, 173-201) is a wide-ranging and eclectic work which discusses folk ornament, symbols and beliefs, often in a mystical and seemingly fanciful way, but it is valuable for an understanding of the origins and nature of Esenin's poetic imagery, and of his "philosophical" outlook. In the course of the article Esenin is critical of Klyuev (IV, 194-195) and Futurism (IV, 195-196), and looks forward to a resurrection of the ancient world of peasant life, under the huge paradise tree of "socialism," which for peasants is a tax-free realm of peace and plenty (IV, 189-191). He concludes by declaring, in a non-Marxist way, that man's faith derives "not from class consciousness, but from consciousness of the temple of infinity which surrounds him" (IV, 201). Many people recall that Esenin disliked theoretical conversations—when asked to theorise or to speak in public, he generally became confused. Nevertheless, he longed to found a literary school of his own, and at this time he no doubt thought that Imaginism was proving just such a school.

In 1920-21 at least thirty books were published by the Imaginists, mostly under the group's imprint, "Imazhinisty." Great audacity and cunning were necessary to obtain paper for these books, and according to Mariengof, Esenin used to go from office to office, promising officials that Lenin would award them a medal if they gave paper to the Imaginists: "And when we needed permission from the Moscow Soviet to open a bookshop, Esenin spoke to Kamenev in the Olonets, Klyuevan manner, rounding his o's and using the familiar 'thou' form in peasant fashion."

Esenin had quarrelled with Gosizdat (the State Publishing House) towards the end of 1919—Shershenevich alleges that Gosizdat had tried to remove the religious words from Esenin's verse—and therefore the Imaginists decided to outwit the law. They printed the names of outlying towns on the covers of their books, knowing that nobody would check up on this because of the country's disrupted transport system. "23 such books were written," claims Shershenevich. "Permission was got for none of them."[1] The Imaginists contrived to have one book printed by the *M. Che-ka* (the Moscow Political Police); another volume, *The Starry Ox (Zvezdnyi byk),* was printed by Esenin in 1921 on the printing press of Trotsky's train![2] Professor Rozanov concedes that the Imaginists left all other literary schools far behind in their energy and enterprise: "They managed to publish their verse under the most unfovourable conditions. The volume

The Foundry of Words (Plavil'nia slov) was printed on hideous wrapping paper and in almost illegible type."

Whether he was planning the edition of volumes, or working in the Imaginists' bookshop, Esenin enjoyed the practical, business aspect of this activity. He was not wholly a dreamer—the book trade clearly appealed to the calculating side of his character. Ryurik Ivnev was displeased by this when he met Esenin again late in 1920:

> He was too occupied with himself, his business, his plans. . . Before me stood a strong, business-like, confident man, outwardly hardly at all changed, but inwardly—quite different. . . At that time living conditions were hard for everyone. . . Against a background of such poverty fine suits and deliberate dandyism seemed out of place and absurd. Of course, this was probably sheer mischief, but he did love to show off the fine cut of his clothes, and his unusual boots, bought God knows where. . .

Esenin's elegant city dress in 1920-21 certainly stood out amidst the general drabness. Poletaev eyed him in 1921: "I looked with amazement at this man, smartly dressed, playing the part of leader of a kind of 'golden youth' in impoverished, hungry, cold Moscow, and capable of such brilliant, profound verse."

In 1919-20 there were several bookshops managed by literary organisations with the official sanction of the Moscow Soviet. Esenin, Mariengof, the second-hand bookseller D. S. Aizenshtadt, and the one-time director of the publishing firm "Altsiona," A. M. Kozhebatkin,[3] all served in the bookshop, the *Artel of Artists of the Word (Artel' khudozhnikov slova)* on Bolshaya Nikitskaya (now Herzen Street). Two other Imaginists, Shershenevich and Kusikov, worked in the bookshop of the All-Russian Union of Poets, in Kamergersky Pereulok. Some memoirists suggest that Esenin did not like serving in the bookshop, and used to prefer sitting out of the way reading a book. In this respect, the bookshop was one of Esenin's "universities." The Imaginists' bookshop on Bolshaya Nikitskaya was very popular, which gave Esenin great satisfaction. Startsev recalls Esenin's words: "It's my shop. I opened it, do you understand?" Although Esenin and Mariengof used to serve behind the counter at times,

Mariengof himself admits that Aizenshtadt was the head and heart of the enterprise. Usually Esenin and Mariengof did not turn up at the shop before 2 p.m., and in the summer of 1921 they merely looked in for an hour or so after dinner, and even that not every day.

Esenin still had a great deal of youthful energy and vitality. Some people even say that 1920-21 was the "healthiest" period in his life, for he worked hard and his fame continued to grow. This may be so, but the harmful aspects of his way of life were to take a heavy toll later. His marriage was broken, and he led a nomadic existence which was to intensify with the years. After Esenin's death, Pyotr Oreshin declared that Esenin's "hooliganism" sprang from his homelessness: "For the last five years he didn't even have a room of his own, and he sought refuge with good friends. . . To tell the truth, Esenin was a bad citizen. He was more a guest in our midst than a citizen, and that is perhaps why he could not regulate his private life." In 1919 and 1920 Esenin lived at various addresses in Moscow. Mariengof recalls: "It so happened that in the spring of 1919 Esenin and I found ourselves without a room. We used to spend the night at male and female friends', in an indescribable room in the hotel Europe ('Evropa'), in Molabukh's train, in the Luxe at Georgy Ustinov's, in short: wherever and however we could." In 1920-21 Esenin and Mariengof shared a room in Bogoslovsky Pereulok in Moscow. Zinaida Raikh gave birth to a son, Konstantin, early in 1920, but Esenin doubted his paternity.[4]

In March 1920 Esenin and Mariengof travelled to Kharkov in the Ukraine and were warmly received by Esenin's good friend, Lev Osipovich Povitsky, in a household where there were some five or six young girls. Povitsky (1890-1974) describes Esenin's stay in Kharkov in idyllic tones:

> Esenin was then in the prime of his creative powers and spiritual health. . . As in Tula, Esenin spent whole evenings in conversations and arguments, he recited his verse, joked and amused himself with all his heart. The girls openly worshipped him, happy and proud that he was living under their roof. Esenin was captivated by one of the

> girls in this group and began a long tender friendship with her. The chaste features of her Biblically stern face evidently had a soothing effect on the "sensual snowstorm" to which he listened too often, and he behaved like a noble and pure knight towards her. She was, perhaps, the only girl who did not become a woman in his hands. . .

Mariengof also refers to this Jewish girl, with her "Biblical eyes"—she was Evgeniya Isaakovna Livshits. Povitsky writes that "there was no trace of wine, carousing or any kind of excesses at our house." A. P. Chapygin, however, claims to have seen Esenin, Mariengof and their friend Sakharov in Kharkov in the spring of 1920: "All three lived in one room. I often found them intoxicated and merry. Whether Mariengof drank I cannot say. S. A. [Esenin] and Sakharov drank."

The Imaginists had come to Kharkov in order to escape for a while from the food shortage in Moscow, and to spread their fame further afield. They decided to give a poetry recital or two, depending on the public's reaction—and in the Kharkov Grand Theatre, before a large audience, the Imaginists presented their wares. One episode of that much-described evening has appeared to many as a particularly shameful blot on the Imaginists' record. Chapygin recalls: "Mariengof pushed out onto the stage the emaciated Velemir Khlebnikov, but the latter, resisting and cowering, had no wish to come out. When he was pushed out he came, but he declaimed in such a way that no one could hear him." Khlebnikov (1885-1922), Futurist poet of fantastic neologisms and quasi-scientific calculations, was noted for his impracticality and "otherworldliness" in everyday life, and for the Imaginists to treat him as they did shows a remarkable insensitivity. Mariengof describes the incident without any compunction, beginning by establishing Khlebnikov's strangeness: he shook hands holding a shoe he was repairing, had eyes like a saint's on an icon, and he had spent the previous night writing illegibly in the dark. According to Mariengof, Esenin had suggested that they should crown Khlebnikov "President of the Terrestrial Globe" in the City Theatre, and Khlebnikov had gratefully agreed. A week later, before a packed auditorium, Khlebnikov stood barefooted, in a cloth surplice, listening as Esenin and Mariengof proclaimed him "President." After every quatrain of mock-praise,

Khlebnikov quietly answered "I believe"—and finally, as symbol of the "Terrestrial Globe," a borrowed ring was placed on his finger. When the owner wanted the ring back after the ceremony, Khlebnikov grew afraid and hid his hand behind his back, saying: "It... it's... the 'Globe'... the symbol of the 'Terrestrial Globe'... And I... you see... Esenin and Mariengof made me 'President'..." Esenin roared with laughter, the owner pulled the ring from Khlebnikov's finger—and Khlebnikov "wept bright tears, as large as those of a horse."

The Futurist poet N. Aseev, upon hearing of the episode, felt indignant, especially as "Khlebnikov had then only just recovered from typhus." There can be no excuse for the Imaginists' behaviour, and Povitsky offers none: "This 'festivity' was a pathetic and vexing spectacle. The Imaginists span the helpless Khlebnikov, almost a paralytic, round in all directions, compelled him to pronounce absurd 'ceremonial' phrases which he repeated with difficulty, and made the sick man a laughing stock in the eyes of an uncomprehending public." The next day Esenin grumbled: "Khlebnikov spoilt it all! I deliberately let him appear first, I gave him the ring so that he should announce loudly: 'I am master of the world!'—and he went and mumbled so that no one could hear."

Yet despite the cruelty of the episode, Esenin was forgiven by the public, as so often during his life, because of his peculiar charm. One memoirist, E. German, declares that, in the Kharkov Theatre, the public was incensed by everyone except Esenin—for one could not be angry with this person, "who seemed inwardly radiant."

In Kharkov the Imaginists also published a volume of verse, *The Cookshop of the Dawn (Kharchevnia zor')*. Besides verse by Esenin and Mariengof, it contained two incantatory poems by Khlebnikov, and some lines by the same author referring to "the Golgotha of Mariengof" ("Golgofa/ Mariengofa") and "the Resurrection of Esenin" ("Voskresenie/ Esenina").

Perhaps shortly after leaving Kharkov, Esenin wrote some seemingly jocular but disturbing letters to Povitsky. Behind the comic misspellings of one letter his instability is evident:

... I live AWL RITE
By the way, it hurts
Ouch, what PANE
I'm thinking of ending
in this little low
                    room
clouds span
          CONFU ION
                    S
I cannot live!
I want to chute myself
... revolv–[5]

After a brief visit to Konstantinovo, Esenin returned to Moscow in April or May. He had not enjoyed his stay in Konstantinovo, and he found Moscow empty too, as is apparent from his letter to Evgeniya Livshits, the girl who had impressed him in Kharkov. Esenin had arranged to meet the nineteen-year-old Evgeniya later in the Crimea, but his letter in reply to hers seems polite and non-committal. He says he was "very much moved" by her letter, he feels lonely in Moscow as Mariengof is not there, he needs to rest, he is overworked with publishing activities–and he ends, with a characteristically distant charm: "Of course, one can't say everything in a letter that one would like to, dear Zhenya! After all, it's better when one sees a person, it's better to talk with one's mouth, eyes, and indeed all one's being, than to trace out these confining letters. I wish you the very, very best. I hope you grow up into a big girl, get married, and everything, everything that you wish. S. Esenin" (V, 84-85). The letter was written with the polite "you" ("vy") form.

By early July Esenin and Mariengof were on the move again, heading this time for the Northern Caucasus. The secret of their mobility was simple–they had a friend, Grigory Kolobov (alias Molabukh), who put a train compartment at their disposal! Kolobov was, it seems, an inspector of the All-Russian Evacuation Commission, and he was in charge of an official carriage in a train. Being an old school friend of Mariengof, he let the two poets travel about in this saloon car whenever they liked. "Not only that," writes Povitsky, "often Esenin and Mariengof drew up the route of their next journey and without much difficulty won the agreement of the owner of the saloon car to follow the route they had devised." These merry travels served a dual purpose: they helped spread the Imaginists' fame, and they were commercially profitable. In famine-ridden Moscow foodstuffs were at a premium—and, by travelling to Tashkent and to the sea, Kolobov and his friends were able to buy dried fruits, nuts, silk cloth, and marine salt which they then re-sold in Moscow at an enormous profit. Hence Kolobov's nickname, "Pochyom-Sol' " ("How much is the salt?")—he speculated on the sale of salt.

Such "criminal" activities were common in the years of famine and hardship—thus, those who had money could enjoy good meals in illegal *stolovye* (dining halls). There are accounts of Esenin eating well in such establishments in 1919-20, and of the privileged gourmets being rudely interrupted by police raids. As Ivnev says, such privileges left a "certain mark on one's character and manners." In 1918 Esenin had eaten in much humbler surroundings, whereas now the "tender hooligan" was prosperous enough to dine well.

Together with Mariengof and Kolobov, he headed south, visiting Rostov-on-Don, Taganrog, Novocherkassk and Baku. Whilst he was crossing the Caucasus a small but highly significant episode occurred, which sheds much light on Esenin's personality and mood at that time. Bored and unimpressed by the Caucasus, he wrote to Evgeniya Livshits and gave an example to illustrate his "sorrow for the departing beloved familiar animal" quality which so contrasts with the "immovable power of what is dead and mechanical":

> We were travelling from Tikhoretskaya to Pyatigorsk, when suddenly we hear shouts, look out of the window and what do we see? We see a small foal galloping with all its might after the railway engine. It was galloping in such a way that we realised at once that for some reason it had decided to outstrip the train. It ran for a very long time, but in the end it began to tire, and at one station it was captured. The episode may strike others as insignificant, but for me it tells a very great deal. The steel horse has conquered the living horse. And this small foal was for me a graphic, dear, dying image of the village

> and the face of Makhno. The village and Makhno in our revolution are terribly like this foal, in the competition of a living force with one of iron. . . I am very sad at present that history is living through a painful epoch of the killing of the living personality, for, you know, the socialism that is developing is not at all what I expected, but a deliberate, definite kind, like a sort of island of St. Helena, without glory and without dreams. In this socialism there is little room for the living, for a person building a bridge into the invisible world, as these bridges are hacked down and blown up beneath the feet of future generations. . . (V, 88).

By August 1920, therefore, Esenin sympathised more with the anarchic revolt of the anti-Bolshevik leader, Makhno, than with the disciplined "iron" will of the Bolsheviks. This mood was not new for him—he had always had vague, mystical and anarchistic expectations of the Revolution. What was new is that he now realised, with unprecedented clarity, that his vague hopes were misplaced—he had "backed the wrong horse" in every sense. There was to be no peasant paradise, no monument to the cow, no "resurrection," no Inoniya. Instead, there was to be iron and the machine, and the power of "death." If in Kharkov, a few months earlier, he had half-jokingly written that his hair was fading (II, 89), now a far greater tragedy had apparently occurred: his Romantic hopes were fading also. From now on, the tone of his poetry was to become funereal. The poet, aged twenty-four, was now "old" (alcohol and promiscuity gave some substance to this myth)—and his soul seemed even older.

The incident of the horse vainly pursuing the train acquired a symbolic importance, and Mariengof describes it at some length also. It became the central episode of Esenin's famous poem "Sorokoust" (II, 93), which, according to Mariengof, was written in the train on the way to Baku. The contest between the living and the steel horse must have appealed especially to the Imaginists, who were partial to equine imagery.[6]

Esenin's attitude to the world, which was essentially that of a Romantic dreamer, had already received a shock a few months earlier, when he visited his native village. In a letter in June he had written of his visit home: "I very much disliked it there—there are many reasons for this, but it's awkward to talk about them in letters now" (V, 84). Esenin's sister, Ekaterina, explains that the village was depressing then for various reasons—there were no matches and nails; there was no kerosene and calico; Esenin's father was troubled by asthma; the old priest, Father Ivan, was stricken by paralysis; old Fyodor Titov was grumbling at the godless Bolsheviks, and so on. During this visit, she says, Esenin wrote the poem "I'm the Last Poet of the Village" ("Ia poslednii poet derevni," II, 95-96). Ekaterina Esenina seems to be disguising the main reason for Esenin's sombre mood in this poem. It was not the poverty of the village, nor the ill health of old friends, which he lamented there, but the imminent encroachment of the "iron guest" (II, 95). Although he lived in the city, Esenin was far from urban in his aesthetic outlook. His images, unlike those of Mariengof and Shershenevich, derived from the countryside, from the same "temple of Nature" as Klyuev. Klyuev, indeed, took sides in the "town versus country" battle some years before Esenin—but now, in 1920, Esenin too was forcibly struck by the impending doom of the village he had loved. During the next two years, and, to a lesser extent, until the end of his life, Esenin expressed in his verse the decline of old-fashioned, non-industrialised Rus. In "The Keys of Mary" he had expected the resurrection of the village, with its ancient culture; now he realised the immensity of his illusion.

Critics usually regard this destruction of Esenin's "patriarchal illusions" as one of the main tragedies of his life. The theme of farewell to the beautiful, "natural" past is indeed at the forefront of much of his subsequent verse—and yet Vladimir Markov may be right in claiming: "There are strong reasons to believe that the 'downfall of village Rus' did not play such a terribly decisive role in Esenin's tragedy. In his last years the peasantry simply was of little interest to him. . ." V. Markov does not discuss this at length, but he does state that Esenin's earlier optimism about the "peasant paradise" was also largely artificial: "Deceiving himself, he pretended to be agitated by the theme of a 'peasant paradise,' and wrote one after another his inwardly false, stillborn, loud long poems" of 1917-18.

Esenin's poetry might seem to refute such a viewpoint,

but the facts of his biography suggest that Markov's scepticism is at least partly justified. Esenin lived more for his verse, and in his verse, than for and in prosaic "real life." He cared a great deal for the inner logic of his lyrical hero's development. In 1917-18 this hero had proclaimed the dawn of a peasant paradise (under Ivanov-Razumnik's influence); now artistic logic compelled him to admit that these expectations were misplaced. The mourning of lost illusions provided him with a new theme of remarkable effectiveness, a theme, moreover, which was congenial to one aspect of his temperament—the quality of nostalgia, bordering at times on sentimentality and self-pity. This may seem an unkind judgment, but the fact is that Konstantinovo was not so radically changed by Lenin's plan of industrialisation and electrification. Even in 1965, the main road was still an unpaved earthen track, bordered by wooden huts. Pigs and geese still wandered along this track, whilst peasant women drew water from the village pump. (Admittedly, more recently there has been much reconstruction in Konstantinovo, to make it into a tourist centre). In 1920, the "changes" Esenin noticed must have been slight, merely a presentiment of possible doom. This is not to suggest that he was "insincere" in his verse. His aesthetic sympathies did indeed lie in the pre-industrial past, and he no doubt identified himself with the logic of his lyrical hero. Nevertheless, he seems to have espoused the cause of old Russia, at least in part, as a means of expressing his own more private sorrow. He mourned the village—but lived in the town. He sympathised with the horse in "Sorokoust"—and did not confess in the poem that he himself was a passenger on the train which defeated the "living horse." Mariengof was unable to distinguish between Esenin's "mask" and his "face,"[7] and Shershenevich felt the same dilemma. Concerning "Sorokoust," Shershenevich writes: "All of Esenin's poems were so closely connected with his life that I cannot even assert *which* resulted from *which* in Esenin: whether because *something* happened to him in his life, he affixed it in his verse, or because he had written lines in *such* a way, he then adjusted his life according to his verse. . ."

Between 1918 and 1920 Esenin spent only a few days in Konstantinovo, and yet this was sufficient for him to begin his truly heart-rending lament for the doomed village. This new poetic theme was all the more effective in that it was out of step with the predominant mood in Soviet poetry. In "I'm the Last Poet of the Village," he predicted the imminent arrival of the "iron guest" (the town, and by implication the Socialist Revolution), with its "black hand," and exclaimed: "Palms that are lifeless and alien,/ In your presence these songs cannot live!" (II, 95). This attitude, as he must have realised, was in direct opposition to the declaration of a proletarian poet, Samobytnik, who wrote in a poem entitled "Machine Paradise" ("Mashinnyi rai"), published in early 1920:

> Celebrate, resound victorious, resurrected realm of Nature,
> Praise the iron-made Messiah, hero of our future days!
> In these palms as dark as twilight lies our liberty unbounded,
> In these muscles made of iron lies the dawn of all mankind.

Esenin did not write many poems in 1919 and 1920 (II, 76-102), but his new themes, of the tender hooligan and the departing village, brought him a wider fame than he had ever enjoyed before. He fulfilled, more successfully than any of his colleagues, the Imaginistic precept of combining high and low, the dirty and the chaste. His poem "Sorokoust"[8] achieved immediate fame and notoriety. In the closing months of 1920 Esenin frequently recited it, and his reception at one stormy meeting in the Polytechnic Museum in Moscow was long remembered. The fourth and fifth lines already provoked some indignant whistles: "You lovers of fleas as songs,/ Don't you want to suck at a gelding?" (The line "Don't you want to suck at a gelding?" is censored by recent Soviet editions, such as II, 91, but was printed in full in the 1920s). The ninth and tenth lines caused even greater alarm:

> [It's good when the twilight teases]
> And pours into our fat backside
> The blood-stained besom of dawn
>
> (II, 91).

Amidst hissing and applause, the president of the evening, the authoritative Symbolist-turned-Communist Valery Bryusov, rose and spoke: "You've heard only the beginning and won't let the poet speak. I hope that those present will believe me when I say that I have some knowledge as far as poetry is concerned. And I declare that this poem by Esenin is the best thing to appear in the whole of Russian poetry over the past two or three years." Ivan Rozanov describes the uproar, but comments: "Yet a week or two later there wasn't, I think, a young poet or simply a lover of poetry in Moscow. . . who was not declaiming the 'red-maned foal.' And then people began to quote these lines in the press too, pinning on Esenin the label of 'poet of the departing village'."

Everyone agrees that Esenin was a marvellous reciter of his own verse, and fortunately for him, he recited splendidly even when drunk. Sergei Konyonkov, at whose studio he was a frequent guest in 1920 and 1921, made a wooden bust of the poet reciting. With one hand he holds the yellow "bush" of his hair; his other hand rests on his heart. This sculpture was placed for a time in the window of the Imaginists' bookshop on Nikitskaya. "Esenin often went out into the street," recalls Ivan Startsev, "–to check on the impression–and he smiled, moved by what he saw." Esenin greatly admired Konyonkov as a sculptor, and also enjoyed the merry hours the Imaginists spent in Konyonkov's studio, singing folk songs, playing the guitar, accordion, and other folk instruments, and drinking vodka. The conversations at Konyonkov's studio seem to have been much in the spirit of "The Keys of Mary," with frequent references to the Bible and the mystical wisdom of the peasantry.

Towards the end of 1920 Esenin had declared war on the town in his verse, but his resistance was couched in funereal terms, for he probably sensed he was fighting a losing (and, indeed, largely imaginary) battle. He spoke of "doom," and the "enemy" with the "iron belly," of the village huts racked by a "fever of steel"; he cursed the "lousy guest" and sang "halleluiah" to his beloved country (II, 91-94). In essence, the "iron guest" is evidently an image of the Revolution. Esenin ended "Sorokoust" by suggesting that this grief makes the peasant take to drink.

In November 1920 his poem "The Hooligan" (II, 97-98) was

published, in which he called himself a hooligan, robber and boor, but also the only singer of village Rus. In that same month he wrote "The Hooligan's Confession" ("Ispoved' khuligana," II, 99-102), in which the twin poles of his recent verse were crystallised with unparalleled clarity. In this poem, the lyrical hero is coarse and tender, desperate and kind; full of provocative vulgarity, and yet also "gently sick with childhood recollections." This poem, which was published in January 1921, was a masterpiece at just the right moment: Esenin could not have timed his "confession" more aptly. It was bound to provoke scandal and indignation—and also compassion and admiration. He presented himself as a hoodlum who, as soon as he is challenged, retreats into the idyllic memories of childhood. It was a brilliant work—and Esenin clearly felt so too, for here he exclaimed for the first time, addressing the peasantry:

> O, if only you understood
> That in Russia your son
> Is the very best poet!
> (II, 100).

He was patriotic in the poem ("I love my country./ I love my country dearly!"), and he even maintained:

> I'm just the same.
> In my heart I am just the same.
> Like cornflowers in the rye, my eyes bloom on my face.
> I spread the golden carpets of my verse,
> And long to speak some tenderness to you...
> (II, 101).

However, a few lines later, he deliberately changed his mood: "Today I feel the desire/ To piss from the window at the moon." (The latter line is censored on II, 101, but was published in full in the 1920s). And so the poem continued, arrogant, crude, and so charming in the poet's evident vulnerability.

"The Hooligan's Confession" is a landmark in Esenin's development. He now lived the role of the tender hooligan both in his everyday life and in his verse. The public had begun to expect this of him, and Esenin, seeking to reveal himself to the utmost as a poet, sacrificed himself to the role his verse had marked out for him. He might say in the poem that he was "just the same" as before, but in fact this was patently not so. Scandals, obscenity and the restless life of a city rake were bound to affect him. Indeed, he himself admitted this in a letter to Ivanov-Razumnik a few weeks later: "Of course, my inner re-orientation has been great. I am thankful for everything that has stretched me internally, and for what has given this form and a tongue to speak. But I have lost in the process everything which formerly gave me joy from my health. I have become more corrupt *(Ia stal gnilee)*. . ." (V, 89-90). And, looking back on his disorderly life of the last two years, Esenin said: "I am surprised that I have managed to write so many short and long poems during this period" (V, 89).

Kruchyonykh noted the poet's outer change by 1920:

> Esenin's portrait at this time is highly indicative. He does not at all resemble his portraits of 1914-16. The feminine softness of his oval face has completely disappeared. His tightly clenched jaws protrude at an acute angle. His lips are closed in an expression of obstinacy and bitterness. His eyes are sunken. His hair falls on his forehead—but not as before; he no longer has soft curls; they are wiry and unruly. And the general expression of his face is no longer one of naive joy and amazement...

When sober, he was calm and charming, greeting his friends with a kiss and a hearty handshake; when drunk, he was bitter, arrogant, intolerant, self-pitying, hypersensitive. As his nervous system became undermined, signs of a persecution mania emerged. Similarly, his belief in himself as the greatest Russian poet assumed unhealthy forms when he was intoxicated or excited. He had numerous verbal duels with Mayakovsky, and he was offensive towards Pasternak. One day in the cafe Domino, at the end of 1920 or beginning of 1921, Ivnev saw Esenin angrily confront Pasternak: "Your poems are tongue-tied. No one can understand them. The people will never give you recognition!" Pasternak replied with venomous courtesy that one should be cautious in playing with the word "people," but Esenin retorted: "I know. . .

that our descendants will say: 'Pasternak? A poet? Never heard of him, although we do know and love the vegetable *pasternak* (parsnip)'." In his letters of this period Esenin finds fault with Klyuev and Oreshin (V, 85-86, 90)–his desire to be Russia's top poet undoubtedly led him to many harsh judgments.

Esenin was essentially a lonely person, even though there was no shortage of drinking partners or women who idolised him. The proletarian poet Kirillov asks: "Did he have any real friends? I doubt it. Esenin was unusually lucky as regards literary success. His fame grew and became more established with every year. Hardly anyone denied his talent. He scarcely had need of a friendly and strong hand. . . He had admirers, patrons, or simply flatterers–and that is perhaps why he did not have any real friends." Mariengof, the person closest to Esenin during these years, comments: "The basic thing in Esenin: fear of loneliness."

The man who–according to Mariengof–loved no one wanted the warmth and recognition of everyone. He had a childish sense of humour, a love of the unusual–and yet this, and his scandals, were evidently an attempt to escape from boredom and dull routine. His appearance as a dandy, with his curly hair carefully set, added to his fame and afforded him some amusement. Yet underlying this was a more serious dissatisfaction with the consistent behaviour required by the conventions of everyday life. Hence his dislike of being tied for long to any idea or any woman; hence, in part, his often expressed desire to confuse everything, to merge heaven and earth, man, animal and tree; hence his attraction to the vagabond life, and to violent distortions of reality, a reality which alcohol, and, ultimately, only death could negate. This characteristic explains much in his life–the reason he felt the need to act and pretend, to shock and impress. He felt compelled to "act the fool": "Because without these eccentricities,/ I cannot live on earth" ("Ottogo chto bez etikh chudachestv/ Ia prozhit' na zemle ne mogu," II, 116).[9] He had to be the picture book peasant, the prophet, the dandy, and then the best poet, the last village poet, and the husband of famous women. This was not merely childishness and ambition: it was an ingrained aversion to anything prosaic, it was in a way a despairing and doomed struggle against death, which repelled and attracted him always, until towards the end of his life death alone was the ultimate friend and enemy. For the sake of this struggle he was to use all the weapons he could: poetry, fame, sex, alcohol, travel, perhaps drugs—and if all failed, there could be but one way out. Should he ever reach the stage of feeling: "In this life there's nothing new in dying,/ But nor, of course, is living any newer"—then boredom would have overcome him for ever.

Chapter Nine: "I Want to Live, Live, Live..." (1921-22)

The year 1921 began with the original four Imaginists re-united in uneasy harmony. Ryurik Ivnev, having left Moscow in March 1919, had returned and rejoined the group in December 1920. Ivnev recalls that, early in 1921, both he and Esenin hit upon the same thought: "that it would be good to go abroad for two or three months, 'to see people and let them see us,' to look at new lands, new cities." They requested permission, and on February 10 Lunacharsky, the People's Commissar of Enlightenment, gave his approval. According to Ivnev, they were about to leave, when Soviet power was established in Georgia and Ivnev loyally returned to the land from which the Mensheviks had expelled him. Probably, he adds, Esenin also had lost interest in the trip abroad. The journey did not take place, and Ivnev and Esenin parted for a further two years.

In February 1921 Esenin applied for the dissolution of his marriage to Zinaida Raikh, and on October 5 they were officially divorced. Also in February he related his brief autobiography to Ivan Rozanov. Here he stressed his Old Believer origins, his links with folk poetry, the influence of his grandfather, his life-long religious doubts–and he offered an explanation of some aspects of his recent literary behaviour:

> People ask me why I sometimes use in my verse words which are considered indecent in society–sometimes I am so bored, so bored, that I feel the sudden urge to get up to some such trick. And anyway, what are these "indecent words"? All Russia uses them, so why shouldn't they be given general recognition in literature too?. . .
>
> Another thing about us poets. Recently there were some elections in the *Poets' Union.* Valery Bryusov was blackballed. Andrei Bely, I and others were elected to the board. Andrei Bely declined, as he was leaving for Petersburg, I got out of it by saying I had no time. That was nonsense, of course. I could have found the time. I really refused because I am completely alien to this union, as to any other.
>
> In general, the longer I live, the more convinced I become that our fraternity, we poets, are a most loathsome lot.

> You ask if the course of my life has been unbroken, straight and even? No, there have been such breaks, scrapes and upsets that I am surprised how I've managed to keep alive and all in one piece up to now. . .

This was clearly the voice of a somewhat dispirited individualist. By now, with the Civil War virtually at an end, Soviet power was more firmly established. The period of "War Communism" (mid-1918 to early 1921) had given way to the New Economic Policy (NEP), introduced in 1921. NEP was intended to encourage the peasants to produce more food by allowing them to sell their own surpluses; but to many people it seemed a renunciation of Marxism. Whilst there was widespread relief that the carnage of Civil War was nearly over, some people, including many "proletarian poets," reacted keenly to the resultant lowering of heroic tension. The excitement of the first revolutionary years was giving way to the *budni,* the day-to-day routine of reconstruction. Esenin, with his deep-rooted fear of boredom and routine, responded predictably to NEP—Mariengof quotes an unpublished folk quatrain Esenin made up on this theme:

> Oh dear me, these Bolsheviks,
> Where the Moscow river licks,
> Underneath the Kremlin roofs
> They've set up their trading-booths.
>
> (Okh, uzh, okh, bol'sheviki,
> Da u Moskv–, da u reki,
> Pod kremlevskoi krovleiu
> Zanialis' torgovleiu.)

In 1921 the literary hooliganism of Esenin and the Imaginists reached unprecedented heights, and the Soviet press was roused to a furore of indignation. In about January the Imaginists published *Golden Boiling Water (Zolotoi kipiatok),* a book of verse by Esenin, Mariengof and Shershenevich. The first section contained Esenin's "The Hooligan's Confession" (including the obscenity quoted on p. 145 above); the second section was Mariengof's "I Indulge in Lust with Inspiration" ("Razvratnichaiu s vdokhnoveniem"); finally came Shershenevich's "Truce with Machines" ("Peremir'e s mashinami"). Mariengof's long poem revealed his customary endeavour to shock at all costs—many of his images are physiological, as he poured verses "whiter than milk" from his "male breasts," and, observing the "coupling" of two towns, raised his hands in prayer: "Socialist god, bestow on them/ Most ecstatic offspring..." Whilst Esenin longed to "piss at the moon," Mariengof addressed the mothers of Russia:

> Sob, mothers. The pink ham
> Of your sons is roasting in the solar
> Frying pan.

Mariengof invited people to bite his "freezing nipples" and promised:

> I will fill
> With new gifts
> The flabby scrota of eunuchs.

Shershenevich's poem in this volume also contained such beguiling concepts as autumn "with the twisted hand of a paralytic," and references to sweat, saliva and urine. One whole page was filled with the following explanation:

HERE
OUR PORTRAITS
SHOULD HAVE BEEN
UNFORTUNATELY
YAKULOV
CELEBRATED
THE NEW YEAR.

This provocative volume did not pass unnoticed. Ivnev claims that Lunacharsky "regarded Esenin and me with a sort of kindness which was touching." "How he could understand and feel everything!," exclaims Ivnev. Nonetheless, Lunacharsky published the following letter in *Izvestiya* on April 14, 1921:

Some time ago I agreed to be honorary president of the All-Russian Union of Poets, but only quite recently have I been able to acquaint myself with certain books published by members of this union. Among others, with *Golden Boiling Water* by Esenin, Mariengof and Shershenevich.

These books, like all others recently published by the so-called Imaginists, are, notwithstanding the undoubted giftedness of the authors, a malicious violation of their own talent, and of humanity, and of present-day Russia.

These books are published illegally, i.e., the paper and printing facilities are obtained in an unlawful manner, disregarding the State Publishing Houses.

The *Glavpolitprosvet* [Central Board of Political Education] has resolved to investigate and to call to account the people assisting the publication and dissemination of these shameful books.

Since the Union of Poets has not protested against this prostitution of talent, soiled, as a preliminary, in stinking filth, I hereby publicly declare that I renounce the title of president of the All-Russian Union of Poets.

A. Lunacharsky

Soviet critics today always emphasise the gulf which really separated Esenin from the other Imaginists. Esenin, they write, was a genuine and important poet, whereas Shershenevich and Mariengof would have passed into oblivion long ago but for their tenuous association with Esenin. There is some truth in this, although present-day Soviet critics clearly seek to absolve Esenin at all costs from the collective sins of the Imaginists. However, even in 1921 Esenin's links with Imaginism struck many critics as unnatural and implausible. There was so much artificiality in the urbanistic, unhealthy imagery of Shershenevich and Mariengof, and it seemed regrettable that the peasant-born Esenin was beginning to invent crude and contrived images. Often critics sharply condemned Shershenevich and Mariengof, and urged both Esenin and the Circassian Alexander Kusikov to dissociate themselves from the other pair. Esenin himself seems to have disliked such efforts at linking him with Kusikov (whom he had known since at least early 1919), and certainly his friendship with Mariengof continued. Nevertheless, as early as 1920 Esenin, on the one hand, and Shershenevich and Mariengof, on the other, undoubtedly differed in their attitude to the role of the "image" in poetry. Esenin disagreed with Shershenevich's view that a poem is a "mechanical" combination of images: Esenin (and Kusikov) regarded the combining of images as "organic" work.[1] A further difference was that Esenin was much more a "Russian" poet. Ivnev felt this, when he wrote to Esenin in 1921: "I often think about you. How closely linked you are with Russia. By your blood, for life and for death. . . Mariengof is the Baltic. Kusikov glances with one eye at the peaks of the Dagestan mountains. Shershenevich is 'without kith or kin'. . . Only you have blood ties with Russia and for this I love you especially. . ." By 1921 it appeared to Professor Rozanov that Esenin, who was now a famous poet, "already felt cramped in the Imaginist circle." Esenin told Rozanov:

> Many people think I'm not an Imaginist at all, but they are mistaken: from my very first independent steps I instinctively aspired towards what I then found more or less realised in Imaginism. But the trouble is that my friends have pinned too much faith in Imaginism, whereas I never forget that it is only one side of the matter, an external. What is much more important is a poetic feeling for the world. This is still alien to Shershenevich, and for a long time Mariengof lacked this poetic content. [They had] only the externals of Imaginism.

In May 1921 Esenin published an article, "Life and Art" ("Byt i iskusstvo," IV, 202-208), which is in part critical of his Imaginist "brothers." Soviet critics nowadays seize upon this article as evidence that Esenin allegedly cooled very quickly towards Imaginism. Above all, they quote his words: "My brothers have no feeling for their native land in all the broad meaning of this word, therefore everything of theirs is so uncoordinated. Therefore they love so much that dissonance which they have imbibed together with the stifling fumes of clownish affectation for the sake of affectation" (IV, 208). Soviet critics also frequently cite Esenin's words in this article that art is inseparable from life (IV, 203, 205), and his declaration: "My brothers do not acknowledge order and concord in the combination of words and images. I wish to say to my brothers that they are mistaken in this" (IV, 205).

Whilst Esenin is undeniably critical here of his brother Imaginists, Soviet scholars exaggerate the extent and the "decisiveness" of this criticism. They generally select one or two anti-Imaginist comments, but fail to place them in their overall context. In fact, "Life and Art" is closely related to Esenin's position in "The Keys of Mary"–he offers here the same vague and mystical classification of images (IV, 205-207), the same abstract categories, the same un-Marxist, "Scythian" attitude to life and to art. He may end his article by stating that art is a "weapon" of life, and life demands only that which is necessary to it (IV, 208)–yet immediately before this he rebukes his "brothers" for lacking the feeling of the juggler of Notre Dame, who prayed before the statue of the Mother of God before beginning his tricks. What is more, Soviet critics fail to point out that Esenin's powerful words castigating the Imaginists' "clownish affectation" ("shutovskoe krivlian'e") are a verbatim repetition of V. Iretsky's condemnation of Imaginism some months earlier, in the journal *Herald of Literature*.

There are other reasons for not attaching excessive importance to Esenin's anti-Imaginist comments in "Life and Art." His further collaboration with the Imaginists was not impaired; Imaginist scandals reached their peak later in 1921, with Esenin playing a leading part; and there is a little-known *Manifesto,* signed by Esenin and Mariengof in September 1921, which is formalistic, nationalistic, and militantly Imaginistic. Despite Esenin's differences with Shershenevich and Mariengof, the writing and publication of "Life and Art" was *not* a decisive turning-point in his relations with the Imaginists.[2]

From March to August 1921 Esenin worked with great care on his first extant dramatic work, *Pugachov* (II, 153-192). It was partly in order to retrace the steps of the eighteenth-century peasant rebel that he made a trip to Central Asia in April and May of that year, a journey he had been contemplating since 1920. Moreover, as he said, "I have a great friend there, Shurka Shiryaevets, whom I have never seen. . ." Esenin had always been attracted more by the East than the West, and he set off hopefully in Kolobov's saloon car. From Samara he wrote a matey letter to Mariengof: ". . . I'm even glad that I've quit that damned Moscow. At present I'm collecting myself and looking inwards. The latest incident really stunned me. Of course I shall not drink like that again. . . My God, what filthy stuff it is. . . A horse (not a foal) again ran after our train, but I now say: 'Nature, you copy Esenin'. . ." (V, 91-92). In the company of Kolobov and a certain Lyova (*not* Lev Povitsky), he travelled gaily on to Tashkent.

The poet Valentin Volpin met him there:

> Esenin arrived in Tashkent at the beginning of May, when spring was already turning into summer. He arrived joyful, excited, and looked eagerly at everything, as if absorbing the luxuriant Turkestan landscape, the remarkably dark blue sky, the morning bray of the donkey, the cry of the camel and all that aspect of the native town which strikes a European as unusual: with its narrow alleyways and eyeless houses, its motley crowd and spicy scents. . .

In the richly-carpeted *chai-khane* (tea houses) Uzbeks and Tadzhiks mingled with Turkmens and turbaned *mullahs,* "and Esenin arrived in such a setting–a young man from Ryazan, straight from famine-stricken Moscow." In his button-hole Esenin cherished a big yellow rose, and at the end of the day he spoke with deep feeling, "although eventually he talked of birch trees and remote Ryazan, as if wishing to stress that his love for these was constant and unchanging."

Most Tashkent poets, recalls Volpin, were hostile towards Imaginism, but they gave Esenin a warm welcome as a recognised poet. On one occasion he recited his verse in the Turkestan Public Library in Tashkent; a few days later he gave a private reading of the completed first draft of *Pugachov* in Volpin's flat.

In Tashkent Esenin at long last met Alexander Shiryaevets (b. 1887), the peasant poet with whom he had corresponded irregularly for over six years. By his adherence to Imaginism Esenin had largely cut himself off from the other peasant poets–in June 1920 he had written to Shiryaevets: "I have almost nothing to do with my old companions, I've parted from Klyuev,

Klychkov has gone away, and Oreshin looks somehow distrustfully at me. . ." (V, 85). Whilst Esenin believed that Oreshin was now writing "bad Communist verse," Oreshin, for his part, was disdainful towards the Imaginists. For Klyuev, Esenin's Imaginism was tantamount to blasphemy—and Shiryaevets too regarded Esenin as a deserter from the peasant camp. Shiryaevets clung on to a belief in the fairy tale elements of life, as seen in the *skazka.* He had written to Khodasevich in January 1917 that he preferred a romanticised view of "the people" to the new "truths" of Karl Marx: ". . . This is all because I don't like the accursed modern times which have destroyed the fairy tale, yet without the fairy tale what life can there be on earth?" In mid-1920 Esenin had told him to come down to earth: "Stop glorifying this stylised Klyuevan Rus with its non-existent Kitezh[3] and its stupid old women, we are not as you make it all seem in your verse. Life, the real life of our Rus, is far far better than the motionless designs of the Old Believers. All this, brother, is a thing of the past, now dead and buried. . ." (V, 86). Shiryaevets remained unconvinced, and, if anything, his attraction to the fairy tale, and his hostility to the modern town, intensified, as is demonstrated by his remarkable 264-page notebook, written in October 1920, which bears the revealing title: *The Monster of Stone and Iron ("About the Town. The Town, the Townsman, and the Countryman in the Poetry of Recent Times").* Towards the end of this treatise Shiryaevets discussed Esenin's recent literary behaviour, keenly regretting that this "prodigal son" had "shamefully exchanged the pipes of Lel' for the raucous trumpet of the 'new art'," and wishing that Esenin would return to the fields of Ryazan.

Such was the background to the meeting of the two poets in Tashkent in May 1921. Esenin had attained national fame as the peasant hooligan cursing the town that enslaved him; Shiryaevets was the obscure peasant who dwelt in outlying Turkestan and remained loyal to his pure peasant origins. Volpin recalls that Shiryaevets "sharply attacked Esenin for his Imaginism," but Esenin "patiently and at length explained to his friend the bases of Imaginism." Several of Esenin's inscriptions on books to Shiryaevets have survived. Apart from two very brief dedications, he also wrote out two lengthier passages. On a copy of *The Hooligan's Confession* (1921), he wrote: "To Alexander Vasilevich Shiryaevets with love and good wishes. S. Esenin. I never loved Kitezh and was not afraid of it, it does not exist and did not exist, just like you and Klyuev. Only the Russian wit is alive, that is what I love and nourish in myself, therefore I am afraid of nothing and it's not the town that shall devour me, but I shall swallow it (with regard to certain comments about my doom)."[4] And in Shiryaevets' album he wrote out a passage from *Pugachov,* which ends with a description of a mother-bear teaching its "foolish" cub its "animal wisdom":

> So that the foolish cub might learn
> Its name and its vocation.
> ....
> I have divined my meaning
> (II, 167).

Beneath this extract in Shiryaevets' album Esenin wrote: "Asia. 1921. May 25." The album entry clearly shows Esenin's self-identification with the "animal wisdom" and "animal soul" of the peasant rebel Pugachov.

From Tashkent Esenin and Kolobov travelled on to Samarkand and perhaps Bukhara, before returning to Moscow in June, laden with flour, currants and dried apricots.

Back in Moscow, where he shared a room with Mariengof in Bogoslovsky Pereulok ("Theologians' Lane"!),[5] Esenin continued to work on the manuscript of *Pugachov.* During this period the controversy between the Imaginists and Lunacharsky deepened. In one of their most famous "scandals," the Imaginists attempted to call a "general mobilisation" in defence of the "new" art. Mariengof recalls:

> At one time it seemed to the Imaginists that formal reaction was raising its head in art. The "Supreme Soviet" of Imaginists (Esenin, Erdman, Shershenevich, Kusikov and I) decided at a secret meeting to declare a "general mobilisation" in defence of left wing forms. In a small secret printing house we printed our "command." At night we went

out onto the streets to stick it up on the fences, walls and columns of Moscow...

The printed leaflet was as follows:

Imaginists of the world, unite!

GENERAL
MOBILISATION
of Poets, Painters, Actors, Composers, Producers and Friends of Active Art.

No. 1
On Sunday, June 12 of this year, a demonstration of the seekers and founders of the new art is planned.

Meeting place: Theatre Square, time: 9 o'clock in the evening.

Route: Tverskaya, Statue of A. S. Pushkin.

PROGRAMME

Parade of forces, speeches, orchestra, verse and brief exhibition of paintings.

Attendance is obligatory for all friends and supporters of active art.

1) the Imaginists,
2) the Futurists,
3) and other groups.

Cause of the mobilisation: the war which has been declared on active art.

Who is not with us is against us!

The leader of active art, the Central Committee of the Order of Imaginists.

Poets: *Sergei Esenin, Alexander Kusikov, Anatoly Mariengof, Vadim Shershenevich, Nikolai Erdman.*
Artists: *Georgy Yakulov, Boris Erdman.*
Composers: *Arseny Avraamov, Pavlov.*
Secretariat: the Imaginist poets *Ivan Gruzinov, Matvei Roizman.*

The next morning, continues Mariengof, Muscovites were bewildered and frightened by the call to general mobilisation, and Esenin, Shershenevich, Kusikov and he were taken to the offices of the *M. Che-ka* (Political Police). Their interrogator there was clearly amused by the episode, but Esenin became afraid, assuring the police: "Father, I am with the Bolsheviks. . . I am with the October Revolution. . ." The Imaginists got off lightly, merely having to tell the "mobilised" crowd the next day that the mobilisation order was rescinded. As they did so, the Imaginists noted with pride the ten mounted military policemen who were keeping an eye on the gathering. That night, at Konyonkov's, Esenin sang a folk quatrain about the events of the day:

Don't you go to the police,
Go and see some woman,
In my noisy ringing youth,
I just love this fooling.

(Ne khodi ty v M. Che-ka,
A khodi k babenke,
Ia valiaiu duraka
V molodosti zvonkoi.)

Mariengof does not offer any exact date for the mobilisation episode, although he continues by referring to *Pugachov* and Esenin's trip to Central Asia, both of which relate to 1921. The mobilisation was called for "Sunday, June 12 of this year." A Moscow archive deduces that this means 1919, whilst the five-volume Soviet edition chooses 1920 (IV, 323). Both of these dates seem mistaken, for June 12 fell on a Sunday in 1921, but not in 1919 or 1920.[6]

Despite the frivolous style of the "mobilisation order" in parodying Bolshevik decrees, its authors were attempting a semi-serious defence of literary freedom. Another Imaginist "stunt" was wholly facetious, for the purpose of self-advertisement—and this was the occasion when they renamed various Moscow thoroughfares after themselves. Mariengof tells that they removed the sign "Kuznetsky Most" and replaced it with a sign saying "The

Street of the Imaginist Esenin"; similarly, they renamed "Petrovka" as "The Street of the Imaginist Mariengof." On the statue of Pushkin they hung a placard, "I am with the Imaginists." The street-naming escapade evidently appealed to Esenin's love of *chudachestva* (eccentricities)—he referred to it with satisfaction in an autobiography (V, 13).

The conflict between the Imaginists and Lunacharsky stemmed, not only from the Imaginists' provocative behaviour in everyday life, but also from a difference of opinion about the "freedom" of writers. In the first three years after the Revolution, poetry had flourished despite the shortage of paper for printing. By 1921, however, many writers began to feel that they were being "stifled." Lunacharsky published a frank article, "Freedom of the Book and the Revolution" in mid-1921, admitting that in its initial stages the Socialist Revolution "is compelled to intensify the spirit of a kind of militarism, to intensify the dictatorship of State power and even, so to speak, its police character." He agreed that "real art, art bearing the stamp of genius or talent, cannot sing in a cage." The State, he declared, requires sincere writers of "agitational" art, but it should not encourage flatterers or forcibly remove sincere writers who are not in full accord with the State's ideals. Then Lunacharsky referred to the Imaginists. The State should make sure that, behind the old forms of art, there are "really sincere groups of artists, and not some sort of individual charlatans who seek to fool the public (such as, for instance, the Imaginists, amongst whom there are some talented people, but who seem to try deliberately to sully their talents). . ." Lunacharsky concluded his article by admitting that in the present harsh times art is of secondary importance, and the State cannot at present allow freedom of printed propaganda. Freedom of the written word is, of course, the ultimate ideal—but only when the spirit of counter-revolution is overcome.

The Imaginists refused to acquiesce, and in the next number of the journal *The Press and the Revolution (Pechat' i revoliutsiia)* the "Central Committee of the Imaginist Order" objected to Lunacharsky's "unsubstantiated phrases" and made the following suggestions:

1. That the People's Commissar Lunacharsky should either stop this flippant persecution of a whole group of poet-innovators, or, if his phrase is not only a phrase, but a firm conviction,–banish us from Soviet Russia, for our presence here in the capacity of charlatans is both insulting for us and not necessary, indeed perhaps even harmful, for the State.

2. That the critic Lunacharsky should confront us in a public discussion on Imaginism, where Prof. Shpet, Prof. Sakulin and other representatives of science and art will be invited as competent judges.

Masters of the Central Committee of the Order of Imaginists
Esenin, Mariengof, Shershenevich (V, 183).

The Imaginists, with their title evidently parodying the Central Committee of the Communist Party, were being deliberately provocative. To call Lunacharsky's attacks "unsubstantiated" was scarcely a strong self-defence–the content of much Imaginist verse could not have been further removed from the sincere "agitational" literature the State required, and nor could some of their recent scandals. In reply to their protest Lunacharsky declared that he did not have the right to banish from Russia poets he disliked, and moreover, even if he had this right, he would not use it. Lunacharsky wrote: "The public itself will soon understand that enormous admixture of clownish clamour and charlatanism which is ruining Imaginism, in his opinion, and which the really talented members of the 'band' will probably soon relinquish." He refused to participate in any debate, realising that "the Messrs. Imaginists will turn such a public discussion into yet one more improper advertisement for their group." Yet, as one critic rightly commented, "one way or another the Imaginists had achieved their aim: they had got yet another 'advertisement'."

On September 12, 1921 Esenin and Mariengof signed a new *Manifesto* of militant Imaginism, for a projected book to be entitled *The Epoch of Esenin and Mariengof (Epokha Esenina i Mariengofa)*:

We supreme masters of the order of Imaginists . . . publicly proclaim for the thousandth time through the body of our works the supremacy of the image over everything else in verbal material. . . We categorically

> reject any concord with the formal achievements of the West, and. . . we ourselves are steadfastly preparing a great invasion against the old culture of Europe. . . We are the turbulent initiators of the epoch of Russia's poetic independence. Only with us is Russian art reaching for the first time the age of self-awareness. . .

As 1922 opened, the underlying rift between the Imaginists became increasingly perceptible. Esenin seemed irritable and nervous. "More than once it was noted," writes Ivan Startsev, that "Esenin was drinking for nights on end and showing little sign of intoxication. When happy, he sang folk quatrains and, screwing his eyes up, passed ironic comments about his drinking companions. But if a relative stranger appeared in their midst Esenin at once changed, becoming suspicious and quick-tempered, and after drinking a few glasses, he began to find fault, brawl, come to blows, and break crockery."

Early in 1922 Kusikov told a meeting of Petersburg writers that the four main Imaginists had split into two directions in their attitude to the image–the "right wing" (Kusikov and Esenin), and the "left wing" (Shershenevich and Mariengof).[7] The "right wing," said Kusikov, regarded the image as a means, whereas the "left wing" saw the image as an end in itself and were not interested in content. A journal report of Kusikov's speech claimed that this declaration was of "historico-literary importance"–and yet Kusikov seems largely to have reiterated the differences mentioned two years earlier by Shershenevich, in his theoretical booklet *2 x 2 = 5.* Nevertheless, Kusikov went abroad in 1922, and settled there, thus parting from Mariengof and Shershenevich.

Esenin's dramatic work *Pugachov* had been published by December 1921, and it was given a very mixed reception. One reviewer, E. Shamurin, stated outright that "only a final break with the 'artistic methods' of the untalented Mariengof and Shershenevich will save the poet and put an end to this absurd, systematic, if not suicide, then self-disfiguration of the artist."

Shershenevich also was fully aware that critics now were virtually unanimous in urging Esenin to break away from the other Imaginists–indeed, Shershenevich began his open letter to Esenin in about 1921 by referring to this very point. Shershenevich advised Esenin to tell his friends, the "Rogachevskys, Razumniks" and so on, "that you have by no means become suddenly spoiled. You are simply developing, getting stronger, and all those features which began to show in your youth have now become clearer."

Esenin himself presumably shared Shershenevich's view that his poetry was developing and getting stronger, but the critical reaction to *Pugachov* surprised and distressed him. He had devoted most of 1921 to the meticulous writing of *Pugachov*–no other major manuscript of his shows such scrupulous revision of the text–and he had placed great hopes on it. Admittedly, there is some doubt about how carefully he studied the historical sources for his drama. When preparing his highly subjective evocation of Pugachov's eighteenth-century peasant revolt, he probably read little background material, despite his protestations to the contrary. Esenin considered *Pugachov* a "really *revolutionary* work," but most critics did not support his opinion. He recited *Pugachov* to the actors of Meierkhold's theatre, but the play was never performed there. It seemed to consist of a series of lyrical monologues, but people found it lacking in scenic action.

Pugachov appears to be one of Esenin's most significant and revealing works, variable in quality but at its best intensely lyrical and rich in language. It may not be a "play," a "drama" (Esenin himself left open the question of its genre), and it certainly is not primarily "historical." Reviewers in 1922 often attacked it on these grounds, condemning the unnatural, "Imaginistic" language of the characters and the excessively complex imagery. Critics rightly felt that Pugachov himself expressed many of Esenin's own moods, but, instead of evaluating the work as a personal statement, they tended to mock its anachronistic flavour. Esenin no doubt read these reviews and was probably hurt by the venom of some critics' reactions. Boris Anibal, for instance, called Pugachov an Imaginist ("a dreamy young man in a top hat"), the other characters comic, the whole piece static and feeble, the action misplaced by 150 years, the thought-content poor, the verse clumsy, the images contrived, and concluded by stating that the poet's work was now in a murky stage under alien influences. Nevertheless, Esenin could derive some consolation from the favourable reaction of such judges as Gorodetsky, Ivanov-Razumnik, Mariengof, and Ehrenburg.[8] Indeed, from the sum total of published reviews, it seems that the majority of critics in 1922 wrote sympathetically about the play, but this was evidently not the general impression at the time. Professor Rozanov states as a fact that, after "Sorokoust," Esenin's "fame began to waver slightly: his *Pugachov* was not a success." This was a bitter blow for Esenin, for, as all the critics appreciated, he had put much of his own soul into the character of Pugachov and some of the minor figures:

> No, no, no! I shall never be willing to die!
> These birds are all circling in vain up above us.
> I want to be a child again, shaking copper from the rye,
> And to raise up my palms like white shining saucers.
> Must I die?
> Can such thoughts find a place in my heart
> When my home still stands in the province of Penza?
> I pity the sun, and I pity the moon,
> I pity the poplar above the low window.
> The steppes and the trees, the groves and the brooks,
> Are blessed, you realise, but for the living.
> Listen, I don't care a damn for the universe,
> If tomorrow I shall be dead!
> I want to live, live, live,
> Live till I shudder in pain!
> Even as a pickpocket, even as a tramp,
> Just to see how the mice leap for joy in the field,
> Just to hear how the frogs down the well sing in ecstasy.
> My white soul is a-foam with apple blossom,
> The wind has kindled the blue flame of my eyes.
> In God's name, teach me how,
> Teach me how and I'll do all you ask,
> I will do all you ask, to ring out in the garden of man!
>
> (Burnov's monologue, II, 185).

Yet the intensity of the above monologue—which Esenin chose

as his only contribution to the Imaginist anthology *The Horse Garden. All the Band,* published in 1922—in a way borders on hysteria. Burnov's cry echoes Esenin's own ignorance of how he should live, how he should "ring out in the garden of man." Parallel to his love of life went an increasingly autumnal mood, a consciousness of his burdened soul and lost youth.[9]

In March 1922 Shershenevich complained in the press that "left wing art" was now being assailed for its lack of realism and its incomprehensibility.

> Things have reached such a pitch that the management of the Polytechnic Museum has categorically refused to let its premises for lectures by the Futurists and Imaginists. . . And if Mayakovsky by means of a strenuous attack has managed to break through the blockade of prohibitions, then as far as the Imaginists are concerned, the Polytechnic Museum (and the Conservatoire and other auditoria) preserve their virginity. Ardent love has turned into ardent hatred and all because of this accursed lack of realism. But as for what kind of joke "realism" is, fortunately no one knows. . . Reducing everything to one level, simplifying everything, by a few meaningless terms—"incomprehensibility," "realism," "vitality". . .

This was the time when "Nepmen" flourished, in a milieu of *cafés chantants,* cabarets and music halls. 1922 is often regarded by Soviet critics today as the most "painful" and "gloomy" year in Esenin's life. Certainly, the poet's mood darkened year by year from 1920 to 1922, and his freshness and health declined. If in December 1920 he had told Ivanov-Razumnik, "I have become more corrupt" (V, 90), a year later he was writing to Klyuev: "My soul is tired and confused at itself and at what is happening" (V, 99). On March 6, 1922, in a further letter to Ivanov-Razumnik, he made it plain that he was tired of his Imaginist rowdyism: "I'm bored stiff at all this running around with my prattling brothers. . . In Moscow I feel wretched. . ." (V, 100, 102).

In March 1922 he published his poem "Mysterious World, My Ancient World" ("Mir tainstvennyi, mir moi drevnii," II, 109-110), which was originally entitled "The Wolf's Death" ("Volch'ia gibel' "). Never before had the poet expressed such active hostility to the town, and, by implication, to the October Revolution, which is strangling the village by means of stone roadways and telegraph poles. Singing a "song of animal's rights," Esenin goes out to greet his own "black death"—and as an analogy to the town's murder of the village, he describes the conflict of man and wolf. Man may shoot the wolf, but the dying animal will tear its human enemy to pieces. Esenin identifies himself with the wolf, and declares that he too will "taste the enemy's blood" with his dying leap, whilst a "song of revenge" shall be sung "on the other shore." As P. Yushin remarks, Esenin's protest was directed, not against the capitalist and "Nepman" town (as some Soviet critics still try to assert), but against the proletarian town, the Socialist changes in the village. Such an attitude to the town, claims Yushin, was to "lead the poet to the verge of an objective break with the revolution"; if he went further in this direction, "counter-revolution would begin, a break with the people." Esenin himself, no doubt, would not have thought of his attitude in such simple Marxist terms, but Yushin's general evaluation is sound. In May 1922, when he went abroad, Esenin was perhaps further from the Bolsheviks than he had ever been. If, when abroad, he discovered that the Russian emigres were even less to his liking, this can have been due, not so much to political perspicacity, as to his strong sense of Russian patriotism and his overwhelming nostalgia for the soil of his motherland.

During the years 1919-22 Esenin maintained a complex relationship with two prominent poets: Vladimir Mayakovsky and Nikolai Klyuev. Today Mayakovsky (1893-1930) and Esenin are generally regarded in the Soviet Union as the two leading poets of those years, and, understandably, frequent attempts are made to show that they respected one another's talent. This may well have been so, but it is clear that no bond of friendship ever arose between the two poets, who sensed one another as literary rivals and enemies. No doubt jealousy played its part in this, particularly on Esenin's side, but serious differences of outlook also contributed. In about 1921, Ehrenburg asked Esenin why he was "so disturbed" by Mayakovsky. Esenin replied:

"He is a poet *for* something, whereas I'm a poet *because of* something *(On poet dlia chego-to, a ia poet ot chego-to).* I myself don't know because of what. . . He will live to be eighty, people will erect a monument to him. . . (Esenin always passionately desired fame, and monuments for him were not bronze statues, but the embodiment of immortality). But I'll die under some fence on which his poems are pasted. But all the same I wouldn't change places with him." I tried to argue with him, Esenin was in a good mood, and he reluctantly conceded that Mayakovsky was a poet, but an "uninteresting" one.

Although Esenin was frequently unjust towards other poets, he had to admit, as Startsev recalls, that "whatever you say, you can't discard Mayakovsky. He will be like a log in literature—and many people will trip up over him." Yet he disliked something about the essence of Mayakovsky's poetry. "I consider Mayakovsky a very striking poet," he told Ivan Rozanov, "but he lacks the spirit of innovation: he stems completely from Whitman.[10] And above all: he does not have a poetic feeling for the world."

The attitude of the peasant-born Esenin towards the urban poet Mayakovsky was complicated by the fact that they belonged to warring literary groups. The Imaginists and the Futurists were constantly at each other's throats, although their animosity seems in part to have been artificially generated, for the sake of publicity. There are amusing reports of altercations between Esenin and Mayakovsky, and the Imaginists in general and Mayakovsky. Once at a banquet in the Press House *(Dom Pechati),* Esenin, somewhat drunk, shouted at Mayakovsky: "Russia is mine, do you understand,—mine, whilst you... you're an American! Russia is mine!" According to N. Poletaev, Mayakovsky replied with icy irony: "Go ahead and take it! Eat it with bread!" At the end of 1920, writes V. Volpin, Esenin was "especially hostile towards the Futurists, denying them any merits and characterising their leaders with very 'strong' epithets." When Lev Povitsky asked Esenin why he was so antagonistic towards the Futurists, he laconically replied: "Because they rob me!" Povitsky comments:

The meaning of these words lay in the fact that Esenin considered

> himself the owner and monopolist of the image *(obraznoe slovo)* in poetry. He claimed that the Futurists, under another mask, resorted to the same Imaginistic method, imbuing it, "as a blind," with a hyperbolic urbanistic content. . . No one and nothing could dissuade him from this peculiar notion of "literary property," created by his own imagination, and his hostility towards the Futurists persisted until his dying day.

Mariengof remembers the fanatical literary disputes of those days, in the Main Hall of the Conservatoire, the Polytechnic Museum, in the poets' cafes on Tverskaya, and on Mondays on the stages of theatres. Mariengof declares: "We Imaginists engaged in persistent polemic with Mayakovsky and the poets who followed him. . . I never went to Mayakovsky's home, and he never came to us. A 'nodding acquaintance,' as they say." Their public disputes must have been lively and often witty. As a rule, Soviet critics today take Mayakovsky's side, for one of the Imaginists' targets was Mayakovsky's politically committed, socially orientated, "agitational," "useful" verse. The Imaginists were essentially non- (if not anti-) Bolshevik, and persistently denigrated Mayakovsky, both verbally and in print. Mariengof called Futurism a "worn-out galosh" and Mayakovsky "the author of the totally untalented *Mystery-Bouffe* and bad feuilleton verse." Shershenevich described Mayakovsky as "the great comic of our day, who imagines himself a lyric poet," and, after Esenin's death, contrasted Esenin with Mayakovsky: "There never were two more different poets. A heart born in the town and its almost hysterical turmoil—that was the poetry of the Futurist Mayakovsky. The proud pathos and unbridled temperament of a river at floodtime, combined with the peaceful calm of country roads...—that was the manner of Esenin."

Many critics, then as now, regarded the two poets primarily as opposites. People often contrast the delicate flute of Esenin with the resonant drum of Mayakovsky; the intimate tender lyricism of Esenin with Mayakovsky's hyperbolic poetry of the market place. One Soviet critic, Yu. Surma, has set the idealistic view of art of the Imaginists against the socially committed attitude of Mayakovsky, for whom the poet was a "master craftsman," a "general," a producer of poetic "material." Certainly the conflict between the Imaginists and Mayakovsky lay deeper than mere personal rivalry, jealousy, and the desire for noisy publicity. The Imaginist Ivan Gruzinov reports a literary dispute, at which Mayakovsky shouted out: "The Imaginists are epigones of Futurism!" To this Gruzinov retorted that Imaginism is a protest against the extreme "naturalism" of the Futurists, and dubbed some of Mayakovsky's work indistinguishable from "the poster and the feuilleton." Lidiya Seifullina recalls that at a dispute in the Polytechnic Museum in November 1920, Mayakovsky sarcastically observed that "the children have killed their own mother"—that is, the Imaginists claimed to have eliminated their "mother," Futurism. The verbal warfare between the Imaginists and Mayakovsky continued for years, so that it is amusingly incongruous to find the Berlin journal *Russian Book (Russkaia kniga),* listing Mayakovsky in 1921 as one of the Imaginists![11] During these years, whenever Esenin mentioned Mayakovsky in theoretical articles, letters, or in the Imaginist declarations he signed, it was always in a hostile tone (IV, 196, 253; V, 97).

At a meeting entitled the "Purge of Modern Poetry," held in the Polytechnic Museum on January 19, 1922, Mayakovsky wittily attacked Mariengof and Shershenevich, but this time spoke sympathetically about Esenin. Such a generous appraisal of his rival came much more rarely, however, from the mouth of Esenin. "Esenin retained a negative attitude towards Mayakovsky all his life," writes Ivan Gruzinov. This is not surprising, as Gruzinov also recalls that Esenin already claimed in 1920 to be "the first, the very best poet in Russia," and complained that "someone was impeding him, someone was not giving him recognition. . ."

A poet who was reluctant to recognise either Esenin or Mayakovsky during the period 1919-22 was Nikolai Klyuev. Klyuev had hailed both the February and the October Revolution, and in 1919 published some poems about Lenin, whom he characterised virtually as the strict but righteous head of an Old Believer monastery. This idiosyncratic "revolutionary" spirit offended many people, and Klyuev soon retired to his northern wilderness, quickly losing faith in the Revolution. Klyuev became increasingly polemical in his poetry of the next three years, jealously defending "Kitezh" and the age-old wisdom and culture of the peasantry, and vehemently attacking everything out of harmony with his vision, such as proletarian poets, the factory, iron, science–and, by implication, the whole course of the Bolshevik Revolution. From 1919 to 1922 Esenin and Klyuev drifted far apart as poets. There were many reasons for this, but a basic psychological difference makes this divergence understandable. Esenin lacked Klyuev's deep-rooted adherence to the Old Believer faith and culture; he was several years younger than Klyuev, and much more adaptable in his aspiration to poetic fame. If Esenin was disturbed by the existence of Mayakovsky, the presence of Klyuev troubled him even more. He no doubt realised how close his own poetic imagery was to that of Klyuev, and hence he constantly felt the need to justify himself and find fault with the latter's poetry. His letters and articles of these years contain continual, often poorly reasoned, criticism of Klyuev, as a lifeless poet, weak in artistic form and belonging to the past (IV, 194-195, 199; V, 86, 90, 93-96), and yet, at the same time, they reveal an admiration for Klyuev's verse and even his outlook (IV, 211, 213; V, 86).

Ivan Startsev noted that Esenin loved Klyuev "with a kind of dual love." This "dual love" can be seen in some of Esenin's letters of this period, where he criticises Klyuev as cunning, yet confesses: "But all the same I'd like to see him" (V, 90–written in December 1920). A year later, in December 1921, he wrote an extremely conciliatory letter to Klyuev: "Peace unto you, my friend! Forgive me for not writing to you during these years, and for writing so little even now. . . I have no way of conveying all that I think and grieve at. But I always remember you, you are always present within me. When we meet it will be easier and more pleasant to express all this without a letter. I kiss you and press your hand. Sergei Esenin" (V, 99). Klyuev retorted, however, by publishing as a separate booklet a polemical poem, or series of poems, *The Fourth Rome (Chetvertyi Rim),* in which he berated the Imaginist Esenin in a crescendo of wrath. In his turn Esenin disparaged Klyuev's religiosity, and also the weak pseudo-Imaginistic images of *The Fourth Rome* (V, 101). Yet at the same time he mentioned that he, Klychkov and Lunacharsky had recently sent some money to assist Klyuev, who was "almost dying of hunger," and expressed the opinion that Klyuev, if only he abandoned his antiquated religiousness, could write better verse than ever before.

Esenin's feelings towards Klyuev were far more complex than his attitude to Mayakovsky. He continually alternated between love and hate, admiration and disdain–Klyuev, his first "teacher," at one time his closest friend, remained for ever his disturbing *alter ego.* On May 5, 1922, five days before he went abroad, Esenin wrote again to Klyuev. The letter, as he himself pointed out, was "purely a business one, without any lyrical outpourings," but Esenin wrote simply and sincerely–promising Klyuev further money if he should be in need ("in this respect, after all, I too owe you a good deal from during my first days"), and frankly expressing his opinion of Klyuev's verse. He told Klyuev, concerning *The Fourth Rome:* "I didn't like the work. It's clumsy and sugary. But, after all, everyone has his own path. I am delighted with many of your other poems. . ." (V, 105). He ended by promising to write to Klyuev from abroad, but no such letters have been traced.

In his verse of 1919-22 Klyuev had repeatedly referred to Esenin, sometimes identifying him as a peasant ally, more often condemning him as an apostate from the true peasant faith. In one poem Klyuev alluded to Esenin as a "good wolf and friend," and there is an undated inscription by Esenin, which seems addressed to Klyuev: "Whatever may happen between us, yet love will remain. However much you may curse me, and I you, all the same you and I are from the same garden, the garden of apple trees, rams, horses and wolves. S. Esenin." Esenin has added in the margin: "We are apple trees and wolves, depending on necessity."

Esenin now felt himself primarily a "wolf," as he had demonstrated in his poem about the "wolf's death." Like Pugachov, he himself might say:

Do you know? People all have an animal soul,
We're all bears, or she-wolves, or foxes,
And life's a gigantic forest for us...
One needs fangs that are powerful, powerful
(II, 168).

Esenin and Isadora Duncan, upon their arrival in New York on the S.S. Paris, October 1, 1922.

Chapter Ten: Enter Isadora (1921-22)

Since late 1921, Esenin's personal life in Moscow had been closely bound up with that of Isadora Duncan. The first meeting of the poet and the dancer has become tangled with legend. One night late in 1921, tells Mariengof, Isadora reclined on a couch in the studio of Georgy Yakulov, with Esenin at her feet:

> She plunged her hand into his curls and said:
>
> "*Solotaia golova!* (Golden head!)"
>
> It was surprising that she, who knew no more than a dozen Russian words, knew precisely these two.
>
> Then she kissed him on the lips.
>
> And for a second time her mouth, small and red like a bullet wound, pleasantly distorted the Russian letters:
>
> "*Anguel!*"
>
> She kissed him again and said:
>
> "*Tschort!* (Devil!)"
>
> After 3 a.m. Isadora Duncan and Esenin left together. . .

Mariengof and Kolobov came away from Yakulov's at dawn: "We walked along the deserted street with heavy hearts." The Imaginists had remained a merry "band" as long as their alliance was unaffected by deep attachments to any one woman. Now, in 1921, the first cracks began to appear in the seemingly unbreakable friendship of Esenin and Mariengof. Soviet critics tend to attribute the eventual break between the two poets to differences in their literary principles, but it is more likely that personal reasons were the first cause. During Esenin's visit to Central Asia in April 1921, Mariengof himself had met a woman in Moscow, the actress Anna Nikritina, who was to be his wife for the next forty years. Mariengof, so cynical in his verse, fell in love—and Esenin mocked his friend's romantic passion. Esenin and Kolobov unflatteringly nicknamed Nikritina "Martyshon," *martyn* or *martyshka* ("little monkey"). Towards the end of 1921, when Mariengof was in love with Nikritina, Esenin refused to stay any longer in Bogoslovsky Pereulok, telling Mariengof: "I cannot and will not sit on the edge of someone else's nest. . ." Their mutual friend, Sakharov, made up a folk quatrain about Mariengof, Esenin and Isadora (or "Duncan" as she is usually known in Russia):

Unwashed Tolya scarcely cheeps,
But Seryozha's friskier.
That's because Seryozha sleeps
With Dunya on Prechistenka.

After their first meeting, Esenin and Isadora Duncan began to live together at Isadora's large apartment on Prechistenka (now Ulitsa Kropotkina). From her side, it was clearly a case of "love at first sight."

Shortly before her death, Isadora Duncan (1878-1927) wrote a candid and moving autobiography, *My Life.* In her book she appears temperamental, vulnerable, superstitious and self-centred; brave, original, inspired, and widely cultured. Of "Scotch-Irish-American" blood, Isadora came from an unstable family background—her father deserted her Irish mother. Isadora herself "decided, then and there, that I would live to fight against marriage and for the emancipation of women, and for the right for every woman to have a child or children as it pleased her, and to uphold her right and her virtue. . ." Disdaining the artificial mechanical movements of classical ballet, the young Isadora strove to perfect her own dance, which would express her spiritual vision. Rousseau, Walt Whitman and Nietzsche were her "dance masters," Beethoven and Wagner her musical inspiration. In Berlin she became known as "the divine, holy Isadora" *(die göttliche, heilige Isadora).* "I had never worn any other dress than the little white tunic, bare feet, and sandals. And my audience came to my performances with an absolutely religious ecstasy. . ." She gave birth to Deirdre, daughter of Gordon Craig, but did not marry; and she longed to found a school where a vast ensemble should dance Beethoven's Ninth Symphony. Love and Art battled within her—and she gave birth to Patrick, son of Paris Singer, but still would not marry. In April 1913 the greatest tragedy of her life befell her—Deirdre and Patrick, her beloved children, were drowned when their chauffeur-attended car plunged into the River Seine. Overcoming thoughts of suicide, Isadora went on living for her school of Dance. She had a third child, who soon died; and during the First World War she usually closed her performances by dancing the *Marseillaise.* She had visited Russia several times—her first visit was in late 1904—and in 1917 Isadora, hating all things bourgeois, welcomed the news of the Russian Revolution: "On the night of the Russian Revolution I danced with a terrible fierce joy. My heart was bursting within me at the release of all those who had suffered, been tortured, died in the cause of humanity. . ." In the spring of 1921, discouraged by her failure to found a school of Dance in the West, Isadora accepted an invitation from the Russian Government to come to Moscow to establish her school. Before leaving London, she was told by a fortune-teller that she would marry: "But at the word 'marry' I cut her short with laughter. I, who was always against marriage? I would never marry. The fortune-teller said, 'Wait and see'." Isadora gladly left the Old World, bourgeois Europe, and eagerly travelled towards the "ideal domain of Communism," to the "beautiful New World that had been created."

Unfortunately her autobiography ends here—the second book she had planned about her years in Bolshevik Russia remained unwritten. Isadora's account of her relationship with Esenin would have given an invaluable insight into Esenin's personality, even though she had but a scanty knowledge of the Russian language. As it is, in 1929 two close associates, Irma Duncan (her adopted daughter, and pupil since 1905) and Allan Ross Macdougall (Isadora's one-time secretary) published a book entitled *Isadora Duncan's Russian Days and her Last Years in France.* They tell that Isadora arrived in Moscow on July 24, 1921. She had been promised a school with a thousand pupils, but had to make do with forty. Despite this setback, she was immediately enthralled by the Communist vision of a new society, and wrote in a newspaper article: "I am convinced that here in Russia is the greatest miracle that has happened to humanity for two thousand years. . . Moscow is a miracle city, and the martyrdom submitted by Russia will be for the future that which the crucifixion was. . . The prophecies of Beethoven, of Nietzsche, of Walt Whitman are being realised. All men will be brothers, carried away by the great wave of liberation that has just been born here in Russia." In Moscow she was given a large house in Prechistenka Street, which had previously been occupied by the Russian ballerina Balashova, who had emigrated to Paris. The house was decorated in opulent bad taste, with cupids and Napoleonic emblems in rococo and Empire style, which Isadora endeavoured to cover up. Her school was formally opened at 20 Prechistenka on December 3—but shortly before then she had met the man who was to make the London fortune-teller's prediction come true. The exact date of this first meeting between Esenin and Isadora Duncan is uncertain. Irma Duncan and Allan Ross Macdougall suggest it was early November 1921: ". . . He was a Russian peasant, tall,[1] blue-eyed, golden-locked. There was something in his moral and poetic make-up of both Robert Burns and Arthur Rimbaud, *Le Poete Maudit . .* "

Isadora was at once captivated by Esenin: she found his face extraordinarily beautiful, even angelic. It is clear that she saw in him not only a fitting lover for the "autumn" of her life, but also, to some extent, a kind of reincarnation of her dead son. Shortly after their first meeting, Isadora danced in the serene calm of her studio, which was dimly lit and draped with blue curtains, whereupon Esenin retorted brutally that he could dance better. To the accompaniment of Kusikov's balalaika, the excited poet danced "like a crazy man." Although Soviet scholars today are reluctant to admit it, first-hand witnesses indicate that Esenin often treated Isadora despotically and cruelly. He evidently felt himself young, virile and infinitely desirable in the eyes of the famous aging dancer from a foreign land. Mariengof even claims—perhaps exaggeratedly—that Esenin's Herod-like despotism only intensified Isadora's delight: "Esenin subsequently became her master, her sovereign. She, like a dog, kissed the hand which he had raised to strike her, and his eyes in which hatred for her burned more often than love. . ." According to Mariengof, when Esenin pushed the enamoured Isadora aside, she rhapsodised: "Ruska lubow!" ("Russian love!").

Isadora was, it seems, a heavy drinker of champagne, cognac and vodka, and Mariengof asserts: "Before he met Isadora Duncan

Esenin did not drink a greater amount or any more often than the rest of us. He used to enjoy a drink in good company—an occasional pleasure and nothing more." Of course, it can be objected that Mariengof was not an unbiased witness—Isadora had helped to weaken the friendship between him and Esenin. True, the theme of drunkenness scarcely occurs in Esenin's verse until 1922. His poems "The Hooligan" and "The Hooligan's Confession" betray no addiction to alcohol, no matter how unstable and sorrowful the lyrical hero of his verse already appeared.[2] Nevertheless, Esenin *had* drunk quite heavily in 1920-21, even if his meeting with Isadora Duncan served to accelerate his movement towards alcoholism. Many of the people closest to Esenin (his friends and relatives) regard Isadora as a destructive element in his life— partly because they feel she caused him to drink more; but partly, perhaps, because it is convenient for them to blame Isadora as a pernicious foreign influence on the poet, thus absolving Esenin's personal weakness.

The Imaginists sought to break up Esenin's relationship with Isadora, and tried to lure him onto a trip with Kolobov to Persia. Once, in late 1921 or early 1922, they put Esenin on a train, but he went only as far as Rostov, from which town he sent a slangy and indignant postcard to Mariengof. This postcard includes the lines: "Greetings to Isadora, Irma and Ilya Ilich.[3] I imagine that the air around them will have been ventilated by now and they have probably already forgotten us. Well, out of sight and out of mind—we shall not, of course, start weeping. . . Damned Persia. Sergei" (V, 99).

The poet promptly returned to Moscow. Irma Duncan claims that he made frequent unavailing efforts to break with Isadora: he often said "adieu" to her and went off with his bundle of clothes, but he always came back to her adoring embrace. "He was a wayward, wilful little child, and she was a mother passionately enough in love with him to overlook and forgive all the vulgar curses and the peasant blows. And so scenes of love and felicity were usually followed by drunken scenes and truancies from Prechistenka."

In February 1922 Esenin accompanied Isadora when she went to dance in Petrograd. The couple stayed at the Hotel

Angleterre. According to Irma Duncan and Allan Ross Macdougall, Esenin soon realised that the hotel had some fine pre-war vintages of wine, and that travelling with Isadora enabled him to order whatever he wanted: ". . . And more than once during their stay at the Angleterre he had to be forcibly carried back to his room by the valets, who found him wandering completely naked and riotous about the halls of the hotel."

They soon returned to Moscow, and on April 12, 1922 Isadora's mother died in Paris. "From that moment, Isadora became more and more restless in Moscow. She felt that she must leave Moscow for a while. This was necessary for two reasons: her health and her school's finances." On May 2, 1922 Esenin and Isadora "were married in the office of the Moscow Registry of Civil Statistics. To all who knew the dancer and her ideas about marriage, this news item, which was cabled to the outside world, came as a shock. But if they could have been told what a simple unbinding ceremony it was–the merest formality! She abdicated none of her ideas about marriage." Irma Duncan and Allan Ross Macdougall continue: "Isadora wanted to take Essenine out of Russia: first, because he was a very sick man, in need of the examination and care of a specialist; second, because he was a poet who required, so she thought, new horizons. . . She wanted to show him all that Europe had of beauty, and all that America had of wonder. . ." They state that Isadora needed the marriage-certificate mainly to satisfy the "interfering" hotel keepers in America.

Just six days after her mother's death, Isadora had sent a telegram to Sol Hurok, the Russian-born impresario in New York:

> S. Hurok 220 W. 42nd St. New York.
>
> Propose tournee twelve weeks or more myself Irma Great Russian Poet Essenin and twenty pupils minimum four performances a week guarante[e] twelve hundred dollars per performances you paying all theatre expenses including voyages large towns orchestra small towns piano.
>
> Isadora Duncan 18/IV 1922.

Hurok reacted favourably to this suggestion, offering Isadora forty thousand dollars for fifty performances. Isadora accepted the offer, and it was decided that the tour in America should last four months, starting in October. Meeting with obstacles from first the United States, and then the Russian, Governments, Isadora's pupils were prevented from joining her outside Russia.

Thus, in April 1922, Isadora planned her trip "abroad," on which Esenin was to accompany her. The poet seems to have imagined that his travels would be brief—he wrote to Klyuev on May 5: "In a fortnight or so I am going to Berlin, I'll return in June or July, or perhaps even later. . ." (V, 105). Yet surely he must have realised that Isadora's tour of America was scheduled to begin in October?

In early May Esenin and Isadora were wed—his second marriage, her first. Nine tempestuous months later they presented reporters with separate disdainful explanations for their union. Isadora told the International News Service in Paris, Feb. 17, 1923: "I never believed in marriage and I now believe in it less than ever. I married Serge only in order to enable him to get a passport to America. He is a genius, and marriage between artists is impossible. . ." Meanwhile, on the selfsame day, Esenin told reporters in Berlin: "I wouldn't live with her again for all the money in America. As soon as I arrive in Moscow I am going to get a divorce. . . I was a fool. I married Duncan for her money and a chance to travel. . ."

Perhaps one should not attach undue importance to these press reports of statements made in anger. It may well be that at times Esenin felt something akin to "love" for Isadora, and he no doubt admired her artistic talent, however grudgingly. In late 1923 he told G. Benislavskaya that he had felt a "great passion" for Isadora for "a whole year": "But then everything passed and nothing remained, nothing. . ." He also allegedly said to Benislavskaya: "In my life I have loved only two women—Zinaida Raikh and Isadora Duncan—and I used to hit them both because of jealousy." In contrast, Mariengof writes:

> Esenin did not fall in love with Isadora Duncan, but with her fame, her world-wide fame. And he married her fame, not her—not an elderly, somewhat heavy, but still beautiful woman with dyed hair. He derived

> pleasure from walking hand in hand with this world-wide celebrity along the streets of Moscow, appearing with her in the Poets' Cafe, at concerts, at theatrical premieres, and hearing behind his back the whisper of many voices in which the two names were interwoven: "Duncan-Esenin. . . Esenin-Duncan. . ."

As well as drinking heavily, Esenin began to dress in even more dandyish clothes. His turbulent life of the past years had made him restless and ever more eager for change. At times his mood by early 1922 seems to have bordered on despair. Memoirists speak of his desire to "withdraw to a monastery," away from the hurly-burly of Moscow. The role of monk-*manqué* may sound strange for one whose monastic aspirations were recently confined to daubing walls, but Esenin made this forlorn declaration with tears in his eyes. Perhaps the lines from a poem he had published nearly seven years earlier passed through his anxious mind: "A skull-capped radiant monk, I'll go/ Across the steppes to monasteries..." (I, 363). The poet complained at this time of kidney trouble, and M. Babenchikov recalls that Esenin

> felt the void of loneliness then more than ever before, having broken with many of his recent friends. He said bluntly of the Imaginists that he now had nothing in common with them, (and never had had). "I'm tired of it all, I want to go away, but I myself don't know yet where to,"—he said to me once. . . In conversations he turned more and more to themes of his youth, sometimes insistently asking: "Have I really changed so much?," sometimes reciting from *Pugachov* with a kind of desperate ardour. . .: "Youth, o my youth, you have taken to flight, like a birdcherry tree on a distant May evening". . .

In 1922, shortly before his departure from Russia, Esenin said despairingly: "I was in the village. . . Everything is crumbling. . . One has to be from there to understand. . . everything is finished. . ." It is unlikely that the poet set out on his journey abroad with a feeling of healthy optimism. An elegiac mood permeates his famous poem "I'm Not Regretting, Calling, or Weeping" ("Ne zhaleiu, ne zovu, ne plachu," II, 111-112), first published in early 1922.

Nevertheless, he did not leave Russia merely as Isadora Duncan's husband and travelling companion. Esenin lived above all for his poetry and his poetic fame—and hence, understandably, he set out with the ambitious dream of conquering Europe and the world by the genius of his verse. "After all, I'm not going there to loaf about London and Paris," he said to Mariengof, "but to conquer." "Conquer whom, Seryozha?," asked Mariengof. "Europe!... Do you understand?... At first, of course, I'll conquer Europe... And then..." Shershenevich recalls Esenin's words: "I'm going to the West in order to show the West what a Russian poet is like. . ."

The critic V. Vdovin has recently revealed that as early as March 17, 1922 Esenin asked Lunacharsky to help him gain permission to go to Berlin for three months in order to publish there his own books and those of the group of poets close to him. On April 3 such permission was given. Shortly before leaving Russia, Esenin cabled to Kusikov, who was already in Berlin, asking him to announce their forthcoming literary recital there (V, 104). Esenin had travelled a great deal within Russia during the past two years—to the Ukraine, the Caucasus, and Central Asia—but he did not feel truly "at home" anywhere: "I want to go away somewhere, yet there's nowhere to go away to. . . I lead somehow a bivouac life, without refuge and shelter, because various idlers. . . have started to visit my house and disturb me. You see, they enjoy drinking with me! I don't even know how to get out of this mess, yet I now find burning myself up both a shame and a pity. I want to start working again. . ." (V, 102).

Esenin wanted "to go away somewhere, yet there's nowhere to go away to. . ." His meeting with Isadora Duncan, and then his marriage to her, offered him the chance to go abroad. Yet, as he had forebodingly sensed in 1920, "I have begun to think that travel is harmful for me. I don't know what would happen to me if by chance I had to journey all round the world?. . ." (V, 87).

This journey was now about to commence. Like another richly national and restless poet, Dylan Thomas, Esenin might have felt: "But I wouldn't be at home if I were at home. Everywhere I find myself seems to be nothing but a resting place between places that become resting places between resting places themselves. This is an essential state of being. . . It may be a primary loneliness that makes me out-of-home. It may be this or that, and this and that is enough for today. . ."

Shortly before Esenin's departure, he and Mariengof exchanged farewell poems. At 9 a.m. on Wednesday May 10, 1922 a tiny plane took off from Moscow on the first regular flight to Germany. In the six-seater Fokker, Kőnigsberg-bound, sat Sergei Esenin and Isadora Duncan, whilst children from Isadora's school waved goodbye until the plane became a speck in the distance.

Esenin's father, Alexander Nikitich Esenin, and his mother, Tatyana Fyodorovna.

Esenin's grandfather, Fyodor Andreevich Titov.

Top: Grigory Panfilov (left) and Sergei Esenin (right), enlarged from a group portrait of the Spas Klepiki boarding school, 1911.

Bottom: Sergei Esenin (third from right) among peasants of Konstantinovo village (c. 1909-10).

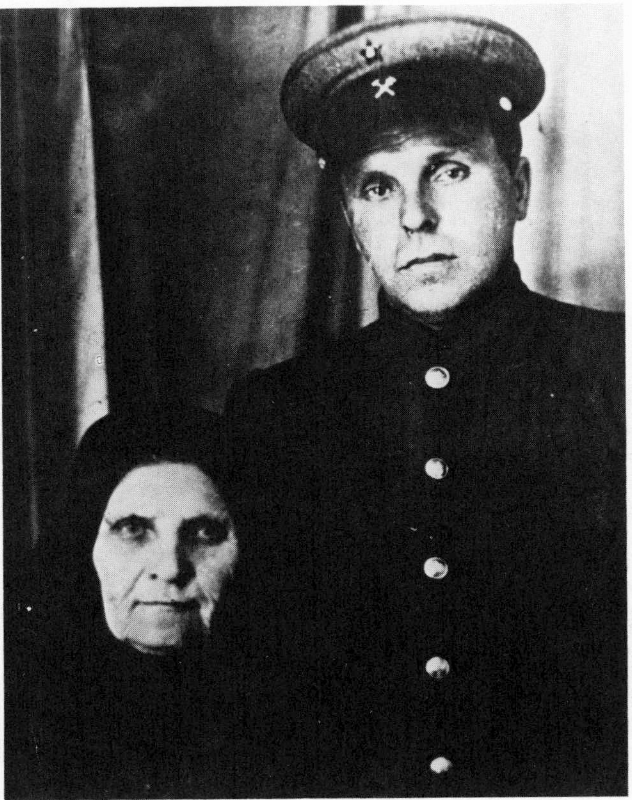

Top: Sergei Esenin (third from rig back row) in group at the Spas-Kl boarding school, 1911.

Left: Esenin's mother with her so Esenin's half-brother.

Esenin with his sisters Katya (l.) and Shura, 1912.

Esenin, c. 1912.

Esenin with his father (left) and his uncle, Ivan Nikitich (right), Moscow, C. 1912-13 (July 13, 191

Esenin, (second from left, back row) with workers at Sytin's printing house, Moscow, c. 1914. Sitting on the floor is Anna Izryadnova.

Esenin's sister Alexandra (Shura) with his son, Yury.

Esenin (left) with Sergei Gorodetsky, Petrograd, 1915.

Esenin (left) with Nikolai Klyuev, 1915-16.

Below: Esenin (right) with Ryurik Ivnev (left) and Vladimir Chernyavsky (centre), Petrograd, 1915.

Esenin, Perhaps c. !915-16, sometime after his literary debut in Petrograd.

Below: Esenin (right) with Mikhail Murashov, Petrograd, c. 1916.

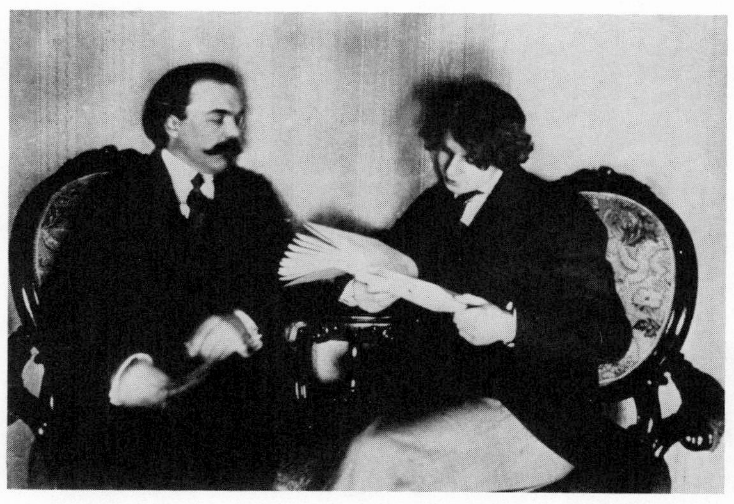

Manuscript of Esenin's poem "Wake me up early tomorrow," 1917.

Разбуди меня завтра рано,
о моя терпѣливая мать!
Я пойду за дорожнымъ курганомъ
Дорогого гостя встрѣчать.

Я сегодня увидѣлъ въ пущѣ
слѣдъ широкихъ колесъ на лугу.
Треплетъ вѣтеръ подъ облачной кущей
Золотую его дугу.

На разсвѣтѣ онъ завтра промчится
Шапку мѣсяцъ пригнувъ подъ кустомъ
И игриво взмахнетъ кобылица
Надъ равниною краснымъ хвостомъ.

Разбуди меня завтра рано,
Засвѣти въ нашей горницѣ свѣтъ.
Говорятъ что я скоро стану
Знаменитый русскій поэтъ.

Воспою я тебя и гостя,
Нашу печь, пѣтуха и кровъ...
И на пѣсни мои прольется
Молоко твоихъ рыжихъ коровъ.

Сергѣй Есенинъ.

1917.

Esenin (left) with Nikolai Klyuev, c. 1916.

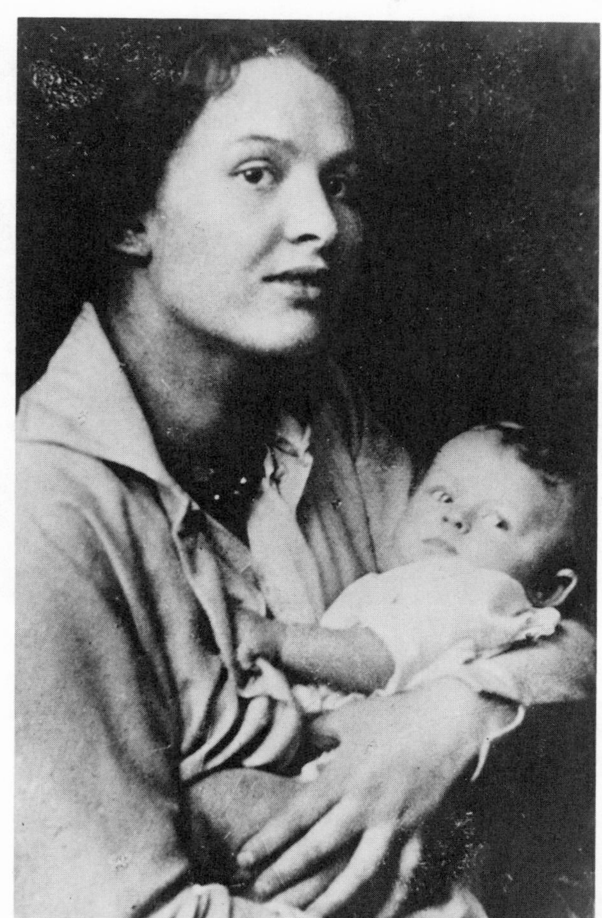

Esenin's first wife, Zinaida Nikolaevna Raikh, with their daughter Tatyana (Tanya).

Below: Esenin (far right) at the unveiling of a statue of the poet A.V. Koltsov, Moscow, November 3, 1918.

Esenin (second from right). From left; Max Zelimovich Perets, Lidia Ivanovna Kashina, El. Ef. Kondratieva, Glafira Lvovna Balmont and Prof. Kozhevnikov. October, 1918.

Zinaida Raikh, with Konstantin (Kostya) and Tatyana (Tanya) (right), the children from her marriage to Esenin.

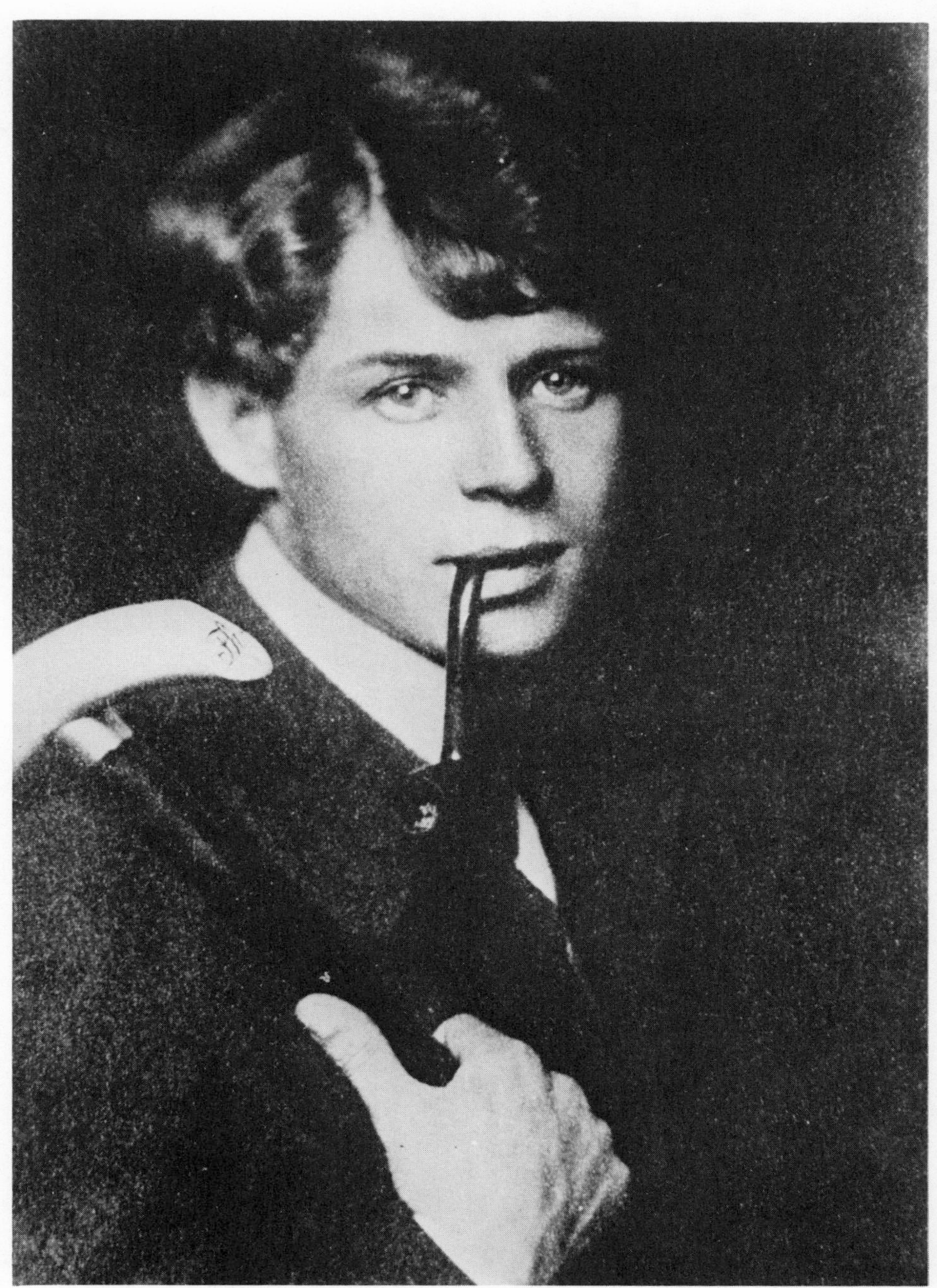

Esenin, c. 1919.

Esenin (left) with Anatoly Mariengof, c. 1919-21.

Esenin (right) with Alexan
Kusikov (left) and Anatoly
Mariengof (centre), 1919.

Esenin (left) with Mariengof (front), and Lev Povitsky, 1920.

Below: Vadim Shershenevich.

Esenin in a group. Standing, Nadezhda Volpin (?), Anatoly Mariengof, Ivan Gruzinov. Seated: Vadim Shershenevich and Esenin.

Esenin (second from left) with the Imaginists Mariengof (left), Kusikov (second from right), and Shershenevich (far right), evidently 1919.

ove: Esenin (right) with
igory Kolobov, c. 1920-21.

ght: Esenin, Rostov-on-Don, July
, 1920 (?).

Esenin (right) with Alexander Sakharov, c. 1920 (?).

Esenin (left) with Mariengof (centre) and Nikolai Erdman (right), c. 1920.

Wooden bust of Esenin by Sergei Konyonkov, 1920.

Esenin's inscription to A.M. Kozhebatkin, December 1921. "To my colleague at cards, vodka and in all our daredevil life, to Alexander Meletevich Kozhebatkin. The Soviet Rasputin, S. Esenin. 1921. December."

Esenin and Isadora Duncan, Berlin [May] 1922.

Esenin and Isadora Dunca, about mid-1922 (?).

Esenin, mid-1922. Esenin has written on the photograph: "S. Esenin 1922 Brussels July[y] 15."

Esenin and Isadora Duncan, mid-1922 (?

Esenin and Duncan, from *The New York Times*, (Courtesy, Dance Collection, New York). The date is given as August 13, 1922. This picture is obviously cropped from the above photo.

Above: Esenin with Irma Duncan (left) and Isadora Duncan (centre), on the wedding-day of Esenin and Isadora (?), Moscow, May 2, 1922.

Right: Esenin, c. 1921-22.

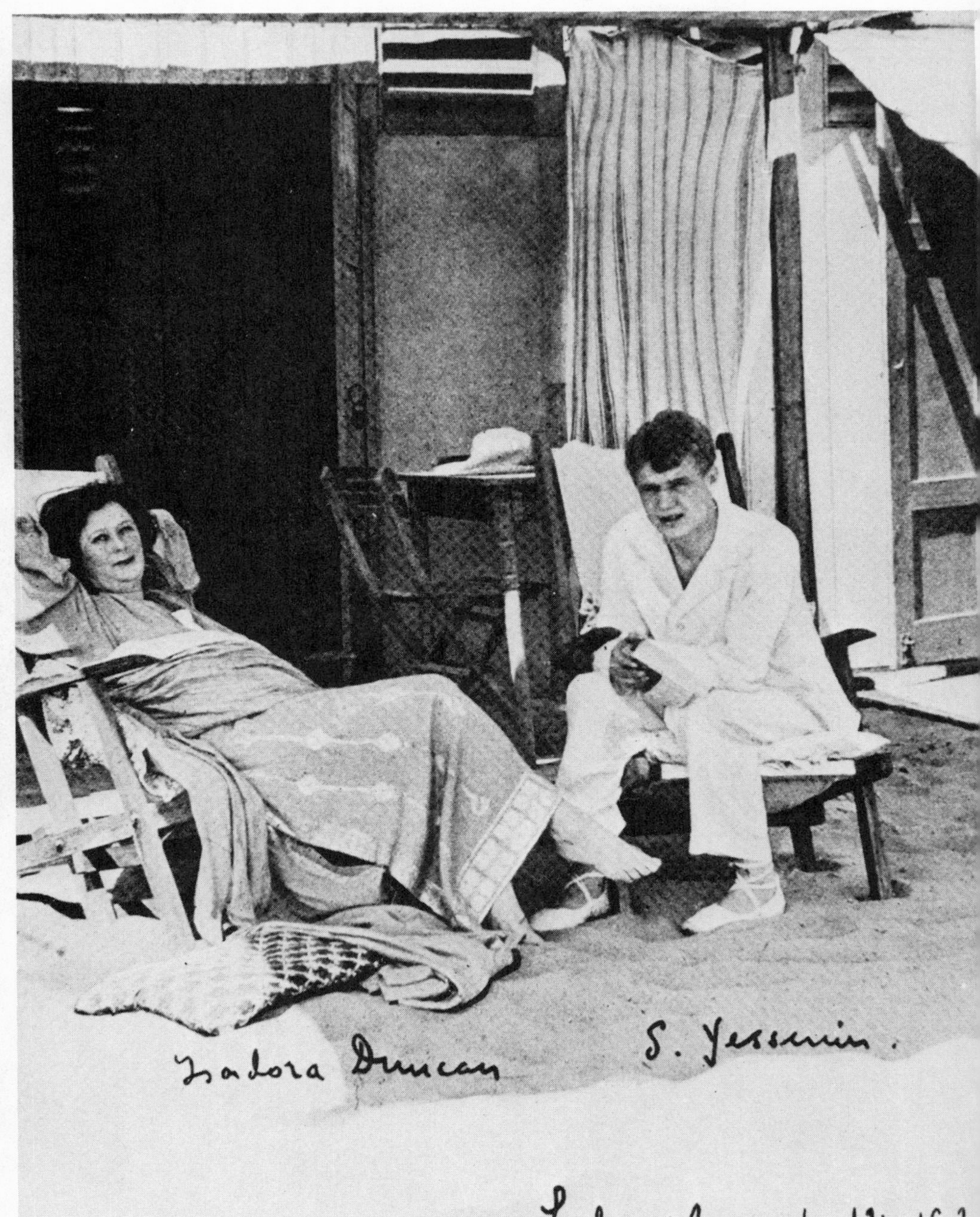

Esenin and Isadora Duncan, The Lido, Venice, evidently on August 14, 1922.
Note: the pictures on the facing page are presumed to be from the same time.

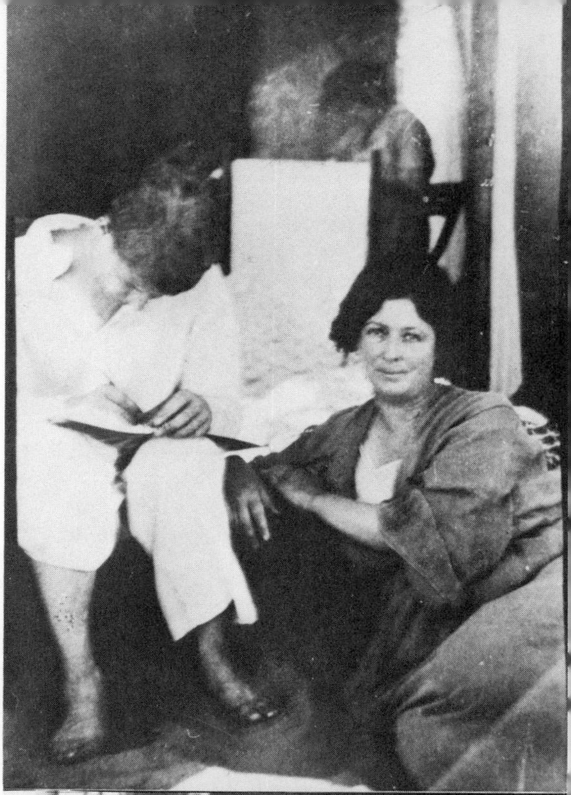

Isadora Duncan and Esenin,
The Lido, Venice, August 14, 1922.

Esenin and Isadora Duncan, 1922 (?).

Esenin, 1922 (?).

Esenin, 1922 (?).

Esenin, c. 1923.

Я знаю что ты настоящий жид.
Ругаешься ты как ярославский вор —
но
Фамилия твоя Лейбман
и чорт с тобой
Что ты жил за границей
Все равно в Могилеве твой дом.

Чекистов

Ха-ха!
Ты обозвал меня жидом!
Нет Замарашкин!
Я гражданин из Веймара
И приехал сюда не как еврей
А как обладающий даром
Укрощать дураков и зверей.
Я ругаюсь!
И буду упорно
Проклинать вас хоть тысячу лет,
потому что хочу в уборную
А уборных в России нет.
Странный и смешной вы народ
Жили весь век свой нищими
И строили храмы божие
Да я-б их давным давно
Перестроил в места отхожие
Ха-ха!
Что скажешь Замарашкин?

Manuscript page from the play *The Land of Scoundrels.*

Об'единение Российских Студентов в Германии.

Перед от'ездом в Африку

в четверг 29 марта 1923 года в 7½ ч. вечера
Klindworth-Scharwenka-Saal,
Lützow-Strasse 76

Единственный за этот год и прощальный вечер

ЕСЕНИНА
и
КУСИКОВА

ЧИТАЮТ:

ЕСЕНИН | Страна негодяев,
Москва кабацкая,
Закрытие Америки и др.

КУСИКОВ | Песочные часы,
Когда вишня в цвету,
Берлинские стихи и др.

ПОСЛЕ: ОБМЕН ВЕСЕЛЫХ МНЕНИЙ.

Билеты: Магазин „МОСКВА", ЛАДЫЖНИКОВА и „КНИГА" Kurfürstenstr. 79, в день вечера с 10—12 и с 6 час. вечера в кассе зала.

Poster announcing the "farewell concert" of Esenin and Kusikov, to be held on March 29, 1923, before their "departure for Africa." The recital was held in Berlin, (Courtesy Alexander Kusikov).

Galina Benislavskaya.

Avgusta Miklashevskaya, 1922.

Miklashevskaya with her son.

Esenin, Leningrad, [April] 1924. From left to right, standing: Vladimir Richiotti, Semyon Polotsky. From lef right, seated: Ivan Pribludny, Sergei Esenin, Grigory Shmerelson and Volf Erlikh.

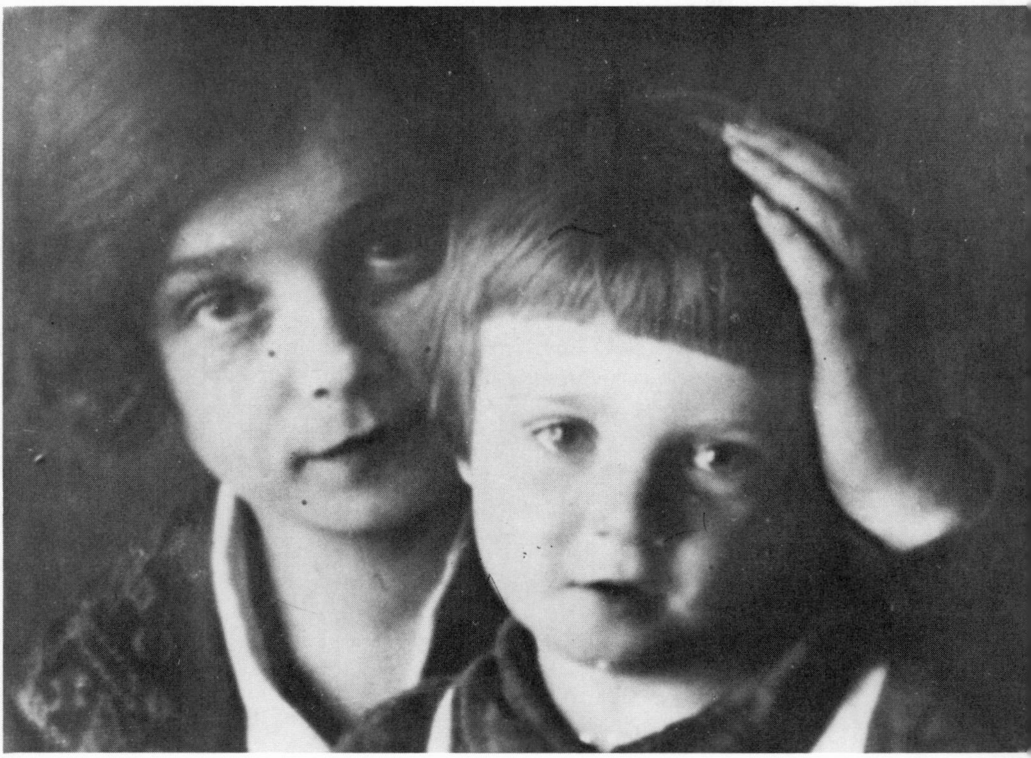

Nadezhda Volpin, with Alexander, her son with Esenin. Apparently on May 7, 1928.

Esenin (centre) with Nikolai Klyuev (left) and Vsevolod Ivanov (right), Leningrad,1924.

Leningrad [April] 1924. From left to right, standing: Vladimir Richiotti, Volf Erlikh. From left to right, seated: Ivan Pribludny, Sergei Esenin, Grigory Shmerelson and Semyon Polotsky.

Above: Esenin, 1924 (May 23?). From left to right are: Sergei Klychkov (?), Ivan Pribludny, Sergei Esenin, N. V. Bogoslovsky.

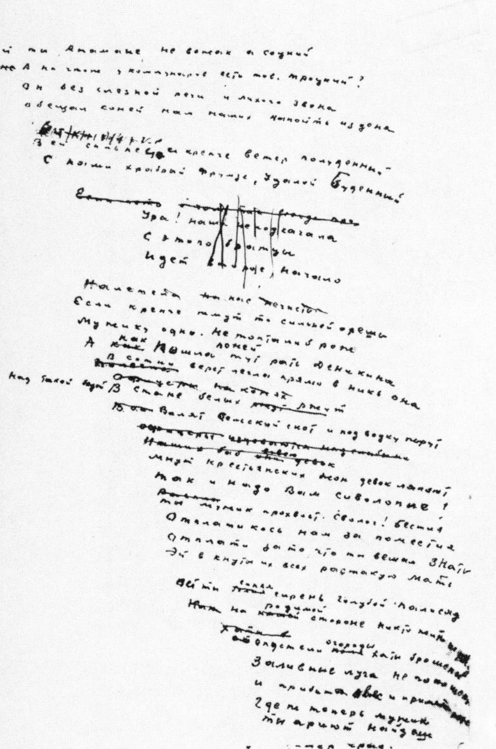

Left: manuscript page from *The Song of the Great Campaign,* written in mid-1924.

Esenin (front left), and the artist Isaak Brodsky (far right), in the artist's studio, Leningrad, 1924 (?).

Esenin with his sister Katya (Ekaterina), Moscow, 1924.

Esenin (left) with Leonid Leonov, Moscow, c. 1924.

Esenin (right) with Vasily Boldovkin, c. 1924.

Esenin with Olga Kobtsova (?), Batum, December 18, 1924 (?).

Esenin (left) with Konstantin Sokolov, Tiflis (?), 1924 (?).

Shagane.

Esenin in a group, Batum, late December 1924. From left to right: N.A. Rudenko, Lev Povitsky, Sergei Esenin, Nikolai Stor, Nikolai Verzhbitsky.

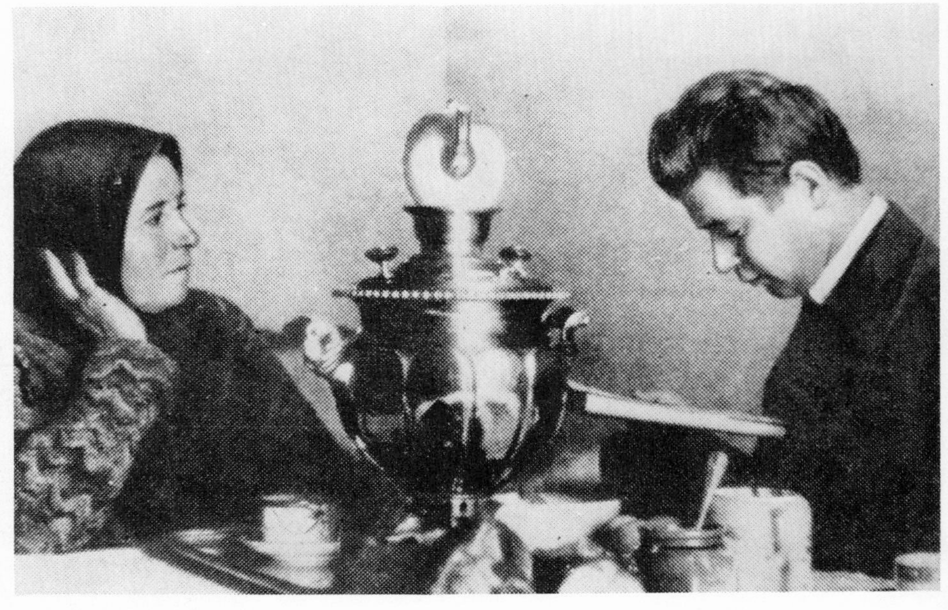

Top: Esenin with his mother, Tatyana Fyodorovna, Moscow, [March] 1925.

Left: manuscript of Esenin's poem "Gentle wind. An evening blue and gloomy." First published March 1926, dated July 1925.

тихий ветер вечер синехмурый
я смотрю широкими глазами
В Персии [Индии] такие ж точно куры
как у нас в соломенной Рязани

тот же месяц, только чуть пошире
чуть желтее и с другого края
Мы с тобою любим в этом мире
одинаково со всеми дорогая

Ночи теплые, ни в вьюгах не воплях
не могу не прославлять не петь их
также девушки здесь обнимают милых
до вторых до петухов до третьих

Ах любовь! она ведь всем знакома
это чувство знают даже кошки
только я с отчизной без дома
От нея сбираю скромно крошки

счастья нет. но горевать не буду
есть везде родные сердцу куры
для меня рассеяны повсюду
молодые чувственные дуры

с ними я все радости приемлю
и для них лишь говорю стихами
оттого знать люди любят землю
что она пропахла петухами

С. Е.

Esenin (back row, right) with Alexander Sakharov (back row, left) and gipsy girls, Moscow, 1925.

Esenin, Moscow, 1925.

Cartoon. "The Robbers from Moscow." 192

Esenin, Moscow [October] 1925. Left to right, back row: Vasily Nasedkin, Alexandra Esenina, Alexander Sakharov, Sergei Esenin. Left to right, front row: Ekaterina Esenin, Sofya Tolstaya.

Esenin, Moscow [October] 1925. Left to right, back row: Vasily Nasedkin, Alexander Sakharov, Alexandra Esenina, Sergei Esenin. Left to right, front row: Ekaterina Esenina, Sofya Tolstaya.

Esenin, 1925.

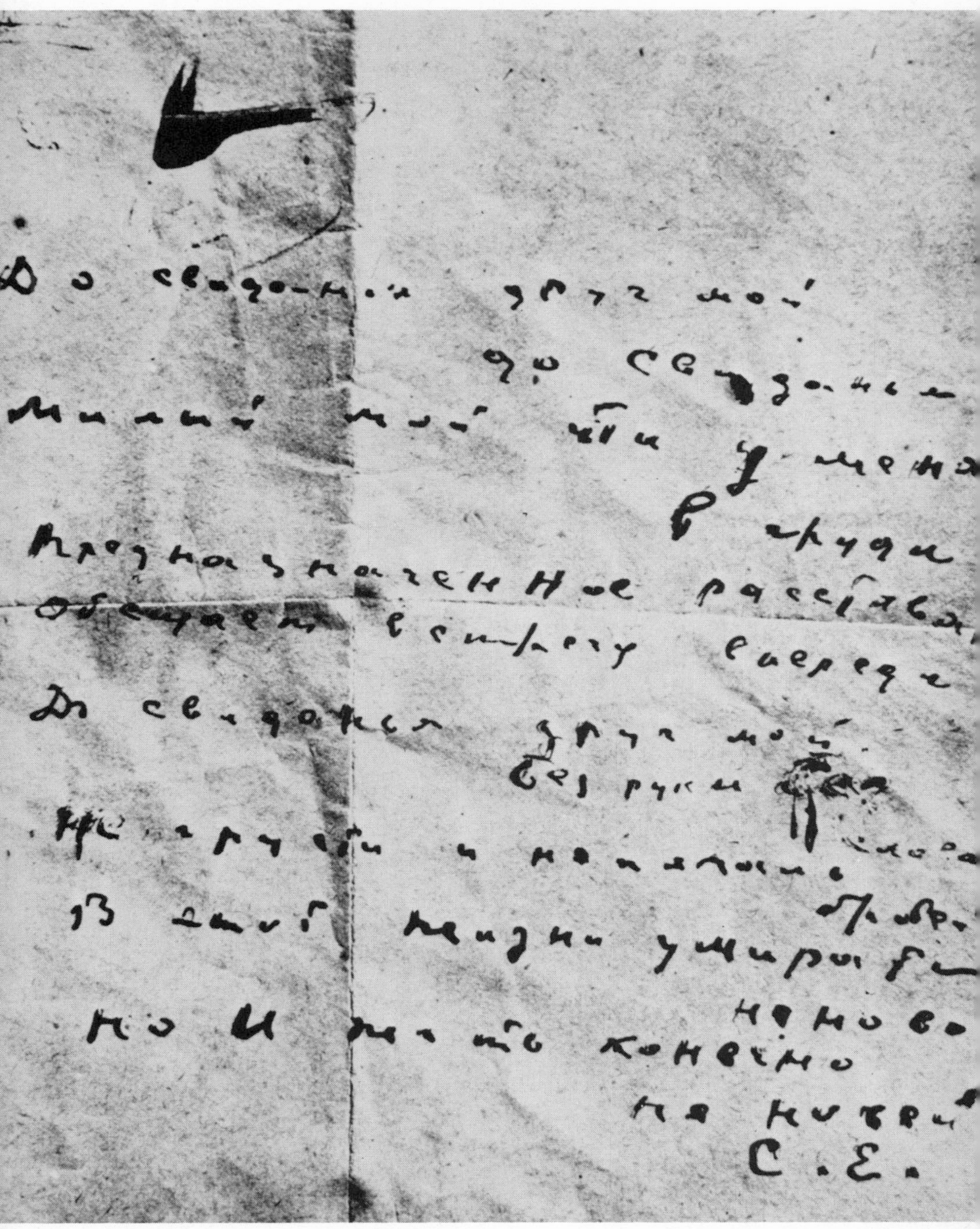
До свиданья друг мой до свиданья
Милый мой ты у меня в груди
Предназначенное расставанье
Обещает встречу впереди
До свиданья друг мой без руки и слова
Не грусти и не печаль бровей
В этой жизни умирать не ново
но и жить конечно не новей
С. Е.

Manuscript of Esenin's last poem, "Goodbye, My Friend, Goodbye," written December 28, 1925.

Room No. 5 in the Hotel Angleterre, Leningrad, December 28, 1925.

Esenin's parents, Alexander Nikitich and Tatyana Fyodorovna, c. 1926-27.

Drawing by Svarog of the dead Esenin, [December 28, 1925.]

ПОЛИКЛИНИКА
ВНУТРЕННИХ БОЛЕЗНЕЙ
И
Общеклиническая Амбулатория
1-го МОСКОВСКОГО
ГОСУДАРСТВЕННОГО УНИВЕРСИТЕТА

ИСТОРИЯ БОЛЕЗНИ

„5" дек 192 5

№

Фамилия Есенин Сергей Александрович 30 лет

Занятие литератор

Адрес:

Диагноз [illegible]

Врач [illegible]

ОСНОВНАЯ ЖАЛОБА [illegible]

Считает себя больным с XI 1925 лет, ухудшение с

УСЛОВИЯ ТРУДА И БЫТА

РАБОТА дневная, ночная, переменная час [illegible]

Дополнительная нагрузка работы час.

Отдых: еженедельный час. в год

Профессиональные вредности

ПОМЕЩЕНИЕ жилое [illegible] в комнате 2 человек, рабочее

ПИТАНИЕ достаточное домашнее столовое [illegible] регулярная горячая пища 2 раз в день

АЛКОГОЛЬ много, умеренно, мало, не пьет с 24

ТАБАК курит, нет, много, умеренно, мало 25 с 15

ПРЕБЫВАНИЕ НА ВОЗДУХЕ [illegible] час. СПОРТ бокс до 27

НАСЛЕДСТВЕННОСТЬ: отец 57 лет [illegible]; мать 55 лет [illegible]

Детей у матери 14 живы 4 [illegible]

Tbc бабка Lues — Alcohol

ПЕРЕНЕСЕННЫЕ ИНФЕКЦИИ Корь 3 Скарлатина 9 Дифтерия 5 Тиф

брюшной сыпной [illegible] возвратный малярия —

Пневмония —

Плеврит с 30 [illegible]

Затяжной кашель, редко, часто, с лет сопровождался t^0 похуданием [illegible]

Венерич. инфекции —

Заболевание суставов — с t^0 без t^0

Другие заболевания Delirium [illegible] + Halluc[illegible] XI 1925 Операции [illegible] 21

This and the following two pages comprise the medical history of Esenin, December 5 1925, compiled in the Polyclinic of Internal Diseases of the First Moscow State University. The bottom of the page refers to "Delerium Tremens and Hallucinations since November 1925."

ИССЛЕДОВАНИЯ ПО ОРГАНАМ

СУБ'ЕКТИВНЫЕ ДАННЫЕ	ДАННЫЕ ОБ'ЕКТИВНОГО ИССЛЕДОВАНИЯ

Органы пищеварения

Аппетит [illegible]	Язык N зубы [illegible]
Диспепт. явл. [illegible]	Желудок N
Боли [illegible]	Кишки N
Стул [illegible] 1-2 д.	Печень [illegible]
	Жел. пузырь N Селезенка [illegible]

Органы дыхания

Кашель сухой, влаж. [illegible]	Груд. кл. [illegible]
Редко, часто с ... лет	Перкуссия [illegible]
Мокрота [illegible]	[illegible]
Знобы [illegible] поты [illegible]	Аускультация [illegible]
t° 37.5 похудание	[illegible]

Сердечно-сосудистая система

Сердцебиение [illegible]	Пульс 84
Одышка [illegible]	Сосуды уд
	Сердце
Боли [illegible]	Перкуссия [illegible]
	Аускультация [illegible]

Мочеполовая система

Мочеиспускание N	Почки [illegible] пузырь
Половая жизнь [illegible] с 21	Отеки [illegible]
[illegible]	Моча

Нервная система

Сон [illegible]	Рефлексы [illegible]
Головн. боли [illegible]	
Самочувствие [illegible]	Дермографизм

Общий вид больн.

Рост ср. Вес	Скелет N [illegible]
Железы	Кожа [illegible] N
	Слиз. оболочки уд
	Мускулатура

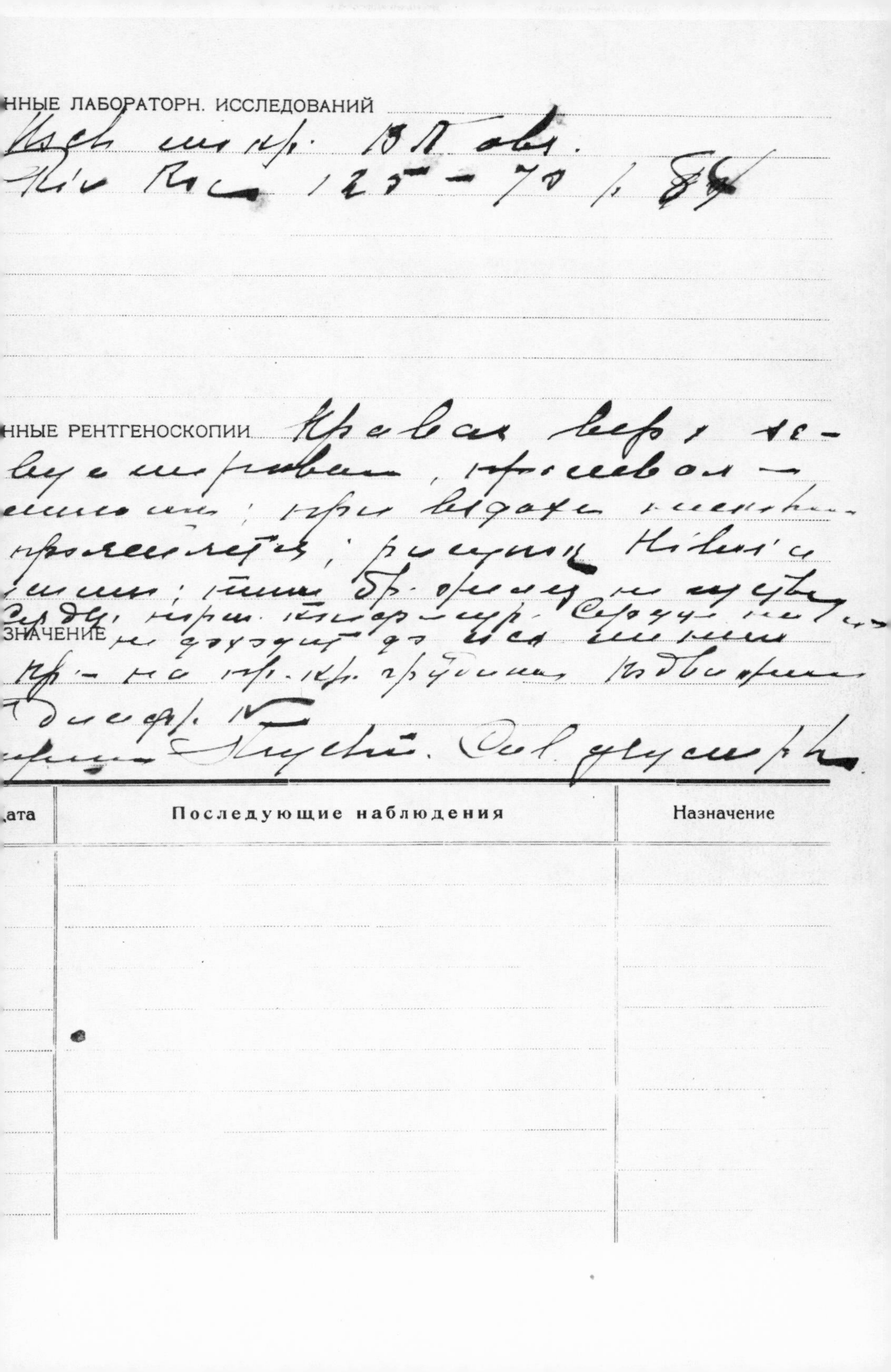

ННЫЕ ЛАБОРАТОРН. ИССЛЕДОВАНИЙ

[illegible] ... [illegible] обыч.
[illegible] 125—70 / 88 [illegible]

ННЫЕ РЕНТГЕНОСКОПИИ [illegible]

[illegible]

ЗНАЧЕНИЕ

[illegible]

Дата	Последующие наблюдения	Назначение

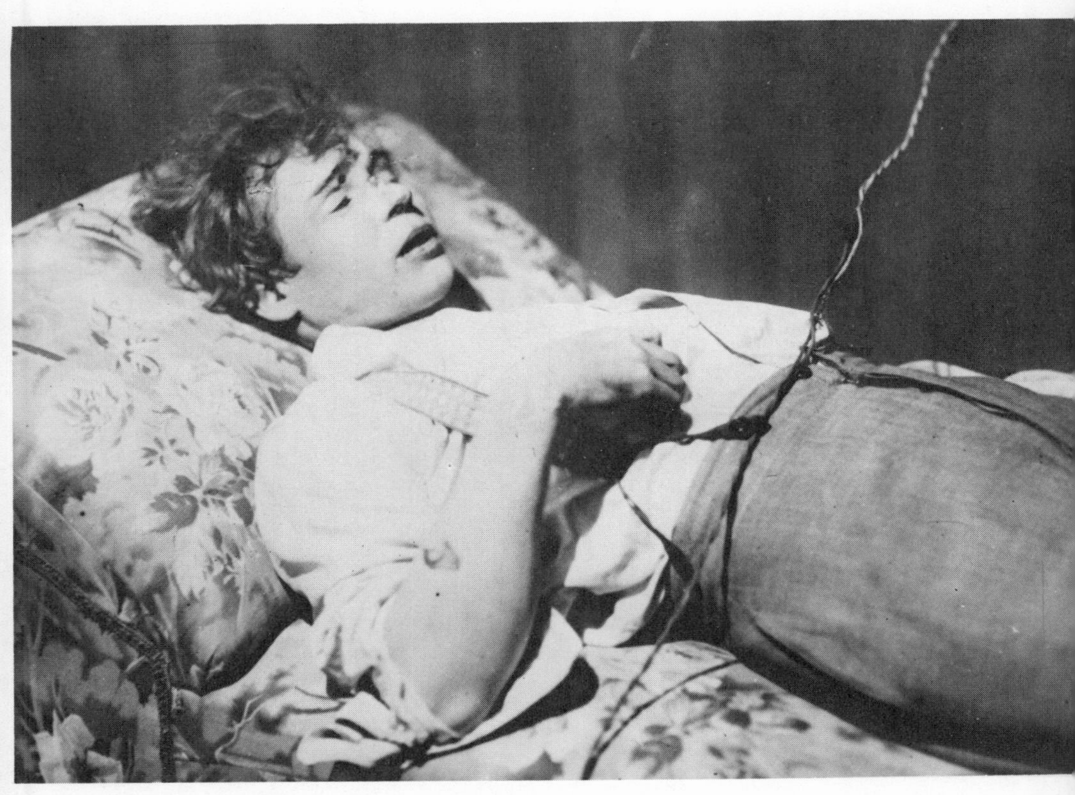

Esenin a few hours after his death, December 28, 1925.

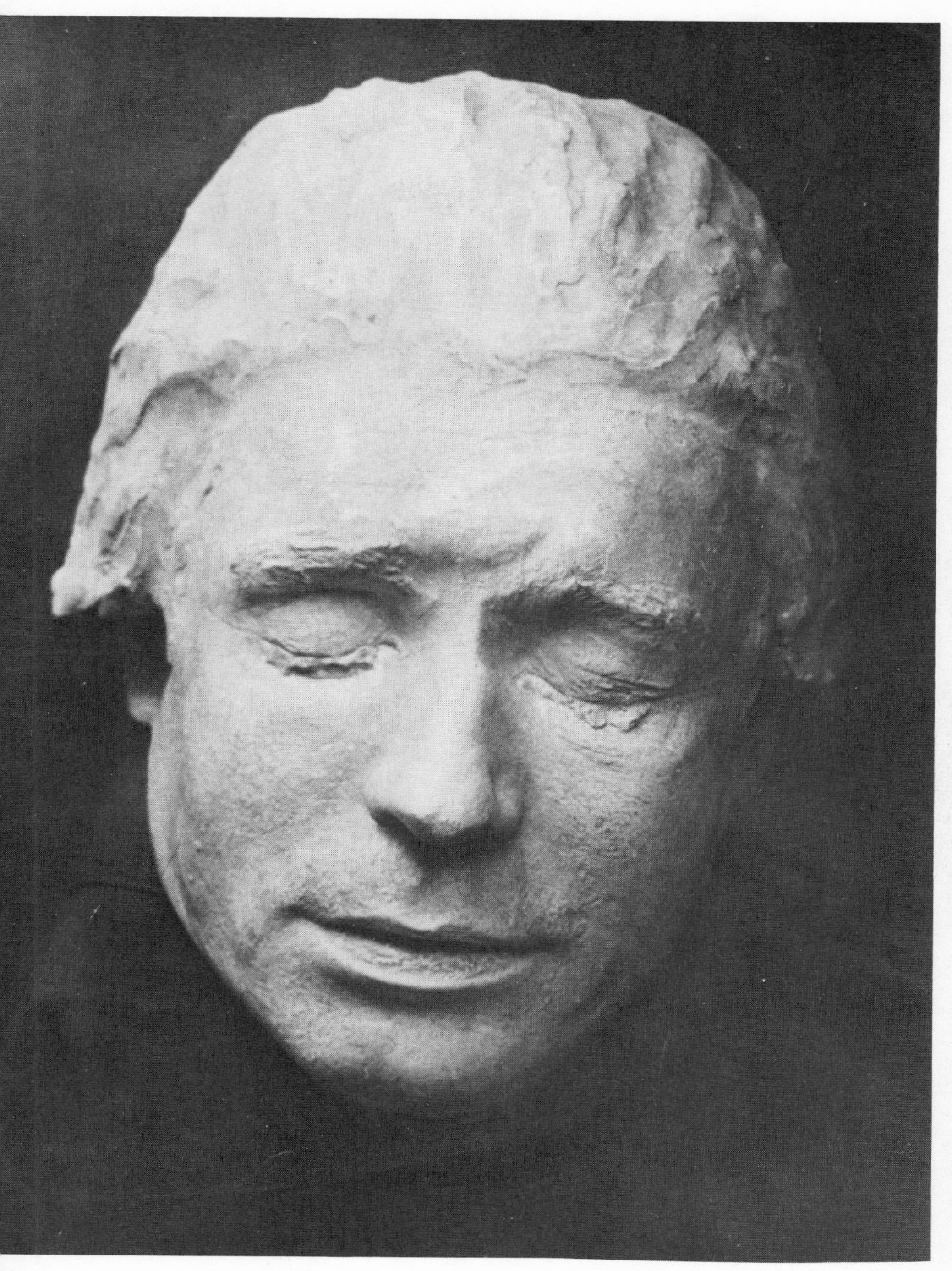

Esenin's death mask, taken by I.S. Zolotarevsky, December 29, 1925.

Esenin in the open coffin, at the Lenigrad Section of the All-Russian Union of Writers, Leningrad, Decemb 29, 1925. Directly behind Esenin's head stands Nikolai Klyuev. Others by the coffin appear to include Vas ly Nasedkin, Sofya Tolstaya and Volf Erlikh.

Esenin in the open coffin, Press House, Moscow, December 30, 1925. Esenin's sister Ekaterina, and his mother are the two women front right. The second woman on the left, hand raised, is Zinaida Raikh; to the right of her, slightly behind, is Meyerhold.

Chapter Eleven: Waterloo (1922-23)

Upon arriving in Berlin on May 11, Esenin and Isadora stayed at the luxurious Hotel Adlon. A Berlin journal noted that he was now completing a new work "The Land of Scoundrels" ("Strana negodiaev," II, 193-250) and that he had signed a contract to go to America. On the day of his arrival in Berlin Esenin handed in two poems to be published by the newspaper *On the Eve (Nakanune).* On May 14 these poems duly appeared: a re-publication of "I'm Not Regretting, Calling, or Weeping" (II, 111-112), and the first publication of "All Living Things Are Marked by a Special Sign" ("Vse zhivoe osoboi metoi," II, 107-108). The poems deeply offended one reader, who commented in a letter to the newspaper *On the Eve:* "I was staggered by this untalented vomit. . ." The reader quoted the first stanza of Esenin's first poem:

I'm not crying, calling or complaining,
All will pass, white smoke from apple trees,
Stricken by the gold of fading,
I no longer shall be young, it seems

and remarked: "Pshaw. Damned abomination. Devoid of rhyme, style or thought. Nothing but the defecation of a brainless head. Many people have been so incensed by such mockery of the Russian language that they cannot vouch for their own behaviour should they meet this vile swine."

It seems inevitable that Esenin, who thrived on provocative conduct, would clash with many of the emigres in Berlin. Moreover, before leaving Russia he is quoted as being extremely hostile towards the emigres Merezhkovsky and Gippius. On Friday May 12 he duly caused his first recorded scandal abroad. He and Isadora entered the Berlin "House of Arts" ("Dom Iskusstv"), to be confronted by a motley ensemble of emigres. Someone suggested the singing of the *Internationale;* Esenin and perhaps Kusikov apparently supported this suggestion; whistles of disagreement arose; and Esenin jumped on a table and began to recite. The various Russian-language newspapers and journals published in Berlin at that time represented differing shades of political opinion. *On the Eve,* being fairly sympathetic towards Bolshevism, accused a reporter from the anti-Bolshevik newspaper *Helm (Rul')* of sparking off this incident. Esenin, writes the *On the Eve* correspondent, declared: "We are the best scandal-makers in the world... Why don't they understand... After all, all Russia is like that." Thus, reports *On the Eve,* "revolutionary Russia was ardently stood up for by her inspired singer, her favourite and faithful son. . . We know that the real Rus. . . can be expressed by the titanic upward flight of Esenin, and not by the despicable hooting of an emigre reporter."

There is something rather unreal about this account of Esenin's first public scandal in Western Europe. It is as if he had been transformed, almost literally overnight, from the *enfant terrible* of Bolshevik Moscow into a "favourite and faithful son" of Soviet Russia. He seems to have been seeking to enrage the emigres. Certainly he loved being different from those around him–and so the robes of Bolshevism might provide a convenient new garb to protect him from dull routine.[1] At all events, Shershenevich in Moscow immediately praised this "revolutionary" act of the Imaginists in Berlin. It is possible also that some of Isadora Duncan's pro-Communist fervour may have rubbed off on the poet. According to an *On the Eve* report, despite the disappointments over her school in Moscow, Isadora had left the country after her ten-month stay "with even more faith in Russia, with even greater expectations, conscious of the fact that in impoverished Russia a new people's soul, in tune with the highest dreams of the whole world, is being created. . ."

On May 14, only three days after arriving in Berlin, Esenin wrote his first reasonably lengthy autobiography (V, 7-10), which was promptly published in the journal *The New Russian Book (Novaia russkaia kniga).* Its tone is extremely crisp and tongue-in-cheek–Esenin may have adopted this air of bravado under the influence of Kusikov, whose lively autobiography had been published in the same journal a month or so earlier. If Kusikov had written about his colourful Oriental childhood and his schoolboy "hooliganism," so Esenin described at length his own peasant origins and childhood escapades (V, 7-8). Whilst Kusikov had written "I'm not a member of the R. K. P." (Russian Communist Party), Esenin capped this by declaring: "I've never been a member of the RKP, as I feel myself to be much more to the left" (V, 9). Like Kusikov, Esenin then listed his own books, and he ended with the following words:

> In Russia, when there was no paper available, I printed my verse, together with Kusikov and Mariengof, on the walls of the Convent of the Passion or simply recited somewhere on the boulevard. The very best admirers of our poetry are prostitutes and bandits. We're all great friends of theirs. The Communists don't like us owing to some misunderstanding. Finally, my most humble greetings to all my readers, and pay a little attention to the sign: "Please do not shoot us!" (V, 10).

In a conversation with Kusikov, reported in *On the Eve* on May 16, Esenin was quoted as saying: "I love Russia. It accepts no other power apart from Soviet power. Only abroad have I understood quite clearly how great are the merits of the Russian revolution, which has saved the world from hopeless philistinism." The *On the Eve* reporter continued, evidently paraphrasing the words of the two poets: "At the present time Imaginism is the predominant movement in Russian poetry. In Moscow alone the Imaginist group numbers about a hundred: the provinces also 'imitate the Imaginists'. . ." Finally, Esenin's plans for the next months were summarised: "S. A. Esenin will be in Europe until October, will visit Paris and London, from where he will fly with Isadora Duncan-Esenina to America. He has signed a contract with the American impresario Hurok for a number of public appearances." (In fact, Esenin never visited England; he travelled to America by boat; and he made no official public appearances there).

Esenin had reason to feel fairly satisfied with his travels so far. If he had not "conquered" Berlin, at least he had made some impact with his poetry. On May 28 *On the Eve* announced that several volumes of his verse were being printed and would soon be on sale in Berlin. (Most of these plans in fact fell through). Some emigre newspapers attacked him, others praised him. Yet Esenin could scarcely be expected to lead a sober and "respectable" life abroad. Ehrenburg writes: "Esenin spent several months in Berlin, pining and of course brawling. His constant companion was the Imaginist Kusikov, who played the guitar and declaimed 'People say of me I'm a scoundrel, A wily Circassian rogue.' They drank and sang. Isadora Duncan tried in vain to calm Esenin; one scene followed upon another. . . Esenin in despair smashed crockery. . ." His relationship with Isadora became even more complex, for Esenin was now uprooted from Moscow and unable to understand German (or, later, French, Italian and English). Moreover, in these new surroundings Isadora received more public attention than he did. According to Mary Desti (who is not always reliable), Esenin often stood on the window ledge of his hotel room threatening to cast himself into the street, and also ordered a vast amount of clothes from a Berlin tailor's: "Sergei took to the niceties of civilisation like a fish to water, and every day thereafter insisted upon a shampoo, private bath, eau de Cologne, powder, perfume." Ehrenburg felt that Isadora wanted to help Esenin but could not. She "possessed not only great talent, but also humanity, tenderness and tact; but he was a vagrant gipsy, who feared most of all constancy of the heart."

Esenin and Isadora had much in common, just as they differed in much. Both were individualists, egoistic and vain; both were "close to the earth" and had a profound awareness of their own bodies (Isadora sought in her dance to express spirituality through her body; Shershenevich felt that Esenin's love of life stemmed from "the feeling of his own body"); both were devoted to their separate arts; both despised bourgeois respectability (herein lies their "revolutionism"); both were restless and uprooted, and had "lost" their children (Isadora's through death, Esenin's by separation from Izryadnova and Raikh); and, it is true, both had a partiality for alcohol and fleeting amorous affairs. Yet their "similarities" were largely tenuous, founded on an unstable emotional affinity of "artistic temperament." No one can accuse Isadora of envying Esenin or begrudging him his success and his talent–even though N. V.

Tolstaya-Krandievskaya may be correct in claiming that the love felt by the aging Isadora contained an element of "tragic greed" for a last great romance. However, the suspicion is often raised that Esenin coveted Isadora's fame and was somewhat calculating in marrying her. It seems improbable that *all* the stories about Esenin beating Isadora, or swearing at her, or speaking disdainfully of her dancing, can be mere fabrication. There was a certain coarseness in Esenin's attitude to Isadora (as to women in general)—whether this should be attributed to his peasant origin is a matter best left for speculation.

Maxim Gorky met the poet and the dancer in Berlin in May 1922, and his description of them is revealing of Esenin's state of mind, although noticeably unsympathetic towards Isadora. Gorky met them at Alexei Tolstoy's flat in Berlin, some six or seven years after first seeing Esenin, and noted that Esenin seemed uneasy, alarmed, "unfriendly towards people": "And it was evident that he was a drinker. His eyelids were swollen, the whites of his eyes were inflamed, the skin on his face and neck was grey and faded, like that of a man who is seldom in the open air and sleeps badly." And then Gorky describes Isadora Duncan dancing in Alexei Tolstoy's flat: "She danced at Tolstoy's, after first dining and drinking some vodka. . . Aging, grown heavy, with a red ugly face, shrouded in a brick-coloured dress, she wheeled and writhed in the cramped room. . ., with a meaningless smile frozen on her fat face." Isadora struck Gorky as "the perfect embodiment of everything unsuited" to Esenin: "Esenin conversed with Duncan by means of gestures, by digs of his knees and elbows. While she was dancing, he sat at the table, drinking wine and frowning as he looked at her out of the corner of his eye. . . And one could feel that he regarded his female friend as a nightmare which was already familiar and not frightening, but which all the same oppressed him. . ." Gorky identified Isadora with the woman described with such revulsion in Esenin's poem "Play, Accordion. Boredom... Boredom..." ("Syp', garmonika. Skuka... Skuka...", II, 123-124). After Isadora's dancing, Esenin recited Khlopusha's monologue from *Pugachov,* and Pugachov's final speech, which moved Gorky till he felt a "spasm" in his throat. Esenin also recited his "Song About a Dog" ("Pesn' o sobake," I, 178-179).[2]

This sad story of a bitch whose seven puppies were drowned prompted Gorky to his famous declaration that ". . . Sergei Esenin was not so much a man as an organ created by Nature exclusively for poetry, for expressing the inexhaustible 'sorrow of the fields,' love for everything living in the world and mercy which–more than anything else–is deserved by man." (This tribute is often quoted, and yet it is strange that Gorky wrote in a private letter in October 1922: ". . . Poetry is love. . . What does Esenin love? He is powerful in the fact that he loves nothing, cares for nothing. . ."). That same evening, in May 1922, Esenin, Isadora, Gorky and others went to the Luna Park, with its side-shows and fun booths, and Gorky noted: "The haste with which Esenin looked at the amusements was suspicious and made one think: the man wants to see everything in order to forget it again as quickly as possible." Then suddenly Esenin turned to Gorky and asked: "Do you think–my verse–is needed? And in general is art–that is, poetry–needed?" Without waiting for an answer, Esenin suggested, "Let's go and drink some wine. . ."

In 1922 Alexei Tolstoy's wife, the poetess Natalya Tolstaya-Krandievskaya, met Esenin and Isadora on the Kurfürstendamm. Esenin was dressed as in a masquerade–wearing a dinner jacket and top hat, with a chrysanthemum in his button hole. Isadora, upon seeing Tolstaya-Krandievskaya's five-year-old son, knelt before the child in the street (in memory of her dead son) and then strode away unseeing, "a figure from Sophocles' tragedies."

Esenin and Isadora left Berlin in June 1922 and began to travel across Germany by car. According to Esenin, they visited Lübeck, Leipzig, Frankfurt and Weimar. Isadora loved travelling in fast cars, and Esenin followed her about, so he claimed, in "silent obedience," as any disagreement on his part made her hysterical (V, 106-107). On June 21 he wrote to Ilya Shneider, who assisted the administration of Isadora's dancing school in Moscow: ". . . The Berlin atmosphere really got me down. At present I can hardly drag my legs along because of my shattered nerves. I'm taking a cure in Wiesbaden. I've stopped drinking and am starting to work. If Isadora were not so extravagant and allowed me to settle down somewhere, then I could earn a great deal of money. . ." (V, 106). In this same letter Esenin made the first of his disdainful dismissals of Western culture from abroad:

> . . . Germany? We'll talk about this later, when we meet, yet life is not here, but in Russia. Here there really is the slow sad decline of which Spengler speaks. Even if we are Asiatics, even if we are foul-smelling, and scratch our backsides unashamedly in public, yet we don't stink as putridly as they stink inside. There can be no revolution here. Here everything is at a dead-end. The only thing that can save and reform them is an invasion of barbarians such as we. There should be a campaign against Europe. . . (V, 107).

A young Polish woman, Lola Kinel, became Isadora's secretary and interpreter in Wiesbaden, and in her memoirs she writes that, after a "series of real Russian libations" in Berlin, Isadora "took Essenine to Wiesbaden for a rest and a cure. It was here that the doctor who examined Essenine told her that his condition was serious; that he must stop drinking for at least two or three months, or she would have a maniac on her hands. Essenine, who had just had a sort of nervous breakdown and suffered from neuritis, promised to comply with the doctor's orders." Lola Kinel continues: "I understood then, too, why Essenine's face was so grey and his lips blue, and why he was often so terribly tense. He had been drinking for several years, drinking heavily, as most Russians do, and this sudden complete stop must have been a bad strain on his nerves. And Isadora's love, very tender and kind, was also a bit too smothering and devouring. . ."

By early July Esenin launched an even sharper onslaught against the West in a letter to Sakharov:

> . . . What can I say about this most terrible realm of philistinism which borders on idiocy? Apart from the foxtrot there is almost nothing here, here they gorge themselves and drink, and then the foxtrot once more. I've not met one human being so far, and see no trace of one. Mister dollar is terribly fashionable, but no one gives a damn for art—the highest thing here is the music hall. . . Even if we are poor, even if we have famine, cold and cannibalism, but to make up for that we have a soul, which people here hire out to others as unwanted. . . (V, 108-109).

Ilya Ehrenburg comments about Esenin: "He swept through Europe and America, noticing nothing. . . Of course in the West then there was not only the foxtrot, but also bloody demonstrations, and famine, and Picasso, and Romain Rolland, and Chaplin, and many other things. . ." Western culture had long been a blind spot for Esenin, and he clearly received a severe shock when he came face to face with the West. His aggressiveness may have been a form of self-defence. "Even if we are Asiatics, even if we are foul-smelling. . ." (V, 107); "Even if we are poor, even if. . ." (V, 109)—this insistent "even if" betrays a lack of self-confidence, as if the Russian peasant felt himself a kind of "poor relation" in Europe.

Esenin had embarked on his foreign travels with a preconceived and deep-rooted hostility to "American" (industrialised, machine-dominated) culture. This was one aspect of his Romantic/peasant aesthetic outlook on the world, but also one of his limitations. His "Russianness," for which he is often praised, contained also an element of narrow nationalism. In 1921 he had told Ivan Rozanov: "My lyric verse is alive with one great love, love for my motherland. Feeling for my motherland is the basic thing in my art." And Rozanov himself made the often quoted statement: "Three loves, I think, moved and enlightened him: love of fame, verse and his motherland. For the sake of these three he was willing to sacrifice everything else: both feeling for women and constancy in friendship, and all other lands and nations." Esenin's love of fame and poetry is unmistakable; his third love, for Russia (especially age-old Rus, the land of the birch tree and the cow) is more intangible, or rather it pervades his whole life and art. Soviet critics today may devise earnest arguments to prove the poet's shrewd understanding of the bourgeois West's failings, but Esenin himself expressed his attitude more pithily in two folk quatrains quoted by Mariengof in the manuscript of *A Novel Without Lies:*

> Europe's mug is clean and swish,
> But I shall not buss her!
> Give to this Imaginist
> His beloved Russia...!

(U Evropy rozha chista
Ne tseluius' s eiu!
Podavai imazhinistu
Miluiu Raseiu...!)

Damn and blast your ugly conk,
Steel-obsessed America!
How I'd love to hear a song
From my native heritage.

(V mat' tebia, iz mati v mat',
Stal'naia Amerika!
Khot' by pesniu uslykhat'
Da s rodnogo berega.)

Esenin's love of Russia, writes Rozanov, "gradually came to consist of memories of childhood. . . His love for his motherland, expressed with such lyrical beauty in his verse, frequently assumed a narrowly nationalistic tone in his everyday conversations." On a copy of *The Keys of Mary* Esenin wrote the following inscription for the poet Evgeny Sokol: "Dear Sokol/ I love Rus/ Forgive me/ But in this/ I am a chauvinist."

Esenin and Isadora continued their travels across Europe. On June 21 they were in Wiesbaden, June 29–Dusseldorf, and July 9–Ostend. From Ostend Esenin wrote to Mariengof: ". . .My dear friend, my closest and best friend, how I'd love to get out of here, out of this nightmarish Europe and back to Russia, to our former youthful hooliganism and all our fervour. . ." (V, 110). By mid-July they were in Brussels, by late July–Paris. Esenin, although bored, was trying hard not to drink. He wrote to Shneider on July 13: "If you could see me now, you'd probably not believe your own eyes. It's almost a month since I had a drink. I've solemnly sworn not to drink before October. It was all brought about by a severe attack of neuritis and neurasthenia, but now that's over too. . ." (V, 113). Mary Desti comments: "Isadora and Sergei spent two very happy months in Paris, with trips to Italy and other places, all forming part of Sergei's foreign education. They devoted much time and thought to the translation and publication of Sergei's poems, which Isadora had arranged for.[3] They were fêted everywhere, and she was as happy as a schoolgirl. Sergei was behaving splendidly, only interested in poems and his work."

Little is known about the poet's stay in Italy in August 1922, although Lola Kinel vividly evokes his mood in Venice–as he glided in a gondola at night, reminiscing about his childhood, and of "beautiful faces and of the most beautiful face he had ever seen, that of a young nun in a Russian convent–a face that was absolutely guileless and pure. . ." Esenin claimed that Lenin was really dead and embalmed (in 1922!), and longed for an English translation to be made of his poems; he said Isadora's fame would die with her, whilst his fame as a poet would live on; and he declared that "everything comes from God. . ." According to Kinel, in Venice Esenin began to drink again, after faithfully sticking to the "water wagon" for more than two months. Kinel remembers his powdered face peering into a mirror in Venice: ". . . Large, roughly-hewn features; deep-set eyes whose blue had turned to a bleary grey; heavy, dark eyebrows, like wings; pale dry skin, and flaxen-blond curls which seemed so youthful and innocent and out of place. . ." There is a series of photographs taken on the beach of the Venice Lido, with Esenin wearing loose, light-coloured "pyjamas" and Isadora looking rather plump. On one of these photographs Isadora's left hand grasps Esenin's left arm, as if anxiously trying to hold on to him.

"Sergei Esenin, poet, together with the dancer Isadora Duncan and A. Vetlugin, left Paris at the end of September for a tour of America." Thus a Berlin journal reported one of the most fateful acts of Esenin's whole life, perhaps indeed the most important since his literary debut in Petrograd in March 1915. (When he at last saw Mariengof again in Moscow, Esenin commented succinctly on his trip abroad: "My Waterloo, Tolya"). Several non-Soviet memoirists declare that Esenin reacted like a child to what he saw in the West, particularly in America, and something of this childish bewilderment at the size of objects can be seen in the poet's own confused memories of the boat on which he travelled to America. The boat's restaurant was "somewhat bigger than our Bolshoi Theatre"; Esenin walked through special libraries, rest rooms, a dance hall, and "about five minutes later" reached his cabin. "I sat down on a sofa and began to roar with laughter. The world in which I had previously lived suddenly seemed to me terribly comic and absurd. . . From this moment I stopped loving beggarly Russia. . ." (IV, 159).

The journey from Le Havre on the *S. S. Paris* took six days, according to Esenin (IV, 160), and the boat steamed past the Statue of Liberty and into New York harbour on Sunday October 1, 1922. Unfortunately, Esenin's introduction to America and Isadora's return to her motherland encountered immediate obstacles. The couple were refused entry and detained overnight on board ship—and the following day they were interrogated by the immigration authorities on Ellis Island, under suspicion of being Bolshevik agents. Although they were released and entered America without further hindrance, the episode caused a blaze of publicity and left a bitter mark, particularly upon Isadora. The misunderstanding was not altogether surprising, considering the anti-Bolshevik mood then rampant in America. New York newspapers on October 2 reported the detention-episode extensively on their front pages. The *New York Tribune* noted:

> Miss Duncan gave out a prepared statement: ". . . We are the representatives of young Russia. We are not mixing in political questions. It is only in the field of art that we are working. We believe the soul of Russia and the soul of America are about to understand each other. . ." . . . While the *Paris* was steaming up the bay Mr. Essenine. . . admired the beauties of the New York skyline. He saw it for the first time through the late afternoon haze, and being a poet went into raptures.

The *New York Times* observed: ". . . Miss Duncan was plainly vexed with the attitude of the Immigration Inspector and said so frankly to the reporters in her suite de luxe on the promenade deck of the *Paris.* She reclined on a couch with her left arm thrown gracefully round the neck of her blonde husband, who had powdered his hair. . . Miss Duncan wore a round white soft felt hat with a narrow black band, a crimson silk gown and red morocco leather Russian boots. . ."

The New York newspapers devoted much space to Esenin's appearance and reactions on board the *Paris.* The *New York Herald* had the impression that, despite Isadora's wrath at being detained,

> her husband, Serge Yessenin, a superblond young Russian poet. . . seemed to regard the incident as rather trivial and capable of swift adjustment. . . Her husband, who is of slim, athletic build, broad shouldered and slim waisted, spoke to Isadora chiefly through her secretary. The husband looks younger than 27, and his dress was no different from that of an ordinary American businessman, being a plain gray tweed. Though unable to speak English, he hung over his wife and smiled approval at everything she said to the reporters. Both appeared to be genuinely in love and took no pains to conceal their mutual adoration. . . Isadora declared that she regarded her husband as the greatest living Russian poet of the imagist brand. She showed a volume of his free verse translated into French. . . The young Russian was entranced by the Manhattan skyline and intimated that he would write about it. . . He prefers to sing of "vagabonds and loafers," and he does not look a bit like either. He said he also had a vast appreciation of bandits and beggars and dogs and cows and other domestic animals. His press notices call him melancholy, but he seems the most cheerful Bolshevist that ever crossed the Atlantic. . .

Isadora spoke enthusiastically of how she had met Esenin: "It was a soul union, and began in her sleep, when her soul 'soared out and met his'." Isadora, though really forty-four, "declared under oath" that she was thirty-eight years old. Esenin himself recalled, upon his return to Moscow, that innumerable reporters and photographers had crowded round them on board the ship. About twenty newspapers, he claimed, immediately published vast articles and photographs of them. These articles "said a little about Isadora Duncan, and that I was a poet, but most of all they spoke of my high shoes and said that I was very well built for athletics and that I would no doubt be the best sportsman in America" (IV, 161). Esenin's amused recollections are supported, for instance, by a report in the *New York World:* ". . . Mme. Duncan's husband came up just then. He speaks

French [sic!], a boyish chap, who looks as though he might make an excellent half-back for any football team–about 5 feet 10 inches,[4] with a blond, clean-cut head set upon a pair of broad shoulders, with narrow hips and feet that might do a hundred yards in about ten seconds. . ."

On October 2 Isadora rejoiced upon being cleared following a two hour interrogation on Ellis Island, whilst Esenin was visibly amused by all the fuss. "When the poet was on his way to the island," noted the *New York Herald* the next day, "he waved a greeting to the Statue of Liberty, remarking in Russian what was liberally translated by the press agent: 'I admire you, old girl, although I must say circumstances prevent me just now from shouting for you.' On the return trip with Isadora he bowed his thanks to the bronze goddess, and after gazing at the skyline declared again that he was surely going to write a poem about it."

These newspaper reports, despite their triviality, do shed some light on Esenin's mental and physical state at the beginning of his American tour. He seems to have been calm, somewhat detached and ironic, and very affectionate towards his wife. He appeared young and cheerful to the New York reporters, and there is no indication that he was drunk or in poor health. He was deeply impressed by the New York skyline, about which he intended to write a poem. Yet, significantly, Esenin proved unable to write verse on such a theme. On his return to Moscow, he exclaimed: "My goodness! How untalented are Mayakovsky's poems about America! Is it possible to express this iron and granite might in words?! It is a poem without words. . ." (IV,160).

The next four months were to produce a disastrous change in Esenin. Whereas his behaviour was relatively sober from June to early October 1922, henceforth–as Khodasevich wrote–"the wedding trip of Esenin and Duncan turned into a hooligan 'tour' of Europe and America. . ." Mary Desti writes: "During Isadora's tour in America, Yessenin's madness began to show itself. He had found that America had not received him as he had expected, and he seemed to hold this as a special grudge against Isadora, insulting her and her country on every occasion. There were many scandals reported in the newspapers, some more or less exaggerated, but there was enough truth in them to make life almost impossible."

There were several reasons for Esenin's bitter reaction against America. He did not know the English language, and being mistrustful by nature, continually imagined that people were laughing at him in America. As Isadora said to Mariengof on her return to Moscow: "And that, combined with his pride! With his unhealthy vanity!. . . And he at once became as angry as a demon." Esenin used to leave abruptly from receptions, and when alone with her grab her by the neck and shout: "The truth! The truth!. . Tell me the whole truth!!. . . What did your American riff-raff say about me?" Isadora gasped that they spoke well of him, but "he never believed me. . . Never. . . Oh, that was so terrible! Such a misfortune!"

The language barrier also thwarted Esenin's desire to conquer America by his verse, and he seems to have grown increasingly disillusioned by this failure. Isadora's dancing used an "international" language; Esenin's poetry was in the incomprehensible Russian tongue.

Feeling neglected in America, he transferred his frustration into other channels. He became extremely jealous of Isadora's fame, and began to believe (or pretend to believe) that America had no appreciation whatsoever for the arts. Mariengof wrote interestingly in 1948 that

> Esenin was incredibly proud and ambitious; he considered himself the first poet of Russia. But he did not have a European name, world fame. Whereas Isadora Duncan did. During their trip to Europe and America he felt himself "the young husband of the famous Duncan." It must be said that worthless journalists, especially transoceanic ones, did not spare his feelings very much. And then there was Esenin's unhealthy mistrustfulness! He saw this "young husband" in almost every glance and heard it in every word. Yet the words were English, French, German–suspicious, mysterious, hostile. He didn't know any languages. And his trip became for him one long torment, torture, insult. He broke. This explains much. Isadora Duncan's guilt, as we would say nowadays, was "objective."

Esenin seems to have decided in America that only by

creating scandals could he draw attention to himself. Unlike the Imaginists' escapades in Moscow, however, Esenin's outbursts in America were more desperate and despairing. In Moscow he might provoke the public's indignation–but those people then listened to, and appreciated, his verse. In America he could merely brawl in a vacuum; scandals for their own sake were a pointless self-sacrifice.

There was one other important factor: alcohol. Esenin arrived in America during the period of prohibition. As a result, both he and Isadora had to resort to "bootleg liquor," which, as Isadora picturesquely remarked when abandoning ungrateful America, was enough to "kill an elephant." Esenin's health became irrevocably undermined by what he drank in the United States.

On October 7 Isadora gave the first of her scheduled performances at Carnegie Hall in New York. Although some memoirists assert that she was no longer capable of dancing, she received favourable press notices for her first concerts in New York after five years. Unfortunately for the success of her tour, however, Isadora could not refrain from addressing the audience at the end of her performances, making idealistic, visionary speeches in praise of Russia and advocating friendship between America and Russia. Her eloquence, together with her transparent dancing costumes, began to clash with the puritanism and anti-Bolshevism of some American towns. A dispatch from Boston on October 22 proclaimed: "Isadora Duncan in Flaming Scarf Says She's a Red. Many Boston Spectators Leave Performance Shocked at her Undress." This report in the *New York Herald* said that Isadora told the audience at the end of her performance: "Life here is not real. . . Americans are wild. Don't let them tame you. I don't let them tame me." The report added that she danced in Boston's Symphony Hall "in a transparent costume that left nothing to the imagination." For this, she was banned from Boston.

Isadora was obtaining great publicity, but indignation at her "Bolshevistic" speeches threatened to bring the tour to a sudden halt. Esenin helped stir the embers of controversy by himself attempting patriotic orations. Although the tour of America was scheduled to last until about February, the disillusioned Isadora announced in early November that her last two performances in Carnegie Hall would take place on November 14 and 15. In fact, the tour continued, but with further mishaps. In early December she declared that she would dance in a New York church on Christmas Eve, but the Bishop of New York intervened and forbade this dance and lecture because of widespread protests. The irrepressible Isadora hit the headlines again on Christmas Day in Brooklyn, by dancing very erratically and performing a premature funeral march for Sarah Bernhardt, who was seriously ill at the time. She told reporters that "doctored" or "etherized" champagne was responsible for the fiasco. "We had some champagne. . . My husband and I are both accustomed to wine. We drank some and it made us both very ill."

During these closing months of 1922, Esenin evidently followed his wife from town to town. Only three letters written by Esenin in America have been published. On November 12 he wrote a long letter to Mariengof from New York, beginning at once in a suicidal tone: "My dear Tolya! How happy I am that you are not with me here in America, in this abominable New York. That would be bad enough to hang oneself" (V, 118). Isadora, although an excellent woman, had lied to him about her "banks and castles": "We sit here without a copeck, waiting to. . . return to Moscow. The best thing I have seen in this world is still–Moscow. . . I will say of myself. . . that I simply do not know how to exist and how to live now. Previously, despite all Russia's privations, we were warmed by the awareness of 'foreign parts,' but now that I have seen these, I beseech God not to let me die spiritually and in my love for my art. No one needs my art here. . ." (V, 118). Esenin continued that he feels his *dusha* (soul), which the Russians have in such abundance, to be quite superfluous in America:

> Dear Tolya. If only you knew how sad I am, then you wouldn't think I had forgotten you, or doubt. . . my love for you. Every day, every hour, first thing in the morning, and last thing at night, I say: Mariengof must be in the shop, now he'll have come home, then Grishka's come, here are the Krotkys, and Sashka, etc., etc. In my head there is Moscow, nothing but Moscow. I'm even ashamed at feeling so

> Chekhovian. . . I have no wish whatsoever to speak that damned English language. I acknowledge no other language apart from Russian and my policy is that if anyone feels interested in talking to me, then let them learn Russian. Of course, in all my movements I seem just as comic to many people as does a Frenchman or Dutchman on our territory. . . (V, 119).

The American tour of Isadora and Esenin approached its turbulent finale. On January 15, 1923 Isadora made her farewell appearance at Carnegie Hall, and the next day the *New York Herald* reported that she danced in a costume "of flaming red" before a half-filled hall: ". . . Miss Duncan said that she and her poet husband, Serge Essenine, shortly will go back to Moscow, and she added that they will never return to America, although she is a native of this country. Essenine sat back stage during her performance. . ." A few days later, the columnist Young Boswell interviewed Isadora for the *New York Tribune*—because "her tour of America has been an interesting failure. . ." Esenin was present as Isadora spoke of her Moscow dancing school. Isadora declared: "Such a school is impossible in America, because there is no democracy in America. . . So long as there is the rich child and the poor child there can be no democracy. . . Every child is born a genius, I think. Those whom the world calls geniuses, when they grow up, are to my mind simply the children who have happily escaped education. Here is a genius.*(She turned to her husband).* Here is young Russia. Mad as a hatter, strong, full of vitality. Poetic!"

Esenin's behaviour in the first few months of 1923 certainly seemed to justify the description "mad as a hatter." On one occasion, apparently in late January 1923, he made some tactless remarks, smacking of anti-Semitism, at a gathering of Russian-Jewish poets at Mani-Leib's in the Bronx. There is some confusion over what exactly happened, but Esenin evidently pronounced the word *zhid* (Yid) several times and caused a scandal.[5] He appears to have been rather drunk, struck Isadora, and eventually had to be held down by force. Esenin was not a consistent anti-Semite—as he himself said, were not his two children from the Jewess, Zinaida Raikh; and his best friend, Mariengof, was of Jewish extraction. In Kharkov he had befriended the Jewish girls at Povitsky's—and, indeed, Esenin had many other Jewish friends during his life. Nevertheless, especially when intoxicated, he was prone to crudely anti-Semitic outbursts, which were clearly one aspect of his "Great Russian" nationalism.

In connection with this incident at Mani-Leib's, and some other occurrences elsewhere, it has been suggested in some non-Soviet memoirs that Esenin was an epileptic. Veniamin Levin relates that, shortly after the Mani-Leib episode, he visited Esenin and Isadora in their hotel. The poet was ill, in bed: "Esenin was rather paler than usual and very polite and considerate with me, and he told me he had had an epileptic fit. I had never heard of this before. Now he told me that he had inherited it from his grandfather. His grandfather had once been whipped in the stables and had contracted the falling sickness, which was transmitted to his grandson. . ."[6] The notion of Esenin's epilepsy is supported by Mary Desti, Sol Hurok, and Avrahm Yarmolinsky. Yarmolinsky, indeed, quotes in full Esenin's letter to Mani-Leib apologising for the incident, which may seem to contain a reference to epilepsy. This letter, which is not included in the Soviet five-volume editions of the poet's works, is effusively apologetic, and, among other things, Esenin wrote: ". . . Towards evening I had another attack *(pripadok)*. Today I lie crushed, both morally and physically. A nurse kept watch by my side all night. A doctor came and gave me a morphia injection. . . I have the same illness that Edgar Poe and Musset had.[7] Edgar Poe used to break up whole houses in these attacks. . . My soul is innocent in this, and my reason, which has awakened today, makes me shed bitter tears, my good Monileib!. . . I ask you for at least a little pity for me. . ." Yarmolinsky deduces that Esenin is referring to epilepsy, and also points out that in a poem of 1923 Esenin described himself as "afflicted by a grave falling-sickness" (II, 141). It might be added that a doctor in Paris in 1923 diagnosed the poet's illness as epilepsy. A report from Paris, dated February 17, 1923, states that Esenin was detained overnight at a police station following a rowdy scandal: ". . .He was booked as 'suffering from epileptic attacks, he had drunk too much'."

Yet, despite all this secondary evidence, Esenin's alleged "epilepsy" seems dubious. No Soviet memoir, published or unpublished, appears to give any hint of this affliction, and nor does his medical report of December 5, 1925. However, it is possible that his nervous attacks (largely induced by alcohol) closely resembled, or were akin to, epileptic seizures. Yet the line he wrote about being "afflicted by a grave falling-sickness" was perhaps a poetic liberty, and a recollection of how people abroad had thought him an epileptic. His "epilepsy" may have been a myth which flattered his desire to be "different."

On February 3, 1923 the controversial couple boarded the U. S. liner *George Washington* and sailed for Cherbourg—but not before Isadora had surpassed herself in a flurry of farewell invective to the American reporters who had plagued her during the past four months. The next day, February 4, the New York press reported the angry leave-taking at length, quoting Isadora's remarks that America does not appreciate art, and that she and her husband are "revolutionists," as all "real artists" are. Isadora's parting attack on America caused great offence, and early in March it was announced that she had forfeited her U. S. citizenship, ostensibly because of her marriage to a Russian.

In these accounts of February 1923, the American newspapers took hardly any interest in Esenin—he was merely the blond poet-husband of the tempestuous Isadora. In early October, he had been described by the press as boyish, athletic and cheerful. Four months later, writes Irma Duncan, Isadora was "worried by the state of her husband's mental and physical health, which his unfortunate experience with bootleg liquor had done nothing to ameliorate." Esenin's health seems to have declined sharply during his American tour. Besides suffering "epileptic" attacks, he was apparently increasingly attracted to suicide. Sol Hurok recalls: "He had talked of suicide in New York, where the Woolworth Building had tempted him; he would jump from the tower, he said, with the manuscript of his last poem in his hand. On second thought, he might fall on an innocent passer-by, even on a baby carriage. He would not like that." He used to brandish a revolver shortly before leaving America (according to Mary Desti), and he may have tried to throttle Isadora. Some memoirs published in the West claim that, not only was he wildly extravagant with Isadora's money in America, but also that he deliberately stole from her, by accumulating clothes and money in suitcases which he then took back to Moscow. If this is true, as seems likely, it must have been a result of his mental unbalance, and perhaps his desire to impress people on his return to Russia.

Esenin's stay in America gave him little of value. Viktor Shklovsky writes: "I remember a conversation we then had about America, about Chicago with its red lift, and, I think, a black carpet in the 'New York Hotel,' a lift of citron-tree wood, and a pale-yellow carpet in the corridor. And that was all. . ." In 1924 Esenin informed the poet Vsevolod Rozhdestvensky that he saw little of America, but befriended a negro there: ". . . He told me about his village, and I told him about the village of Konstantinovo. And we both felt good and sad. He was a good man, and we two then spent many an evening together. When I had to leave, I kept inviting him to Moscow. . . He promised to come. He was the only person I liked in America. . ." Vladimir Chernyavsky relates that Esenin spoke confusedly about the West after his return to Russia, "as if glad that he hadn't accepted Europe and it hadn't accepted him. Yet one could see that this had wounded him. . . But it seems that America had disturbed him most of all. He had a feeling of envy mixed with hatred for America. . . He did not conceal that his return home was a flight from the West and from love."

Esenin was "disturbed" far more by America than by Western Europe. He himself admitted that his "vision" became changed especially after seeing America (IV, 158), and he devoted his sketch "The Iron Mirgorod" ("Zheleznyi Mirgorod," IV, 158-169) almost exclusively to his impressions of that country. Throughout this sketch, his admiration for the grandeur of America's industrial culture is apparent. He is aware that advertising is of enormous importance in America—but "it's devilishly well done!" (IV, 165). He realises that the Redskins have been decimated and corrupted by the white man in America—but, seeing the huge Brooklyn Bridge, he feels that "no one will regret that the wild Hiawatha no longer hunts deer here" (IV, 164). He acknowledges that Russia as yet lies far behind America's development, with nothing to rival Broadway's sea of neon-signs: "When one beholds or hears all this, one is involuntarily struck by Mankind's potential, and one begins to feel ashamed that here in Russia people still believe in the bearded grandfather and trust in his mercy. Poor Russian Hiawatha!" (IV, 166).[8]

Esenin's admiration for America as the land of electricity and ferro-concrete marked a considerable change in his outlook. After visiting America, he began to advocate that Russia should follow the example of the United States. Naturally, his Romantic, pre-industrial sympathies were too deep-rooted to be swept away without regret overnight, but this was one definite result of his travels abroad. He had hoped to conquer America by his verse—and, instead, had himself succumbed to the compelling power of America's industrial might.

Towards the end of "The Iron Mirgorod," Esenin discussed American artistic culture, and in much he seems to have echoed Isadora Duncan's scornful views. In general, "The Iron Mirgorod" is a naive and feeble work (as is admitted by memoirists such as Voronsky, Ivnev, Poletaev and Ehrenburg). Esenin probably knew little about the arts in America, except what he learned from his cultural contacts with the Russian-Jewish community. Nevertheless, either by his own intuition, or through the promptings of Isadora, he was able to observe: "The power of ferro-concrete, the grandeur of the buildings, have cramped the American's brain and narrowed his vision. . . Europe smokes and discards the cigarette end, America picks up the cigarette ends, but out of these stubs something grandiose is growing. . ." (IV, 169).

The return of Isadora and Esenin to Europe was not a heroic retreat. "Isadora had much to say about this return trip," writes Mary Desti. "Sergei was never sober on the boat, as he had no difficulty in getting all the drink he wanted." On board ship Esenin wrote to Kusikov, who was living in Berlin. The letter (which has not been published in the Soviet Union) was in his usual neat handwriting, and he seems to have been sober at the time:

> Dear Sandro!. . . I'll tell you about America later. It's the most frightful trash. . . Sandro, Sandro! I am filled with deadly, unbearable longing. I feel foreign and superfluous here, but when I remember Russia, and remember what awaits me there, I have no desire to return. If I were alone, if I did not have any sisters, then I would throw up everything and go off to Africa or some such place. It is sickening for me, a *legitimate* son of Russia, to be a stepson in my own land. I am fed up with the bloody condescending attitude of those in power, and even more sickened by having to put up with the fawning behaviour of my brethren towards them. I can't stand it! By God, I can't. . . Listen, dear friend!. . . I am ceasing to understand what revolution I belonged to. I can see only one thing—that it was neither the February nor the October, evidently. In us there was and is concealed a kind of November. . . Atlantic Ocean, February 7, 1923.

On the evening of Sunday February 11, 1923, the *George Washington* arrived in Cherbourg. Reporters in Paris were only too eager to interview Isadora about her experiences in America, and, when she was not to be found, they indulged in malicious gossip about her "blackened eyes," resulting from "maltreatment at the hands of her untamed Russian husband, Serge Essenin. . ." Mary Desti met Isadora and Esenin upon their arrival in Paris.[9] Isadora was unmistakably anxious—she had cabled to Desti, who was then living in London, "If you would save my life and reason, meet me in Paris arriving *George Washington.* Love, Isadora"; and when Isadora stepped off the boat-train in Paris, she said frantically to Desti: "Now, don't try to understand anything. I will explain later. Only whatever you do, forget that I'm the great artist. I'm just a nice intelligent person who appreciates the great genius of Sergei Yessenin. He is the artist; he is the great poet. . ." Although short of money, Isadora and Esenin immediately took rooms in the exclusive Hotel Crillon, with Desti occupying an adjoining room. Esenin had a little attache case, which Isadora said he never let out of his hand, except when he slept. When Desti suggested Esenin may have some money there, Isadora laughingly denied it: "Why, my dear, we haven't a penny in the world. . . For the past two weeks we could scarcely pay for our hotel and our food. I didn't mind for myself, but I hated Sergei getting such an ugly impression of America. It's a terrible shock to the artist. You see, he knows absolutely nothing about money."

Desti describes the dinner she had with Esenin and Isadora: ". . . Sergei recited some of his poems, and truly looked like a young god from Olympus, Donatello come to life, a dancing faun. . ." But soon Esenin disappeared, and Isadora told Desti: "When he drinks, he becomes mad, quite, quite mad, and he thinks I am his greatest enemy. . ." Isadora referred to Esenin's resemblance to her dead son, Patrick: ". . . No, you must help me to save him; get him back to Russia. He'll be all right there. He is a great genius, a great poet, and they know how to take care of their artists." Esenin returned to the hotel in a frenzy, smashed the furniture, and was taken to a police station, where a doctor examined him and declared him to be an epileptic. Isadora, after some hesitation, opened Esenin's attache case—

> and to her amazement found it filled with American money, all in small amounts; even silver—about two thousand dollars. "My God, Mary, can it be possible? No, I can't believe it. Poor little Sergei. I'm sure he didn't really know what it was all about. Never having had any money in his life and seeing it scattered about so lavishly, his peasant cunning came to the fore, and unconsciously he decided to save some of it. Most likely for those who needed it so badly in his own country."

Isadora and Desti then went to a hotel in Versailles, where the doctor asked Isadora if she objected to Esenin being kept in an institution:

> The police would free him only on condition that he leave the country immediately. Isadora sent the maid with the last money she had in the world. We had purchased two tickets, and the maid accompanied Sergei to Berlin, where he had many friends and where the Russian Government was represented. Between the time the maid left us and nine o'clock when the train left for Berlin, Isadora lived in terror. Sergei got all his trunks, including the attache case, with only enough money to pay his way to Berlin.

The hotel-wrecking episode was widely reported in the Parisian and American press, and Desti's account of Esenin's behaviour suggests that his instability had reached a dangerous level. The relationship between Esenin and Isadora was now close to the breaking point. In America Isadora had denied reports that Esenin had ever blacked her eyes or beaten her; now, in Paris, she once more defended her husband and even claimed that the poet was suffering from shell-shock. In a poem of early 1923 Esenin voiced his disillusionment with his love for Isadora:

> ... In this woman I looked for happiness,
> But by accident found my doom.
>
> I'd not realised that love's an infection,
> I'd not realised that love is the plague...
> (II, 125).

Esenin arrived in Berlin, where newspaper reporters proceeded to interview him in their avid search for gossip. He evidently obliged them by making some scathing comments about Isadora. A "Special Cable Despatch to the World" from Berlin on February 17 proclaimed: "ISADORA DUNCAN'S POET-HUSBAND ON WAY TO RUSSIA FOR A DIVORCE," and quoted Esenin as saying: "I found America a country which did not appreciate art and is filled with crass materialism. Americans think they are wonderful people because they are rich, but I prefer poverty in Russia." In a notable example of the "pot calling the kettle black," Esenin said (according to a press cutting dated Berlin, February 24): "I love Isadora madly but she drank so much I could not stand it any longer. . ." Yet in a sense Esenin's claim is not so farfetched. Isadora did indeed live extravagantly and drink generously, although she could control herself far better than he could. Her way of life set a pace which even Esenin could not maintain for long. A sensational interview published in the Berlin *8-Uhr Abendblatt* on February 19, 1923 reports him as saying he was "glad to have got rid of his wife at last" and that he "never wanted to see her again in his life":

> . . . He wanted above all to be *alone,* without his wife, of whom he

> seems almost incredibly afraid. . . "It was hell," he says, "which I bore for six months. But then I couldn't stand it any longer, and now I feel well again for the first time since the day of my marriage, as a free man, dependent on no one." Agitated, pale, quite beside himself, he speaks of his marriage, and his young Dorian-Gray-face darkens.

This article was headed:"Lieber in Siberien–als Gatte der Duncan zu sein" ("I'd Rather Be in Siberia Than Be Duncan's Husband"). Vladimir Chernyavsky cites Esenin's words about Isadora, after his return to Russia: "Don't say she's old, she's not; she's a beautiful fine woman. But her hair is quite grey–like snow. You know, she's a real Russian woman, more Russian than all of them there. She has our soul, she understood me"–but Chernyavsky then adds: "Yet the endless follies of Duncan who was. . . jealous and demanding, never letting Sergei leave her side for a minute, exhausted him, and he fled from her."

In Berlin Esenin may have spoken disparagingly of Isadora, who was suffering from a fever in France–but his state of mind was evidently unbalanced. Isadora was "bombarded continually with telegrams from Sergei and his friends in Berlin," writes Mary Desti, "saying he would certainly commit suicide unless Isadora returned to him. Sergei's telegrams usually read like this: 'Isadora browning ('browning' meant 'shoot' to him) darling Sergei *lubish moya* darling scurry scurry' (meaning 'hurry hurry')–five or six telegrams a day; all of which kept Isadora's temperature soaring." Isadora determined to drive to Berlin to see Esenin: "I don't care what he has done, I love him and he loves me. The thought that some harm may come to him drives me mad. . ." On a Berlin street poet and dancer were ecstatically reunited, and they celebrated the reunion by throwing a grand Russian-style feast in the Palace Hotel. It was an evening of vodka, Isadora and song–but, alas, the "poor wild creature" (so Mary Desti describes Esenin) and Isadora soon quarrelled that night, and Esenin smashed everything and hurled abuse at Isadora and Mary Desti, in "one of the most violent fits of madness." The next day was just as tempestuous, and Isadora ran away from Esenin for a few hours. She told Mary Desti that "he had said something so horribly brutal about her children that she simply had to leave, and walked out of the hotel. He might do what he liked, and say what he liked, but to touch that wound in her heart was too much. He spoke constantly of his own three children, one by his first wife before he was eighteen [sic], and the others by his second wife, who was now Frau Meyerhold, the wife of the famous producer, to whom Sergei gave her and the two children. . ." Yet, after a few hours, he and Isadora were together once more. "A general family council then took place," writes Desti, "and Isadora decided we should all go to Russia. But first it was absolutely necessary to go to Paris to rent or sell the Rue de la Pompe house and furniture, then take her clothes and books with her to Moscow, where she intended going for life, where she would continue her school in spite of all difficulties, and where Sergei would write marvellous poems. Dreams, beautiful dreams!"

Roman Gul, who had seen Esenin in Berlin in May 1922, observed him there again after the poet's tour of America: "He was deathly pale, and he was never sober." Gul depicts Esenin reciting "Moscow of the Taverns" ("Moskva kabatskaia")–he was dressed in black, in a dinner jacket and patent-leather shoes. "His face was terrible because of all the violet powder on it." His face, handsome in adolescence, "was now ill, deathly, with a hollow, blue-pink glow. His golden hair and dark blue eyes seemed as if from another face that had been lost in Ryazan. When Esenin finished reciting, he gave a faint smile, took his glass and drank it all at one go, like water. Such things cannot be described. In everything: the way he took it, the way he drank and then put the glass down–there was something doomed, 'nearly finished,' in Esenin. . ." At five in the morning Esenin and Gul left the German aviators' club. Esenin, now more sober, said: "You know, you know, I love nothing at all. Nothing... I love only my children. I love them. My daughter is beautiful–blonde. She stamps her foot and shouts: 'My name is Esenin!...' What a fine daughter.... I should return to Russia, to my children... but I just rush around... I love Russia very much. And I love my mother. And I love the revolution. I love the revolution very much."

Esenin once confessed to a friend: "You know, I wrote nothing for almost two years, when I was abroad" (V, 147). This is not wholly accurate, for the poet could hardly have survived had he entirely abandoned his main aim in life during these months in Europe and America. Nevertheless, his works of this period constitute the most actively despairing phase in his poetry.

On March 20, 1923 he wrote an introduction for his Berlin volume, *A Brawler's Poems (Stikhi skandalista):*

> Introduction. I feel I am a master in Russian poetry and therefore drag words of all shades into my poetic speech—there are no such things as dirty words. There are only dirty ideas. My utterance of a bold word embarrasses not me, but the reader and hearer. Words are citizens. I am their general. I lead them. I'm very fond of rough words. I line these up like recruits. Today they are clumsy, but tomorrow they'll be like the rest of the army in the line-up of my speech. The poems in this book are not new. I have chosen the most characteristic ones and what I consider the best. The last four poems, "Moscow of the Taverns," are here published for the first time. Sergei Esenin. Berlin March 20, 1923.

In mid-1923 *A Brawler's Poems* was published in Berlin. The poems in this volume are funereal, full of "coarse" words and the death-wish—yet Esenin was justified in regarding them as his best and most typical works. The book contained much of his most powerful verse and was extremely impressive. The contrast between *A Brawler's Poems* and the volume *Selected Works (Izbrannoe),* published by Gosizdat in Moscow in late 1922, is enormous—they might almost have been written by two different poets. *Selected Works* contains a preponderance of pre-1918, optimistic, pastoral verse; whereas *A Brawler's Poems* has mostly the gloomier pre-1918 poems, together with Esenin's more recent dark creations: "Sorokoust"; "The Hooligan's Confession"; "Mysterious World, My Ancient World."

The only new pieces in *A Brawler's Poems* were four poems, published together without a break under the heading "Moscow of the Taverns." Written abroad in 1922-23, though perhaps partly reflecting the Pegasus Stall milieu, these poems (II, 119-126) introduced a new theme into Esenin's verse: the theme of drunkenness and promiscuity. The two poems which have been linked with Isadora Duncan's name (II, 123-126) were not published in Russia during Esenin's lifetime. In 1923-24 he combined various works under the general title *"Moscow of the Taverns,"* and this cycle won him considerable popularity or notoriety, but also helped bring his whole poetic career into posthumous disrepute. The setting is the tavern, the inhabitants are prostitutes and bandits, syphilitic accordionists, down-and-outs seeking to drown their misery in alcohol and dreams. After his death, controversy surrounded critics' evaluation of these poems. To some they seemed the essence of Esenin, who, they declared, glorified drunkenness and debauchery; others sensed that the poems really reflect his lonely despair, from which he would gladly have escaped. Written in a universally understandable, non-Imaginistic language, these poems immediately appealed to thousands of Russians who saw in them a reflection of their own anguish. In the two works not published in Russia during the poet's lifetime, Esenin expressed a cynical view of life and love: "Our life is sheets and bed./ Our life is a kiss, and then into the whirlpool" (II, 126), and he appeared to be resisting thoughts of suicide: "I'll not put an end to myself" (II, 124), "I shall never die, my friend" (II, 126).

Whilst abroad, Esenin evidently worked on the prototype of "The Black Man" ("Chernyi chelovek," III, 301-306), which in its extant form was written in November 1925.[10] He recited, it seems, an even more tragic version of this poem to various friends shortly after his return to Russia. "The Black Man" represents the depths of despair, and a struggle against alcoholic hallucinations and a troubled conscience. At the climax of the poem, the hero hurls his walking stick at the "black man" who taunts him—and finds himself alone, with a broken mirror. (In his fits of rage, Esenin tended to smash windows and mirrors). "The Black Man," so candidly self-indicting, shows the extent of the poet's unbalance after his years in Moscow's bohemia and his visit to Europe and America. "In the last two years of his life," writes S. A. Tolstaya, "Esenin recited this poem very rarely, he didn't like speaking of it and looked upon it with distress and pain. He recited it only in moments of extreme intoxication and when in an especially dark state of mind."

Apart from "The Black Man" and the poems entitled "Moscow of the Taverns," the only other substantial poetic achievement of Esenin's months abroad was his verse-play *The Land of Scoundrels* (II, 193-250). This was begun before he left Russia,[11] and published only in part during his lifetime. Although set in Russia, *The Land of Scoundrels* is unique in Esenin's verse in reflecting to some extent something that he actually saw abroad—namely, America's industrialisation and the New York Stock Market (II, 212-213). The cloak-and-dagger story line of *The Land of Scoundrels* is fairly infantile, and the artistic merit of the play is slight. As is generally recognised, the most significant aspect of the work is the contrast between the two leading figures—the anarchistic peasant rebel and bandit Nomakh (that is, Makhno), and the Soviet Commissar Rassvetov. The balance between anti-Soviet and pro-Soviet views is so delicately poised that some emigre critics exaggeratedly claim the play as violently anti-Soviet, whilst most recent Soviet critics declare that Esenin is basically on the side of the Bolshevik Rassvetov.

Certainly, Esenin's attitude towards Nomakh is ambivalent. He sympathises emotionally, intuitively, with the anarchistic peasant rebel. Several of Nomakh's lines are almost identical with lines from Esenin's lyric verse, whilst one speech (II, 243-244) is unmistakably akin to those poems where Esenin depicts his own present hooliganism and recalls his happy childhood. In the handwritten rough draft of one scene, the poet described Nomakh in the stage directions as "sitting fully clothed, in a top hat and opera cloak"—that is, very like the Imaginist Esenin! (In the final version, Nomakh is merely shown as "sitting, wearing a hat," II, 239).

In the manuscript of *The Land of Scoundrels,* Esenin let Nomakh comment thus upon the achievements of the Revolution:

... The self-same rogues have come
The self-same thieves

And by the law of revolution
They have taken everyone prisoner.
Well, to the devil with all this, to the devil!
I am far from complaining.
Bandits aren't supposed
To feel lyrical sadness...

(... Prishli te zhe zhuliki
Te zhe vory
I zakonom revoliutsii
Vsekh vziali v plen
No k chertu vse eto k chertu!
Ia dalek ot zhalob
Liricheskaia grust'
Banditam ne polagaetsia...).

Most of these lines have not, it seems, been published in the Soviet Union. Yet, despite his autobiographical affinity with Nomakh, Esenin understood intellectually that Russia perhaps needs the discipline and industrialisation advocated by Rassvetov. This conflict within the poet was to remain until the end of his life—the contradiction between heart and head in his hopes for Russia's future.

From Berlin Esenin and Isadora returned to Paris, where Esenin's drunken outbursts continued. In about April 1923 he was involved in a scene at a Russian restaurant in Paris. Details of the affair are confused, but it appears that Esenin was drunk and insulted some ex-Tsarist officers, who retaliated by forcibly removing some of his clothes and beating him. The episode became well-known in the Soviet Union, where it is curiously regarded by some as evidence of the poet's "democratic" views. When he returned to Russia, Esenin allegedly claimed: "Yes, I caused scandals, but I caused them well, I caused scandals on behalf of the Russian Revolution."

In a letter to Mariengof in the spring of 1923, Esenin wrote: "God! I could even hang myself from such loneliness" (V, 122). This seems to have been more than a mere turn of phrase—indeed,

Sewell Stokes quotes Isadora as saying: "What a perfectly absurd idea it is that the more people talk about suicide, the less likely they are to commit it. Yessenin. . . was always threatening to kill himself. At a dinner party I gave one night in Paris, he tried to hang himself. When my guests were shown into the dining room they discovered him suspended from the lamp. But he was not dead. So they only laughed. They told me it was very silly of me to worry, that he was only trying to frighten me. . ." If this is accurate, it may be the adult Esenin's first recorded suicide attempt, although he is also said to have contemplated suicide in New York and to have threatened self-destruction in Berlin.[12]

After one mirror-smashing incident in late May Esenin was apprehended by the police, and Isadora decided to have him treated at a *Maison de Santé*. His behaviour aroused the bitter ire of the emigre Dmitry Merezhkovsky, whose salon Esenin had attended in Petrograd in 1915. In the Paris newspaper *L'Eclair* on June 16, 1923, Merezhkovsky accused Esenin of being a drunken brawler and wife-beater, and mocked Isadora's dancing and revolutionism. Isadora, ever-ready to rebut venomous attacks, wrote a long letter of protest, refuting all of Merezhkovsky's accusations and implicitly defending the right of a genius such as Esenin to be drunken or mad. In 1924-25 Esenin was to recall Merezhkovsky's article and hurl crude abuse at both Merezhkovsky and Gippius (IV, 231-232).

After the poet's release from the *Maison de Santé,* Isadora resolved to sell off her furniture in the Rue de la Pompe, let her house on a long lease, and travel to Moscow with her uncontrollable husband. As everyone realised, it was high time for Esenin to return to Russia.

Esenin, c. 1922-1923.

Chapter Twelve: Soviet Rus (1923-24)

When Esenin stood once more on Russian soil, after an absence of fifteen months, he is said to have wept and kissed the earth. Ilya Shneider, who met the couple at the railway station in Moscow in early August, recalls that Isadora remarked to him in German, indicating Esenin: "I have brought this child back to his native land, but I no longer have anything in common with him. . ." The poet's relationship with Isadora, never very stable, had markedly worsened since about February 1923. After a few days together in Moscow, they quarrelled once again, and Esenin disappeared. Shortly afterwards, in mid-August, Isadora and Irma departed for the Caucasus, where Isadora was to dance and also recuperate. Esenin saw her off as she left Moscow by train, and even promised to come later to the Caucasus or Crimea—but in fact this was the end of their life together.

In the past six months he had been bound to her not so much by affection as by his practical dependence on her when abroad. Now, back in Moscow, he sought to enjoy his regained freedom. Isadora herself presumably realised that her grand romance with the young Russian was over, even though she sent several tender telegrams to her husband from the Caucasus:

> Moscow. Prechistenka 20, to Esenin.
> Kislovodsk...
> Darling very sad without you hope you come here soon I love you forever Isadora

and shortly afterwards, when Esenin had already moved back to his old room in Bogoslovsky Pereulok:

> Petrovka Bogoslovsky 3. To Mariengof and Esenin.
> Baku...
> Leaving Monday for Tiflis Come there Telegraph departure Orient I love you forever Isadora.

These were the forlorn loving words of a forty-five-year-old woman to her young errant husband. Desti claims that "to her dying day" Isadora declared that she felt Esenin's "blue eyes looking into hers," and in 1927 Sol Hurok saw Isadora in Paris:

> Isadora herself was sadly changed. Her beautiful body was shapeless with flabby muscles and fat; her hair was dyed a dreadful shade of reddish-purple. But behind the still-beautiful eyes in her parchment-yellow face, as she talked, lay the irreparable loss of her love, the great love of her later years. Cruel, contemptuous, taunting, openly unfaithful, Serge Essenine had embodied her dream of immortal beauty mortally young, and she had given him everything with an Olympian generosity.

Some sources wrongly assert that Esenin and Isadora were divorced after they parted, but in reality, although Isadora contemplated such a step, no divorce took place. As for Esenin, he apparently spoke conflictingly of Isadora after their parting: some memoirists say he was afraid of her or abused her, others that he remembered her fondly. In late August 1923 Esenin wrote to Isadora: "I often remember you with all my gratitude to you. . . I wish you success and health, and that you should drink less. . ."

From abroad, Esenin had sent many warm letters to Mariengof, despite their premonitions of estrangement when parting in 1922. In August 1923 Mariengof, then by the Black Sea, received a telegram: "I've arrived Come Esenin"—and Mariengof hastened to Moscow, rejoicing that "my only friend has returned." In Moscow the two poets met, with Mariengof noting Esenin's European clothes, light walk and beautiful golden hair: ". . . Only his eyes. . . I couldn't understand it. . . strange—they weren't his eyes." And Esenin proceeded to give his impressions of abroad:

> —. . . In Venice the architecture's not bad... only it st-i-inks!... And in New York I liked best of all a monkey owned by one banker... and in Paris... I was sitting in a pub... up comes the garçon... and says: "You, Esenin, are deigning to eat here, whilst we, Guards-officers, have a serviette under our arm"... "You're lackeys?," I asked... "Yes!

> lackeys!..." "Then"–I said, "give me some champagne and quit talking!"... That's how it was!... well, I translated your verse... published my book in French... only there was no point... no one needs poetry there... And as for Isadora–adieu!. . ."

Then he recited "Moscow of the Taverns" and "The Black Man" to Mariengof, and that evening, in some bohemian tavern, Esenin got drunk, swore, broke crockery, overturned tables, tore and scattered ten-rouble notes–and was carried home, unconscious, with foam on his lips, his cheeks and forehead sheer white. Mariengof comments: "That was the day–of our first meeting. . . I remembered the poem about 'the black man.' And I felt afraid. . ."

The next day Esenin transferred his heavy American trunks to Bogoslovsky Pereulok–trunks full of elegant European clothes, which he guarded with abnormal fervour. Mariengof noticed a sad change in Esenin–whereas, before his foreign trip, the poet's scandals were calculated and cunning (he hurled unbreakable plates on the floor, and broke windows after first taking the precaution of protecting his fist), now they were uncontrolled and sick.

Trotsky had written that Esenin "will come and tell the story himself" of his foreign travels. On August 21 the poet duly spoke of his journey abroad before a large audience at the Polytechnic Museum in Moscow. As so often in his life, the evening followed a predictable pattern. Esenin attempted to make a speech, but was incoherent, perhaps drunk; the audience was incensed; he then began to recite his verse brilliantly, and all was forgiven–the evening ended amidst tumultuous applause.

As if answering Trotsky's prediction, in August Esenin began to write "The Iron Mirgorod" for publication in *Izvestiya.*[1] On August 22 the first part of "The Iron Mirgorod" was printed, striking many people by its inadequacy. Indeed, a biting parody of this first part appeared in the newspaper *Pravda* some six days later, mocking the poet's arrogance and affectation. Perhaps as a result of this rebuke, Esenin seems to have toned down his egocentricity for the second part of "The Iron Mirgorod," published in *Izvestiya* on September 16. Nevertheless, despite these attempts, both oral and written, the poet failed to give any coherent account of his journey abroad, from which he had returned dissatisfied and irritable. What could he tell? He had seen little, written little, drunk a great deal, and felt very homesick.

At about this time, he wrote his second brief autobiography at the request of a literary acquaintance. Although he wrote this autobiography whilst sitting in the Pegasus Stall, Esenin unmistakably kept in mind that it was intended for a Soviet audience. He asserted that as a child he "had little belief in God" (V, 11); he omitted the fact that the boarding school he attended was a Church school (V, 12); he tendentiously discussed his stay in Tsarskoe Selo in 1916, claiming that he was put in a disciplinary battalion for refusing to write verse in honour of the Tsar (V, 13); he declared that he left Petrograd in 1918 "together with the Soviet government" (V, 13); and he briefly referred to his trip abroad, concluding with the words: "I am pleased most of all with the fact that I have returned to Soviet Russia. We shall see what happens next" (V, 14).

The text of this autobiography, as published in V, 11-14, omits one significant detail which was, however, published in 1926 and which can still be seen today in Esenin's manuscript. Esenin wrote, after listing his books (V, 12): "During the Revolution I was noted by Trotsky as a fellow traveller," and then he continued, as published on V, 12: "I am extremely individualistic. I stand firmly in support of the Soviet platform."

Trotsky's name is now erased in the Soviet Union, not only from "The Iron Mirgorod" and this autobiography, but also from two poems Esenin wrote in 1924.[2] No Soviet edition today mentions these omissions, or that Esenin greatly respected Trotsky, whom he met in person after his return to Russia. In his book *Literature and Revolution (Literatura i revoliutsiia),* Trotsky named Esenin as one of the "literary *poputchiki* [fellow travellers] of the revolution," whose art is "more or less organically linked with the revolution, although it is not the art of the revolution." Trotsky incisively characterised Klyuev as ornamental, static, anti-urban, with his dream of a rich peasant kingdom, and asked: "What will be Klyuev's further path: towards the revolution, or away from it? Probably, away from the revolution: for he is too imbued with the past. . . It seems that Klyuev is on the decline." Immediately after discussing Klyuev, Trotsky turned to Esenin:

> Esenin (and the whole group of Imaginists–Mariengof, Shershenevich, Kusikov) stands somewhere at the intersection of the lines of Klyuev and Mayakovsky. Esenin's roots are of the village, but not as deep as Klyuev's. . . Esenin is not only younger, but more flexible and plastic, more open to influences and possibilities. . . Esenin boasts of being a mischief-maker and hooligan. Admittedly, his mischievousness, even purely literary ("Confession") is not very frightening. But without doubt Esenin has reflected the pre-revolutionary and revolutionary spirit of peasant youth, who have been driven to mischief and recklessness by the shattering of the village's structure. . .

Trotsky continued that Imaginism slows down Esenin's dynamism, because it overloads a work with images: "At all events, Imaginism is not a literary school from which one can expect any important development." Trotsky dismissed Esenin's Pugachov as a "sentimental romantic": "Pugachov himself from head to foot is Sergei Esenin: he wants to appear terrifying, but he can't. . . If Imaginism, which hardly had any existence, is totally spent, nevertheless Esenin's future lies ahead. . ."

Esenin had not, as yet, formally broken with the Imaginist movement, although in "The Iron Mirgorod" he seemed to agree with Trotsky–Esenin wrote that, when abroad, he felt that " 'Imaginism' has dried up" (IV, 159). Esenin may have felt flattered by the attention of one of the Revolution's outstanding political leaders, and he was excited when, one day, he was summoned to meet Trotsky in the Kremlin, to discuss the possibility of publishing a journal. Mariengof remarks that the former terrorist, Yakov Blyumkin, arranged for Esenin and Mariengof to meet Trotsky: "And the happy Esenin ran to wash his hair, which he always did when he wanted to look a little more handsome and poetic." According to Mariengof, Esenin gave Trotsky a copy of the Imaginist journal *Hotel for Travellers in the Beautiful (Gostinitsa dlia puteshestvuiushchikh v prekrasnom),* the first issue of which had appeared in Moscow at the end of 1922. Although there was some talk of publishing a new journal, such plans came to nothing. Nevertheless, Esenin distinctly admired Trotsky. In

1926 Oleg Leonidov wrote: "L. D. Trotsky followed Esenin's work with great interest. He conversed with the poet on several occasions, trying to give him encouragement. And after such conversations with Trotsky Esenin went away calm, contented, dreaming of becoming a 'State,' national poet, and, half-jokingly, half in earnest, called himself 'State property'." V. Nasedkin, who knew Esenin well in 1925, claims: "Esenin considered Trotsky to be the ideal complete type of man."

Admittedly, Esenin's admiration for Trotsky was perhaps not primarily political in nature (although he never mentioned Stalin in his verse, a fact which may have contributed to the poet's official disfavour in the Soviet Union during Stalin's dictatorship). Esenin probably held Trotsky in esteem largely for his tolerance on questions of the Party's control over literature. During the years 1923-25 some zealously Marxist critics and literary organisations sought to belittle and even deny the achievements of non-orthodox writers such as Esenin. Trotsky's attitude, like that of the editor of the journal *Red Virgin Soil (Krasnaia nov')*, A. Voronsky, was less rigid. Trotsky wrote in 1923:

> We believe that comrade Voronsky is carrying out–on the Party's instructions–major literary-cultural work. . . We are well aware of the political limitations, instability and unreliability of the *poputchiki.*[3] But if we discard Pilnyak. . ., the Serapion Brothers and Vsevolod Ivanov, Tikhonov and Polonskaya, Mayakovsky, Esenin,–then what will really be left apart from as yet unpaid promissory notes for the future proletarian literature?. . . The sphere of art is not one in which the Party is called to command. The Party can and must protect, assist, and only indirectly lead.

Esenin undoubtedly derived support and encouragement from this undoctrinaire attitude of Trotsky and Voronsky. After the chaotic freedom of the first years of the Revolution, when the Imaginists published their provocative volumes, rigid Marxist dogma was now straining at the leash. Esenin evidently realised this when he returned to Moscow from abroad. Shortly after his arrival, he went to see Voronsky at the editorial office of *Red Virgin Soil.* Voronsky was struck by his dandyish European clothes and heavily powdered cheeks, but noted the duality in the poet, who also seemed to be a simple, melancholy, charming Russian, with a vague "lunar" smile: "When taking his leave, he observed: 'We will work together and be friends. But bear in mind: I know you're a Communist. I also am in favour of Soviet power, but I love Rus. In my own fashion. I will not allow myself to be muzzled, and will not dance to anybody's tune'... He said this with a smile, half-joking, half-serious."

From 1923 until his death, Esenin became a regular contributor to Voronsky's *Red Virgin Soil,* where his poems usually occupied first place in the poetry section. Voronsky, who was well-disposed towards Esenin, was himself subjected to the pressure of increasing, and finally irresistible, ideological criticism. In December 1923, when Esenin was already a regular contributor to *Red Virgin Soil,* Voronsky published a long article in defence of the fellow travellers: ". . . It must be confessed that many fellow travellers are very bad as far as Communism is concerned—that's why they are fellow travellers. But they are, in artistic respects, the most powerful flank of contemporary literature. . ."[4] Among the fellow travellers Voronsky numbered Mayakovsky, Esenin, Pasternak, Babel and Gorky: ". . . In essence, our proletarian writers. . . as a whole have not yet passed beyond the stage of imitating some or other of these writers." Voronsky objected to the anti-fellow traveller campaign of some supporters of "proletarian literature":

> It will do no harm to emphasise that this whole literary campaign has assumed the character of a downright persecution, not only of a number of non-Party writers, but also of those Communists who are held guilty of shutting their eyes to, and encouraging, them. Petty political intrigue has been introduced into literature. . . and an atmosphere is forming which is so hostile to literature that writers are now finding it hard to breathe. Intermediate writers are being treated as second- and third-class citizens. . . This question is now so acute that the Party. . . really must say its deciding word. . .

During the last two years of his life, Esenin was bitterly attacked by certain narrowly Marxist, proletarian critics, who were not above using his drunken scandals as evidence of his artistic and political impropriety. Soviet scholars today often claim that Communist Party leaders (such as Kalinin and Kirov) took a kindly interest in Esenin in 1923-25,[5] and it is indeed true that the higher Party functionaries patiently tolerated a great deal from Esenin. Nevertheless, the picture of a paternal Party is somewhat over-simple. A. P. Chapygin observes: "I will not name names, but whenever I happened to speak with leading figures in the social and political world, these people always spoke abusively of S. A. [Esenin]. I know that in Moscow only A. K. Voronsky regarded the poet with love and benevolence." Shershenevich blamed his "contemporaries" for Esenin's death: "Esenin had returned from abroad. The newspapers persecuted him, the public did not read him or listen to him. Esenin did not know what to do. . ."

Walking along Tverskaya one evening, in the autumn of 1923, Esenin said to Gruzinov: "Politics are a delicate matter. Politics require intelligence. Take Sergei Gorodetsky for instance. He's a fool. He's plopped into the mud." Yet Esenin, although no simpleton, was politically uneducated. Innokenty Oksenov writes: "He lacked what is called a world outlook, even the rudiments thereof—and people who met Esenin know what a chaos of ideas, concepts and biases reigned in his golden head. . ." Then, in the typescript of these memoirs, come several lines which have been crossed out by someone: "(If this had been understood for one moment by those dullards and scoundrels, those petty enviers, who under the influence of drink clashed with the poet and who—it is terrible to say this, but one must—beat him, tormented him,—then probably Esenin's tragic end would at least have been postponed, and in his last years the poet would not have looked so wild, glancing from side to side, literally like a hunted animal)."

Esenin's life had now entered a minor key—and yet, strangely, a very different picture emerges from recent Soviet critical works, which endeavour to prove that, in his last two years, Esenin "overcame his spiritual crisis." Certainly, in 1924 and early 1925 the poet made a greater effort than ever before to understand and accept Soviet Russia, Bolshevism, Marx, and the general development of the October Revolution. This is reflected in many of his works of this period, even though his "contradictions" are often apparent and his shorter lyric poems are mainly elegiac. However, memoirs and critical literature of the 1920s make it clear that Esenin's gradual recognition of the Revolution was painfully slow and uneven; the poet was capable of anti-Bolshevik tirades and seldom knew peace of mind during his final years. There is virtual unanimity in the memoirs of those who met Esenin after his return from abroad: the poet was "a broken man," "a different person," ill and irritable. These descriptions occur again and again (for instance, in the memoirs of R. Ivnev, L. Kleinbort, A. Mariengof, N. Poletaev, L. Povitsky, Vs. Rozhdestvensky, V. Shershenevich, I. Startsev, and G. Ustinov). Yet recent Soviet critics portray the matter quite differently. In the Soviet Union today, Esenin's last two years evidently have to be shown as following an upward pattern of recovery. Such an interpretation is far from objective—hence P. F. Yushin quotes none of the eyewitness memoirs describing Esenin on his return from abroad, and instead seeks to argue that "The Iron Mirgorod" (an article derided by many, mocked in *Pravda,* and, according to A. Voronsky, "written reluctantly") represented the poet's "mature" mood in late 1923.

Esenin, in fact, had lost almost everything by late 1923. In September he published a poem which included the lines: "I've no love for the village or city,/ How could I have kept this love?" (II, 115). In October-November another poem of his appeared for the first time, in which he depicted himself as a "street rake" and "mischievous idler," and, although "a good friend to animals," declared:

> I wear my top hat not for women—
> My heart hasn't the strength to live in stupid passion...
>
> I have no friends among people
> (II, 118).[6]

He had broken with Isadora, just as earlier he had parted from Zinaida Raikh—he clearly sensed by now that love for women would never bring him happiness. His friendship with Mariengof was soon to end—and it seems that he was left once more with nothing but the great love of his life: poetry. Yet, even here, a certain disillusionment is evident. Rozanov states that, for Esenin, "fame was more precious than life"; Mariengof felt that "Esenin would sacrifice his life for this stupid, this wonderful, this terrible *fame.*" Hence Esenin's recognition that fame was not worthwhile would be a considerable admission of defeat–and he wrote in a poem first published in late 1923: "I didn't seek either fame or peace,/ I'm aware of the vanity of this fame" (II, 127). Probably his humiliating experience in America had brought him this awareness–but the desire for fame was, of course, too ingrained in him to be abandoned, and he was blatantly inaccurate in claiming that he had not sought fame. In his last two years he strove to emulate the greatest Russian poet, Alexander Pushkin (1799-1837). One frosty winter night Voronsky saw Esenin wearing a top hat and long Pushkinian cloak. Voronsky asked Esenin the reason for this masquerade: "He smiled an absent-minded, somewhat mischievous smile, and replied simply and naively: –'I want to look like Pushkin, the best poet in the world. . . I'm very bored.' He seemed like a capricious and hurt child."

Mariengof comments that Esenin tragically passed from tippler to drunkard to alcoholic: ". . . Yes, he could lose and did lose everything. Both money from his pocket and shame from his soul and his last friend and the woman he loved, and his hat from his head and his head in a pub–but not his poems! His poems were his heartbeat, his very breath."

A poet's gift–is to soothe and harass,
He bears the stamp of fate.
On earth I wanted to marry
A white rose to a pitch-black toad...
(II, 129).

Shortly after his return to Moscow, Esenin met a woman, the actress Avgusta Miklashevskaya (b. 1891), to whom he dedicated a cycle of poems, "A Hooligan's Love" ("Liubov' khuligana," II, 131-144). They were introduced by Mariengof's wife, Anna Nikritina, a fellow actress at the Kamerny Theatre in Moscow–and Miklashevskaya recalled some forty years later: "For a whole month we met every day. We wandered a great deal about Moscow, and made lengthy excursions outside the town. It was early, golden autumn. Yellow leaves rustled underfoot. . . –'With you I am like a schoolboy'. . .–said Esenin gently, in surprise. And he smiled." In 1948 Mariengof wrote of the heroine of "A Hooligan's Love":

> The figure of the woman was not invented. In general Esenin did not invent in his verse. Everything really happened. This is his strength and his limitation. Avgusta Leonidovna Miklashevskaya, an actress at the Kamerny Theatre, Nikritina's friend, really did have "autumnal tiredness in her eyes" and "glass-like smoke in her hair."[7] I used to like saying that I was fond of ugly beauties. But Miklashevskaya, Gutya Miklashevskaya, was a beautiful beauty. A beauty! Ah, such a beauty!... In those far-off days. Tall, slender, with a stern, slightly cool expression, and–eyes! eyes! the colour of walnut, beautiful in their Slavic sorrow. I would say: in their unhappiness. And their love was pure, with poetry, with bouquets of white roses, with romanticism. . . and to a certain extent it was contrived, contrived for the sake of a new lyrical theme. That is Esenin's paradox: contrived love, a contrived biography, contrived life. One might ask: why? And the answer is: in order that his verse should not be contrived. Everything, everything–was for the sake of his verse.

Mariengof's words seem remarkably apt. After the apparent cynicism of the love theme in "Moscow of the Taverns," Esenin's lyrical hero–so close to Esenin himself, although "to a certain extent... contrived"–passed into autumnal resignation. In his verse, the scandals were over, it was the lull after the storm–and Esenin's lyrical hero asserted: "Intrepidly I can declare:/ I bid farewell to rowdyism" (II, 135). In reality, this farewell to hooliganism was wishful thinking, a poetic truth–as Mariengof crudely said to Miklashevskaya: "You schoolgirl, you imagined you could reform him! He doesn't need that! Come what may, he'll run away from you to some prostitute. . ." During these months in late 1923 when Esenin dedicated his love poems to Miklashevskaya, he had various casual affairs, making at least one woman (Nadezhda Volpin) pregnant. Ivnev, doubting Esenin's ability to love, wrote: "He often even 'invented' his love—as it was with the actress M., to whom he sent flowers every day, whilst at the same time complaining to his friends that he was bored with her." Esenin and Miklashevskaya do not appear to have lived together; after 1923 they met very seldom.

The seven poems of "A Hooligan's Love" have provoked divergent critical reactions. They are "love poems" of a peculiar sort: melancholy, wistful, resigned, without passion. No wonder "autumn" pervades these pages: the autumn of the poet's farewell to hooliganism, and the autumn of his beloved's hair and eyes.[8] In "A Hooligan's Love" it may appear that Esenin is preoccupied with himself, rather than his beloved—he stresses the theme of his former hooliganism, and the scandals to which he bids farewell; and he seems to regard his beloved as a springboard for his own rebirth: "This autumnal gold,/ This lock of whitish hair—/ It all has come as the salvation/ Of the restless rake..." (II, 137). His own soul is "like a yellow skeleton"; he mocks his fashionable clothes; he is aware of his international ill-repute, creating terror from Moscow to Paris (II, 141).

Yet the cycle should not be regarded as merely egoistic, with the poet projecting his own autumnal mood onto Miklashevskaya. Miklashevskaya herself was then a forlorn beauty, and Esenin evoked her own state of mind—she had indeed been "drained by someone else" (II, 135), "another person's lips" had indeed dispersed her "warmth" and the "tremor" of her body (II, 139).[9]

Some critics have been excessively harsh towards the sad, passionless tone of "A Hooligan's Love." Kruchyonykh, for instance, exclaims, concerning Esenin's reference to his beloved's "dead" soul (II, 139, lines 5-8): "Love in a cemetery! Others would flee from this, but our poet is drawn towards this 'joy,' towards this body (necrophilism?!). . . The poet endowed his beloved with his own spiritual devastation and hopelessness—and could find nothing in love to heal him." In contrast, several recent Soviet critics rightly point out that, in "A Hooligan's Love," Esenin showed respect and gentleness towards his beloved, unlike his coarse disdain for the "lousy bitch" in "Moscow of the Taverns."

Nevertheless, in this cycle–where the "light blue fire" of love flares up at the beginning, only to peter out by the end–Esenin clearly kept one eye on the "customer" (his reader), whom he sought to interest in his fate. This he managed brilliantly, by concentrating almost solely on his own past, present and future, his own decline and possible regeneration. By ridding his verse of its Imaginistic complexity, and paring it down to universally comprehensible simplicity and a predictably recurring rhythmicality, he appealed to a wider public.

Several critics in the 1920s–such as Yu. Tynyanov, N. Aseev, V. Druzin, A. Kruchyonykh and P. N. Medvedev–felt that Esenin sacrificed stylistic subtlety (imagery, sophisticated rhythms and rhymes) and thematic variety in his last years. Voronsky observes that, during this period, Esenin was hostile to technical experimentation in poetry–Esenin said: "One must write as simply as possible. That is more difficult." One means of writing "simply" was to limit his poetic themes–that is, to bring into bold relief his own errant and tragic fate. Admittedly, in 1924-25 Esenin wrote several long poems about Soviet Russia, but their artistic quality was not always high. "All of Esenin's subsequent history," claims Professor Rozanov, "was the gradual narrowing of his organic themes and the incipient devastation of his soul." Yet the lyric poems of his last two years are in many ways his most effective–certainly they have a more universal appeal than his "Klyuevan" pre-1917 poems, his "Scythian" revolutionary efforts of 1917-18, or his more complicated Imaginistic works of 1919-21. Stylistically these short lyrics of 1923-25 are less rich, with a tendency to self-repetition–but they have an emotional impact which makes up for these defects.

In his last two years, more than ever before, Esenin's verse became "a lyrical novel." Valentina Dynnik states that, in his poems, the reader "awaited news about the fate of the lyrical hero." "The reader looks upon his poems as documents," noted Yu. Tynyanov in 1924, "as a letter received in the post from Esenin." No other Russian poet during these years had such an immediate effect on the reader. Gorodetsky comments: "He lived from one poem to another."

Nothing else remained for him but his verse: his "love" for Miklashevskaya was short-lived and, as Mariengof says, to a certain extent "contrived." Isadora continued for a while to pursue his love at a distance, but on October 9, 1923 a telegram reached her in Yalta: "Don't send any more letters telegrams Essenine he is with me and won't join you must count on his not returning to you. GALINA BENISLAVSKAYA." Isadora returned to Moscow in mid-October, but Esenin walked out on her for the last, irrevocable time shortly afterwards. He had drafted a telegram to Isadora when she was in Yalta: "I said in Paris that I would leave you in Russia [You have made me bitter] [I love you but] I shall not live with you [I have married] Now I am married and happy and wish you the same. Esenin."

Galina (Galya) Benislavskaya (1897-1926) worked for the newspaper *The Poor (Bednota)* and had first met Esenin in the autumn of 1920. In the last two years of his life, she seems to have been his guardian angel, taking care of him and managing his literary affairs. Whilst her relationship with Esenin was probably not as platonic as is sometimes made out, her devotion to the poet was profound and largely selfless. Mariengof recalled many years later: "After Esenin's return from America, Galya became the person closest of all to him: his beloved, friend and nurse. His nurse in the highest, most noble and beautiful sense of this word. . . I think I have never met in my life a greater self-sacrifice than Galya's, a greater devotion, lack of squeamishness, and, of course, a greater–love. She devoted herself completely to Esenin, demanding nothing in return. And, to tell the truth,–receiving nothing." Miklashevskaya (who, after all, might have resented Benislavskaya as a rival in late 1923) declares: "She was beautiful, intelligent. . . Two dark plaits, considerate intelligent eyes, which looked a little distrustful. A smile that was always restrained, concealed. She had so much love, strength, and the ability to appear calm!. . . Every time I met Galya, I was delighted by her inner strength and spiritual beauty. I was struck by her great love for Esenin, which could put up with so much if he required it." From perhaps late September 1923

Esenin began to live at Benislavskaya's—and, until mid-1925, she was his most loyal friend and assistant.

Mariengof's own friendship with Esenin appears to have ended or cooled unexpectedly in late 1923. Upon his return to Moscow in August Esenin had almost immediately resumed his communal life with Mariengof. Yet soon they drifted apart—and no one really explains why. Unconvincing suggestions have been made that Esenin blamed Mariengof for not giving financial help to Esenin's sisters whilst Esenin was abroad, and for "making" him divorce Zinaida Raikh.

The fact remains that, as Mariengof wrote: ". . . Upon his return 'our life' came to a sudden end—'we' split into 'I' and 'He'." In part, there were probably no "reasons" for the break—the behaviour of quarrelling friends is not always "rational," especially when one friend, like Esenin, is addicted to alcohol. Nevertheless, the personal conflict seems to have been hastened by differences in literary matters. Esenin's enthusiasm for Imaginism, already wavering in 1921, had diminished further during his stay abroad, even though he still called himself an "Imaginist" in 1923. Whilst Esenin was outside Russia, Mariengof had achieved a dominant position in Imaginism, especially on the pages of the newly-founded journal *Hotel for Travellers in the Beautiful.* Esenin allegedly took offence when placed last alphabetically in a list of Imaginists published there—instead of Esenin preceding Ivnev, Mariengof etc., Mariengof craftily decided the order according to their first names: Anatoly, Ryurik, Sergei. . . Apart from this feeling of "personal resentment" (V, 125), Esenin had declared in "The Iron Mirgorod" that he realised abroad that "the 'Imaginism' propounded by me and my friends has dried up. I felt that the important thing was not similes, but what is organic" (IV, 159). Ivnev wrote in 1926 that, after his foreign travels, Esenin "began to suffocate in the narrow circle of Imaginism": ". . . However, being very circumspect and cautious, despite his effusiveness, he did not break completely with Imaginism. He suddenly transferred his dissatisfaction with Imaginism onto Mariengof. He began to distinguish between two kinds of Imaginism. One—the odious, Mariengof kind, with which he 'would fight,' and the other–his own, Esenin-type, which he 'recognised' and would not 'abandon'." When the third number of *Hotel...* was being prepared at the beginning of 1924, Esenin after much hesitation published some of his "Moscow of the Taverns" poems there–but he refused to participate in the fourth and, as it turned out, final number of the journal, issued in mid-1924.

Thus, states Mariengof, "at first our literary paths diverged," and then the "path of friendship" parted between Esenin and Mariengof. In 1924 Mariengof went to Paris for a while, and upon returning to Moscow, met Esenin by chance in a cafe. "We had not seen one another for several months. When I left Russia I had not managed to say goodbye to him. And yet there had been no quarrel. It was simply that our relationship had cooled." The bleary-eyed Esenin gazed in an unfriendly way at Mariengof, and said: "I'll eat you up!" Mariengof explains that Esenin meant "eat up" in literary matters. "And that was our quarrel. Our first for six years. A month later we met in the street and, without greeting one another, averted our eyes." Anna Nikritina, whom Mariengof married, writes that there was no "quarrel," but a drifting apart, with Esenin jealous of Mariengof's position in *Hotel for Travellers in the Beautiful:* ". . . When drunk, Esenin spoke badly of Mariengof. But nonetheless Mariengof did not stop loving Esenin, nor Esenin Mariengof. . ."

Drifting away from his alliance with Mariengof, Esenin turned once more to the peasant poets–a somewhat surprising reversion to his searches of 1918, to the poets who had subsequently with one voice condemned his Imaginism. Mariengof noticed Esenin's eye straying towards the peasant poets:

> He sat for hours with Oreshin, Klychkov and Shiryaevets in a basement room of the Pegasus Stall. They quarrelled, shouted, drank. Esenin wanted to be the leader. In the projected journal *Russians* he demanded:–Dictatorship! Oreshin retorted maliciously and sombrely with a rude sign. Klychkov grinned whilst hating him with a profound envy. Esenin went off to Petersburg and brought back Nikolai Klyuev with him. Klyuev clasped his lesser literary brethren in his pastoral embrace, kissed them threefold on their lips, and addressed Esenin affectionately as "Seryozhenka". . .

According to Mariengof, whilst Esenin wooed Klyuev's support for his "dictatorship" in the journal *Russians,* Klyuev was more concerned with obtaining a new pair of shoes at Esenin's expense. When the shoes were ready, Klyuev wrapped them up and slipped out of Moscow in the dead of night, saying goodbye to no one.

Klyuev's visit to Moscow was evidently in October 1923. His relationship with Esenin, both personal and literary, remained highly complex. Although Klyuev had berated the Imaginist Esenin in *The Fourth Rome,* he still felt that Esenin and he were "spouses." For his part, Esenin apparently made some scathing comments about Klyuev after returning from abroad. Yet in 1924 he told Erlikh: "Klyuev was my teacher"–Esenin was certainly not as ill-disposed towards Klyuev as was A. Nazarova, a friend of Benislavskaya, who called Klyuev one of the "leeches clinging on to Esenin." Benislavskaya herself found Klyuev "repulsive," hypocritical, cunning, envious and base. Miklashevskaya also met Klyuev during his visit to Moscow, and took a strong dislike to him: "Klyuev again said that no one needed Esenin's verse now. This was the most terrible and painful thing for Sergei, and yet Klyuev kept on repeating that his poetry was superfluous. He even went so far as to say that the only thing left for Esenin was to shoot himself. After meeting me Klyuev spent a long time trying to persuade Esenin to return to Duncan." Esenin, of course, had no intention of going back to Isadora, and instead Klyuev returned to Petersburg, without concluding any new literary alliance with Esenin.

Esenin dreamed of founding a journal, although he lacked the organisational tenacity for such a task. If in his poetry he increasingly sought to emulate Pushkin, so, in his plans for a journal, Nekrasov was his model. "I want to organise a journal. I shall publish a journal. I shall work like Nekrasov," he said to Ivan Gruzinov. During the early part of 1924 Esenin planned to edit *The Freethinker (Vol'nodumets),* in opposition to Mariengof's *Hotel for Travellers in the Beautiful*–but nothing came of this proposed journal, in which he hoped to publish works by, among others, Ivnev, Gruzinov and some of the peasant poets.

On November 20, 1923 an incident occurred which raised a storm in the Moscow press and demonstrated how hostile many sections of the public now were towards the drunken poet. Briefly, what happened was that four poets–Esenin, Oreshin, Klychkov and Ganin–were slightly drunk in a Moscow tavern and began to argue. During their argument the word "Yid" was used several times; a Jewish customer complained to the police; and the four poets were taken to a police station. There Esenin behaved provocatively, rang up the Communist poet Demyan Bedny, and grumbled on the phone that "one Yid" had caused "four Russians" to be arrested. Bedny indignantly refused to help such "scoundrels," and the four poets spent the night in jail. This episode might have passed more or less unnoticed had not a critic, L. Sosnovsky, printed a long and malicious account of the events in the newspaper *The Workers' Paper (Rabochaia gazeta)* on November 22. Clearly Sosnovsky was prejudiced against the fellow travellers, for he wrote: "I believe that if one were to scratch a few more of the fellow travellers, then beneath their Soviet skin one would find a by no means Soviet essence. It will be very interesting to know what literary doors will be open to these Soviet ponces after they leave the police station, and how great will be the patience of those who unsuccessfully bother with such fellow travellers in the hope of transforming them. . ." Now that the episode was widely known, the four poets published a brief letter in the newspaper *Pravda* on November 30, indicating that the incident would be examined by a comrades' court of the Central Bureau of Press Workers. On December 2 the matter was discussed at the Writers' Union. Esenin allegedly declared at this meeting: "We were sitting in a pub, drinking and talking about publishing a journal. . . We wanted to go to Trotsky and Kamenev to ask for money. . . But some bloke was eavesdropping. I said: 'Pour some beer in his ear.' He called me a Russian boor, and I told him he was a dirty Yid *(zhidovskaia morda).*" All four poets professed their loyalty to the Soviet government (as if this would excuse their behaviour), and Ryurik Ivnev suggested that the poets' explanations be accepted and that Demyan Bedny and Sosnovsky be rebuked. On December 10 the incident was investigated in the Press House, and the evidence given was widely reported in the press. (By a sad irony, Esenin had hoped to celebrate the tenth anniversary of his literary activity on that selfsame day). The four poets were accused of "anti-social, hooligan and Black Hundred behaviour"; Sosnovsky was the chief prosecutor, with Demyan Bedny as one of the witnesses; whilst many people spoke out in defence of the poets.[10] Mariengof provided rather ambiguous support, stressing that Esenin "had become an inveterate drunkard this year and cannot be examined and judged as a normal person. He is simply in need of a cure." Mariengof is quoted as saying that Esenin was now "close to delirium tremens." Esenin made a "speech" which, according to the newspaper *Evening Moscow (Vecherniaia Moskva),* "tended to confirm the medical opinions about him." Sosnovsky maintained that the incident was symptomatic of a disease dangerous to society, and added: "Esenin's anti-Semitic outbursts in America are well-known. We cannot tolerate it that people should take Esenin as a yardstick for Soviet literature." One reporter hostile to Esenin quoted disapprovingly the "defence" of Esenin offered by some Party members: "Now really, how can Esenin be an anti-Semite when he's had eight or so mistresses who were Jewesses. . ."

The incident, and the general behaviour of the four poets, especially Esenin, was debated in the Press House from 8 p.m. until 3 a.m., and the verdict was postponed for several days. Clearly much of the Moscow press hoped for a strict verdict, but in fact the Court decided merely that the four poets should be subjected to "public censure" for their anti-social and anti-Semitic behaviour, and that they should henceforth be allowed "to continue their literary work as before." At the same time, Sosnovsky was rebuked for basing his article on insufficient facts and for abusing the incident in order to "attack some of the existing literary groups."

Although the matter was now officially closed, the newspaper *The Workers' Moscow (Rabochaia Moskva)* promptly mounted an indignant campaign against Esenin and in defence of Sosnovsky. For several days letters from workers were published in the newspaper, protesting against the lenient verdict of the comrades' court. The chief target was Esenin, "the ringleader in this whole incident." One worker journalist declared that Esenin should have been dealt with "as we workers dealt with our masters before the revolution"; another Communist asserted that "there is no place in our family for depraved cocainists such as Esenin!"; various people wrote in to advocate that Esenin and co. should be tried by the People's Court—many letters published in *The Workers' Moscow* demanded nothing less than the expulsion of Esenin from the ranks of Soviet literature.

This episode had considerable repercussions in the Soviet press. Esenin's weakness for alcohol and scandals was now brought out into the open and regarded as a fair subject for comment. Parodies of his verse were published (for instance, in the journal *Dawn [Zori]*, dated December 16), and the satirical journal *Crocodile (Krokodil)* on January 13, 1924 printed a large cartoon showing incongruous pairs of Communists and anti-Communists peacefully co-existing on Noah's Ark. One of the pairs depicted Esenin, a slim lad in shirt and trousers, leaning drunkenly over the side of the Ark, vomiting, whilst Sosnovsky towers above him, sympathetically feeling Esenin's forehead with one hand, whilst his other hand rests consolingly on the poet's back.[11]

In the previous few months Esenin had been criticised in the press for his arrogance (concerning "The Iron Mirgorod") and for his "coarse crude verse"—but only now were his drunken scandals openly reported. Boris Volin, editor of the satirical journal *Red Pepper (Krasnyi Perets)* and initiator of the anti-Esenin campaign in *The Workers' Moscow,* now went so far as to publish a lengthy report of an earlier "scandal" of the poet, which had occurred on September 15, 1923. On that occasion Esenin, when extremely intoxicated, had overturned tables and chairs, and had broken crockery in the Pegasus Stall, and when conducted to the police station had called the policemen there "scoundrels, bribe-takers, rogues, parasites, old gendarmes, and villains." At 5 a.m. the next morning, when Esenin had sobered up and was taken for questioning, "some girls he knew came and gave him a comb and some powder so that he might tidy himself up."

Although in his verse of late 1923 Esenin was "bidding farewell to rowdyism," during these first months after his return from abroad he was frequently brought drunk to various Moscow police stations, where he was charged with "hooliganism, resisting the authorities, and insulting the representatives of authority." His inability to refrain from anti-Semitic outbursts when inebriated was particularly damaging, although most memoirists reject the notion that he was in any way a rabid anti-Semite. Nevertheless, the charge stuck, and several posthumous detractors of the poet stated categorically that he was an anti-Semite, whose scandals were "political" (presumably anti-Soviet) in character.

Voronsky, the editor of *Red Virgin Soil,* was right in objecting to the nature of the press campaign against Esenin. Had Esenin been a "Communist" poet, certain sections of the press would have been less vehement; instead, people like Sosnovsky and Volin used his scandals in an attempt to discredit the fellow travellers in general.

One evening, after drinking himself unconscious, Esenin was carried to Ivan Startsev's flat: "When he started to come to, he began to cough non-stop, bespattering the sheets with blood." In the following months, he was to cough blood on several occasions. Alcohol was proving too strong even for Esenin's constitution. Evidently some people regarded his rowdy behaviour as hostile to the Revolution, but he defended himself to Volf Erlikh: "Do you really think I'm a counter-revolutionary? Don't be daft! If I were a counter-revolutionary I'd behave quite differently! I'm simply—at home. Do you understand? I'm at home! And if I don't like something, then I shout out! That is my right. Precisely because I am at home. I wouldn't allow a White Guard to speak about Russia the way I do. . ."

Yet, though Esenin claimed to be "at home" in Soviet Russia, it was his very homelessness which struck many friends. He had no room of his own, notes Poletaev: ". . . Yes, this man was homeless—he was born that way and lived thus of his own accord. He was sure he was a welcome guest wherever he went." Yet this "homelessness depressed him greatly," writes Startsev. "His position really was very difficult. His manuscripts and things were scattered about various rooms in Moscow. . ."

One of the four poets involved in the anti-Semitic trial, Alexei Ganin, was soon executed by a firing-squad as a counter-revolutionary. Esenin, in contrast, entered a sanatorium for nervous complaints in mid-December 1923. His illness was presumably precipitated by the controversy of the previous weeks.

In December Esenin was hoping to publish *Moscow of the Taverns,* but on December 28 Valentin Volpin informed him that GUM (the State Department Store) had refused to print the book. Probably the censor found fault, among other things, with the tone of "Play, Accordion. Boredom... Boredom..." (II, 123-124)–although this poem had been published in Berlin in 1923, it was "banned by the censor" in Moscow and not printed in the Soviet Union during Esenin's lifetime. When eventually the cycle of poems, "Moscow of the Taverns" was issued in a book of that title in mid-1924, no publisher's name appeared on the cover.[12]

In a poem of 1923 Esenin had touched upon the theme of religion, absent from his poetry for several years: "... I'm ashamed that I believed once in God,/ I am pained that I don't believe now" (II, 129). On January 1, 1924, in a foreword for some projected edition of his works, he sought to explain away the period of his early religious verse:

> . . . I do not regard this stage as belonging to me creatively. It was a condition of my upbringing and that milieu in which I moved during the first period of my literary activity. . . I am not at all a religious person, nor a mystic. I am a realist, and if there is something in me too obscure for a realist, then it is romanticism, but romanticism not of the old, tender type adored by ladies, but the most down-to-earth kind which pursues adventurist aims in subject matter rather than rotten moods about Roses, Crosses and all such trash. . . I would ask my readers to treat all my Jesuses, Mothers of God and St. Nicholases as fairy tale elements in poetry. I cannot deny this stage of mine by erasing it, just as the whole of mankind cannot wash away the period of two thousand years of Christian culture, but all these Church proper names must be regarded like names which for us have become myths: Osiris, Oannes, Zeus, Aphrodite, Athena etc. . . (IV, 225-226).

At a time when certain sections of the press were extremely hostile to him, and he himself had "never been so tired," after the "endless drunken nights" (II, 149), Esenin was probably grateful that Voronsky now published a long and incisive "literary silhouette" about him in *Red Virgin Soil.* Voronsky, one of the most perceptive writers about Esenin's personality and poetry, observed, among other things:

> . . . Esenin is above all indifferent to politics *(apolitichen).* The poet aims his hatred of the iron guest not so much against the actual course of the revolution as against the age of steam and electricity in general... Esenin is an exceptionally talented poet, the likes of whom in Russia can be counted on the fingers of one hand. Yet this poet quite often creates works that are utterly harmful. This comes about because he is totally unwilling to work by the sweat of his brow on patching up his tattered outlook on the world. He is not at all bothered by this. On the contrary, the poet seems deliberately to emphasise his disharmony, he makes a principle out of his contradictions, cultivates them,. . . assiduously shows them. As a result one sees a pose, something affected, coquettish, as if he were changing clothes before the reader's eyes. No wonder Esenin talks about pursuing "adventurist aims in subject matter". . . One cannot say that Esenin's poetic moods do not correspond to his real feelings and frame of mind, but the poet has no desire to synthesize them. On the contrary, he plays on discords. And this is very dangerous. . .

Voronsky then discussed "Moscow of the Taverns," which he regarded (with insufficient grounds) as a milieu glorified by the poet. Voronsky continued:

> The moods expressed in "Moscow of the Taverns" are dictated, in the first instance, by loss of faith in our revolution, in its meaning, its victory, its life-giving creative transforming basis, its future scope. . . When it became clear that the revolution is a difficult, bloody, slow affair, with its prosaic aspects,. . . and that it demands business-like preparatory work, and not abstract enthusiasm, fervour, dreaminess etc.,–then some people began to waver and doubt, and dispirited moods, disillusionment, downright decadence appeared. . . As a result we have such literary phenomena as "Moscow of the Taverns," where the demand for miracles, transformations, unrealised hopes is replaced

> by drunken intoxication, and a tendency to protest and fight degenerates into drunken scandals. In Esenin's verse about tavern Moscow loss of purpose, spiritual prostration, a profoundly anti-social attitude, . . the disintegration of the personality are fully apparent. . . These moods are seeping into the midst of proletarian writers, of Communists and our young people; a broad river of home-brewed alcohol is now streaming across the whole of Russia. . . Esenin assures us in his latest verse that he is saying farewell to hooliganism, but he is taking rather a long time about it. A legitimate doubt creeps in that he is talking about this farewell only for "adventurist aims in subject matter." And yet Esenin loves the peasant, "animality," the sunsets. . .

Voronsky noted that Esenin had now apparently left Imaginism, and ended his article: "He is one of the most subtle and tender lyric poets of our times,. . . but the inner collapse of his poetic personality, elements of ideological decay threaten to destroy him."

On January 21, 1924 Lenin died, and Esenin is said to have stood by the dead leader's coffin. It seems improbable, however, that he was deeply moved by Lenin's death. (Unlike Klyuev, Esenin had never as yet mentioned Lenin in his poetry). One critic, V. Polonsky, wrote in 1926 that Esenin "looked upon Lenin with enthusiasm, but Pugachov was more essentially close to him"—that is, he really preferred undisciplined revolt to a disciplined revolution.

At all events, Lenin's death scarcely had a "sobering" effect on the poet. Shershenevich wrote to Kusikov on January 23, 1924: ". . . As for Sergei, he has left the sanatorium and again caused a scandal. . . Again his Jewish speeches, gendarmes and all the other charms of a man who thinks he can get away with anything. I am very sorry for Seryozha, but I don't like sheer stupidity. Good luck to him! As a human being he is finished, vodka has dealt him the final blow; may God grant that he is not finished as a poet."

By February 1924 Esenin was once again in hospital, this time after damaging his arm in mysterious circumstances. (He had fallen through a basement window and cut his wrist, evidently when drunk. Some people regarded this as a suicide attempt; others claim it was an accident or the result of a drunken hallucination. His arm was operated on, leaving a scar). Whilst in hospital, Esenin wrote the poem "Youthful Years of Unruly Glory" ("Gody molodye s zabubennoi slavoi," III, 7-8). Sofya Vinogradskaya recalls him sitting in the hospital bed, hoarsely declaiming the poem: "Before us was not a poet reciting his verse, but a man telling the terrible truth of his life, crying out about his torments."

> ... I don't know if my last hour lies afar or near me,
> Once my eyes were gleaming blue, now they are so bleary.
>
> Where are you, my happiness? Sorrow, gloom, confusion.
> In the fields? Or in the pub? Nothing but illusion...

The poet had been involved in an incident at the Pegasus Stall in early February, and was liable to imprisonment. Apparently to avoid this, his stay in hospital was prolonged.

He came out of hospital in March, and at about the same time the third number of the Imaginist journal *Hotel for Travellers in the Beautiful* was published. Esenin's signature stood here beneath those of Mariengof, Shershenevich, N. Erdman and Ivnev, under the theoretical *Eight Points (Vosem' punktov,* IV, 261-264). Imaginist theory had become much less provocative since the *Declaration* of 1919—in June 1923, in *Almost a Declaration (Pochti deklaratsiia,* IV, 257-260), the Imaginists had prescribed, not "the image as an end in itself," but "the image of man," "the image of the epoch," "psychologism," "strict logical thought," and the organic image (IV, 260). So now, in *Eight Points,* they advocated the need to "idealise and romanticise life," to struggle for "a new feeling for the world," for "the abolition of the serfdom of consciousness and feeling" (IV, 263-264). They remained implacably hostile to Futurism and prosaic proletarian poetry—but the fire had gone out, they now looked more soberly upon the "buffoonery" of their earlier scandals (IV, 259).

Although he signed the *Eight Points,* Esenin was now an Imaginist more through inertia than conviction. At about this time he wrote one of his most famous poems, "Letter to Mother"

("Pis'mo materi," III, 9-10). The theme of this poem—the drunken son assuring his grieving old mother of his filial love and promising her that he will see her again before he dies—is undeniably effective, and the poem, with its eternal, universal theme, has been set many times to music. The poet undoubtedly sentimentalised the picture of his mother—a strong-willed, heavy-jawed woman not yet fifty years old—but, viewed from the standpoint of his lyrical hero, the poem has deep artistic truth.

Shiryaevets asserted in a letter of April 4: "About three days ago I came across Esenin on the Arbat. We went, of course, into a beer hall, listened to the accordionists and gave ourselves up to lyrical outpourings. He was cheerful as ever, intends to go to the village in summer, and has written many new works." Perhaps Esenin seemed cheerful that day, but his general mood was very different. The medical report of a psychiatric clinic had stated on March 24, 1924 that he was "suffering from a serious nervous and mental disease, expressed in grave attacks of derangement and fixed thoughts and inclinations." Galina Benislavskaya had written to Esenin on February 8, begging him to abandon his drunken escapades, which are "worse than any kind of diarrhoea": ". . . After all, you are suffering from a mental disorder, and this is more terrifying and unpleasant than a stomach upset. . ." On April 6 Benislavskaya wrote a long, candid letter to the poet, imploring him to appreciate her devotion, and admitting that she herself was "on the brink" because of the strain of her efforts on his behalf. She declared that Esenin was now "completely alone," with "unhearing ears" and "unseeing eyes":

> . . . Nowadays you're somehow "unreal." You are continually absent. . . You have totally withdrawn into yourself, you are continually turning your soul, your experiences, your feelings inside out. You see other people only insofar as you find in them some echo for your introspection. Look how intolerant you have become towards everything which does not coincide with your views. . . This is unhealthy in you, and it is no doubt connected with your general state. Something has atrophied in you at present, and you have cut yourself off from the living world. . . You wander distractedly through life, seeing no one and nothing. . . If you want to recover, then work

> a little upon yourself... You're by no means as weak as you make out. Don't shelter behind the hopelessness of your position. That is nonsense!. . .

In April Esenin went to Leningrad. "We live in a fluid age," he said, "and I understand nothing therein." I. Oksenov recalls: "When Esenin. . . was asked whether he ever went home to the village, he replied: 'I find it painful to visit them. Father sits beneath a tree, whilst I feel all the tragedy of what has befallen Russia'."

It seems clear that now, especially when drunk, Esenin expressed wildly anti-Bolshevik sentiments, and it is not only emigres such as Khodasevich and Georgy Ivanov who allude to these outbursts. Ivan Evdokimov, a writer who met Esenin quite often in 1924-25, refers to the sober-drunk alternation of Esenin's life in 1924:

> . . . When drunk he was arrogant, coarse; he swore, shouted and slobbered. . .; he waved his arms about and smoked a lot. The impression he made was painful, unpleasant, often repulsive. He was always railing against someone or other, often against writers and poets, and even more often against the peasants, whom he described in most monstrous expressions. He made ironic comments about Soviet power, or passed anti-Semitic utterances with relish and ardour, pronouncing the word "Yid" with a kind of bitterness and disdain.

Vladimir Chernyavsky met the poet in Leningrad in 1924, after an interval of six years. When Chernyavsky suggested that he should drink less, Esenin became terribly agitated:

> "I can't help it, why don't you understand, I can't help drinking. If I didn't drink, do you think I could endure all this?..." . . . The more he drank, the more blackly and bitterly he spoke about the present age, about "what they are doing," and that "they" had "deceived" him. . . In this torrent of complaints and demands there was incredible nationalism, and hatred of the Jews, and. . . a new future revolution in which he, Esenin,–not with his verse, but with this hand–would beat, beat. . . whom? He himself could not say. . .

One morning Chernyavsky awakened Esenin at 11 a.m., and the poet at once began to drink on an empty stomach: ". . . He again said that 'they are everywhere, don't you see, everywhere,' that 'they have left nothing, nothing at all,' that he could not stand it. . . and one did not know where the real truth lay for him–in this. . . aimless hatred or in the lyrical calm of his poetry about his reborn homeland."

On April 14 Esenin gave a recital of his poetry in the Lassalle Hall (formerly the Hall of the City Duma) in Leningrad. He was due to make a speech "about vileness etc. in literature," "a challenge to the non-fellow travellers." His attempt at oratory was nearly disastrous. Memoirists recall that he was drunk, incoherent, made "some two-edged comments about the Jews"–but, when a scandal seemed imminent, he began to recite his verse, and at the end, exhausted, he was raised aloft in triumph.

One day in Leningrad, the writer Mikhail Zoshchenko met Esenin on the Nevsky Prospekt. Esenin was pale, taciturn, sullen and depressed. At the poet's suggestion, they went into a beer hall, where he began to drink:

> . . . To distract him, I asked him to recite some verse . . . He stood up and recited the poem "The Black Man." People gathered round our table. Someone said: "It's Esenin." Almost the whole beer hall gathered round. A minute later, Esenin was standing on a chair, gesticulating and reciting his short poems. He recited marvellously, with such feeling, such pain, that everyone was shaken. I have seen many poets on the stage. I have seen their remarkable success, I have seen the ovations and rapture of crowded halls, but I have never seen such feelings and such warmth as people felt for Esenin. Dozens of hands bore him up from the chair and carried him to a table. Everyone wanted to clink glasses with him. To touch him, embrace him, kiss him... I left the beer hall.

Although he met the young Leningrad Imaginists (Erlikh, Richiotti, Polotsky, Shmerelson) whilst in Leningrad in April, Esenin declared: "I am not a peasant poet, nor an Imaginist–I am simply a poet." (In the summer of 1924 I. Oksenov noted his words: "I don't want to reflect the peasant masses... I am simply a Russian poet, not a politician. . . a poet, that is a theme, art is not politics, it remains, art is. . ."—and here he gesticulated vehemently). Yet, despite the fact that he was scarcely enthusiastic about politics and Bolshevism at this time, Esenin now worked on his first poem about Lenin, which was allegedly a long poem, *Guliai-pole,* of which only a brief extract has survived. Artistically, the extract "Lenin" (III, 231-235) is second-rate, a piece of weakly-felt rhetoric—and critics were not slow in voicing their censure. Moreover, the draft version of this work contains some lines unpublished in the Soviet Union. In its published form, the poem shows Lenin as a "rebel," "stern genius," "shy, simple and dear," "like a sphynx before me," and very unlike conventional romantic heroes (III, 232-233). A few variants from Esenin's original manuscripts have been published in the Soviet Union, but it should be pointed out that Esenin also wrote that Lenin "looked at you rather like an apache" ("gliadel nemnogo kak apash'") and "looked at you like a Russian hooligan" ("smotrel kak russkii khuligan"). This does not, of course, prove Esenin's disrespect for Lenin—the poet constantly endowed people in his verse with his own characteristics, be it Pugachov, Nomakh/Makhno, or Pushkin. Nevertheless, the closing lines of the poem betray the alienation Esenin felt towards the Bolsheviks. He portrays Lenin's disciples as stern and sullen, "chaining the country in concrete" (III, 235).

By early May Esenin had returned to Moscow, and on May 15 an event occurred which by all accounts made a shattering impression on him. On that day, the peasant poet Alexander Shiryaëvets died of meningitis.[13] Although he had not met Shiryaevets very frequently since returning from abroad, Esenin was undoubtedly well-disposed towards the Volga poet. Nevertheless, the intensity of his reaction to Shiryaevets' sudden death was surely due to the intimations of mortality it awoke in his darkening consciousness. "Only worms come back to life," he said. "The best creatures depart forever, without return." Memoirists recall that he was overwhelmed by Shiryaevets' death. N. Zakharov-Mensky states: "Probably not many people know that the late poet A. Shiryaevets, who was given a civil burial, was before this and with the personal participation of S. Esenin, given a religious funeral service by a priest observing all the rites of the church." Perhaps a few days after Shiryaevets' funeral, Esenin wrote the poem "We Are Now Gradually Departing" ("My teper' ukhodim ponemnogu," III, 11-12), originally entitled "To My Coevals" ("Rovesnikam"). This elegy, one of Esenin's masterpieces, expresses gratitude for the beauty of our all-too-brief life.[14]

One day, after his return from abroad, Esenin had quoted to Mariengof what he called Turgenev's "marvellous" lines about life: ". . . One must calmly accept life's few gifts, and when one's legs give way under one, sit down by the roadside and look at the passers-by without envy and annoyance: for they too shall not go far." This elegiac calm was to characterise many of Esenin's best poems of 1924-25.

In his last restless years, he was unable or unwilling to remain for long in one place. Yet, despite his homelessness, he still felt an emotional tie with his birthplace, his spiritual home. "Do you know why I'm a poet," he asked Erlikh, "whilst Mayakovsky is of indeterminate profession? I have a homeland! I have—Ryazan! I came from there, and whatever may happen, I shall return there! But he hasn't got a thing. . . You can't be a poet if you've no homeland." Voronsky recalls:

> In his last two years Esenin continually intended to go to the village and live there properly. He knew he was ill, and he seemed to be seriously afraid of his illness. He felt great nostalgia for the simple, uncomplicated life, for simple human relationships and simple things. It would be good, he thought, to occupy oneself with everyday, ordinary, clear-cut, tangible matters, to have a garden with lime trees, to talk of hay making and the harvest, to spend a quiet idyllic evening. . .

Towards the end of May Esenin travelled to Konstantinovo, visiting his native village for the first time in over two years, together with his friend Sakharov. Although he stayed there for only a few days, his visit moved him on June 1 to write a poem, "Return Home" ("Vozvrashchenie na rodinu," III, 13-16), an elegy to the changed village. The village is so poor that "even a cow could weep"; he does not recognise his father's house;[15] his grandfather deplores the new atheism; and only the poet's young sisters rejoice at the new Communist order. "Here is my sisters' life,/ My sisters', but not mine," reflects the poet–"Of course, even Lenin is no icon for me,/ I know the world.../ I love my family..." (III, 15-16). Esenin says that he is not a Communist (III, 15), he has never read Marx and Engels (III, 16). The poem lacks bitterness, however–Esenin loves the village, no matter how much it, and he, have changed, and he accepts these changes calmly, even lethargically.

"Return Home" shows the marked influence of Pushkin (for example, Pushkin's "... I Have Visited Again" ["... Vnov' ia posetil"])–and in mid-1924 Esenin wrote in answer to a questionnaire: "Pushkin is my favourite poet of all. With every year I feel him more and more to be the genius of the land in which I live. . . To understand Pushkin properly, one needs to possess talent" (IV, 228). Back in Moscow, on June 6 Esenin recited his newly-written poem "To Pushkin" ("Pushkinu," III, 17-18) at a public meeting to celebrate the 125th anniversary of the great poet's birth. Esenin stood at the foot of Pushkin's bronze statue on Tverskoy Boulevard and declaimed his poem to Pushkin, in which he compared himself with his illustrious predecessor: "Blond, almost white-haired,/ Shrouded in the mists of legend,/ O Alexander! You were a rake,/ As I today am a hooligan." Looking at Pushkin's statue, Esenin (who had always longed for such fame) declared: "I would die of joy right now,/ If I were granted such a fate./ But, destined for persecution,/ I shall yet sing for long.../ So that my steppe-like singing/ Might resound like bronze" (III, 17-18). By September 1924 Voronsky was one of the first, if not the first, to note that "Sergei Esenin, one of the most gifted contemporary poets, after erring in the ravines of Imaginism, has, with great advantage both for himself and for his readers, returned–let us hope, lastingly–to Pushkin."

In June Esenin again visited Leningrad, where he met several people from his Petrograd past, including Ivanov-Razumnik and Klyuev. Ivanov-Razumnik comments on Esenin's "illness": ". . . This illness itself resulted from the impossibility of writing and breathing in the oppressive atmosphere of the Soviet paradise. I know about this from a conversation with Esenin. . ., when he visited me in Tsarskoe Selo in the summer of 1924. . ." Ivanov-Razumnik wrote this in emigration, and Soviet critics might claim that he was biased. Nevertheless, Esenin noticeably defends "free" art in his brief autobiography, written on June 20, 1924:

> Above all I love the manifestation of that which is organic. Art for me is not the intricacy of patterns, but the most essential word of that language in which I wish to express myself. Therefore the Imaginist movement, founded in 1919 by myself on the one hand, and Shershenevich on the other, although it turned Russian poetry formally along a different channel of perception, nonetheless gave no one the automatic right to claim he had talent. At present I reject all schools. I believe that a poet simply cannot adhere to any one set school. That binds him hand and foot. Only a free artist can voice his free word (V, 18-19).

The manuscript of Esenin's autobiography appears to have been cut at this point.

Yet, in August 1923, he had professed his "love" for Communist construction: "Even if I'm not close to the Communists as a Romantic in my poems,–I am close to them in my intellect and hope that, perhaps, I shall be close to them also in my poetry" (IV, 159-160). The volume *Moscow of the Taverns,* summarising his crisis of 1921-23, was issued in mid-1924. It was time that he stopped "hanging his head" (II, 119,121) and "screwing up his eyes" (II, 105); he now had to bring himself to "look into the fateful face" (II, 121) of the new Russia. In September-October 1924 the long poem "Song of the Great Campaign" ("Pesn' o velikom pokhode," III, 236-255) was published on three separate occasions, and Esenin evidently hoped that Communist critics would approve of his attempt at a revolutionary work. Nevertheless, despite his good intentions, the poem is not one of his most memorable creations. Valentin Volpin remarked in a letter to the poet on August 18: ". . . By chance I read your 'Song of the Great Campaign.' I was very pleased by certain of its passages, its extreme musicality and its general construction. Though I must say that, taken as a whole, it is not 'Esenin-ish.'

Do you know what I mean?. . ."

Volpin's feeling that this new work was not "Esenin-ish" was shared by many critics, and until the end of his life Esenin had great difficulty in convincing people that his pro-Soviet verse really stemmed from his heart. In the revealing poem "Soviet Rus" ("Rus' sovetskaia," III, 21-24), written in mid-1924, he depicted himself as a "foreigner in his own land," who seems like a "surly pilgrim" to the villagers of Konstantinovo. The village has changed so much–his father's house lies in ashes, the young Communists sing the agitational poetry of Demyan Bedny, a lame soldier of the Red Army reminisces about the Civil War,–and Esenin can but observe all this as an acquiescing outsider, blessing the young generation whose songs, although perhaps more interesting, are not his songs: "My poetry is now no longer needed here,/ And it may be that I am also now not needed..." (III, 23). He accepts his superfluity philosophically, declaring that he will always sing the praises of "the sixth part of the earth, which bears the short name 'Rus' " (III, 24)–but, significantly (and contradictorily), he says he will not write poetry in honour of the Revolution: "I'll give up all my soul to May and to October,/ But I shall not surrender my dear lyre..." (III, 24). These lines show a basic contradiction in all of Esenin's pro-Soviet verse of this period, in all his endeavours to portray the Revolution and its achievements. He wanted, rationally, to feel these themes in his heart ("I'll give up all my soul...")–and yet, at the same time, he was reluctant to dedicate his poetic talent to these aims ("I shall not surrender my dear lyre..."). This inner contradiction perhaps partly explains why "Soviet Rus," although valuable as an autobiographical statement, is somewhat prosaic in style: in his efforts to achieve "Pushkinian" simplicity, the verse tends to be lifeless. Certainly, some critics were unimpressed by the style of these poems, and not everyone welcomed his attempts at "revolutionary" works, doubting his sincerity and general aptness for such topics.

Esenin himself may not have been really content with these poems. Ivan Rozanov writes: "He was too enclosed in his own individualism, and yet when he tried to tackle large themes, for instance, about the new Russia, he himself did not derive satisfaction from these poems, so I have heard, because—though he rushed at these themes as 'the most ardent fellow traveller'—he was not organically linked with them." "He took the line of least resistance," states N. Poletaev, "publishing in journals his so-called 'Pushkinian' verse, for which critics praised him, but which did not satisfy him as a master." Yet V. Kirillov recalls that, when he asked Esenin in late 1925 whether he valued his revolutionary pieces, Esenin replied: "Yes, of course, they are very good works, and I like them. . ." His "Poem About the 36" ("Poema o 36," III, 256-272), written in August 1924, is repetitive, diffuse, and over-simple.

Artistically, the elegies are Esenin's outstanding works of this period, such as "This Sorrow Cannot Be Abated" ("Etoi grusti teper' ne rassypat'," III, 19-20). Early in August he again visited Konstantinovo, this time in the company of the young, handsome, devil-may-care poet Ivan Pribludny (1905-1937), and it was during this brief stay that he wrote his third great elegy of mid-1924, "The Golden Grove Has Ceased to Speak" ("Otgovorila roshcha zolotaia," III, 26-27).

The months from May to August had been an extremely prolific period in Esenin's writing. (He had confessed to Benislavskaya on July 15: "I'm working at top speed, as if I were in a hurry to get things finished in time," V, 130). Both in his "pro-Soviet" verse and his elegies, his poetic style was now shorn of Imaginistic boldness and excesses, so that it comes as no surprise to read the following letter in *Pravda* on August 31: "To the editors. We, the creators of Imaginism, hereby publicly announce that the group of Imaginists in its previously known composition is declared by us to be dissolved. Sergei Esenin, Ivan Gruzinov" (V, 184). Ivnev, one of the "dissolved" group, recalls their reaction upon reading this letter in *Pravda:* "All this was very amusing, and we laughed a great deal." Amused or not, the disbanded group hit back with an outspoken public attack on Esenin, not only accusing him of never keeping his word, but also alleging that "Esenin in our opinion is hopelessly sick both physically and mentally, and this can be the only excuse for his actions. . . Thus the 'dissolution' of Imaginism is merely one further proof of Esenin's own dissoluteness."[16]

The Imaginist group, with which Esenin had at last officially broken, now had but a nominal existence. Its official organ, the journal *Hotel for Travellers in the Beautiful,* ceased publication after its fourth issue, despite the announcement that "No. 5 will be published on August 15." Moreover, the Imaginist cafe, the Pegasus Stall, was closed down in 1924, a fact to which Esenin alludes in a letter to Benislavskaya (not included in the five-volume Soviet edition): ". . . Yes! It's a shady affair concerning the Stall. Mariengof is going to Paris. You or I can draw our own conclusions from this. He's a worse thief than Pribludny. . . So you're wrong in rejoicing at its closure. And where is my money? I didn't open the *Association* for these rogues. . ." This was at the time of Esenin's open break with Mariengof, whom he now called untalented.

In fact, in September Esenin withdrew, not only from Mariengof and the Imaginists, but from Moscow as a whole, for in that month he journeyed south to the Caucasus. Throughout 1924 he had contributed regularly to the journal *Red Virgin Soil.* During this period there was lively discussion about the Party's policy regarding literature: Voronsky, Trotsky and others rejected the assertions of the *On Guard (Na postu)* group that proletarian literature was the strongest and deserved a privileged position. On May 9, 1924 Esenin, and other fellow travellers, had signed a letter addressed to the Central Committee of the Communist Party, protesting against the demoralising attacks of such journals as *On Guard.* Voronsky acted as editor-in-chief of *Red Virgin Soil* for the first five numbers of 1924 (up to, and including, the August-September issue), but thereafter his name merely stood first in a bracketed editorial trio: A. Voronsky, F. Raskolnikov, Vl. Sorin. In late 1924 Esenin declared that he would stop contributing to the journal if "Voronsky's line" were altered (V, 135), but in fact Voronsky remained on the editorial board throughout 1925, and Esenin was the poet most regularly printed in *Red Virgin Soil* during that year.

For nearly a year Esenin had been living mainly at Galina Benislavskaya's on the seventh floor of Pravda House in Bryusov-sky Pereulok. During the first eight months of 1924 he appears to have formed no deep romantic attachments. On August 14 he wrote from Konstantinovo to Anna Abramovna Berzin (1897-1961), who worked for the State Publishers: "The nights are marvellous here, with moonlight and–however strange it may be with autumn near–dewless. But they all pass without love, and all I can do is remember the past. . ." (V, 132). Admittedly, there is one rather frantic note from Esenin to Berzin: "Dear, beloved Abramovna. Forgive me, forgive me. . . I love you, love you. Farewell"–but he does not seem to have been profoundly in love with her, although her letters to the poet indicate that she loved him. According to Sofya Vinogradskaya, Esenin once disappeared for three days to visit Isadora Duncan, but he soon fled from her, imagining that he was being pursued. Whether or not this is true, Isadora herself left the Soviet Union for ever at the end of September 1924, and travelled to Berlin.

All Esenin could do was "remember the past"–as in the poem "The Son of a Bitch" ("Sukin syn," III, 38-39), a nostalgic recollection of his youthful unrequited love for an elusive "girl in white."[17]

Chapter Thirteen: Caucasian Interludes (1924-25)

There seems to be no overriding reason for Esenin's journey southwards in early September. His departures happened suddenly, on impulse, whilst his inner restlessness and "out-of-homeness" kept him on the move. There were literary reasons too, for Esenin was well aware that the Caucasus had attracted great Russian writers of the past: Griboedov, Lermontov, and, above all, Alexander Pushkin. It is not by chance that his first Caucasian poem, "In the Caucasus" ("Na Kavkaze," III, 28-30), gives such a prominent place to these writers (as well as seeking to discredit his contemporaries, Mayakovsky and Klyuev). Moreover, Esenin continues here his literary "farewell to bohemianism" and claims that in him there has matured "a poet with a great epic theme." Rather more convincing in this poem was his admission that he came to the Caucasus "not knowing the reason," whether to weep over Griboedov's grave or lie in wait for his own last hour (III, 29). Arriving in Baku, "he said that he had nothing to do in Moscow," recalls Lev Fainshtein, "and that he would definitely go to Persia"—his longstanding partiality for the East may also have prompted his travels.

On September 17 he wrote from Tiflis to his sister Ekaterina. This letter is not published in the five-volume Soviet edition, but a typewritten copy (not the original) in a Moscow archive shows that Esenin wrote, among other things:

> . . . Find out how the Voronsky affair ended. It will be terribly unpleasant for me if the *On Guard* people eat him up. It'll mean then: beat the drum and open up shop. It is absolutely impossible to write according to a given line. That would bore anyone to tears. I am working a little. Tomorrow I'm going to Baku, and then to Kislovodsk. Vardin is very kind and considerate to me. He is a marvellous, simple and sensitive person. All that he does in literary policy he does as an honest Communist. The only trouble is that he loves Communism more than literature. . .[1]

Esenin duly travelled to Baku, an oil city on the Caspian Sea.

There Pyotr Chagin (1898-1967), second secretary of the Azerbaijan Communist Party and editor of the newspaper *Baku Worker (Bakinskii rabochii),* took a friendly interest in his fate. In late September *Baku Worker* willingly printed many of his poems on its pages. The newspaper and its editor clearly sought to encourage Esenin to accept "Soviet reality"—on September 25, for instance, a sympathetic article about Esenin's poetry in *Baku Worker* implied that he should read Marx and Engels and become imbued with the ideology of the working class: ". . . One cannot live in emptiness and hooliganism. There is no return to what is old. Therefore the choice is: either emptiness and death, or join the new faith and the new Moscow of the workers. . . Esenin will go to where there is life and living people." In Baku, in the event of the poet being discovered drunk in public, the local authorities were instructed to escort him home safely and pursue the matter no further. On October 5 Esenin wrote a short poem: "Ah, My Life..." ("Ekh zhizn' moia..."), which includes the sad lines: "The glass will be empty,/ Just as life is empty..." A day or two later he left Baku and travelled to Tiflis (present-day Tbilisi) in Georgia.

In Tiflis the poet lived at first in the hotel *Oriant* (Orient), but soon began to stay alternately with Nikolai Stor and Nikolai Verzhbitsky, journalists of the newspaper *Dawn of the East (Zaria Vostoka).* In mid-October Esenin appeared determined to travel to Teheran, although he admitted "why the devil I'm going—I don't know" (V, 136). On October 21 he wrote to Anna Berzin, suggesting a week's visit "to Constantinople or Teheran" (V, 137). His desire to see Persia persisted into 1925, but there seems to be no serious evidence that he ever actually visited that country. Esenin was too talented a poet, and too undisciplined a person, to be permitted such a hazardous journey. In mid-October he and Verzhbitsky apparently quarrelled in a Tiflis restaurant, and decided to fight a duel. Nikolai Stor had a pistol and was to act as Esenin's second, but the duel was prevented by mounted police who had evidently been informed by a waiter from the restaurant. Next morning Esenin inscribed the following words on a copy of his book *Transfiguration:* "To comrade Stor, in memory of Tiflis, the horsemen and so on.

Sergei Esenin. 18/X 24" ("t. Storu na pamiat' o Tiflise vsadnikakh i prochem Sergei Esenin 18/X 24"). One writer, S. Mar, claims that the poet participated in "drunken brawls in the taverns of Tiflis, where so often Georgian poets saved Esenin from a Caucasian dagger."

Nonetheless, on October 20 Esenin assured Margarita Livshits: ". . . I lead a dull life. . . In general, I've lost interest in drinking. It seems I really have sown my wild oats. . ." (V, 137). And he told Benislavskaya: ". . . I think I won't be returning very soon. The point is that I have nothing to do in Moscow. I'm tired of pub-crawling. I shall live a while in Teheran, and then go to Batum or Baku. . ." (V, 138). Benislavskaya had the impression that at this time Esenin was in fairly good health.

Esenin befriended many of the hospitable young Georgian poets in Tiflis—Titsian Tabidze (1893-1937), Paolo Yashvili (1895-1937), Georgy Leonidze (1899-1966) and others. He spoke of translating some Georgian poetry into Russian, but, as in his plans for editing a journal, his words were not turned into actions.

In early December Esenin transferred from Tiflis to the Black Sea port of Batum, where his old friend Lev Povitsky was waiting to welcome him. On December 12 the poet wrote to Benislavskaya that he was "very ill" and was missing Moscow (V, 141). After a few days in a hotel he moved to Povitsky's quiet little house by the sea, but Povitsky recalls that Esenin drank heavily in Batum: "At dinner he used to drink a bottle of cognac, that was his usual dinner time norm. He hardly used to touch his food." Esenin agreed to Povitsky's suggestion that he be locked in his room in the mornings when Povitsky went to work, and at 2 p.m. Povitsky used to return and they dined together. After that, Esenin was free to do what he liked for the rest of the day, but in this way he was able to concentrate on writing poetry during the mornings.

In Batum, whilst appreciating the pleasant warm weather, the poet felt bored and restless. Once, when tipsy, he started to polish the shoes of women passing by in the street; another evening he arrived drunk at a literary "trial" of some Futurist poets, and hurled obscenities at them; and this same boredom pervades his poem "Batum" (III, 78-81), with its nostalgic refrain:

Every day
I go down to the harbour,
Bid farewell
To those I never knew,
And I gaze more sadly,
Even harder
Into the magic, far-off blue.

In a letter to Benislavskaya on December 20, he mused: "Perhaps everything in the world is a mirage, and we only seem to one another to exist" (V, 147).

Esenin evidently fell in love, or had an affair, with a certain "Miss Ol" (also known as "Miss Oll," "Miss Olli," and "Ol-Ol") soon after arriving in Batum.[2] His Tiflis friends followed his progress with interest. "How are your plans for the future with Miss Oll," inquired the artist Konstantin Sokolov on December 17: "If all this is from the bottom of your heart and what is so essential for us all, then I could only wish happiness for your tired and tortured soul. . . I kiss Miss Oll's hand and wish that she may love you simply, profoundly, in a truly Russian way. . ." Nikolai Verzhbitsky, whose letters to Esenin sometimes have an alcoholic aroma, wrote more flippantly to the poet on December 18: ". . . Write me a long letter. About your state of mind, your sudden love,. . . about your dear host Lyova. . . And so, Serga—don't drink milk, also avoid water, and above all—beware of tea. These drinks will be your ruin. Cover Kuku and Mogilevsky with kisses, embrace Lyova, and do what you want with Miss Olli. Write. Nik. Verzhb." Povitsky recalls that "Esenin offered his hand and heart to. . . a girl in Batum, 'Miss Ol.' That's the nickname he himself gave her. . . She was aged about 18, in her looks resembling a high school girl of former times. She was well read, with an interest and inclination towards literature, and she greeted Esenin rapturously. They soon became intimate friends, and Esenin spoke of marriage. . ." The girl wanted to be Esenin's wife, but Povitsky then learnt from local people that "Miss Ol" and her relatives were "engaged in contraband trade with Turkey, or perhaps in an even worse business. . ." Povitsky conveyed this information to Esenin, and later the poet broke with her completely. In late January 1925 Esenin referred to "Miss Olli" in a letter to Verzhbitsky: ". . . I told her to go to the devil. And indeed I was only joking about marriage. I'm not one to be tied to those shafts. . ." (V, 154).

Despite his closeness to "Miss Ol," in his verse of mid-December Esenin wrote of another woman he met in Batum: a certain Shagane. On January 1, 1925 the newspaper *Baku Worker* published the most famous of his *Persian Motifs,* "Shagane You Are Mine, Shagane!" ("Shagane ty moia, Shagane!," III, 98-99). He mentioned her in another of his *Persian Motifs* written in December (III, 100), and, some months later, again included the name Shagane (or the shortened form Shaga) in some poems of this cycle (III, 109, 111, 115, 117). Shagane has been identified with a Batum schoolteacher, Shagane Nersesovna Talyan (b. 1900). She was evidently a mere passing encounter of the poet, who was probably moved more by her evocative name than by any promptings of profound love. (Incidentally, the Armenian Shagane–like the Russians Lidiya Kashina and Avgusta Miklashevskaya, and the American Isadora Duncan–was already a mother before Esenin met her). Some doubts have been cast upon the authenticity of the figure of "Shagane." When Esenin's volume of poetry *Persian Motifs (Persidskie motivy)* was published in mid-1925, it bore the dedication: "To Pyotr Ivanovich Chagin with love and friendship." A feuilletonist, Sem. Narinyani, has suggested that the poem "Shagane ty moia, Shagane!" was originally "Chagane ty moia, Chagane!"–that is, a fictitious name based on the surname of Chagin. This may be only a hypothesis, yet on January 15, 1966 Chagin's own wife, in Chagin's presence, asserted that the feuilleton version is indeed true.

On December 25, whilst Esenin was in Batum, Galina Benislavskaya and Esenin's two sisters, Katya (Ekaterina) and Shura (Alexandra), left Moscow to spend a few days in Konstantinovo. On December 30 Ekaterina wrote to her brother, telling him of this visit:

> . . . We now have a nice, new home, there will be four rooms in the hut but you won't get any of them, we've decided to give you the old hut. We'll repair it and you will live there, we'll make it not in the town manner, but simple, like everyone else's. We'll leave the icon hanging there and the icon lamp too. In short, everything will

be in the old style, whereas in the new hut everything will be after the new fashion. . . You know, we heard Mother and Father singing, that was really good and I joined in at times, but somehow I can't manage it the way they do. . . All of us together, Mother, Father, Galya, Shurka and I sang "The Evening Knit Its Black Brows" ("Vecher chernye brovi nasopil"), we really like this poem, but Mother liked best of all "Soviet Rus." She says that you know how to write really well. . .

At the end of December, the weather broke in the Caucasus, and Batum was buried in snowdrifts. Earlier in the month, tropical rain had beaten against the window panes; now, as waves roared and snowdrifts mounted, Esenin was confined to Povitsky's house for the last week of the year. He passed the boring hours by improving his billiards.

By the end of January 1925 Esenin was eager to leave Batum and revisit Baku and Tiflis. In late February he stayed briefly in Tiflis and Baku, before returning to Moscow at the beginning of March.

During his months in the Caucasus from September 1924 to late February 1925, Esenin produced a large number of works. In Batum in December the poet himself felt that he was "working and writing devilishly well" (V, 145). "I feel enlightened, I don't need this stupid noisy fame. . .," he told Benislavskaya.

I have understood what real poetry is. Don't jump to the conclusion that I have stopped polishing my poems. That is not so. On the contrary, I have now become more demanding about form. The point is that I have arrived at simplicity and can calmly say: "So what? We're bare at the best of times. From now on I'll use verbs as rhymes."[3] . . . It happens very rarely in life that one writes so much and so easily. It's all a result of my being alone and concentrated in myself. People say I've grown much better-looking. Probably because I've seen something and have calmed down. . .(V, 147, 149).

The prevailing Soviet view today is neatly expressed by L. G.

Yudkevich: "This was the 'Boldino autumn' of Sergei Esenin."[4]

This opinion should not, however, remain unchallenged. His poetry of this period was prolific, but, with few exceptions, artistically poorer than his previous general standard. The quality did not match the quantity. As Voronsky observed in March 1925: "Many (not all) of his Caucasian poems are mediocre and for Esenin quite weak. It appears that in this respect the climate of Georgia was by no means beneficial for him." Also in March 1925, the critic A. Lezhnev, whilst welcoming the poet's attempt to break with the past and to renew his severed links with society, nonetheless criticised certain "false notes" in his recent verse, and commented: "Another fault of Esenin's latest poems is their monotony, their lack of variety in methods, rhythm, mood and tone. The poet is patently repeating himself."

Much of what Esenin wrote was in the unpretentious, but undemanding, form of short iambic lines. Many of the poems reflect his attempt to come closer to an understanding of "Soviet reality"; yet most of them are undistinguished as poetry. "The Ballad About the Twenty-Six" ("Ballada o dvadtsati shesti," III, 31-37) is particularly uninspired—the refrain "There were 26 of them,/ 26" is shamelessly over-used, and numerous sections are repeated wholesale in the second part of the poem. "In Memory of Bryusov" ("Pamiati Briusova," III, 42-43) is feeble, and "Stanzas" ("Stansy," III, 44-47) further exemplifies the impoverishment of Esenin's poetic language, even though, from the Soviet point of view, it marks the poet's continuing ideological progress. Esenin declares: "I want to be a singer/ And a citizen,/ So that for everyone,/ As an example to be proud of,/ I might become a real/ And not a step-son—/ In the great states of the U.S.S.R." Yet he then refers flippantly to his drunken scandals and skirmishes with the police in Moscow; he proclaims: "I'm not a canary!/ I'm a poet!/ And not to be compared with any old Demyans" (a disdainful thrust at Demyan Bedny); and he finds prosaic and scarcely wholehearted words to describe Lenin, Marx and the new era. He exhorts himself: "Come on, Sergei,/ Let's sit down quietly to Marx,/ Let's sniff the great wisdom/ Of his boring lines." Earlier in the year he had been "full of thoughts of my merry youth" (III, 26); arriving in the Caucasus he was "full of thoughts" of the great, dead Russian poets (III, 29);

now he was "full of thoughts of industrial power" (III, 47). Voronsky singled out "Stanzas" as "weak and unconvincing," and stated: "It is probably too early for Esenin to start writing about Marx and Lenin, but it is very opportune and to the point for him to study them attentively, not for the sake of a witty remark, but in order to revise some aspects of his poetry. . ."[5]

Some works of this period are, however, richly autobiographical. In "Departing Rus" ("Rus' ukhodiashchaia," III, 48-52) the poet regrets that he has been caught between two generations and been insufficiently linked with the heroic age: "I'm not a new man!/ Why conceal this?/ I've remained with one foot in the past,/ In seeking to catch up with the steel army,/ I slip and fall with my other foot..." "Letter to a Woman" ("Pis'mo k zhenshchine," III, 57-60) is a sincere confession, which seems to contain reminiscences about his marriage to Zinaida Raikh. "My Life" ("Moi put'," III, 130-136) is touchingly natural in its memories of early childhood and first love, even though at times Esenin deliberately distorts the chronology of his life story. "Anna Snegina" (III, 273-300), the longest work of his Caucasus period, reads easily, and is especially moving in its lyrical sections evoking the painful memories of unrequited love (III, 278, 300). Nevertheless, the poem is nowadays somewhat overrated by Soviet critics because of its historical "realism," so unlike Esenin's wild cosmic revolutionary poems of 1917-18. Incidentally, the narrator-hero (who is largely autobiographical) takes almost no active part, and very little interest, in the historical events which form a background to the work.[6]

Many of Esenin's poems at this time were in the form of "letters"—after his "Letter to a Woman" and what amounted to an open letter to the Georgian poets ("To the Poets of Georgia," ["Poetam Gruzii"], III, 61-64), he composed "A Letter from Mother" ("Pis'mo ot materi," III, 65-68), "Reply" ("Otvet," III, 69-72), and "Letter to Grandfather" ("Pis'mo dedu," III, 82-86).

Much of this verse lacks life and illumination, despite the poet's claim in "Stanzas" that in his eyes was "the light of wondrous insights" (III, 45). In January 1925 he wrote a weak poem about Lenin, entitled "Captain of the Earth" ("Kapitan zemli,"

III, 124-127). Lev Povitsky recalls that *Baku Worker* rejected the poem, and it remained unpublished during the poet's lifetime.

During this Caucasus period, Esenin also began work on his cycle of "Persian Motifs", and hoped to publish a volume under the title *The Rowan Tree Bonfire (Riabinovyi koster).* Three books of his poetry were issued. *Soviet Rus,* published in Baku at the end of 1924, contained his most recent verse. Pyotr Chagin, in his foreword to the book, stressed that Esenin's poetry was now in a transitional stage, from intimate lyricism to social, "civic" themes, from the tavern to the crowded street, from the *kulak* hut to the revolutionary masses: ". . . In these poems Sergei Esenin *is already more than a fellow traveller, he is already our sputnik* [close companion]. . ." In January 1925 *The Soviet Land (Strana sovetskaia)* was published in Tiflis. Like the Baku volume, this latest collection of his verse consisted mainly of his longer "pro-Soviet" poems of the past few months. Of greatest interest, perhaps, was the book *Poems [Stikhi] (1920-1924),* badly printed but well selected. The critical reaction to this retrospective volume was generally favourable. Professor Rozanov, under the pseudonym Andrei Shipov, reviewed it perceptively early in 1925:

> It seems that no living lyric poet evokes the reader's sincere sympathies. . . as does Sergei Esenin. This stems not so much from the extent of his lyric talent as from its qualities. In some respects Esenin should without doubt be inferior to some of his contemporaries: he lacks the sweep and crude strength of Mayakovsky, the cultural saturation of Mandelstam, or the dazzling lyrical intensity of Boris Pasternak, but he has a quality which is perhaps the most valuable of all for a lyric poet—the ability to reach the reader's heart and even—a thing to which we are now especially unaccustomed—the ability at times to move and touch us. . . Esenin propounds nothing, summons us nowhere, poses and resolves no questions of worldwide importance, he tells only about himself, exclusively about himself. . . But Esenin's "I" is not the "I" of a proud individualist or egoist: it nearly always sounds like "we". . . Another cause of Esenin's exceptional success, apart from his emotional qualities, is the fact that he is simpler than the other poets, more in the traditions of Russian literature, especially in this book where he clearly abandons Imaginism and approaches the methods of Pushkin's poetry. Mandelstam and Pasternak are too

> intellectual as poets, in the last resort they are poets for the few. . . Esenin, on the other hand, can be understood by everyone from the lowly to the grand. . .

Esenin had been absent from Moscow for most of the past six months, and as he stepped out onto the platform of the Kursk station, he was eagerly met by Galina Benislavskaya, his sister Ekaterina, and Ekaterina's suitor, the poet Vasily Nasedkin (1894-1940). Nasedkin states that, during his stay in Moscow (from about March 1-27), Esenin got drunk only four or five times, and without causing any scandals: "He even boasted that the Caucasus had reformed him. He looked very well, and had put on weight. . . During the first week he was extraordinarily cheerful and lively. . ." At Nasedkin's suggestion, Esenin recited "Anna Snegina" to members of the *Pereval* group,[7] but the poem was coolly received. Nasedkin later recalled that this "Pereval" failure "seems to set the tone for the whole of 1925. In that literary year Esenin had quite a few such failures, certainly more than in any previous year."

It may have been on March 5 that Esenin first met Sofya Andreevna Tolstaya (1900-1957), a granddaughter of Lev Tolstoy. She is said not to have been particularly beautiful, but to have had a certain appeal, in addition to the aura of her famous name. At much the same time Esenin's mother arrived in Moscow from the village, and she spent two or three days with her three children in Benislavskaya's flat. The poet was tremendously pleased by this brief family reunion. A photograph of this visit shows him reciting "Anna Snegina" to his mother, as they sit at a samovar-adorned table. Nasedkin noted, however, that in the second half of March Esenin wrote nothing and "reached for the bottle." Nearly every night one or two chance acquaintances came back with him and spent the night at Benislavskaya's.

Esenin had never intended this stay in Moscow to be protracted, for he wanted to return soon to the Caucasus. Towards the end of the month, he was thinner, irritable, and "far from happy. On the eve of his departure, completely sober, he wept for a long time. On his last day a sad smile. . . never left his face. He really did have the look then of a man oppressed and persecuted." His attraction to Sofya Tolstaya evidently began to spoil his relationship with Galina Benislavskaya—on March 21, clearly in reply to some protest from Benislavskaya, he wrote her a note: "Dear Galya! You are close to me as a friend, but I don't love you at all as a woman. S. Esenin." On March 27 he set off for Baku.

From the outset his journey seems to have been plagued by misfortune. On April 8 he wrote to Benislavskaya that bandits had robbed him of his coat and money, and he had caught a severe chill—"something like periostitis. The pain is terrible" (V, 161). In the middle of April he bathed in the sea during a strong wind, and doctors diagnosed his resultant illness as "galloping consumption." Some confusion surrounds the exact causes and nature of his illness in Baku. Esenin later told Nasedkin:

> We were driving in a car, and went into the mountains. You know, it's cold in the mountains, and I was wearing only a shirt. Next day blood poured from my throat. I was very scared. Chagin summoned some doctors. "If you don't stop drinking, then you'll be dead in three months,"... they said, and they put me in hospital. Holiday time, Easter, and there was I in hospital. I thought I was dying. In one day I wrote two poems: "There Is One Good Song..." ("Est' odna khoroshaia pesnia...," III, 141-142) and "Well, Kiss Me, Kiss Me" ("Nu, tselui menia, tselui," III, 143-144). . .

Volf Erlikh recalls: "In May I read in the newspapers that Esenin had tuberculosis of the throat," but Erlikh adds that Esenin denied any such illness: " 'Lies. I simply lost my voice through drinking. In the Caucasus I ran out into the snow with an open neck, I wanted to catch a chill. But it didn't work out.' He was silent for a moment, and then stood up determinedly...—'But I shall die all the same. And very soon'."

Evidently during this visit, A. Voronsky met Esenin in Baku. The poet stood by the unfriendly sea, smiling absent-mindedly and coughing: ". . . His whole figure seemed doomed and quite superfluous here." In a country house outside Baku, Esenin drank, caused a scandal, and then wept and said to

Voronsky: " 'I have nothing left. I am afraid. I have no friends, no one close to me. I love no one and nothing. Only my verse remains. I have given everything for my verse, do you understand, everything. There you see a church, the village, the horizon, the fields and forest. And all that is now far from me.' He wept for over an hour."

Yet Sofya Vinogradskaya attests that Esenin derived no pleasure from his poems once they were completed and published:

> "It's no longer mine, it's already someone else's when it's completed... What am I left with? I tear it out of myself, write it, and it goes away from me, and I am left with nothing..." He used to say this angrily, in a kind of frenzy. He felt a martyr to his own verse... He was angered by the fact that all his thoughts, all his feelings were poured into his poems, thus leaving nothing for himself. Yet he could not stop writing. And in the intervals between he fell ill, he drank... Outside his poetry he was bored. . . He said he envied those who served, worked and studied. Whereas he didn't know what to do with himself and his time when he wasn't writing poetry. His poetry took up his whole being, his whole life was in his verse, outside his verse there was nothing.

In April and May—perhaps partly because of the criticisms voiced by Voronsky in March—Esenin reverted to the writing of lyric verse. The Caucasian winter of long poems was over; from now on the poet was to devote himself to the genre most natural to him: the short autobiographical lyric. The tone of Esenin's poems, as he lay in hospital with suspected tuberculosis of the lungs, was understandably funereal. If he entered hospital in about mid-April, by the end of the month he was evidently well enough to be discharged, for on May 1 he attended a May Day celebration of the workers in one of the districts of Baku.

Only in one poem of this period did Esenin look beyond himself. In "Comfortless Watery Moonlight" ("Neuiutnaia zhidkaia lunnost'," III, 156-157) he declared that he no longer loved the beggarly Russian countryside: "I don't know what will become of me.../ Perhaps I'm unsuited for the new life,/ But all the same I want to see/ Poor beggarly Rus clothed in steel." Despite this advocacy of Russia's industrialisation, Esenin remained predominantly self-obsessed during the last months of 1925. Even the moon, his favourite image, has a "consumptive light" in this poem—thus the sick poet transferred his supposed illness to the celestial body.

By May 11 Esenin was in hospital again, suffering, so he claimed, from "catarrh of the right lung" (V, 162)—but doctors who examined him took a graver view of his condition. On May 12 he wrote to Benislavskaya: "I am forbidden to drink. There really is something wrong with my lungs" (V, 164). He was advised to recuperate in Abas-Tuman, a Georgian health resort, but he did not go there. Indeed, throughout 1925 he seems to have resisted most attempts to improve his declining health, although he realised that a cure was essential. He was out of hospital again on about May 17, and returned to Moscow at the end of the month, looking thin and jaded.

Early in June he made an ill-starred two-day excursion to Konstantinovo, to attend the wedding of his cousin. Nasedkin admits: "Before this trip I, like everyone who knew Esenin, had considered him to be a relatively healthy person. But here in the village, he was completely beside himself. His caprices assumed painful and clearly unhealthy forms. . ." Esenin attempted to excuse himself in two ways—first, he objected to some "prostitute" whom his friends had brought from Moscow to the village; and, secondly, he claimed he had reacted with anguish to "the peasant stagnation, ignorance and greediness" which he had met in the village.

I. G. Atyunin writes of Esenin's last visits to the village: "When in the village he used to drink and brawl all the time, he broke windows and tried to beat his mother unmercifully. . ." Esenin would sing obscene songs, or sob at the awareness of imminent death: "In his last months his dream was to build a house in the garden and live with his family in the village."

Back in Moscow Esenin was advised by Nasedkin to settle down and discipline himself, and he agreed: "Perhaps I should marry S. T[olst]aya and start leading a quiet life." Vladimir Chernyavsky comments: "Sergei Esenin and Sofya Tolstaya—this combination appealed to him. . ." (Some memoirists recall a time when Esenin allegedly thought of marrying Chaliapin's daughter or niece: "You know, it would sound marvellous: Esenin and Chaliapina... Eh?... Shall I marry her?"—perhaps he viewed marriage with Lev Tolstoy's granddaughter in much the same light). According to Mariengof, Sofya Tolstaya looked "impossibly like her grandfather. All she lacked was a bald patch and a grey beard. . ." At first Esenin hesitated about marrying her. "Well, I ask you, marriage!," he said to Erlikh. "Why should a person like me get married? What am I left with in this life? Fame? My God! I'm not a child, you know! Poetry? Perhaps... But no! That too is leaving me... Happiness is muck! It doesn't exist. And as for my private life!... I have sacrificed that for what I no longer possess... Where is my life? Where are my children?. . ."

Nevertheless, on June 16 Esenin informed his sister Ekaterina: "I am marrying Tolstaya and going to the Crimea with her. . ." (V, 165). As a preliminary to marriage, writes Nasedkin, he "left Galya Benislavskaya completely" and "somehow hesitantly, almost unwillingly, began to move to his new place of residence." This break with Benislavskaya was extremely painful, for she had been the poet's closest confidante for well over a year. Sofya Vinogradskaya observes: "When the break occurred between him and Benislavskaya, Esenin realised that he had lost his most valuable support in life—his friend... After this, he seemed to lose confidence in people's love for him."

Esenin did not officially register his marriage with Sofya Tolstaya until September 18, although he lived with her from June onwards. During June he drank relatively little, and there were those who thought that his projected marriage to Tolstaya might prove a lasting beneficial influence on his behaviour. Yet there were also sceptics who regarded this as merely one more episode in the poet's life. It seems that the couple were ill-matched and had little in common. Whilst some memoirists praise Tolstaya, Esenin is said to have wept and declared that "nothing will come of the marriage. . ." Tolstaya's flat, with its innumerable portraits of Lev Tolstoy, displeased the poet—by July he was writing to Verzhbitsky: "Little good will come of my new family, everything here is too much imbued with 'the grand old man,' he is so omnipresent, on the tables, and in the tables, and on the walls, and it seems even on the ceilings, that there is no room left for living people. And that oppresses me. . ." (V, 167).

The troubled relationship between Esenin and Tolstaya is reflected in some notes and telegrams they sent one another. (Esenin's messages are here printed in italics).

> Sergei, my dear, come quickly. I want to see you very, very much. So terribly sad. Your Sonya.
>
> *I don't know what to say. You will see me no more. For no reason. I love you, love you.*[8]
>
> . . . Keep well, my dear. In my thoughts always with you. S.
>
> *I feel well will see you soon love Sergei.*[9]
>
> Sergei, my dear, I didn't want to wake you. Come to me at my work (Prechistenka 11) or ring (2-26-90)... For God's sake remember what you promised, otherwise I will feel anxious. I kiss you. Sonya.
>
> *Sonya. Forgive me for insulting you. You yourself are to blame... I'll ring. Sergei.*

After Esenin's death, Sofya Tolstaya's attitude to him was described by her mother in a letter: ". . . Her love for him evidently knew no bounds, and, as she herself used to say, in her love there was much that was maternal, as for a sick child."

Esenin was now haunted by the idea of death. "He was drawn towards the balcony, towards windows," writes Volf Erlikh. "He stood by the open window and looked down. I went up and touched him on the shoulder. —'Sergei! Don't look down so long. It's not good!' He turned his dead-white face towards me. —'Ah, *katso!..*[10] How boring it is!' " He was beginning to fear loneliness in the early hours of the morning—one day he wakened Erlikh at 3 a.m. and together they went for a stroll around Moscow. At 5 a.m. Esenin said: "Listen... I'm a doomed man... I am very ill... Above all—cowardly... I am very unhappy. I have nothing in life. Everything has betrayed me. Do you understand? Everything! But that's not the point... Listen... Never pity me! Never pity me, *katso!* If I ever notice that... I will kill you! Do you understand?"

"If you ever feel the desire to write about me, then write: he lived only for his art and only with this passed through life."

Several selected volumes of Esenin's poetry were issued by mid-1925: *About Russia and the Revolution (O Rossii i revoliutsii), The Cotton Print of Birch Trees (Berezovyi sitets),*[11] *Selected Verse (Izbrannye stikhi).* These books all tactfully omitted his tavern verse and republished works chiefly of his earlier years. Of greater interest was the publication of the volume entitled *Persian Motifs,* perhaps towards the end of June. This book contained ten poems of the "Persian Motifs" cycle, plus the autobiographical "My Life" and four sad short lyrics of 1924. The ten "Persian Motifs" (III, 94-112) had all been published previously, but never before united into one cycle. Esenin, not having visited Persia, had three main sources of "local colour." Firstly, he had observed the oriental aspect of such towns as Samarkand and Tashkent (in 1921), and Baku, Tiflis and Batum (especially since late 1924). He also derived information and inspiration from the travellers' tales of those who had actually visited Teheran and Shiraz. Chagin's brother, Vasily Boldovkin,[12] who had served in the Soviet Embassy in Teheran, regaled the poet with many eyewitness tales. Finally, Esenin consulted several poetic sources which conveyed the atmosphere of the East. He probably knew Shiryaevets' Turkestan poems, *The Turquoise Tea House (Biriuzovaia Chaikhana);* he is said to have read with interest Bryusov's translations of Armenian poetry; and he had presumably noted Klyuev's (and, even more, Kusikov's) attachment to the East. More important still, he apparently read some ancient Persian poetry in Russian translations.[13] Nevertheless, Esenin's "Persian Motifs" remain very Russian in feeling, even though he mentions Oriental places and poets, roses and nightingales, tea houses and black veils. The poet is continually glancing towards far-off Russia and the "girl in the north," and it is no surprise when he finally decides to "return to Rus." The poems are calm, warm and melodious, and yet their importance and merit are exaggerated by Soviet critics today. The style of many of the "Persian Motifs" seems mechanical and stilted, and the verse form over-simple. Only three poems of the cycle enjoy wide popularity (III, 96-100). Present-day Soviet critics wish to imply that the poet saw life in 1924-25 in a rosier hue, and hence they hail the "Persian Motifs" mainly because of their contrast with "Moscow of the Taverns."

Esenin was very pleased in June 1925 at the decision of Gosizdat (the State Publishers) to issue a large collection of his poetry. On June 17 he suggested a contract: 10,000 lines of his verse to be published at a rouble a line, with 2000 roubles to be given to him at once, and the remaining money to be paid at 1000 roubles a month, commencing on August 1. All the conditions were accepted except for the immediate single payment of 2000 roubles, and on June 30 the contract was formally signed. "The poet provided for his life for many months to come," observes Ivan Evdokimov. In August Nasedkin wrote to Esenin: "When Mayakovsky heard about the terms of the publication of your works, he fell ill with a nervous disorder. Because of envy." No other poet received as much as a rouble a line from the State Publishers.

Esenin said to Ivan Evdokimov, who worked at Gosizdat: "Evdokimych... I've written about fifteen thousand lines. You know, I'll select the very best, about ten thousand. That will be enough: there will be three volumes. My first 'Collected Works,' you know... Now I'll get down to work." Yet Evdokimov adds that, when Esenin brought along some manuscripts for this forthcoming edition, they were in a chaotic condition—a mixture of handwritten poems and cuttings from newspapers and journals, without plan and without any chronological order, "a complete muddle." A temporary halt in overcoming this chaos was caused by the poet's sudden departure from Moscow at the end of July, not long after again visiting Konstantinovo. Voronsky was to recall: "When people advised him to undergo medical treatment, he pleaded with his invariable smile that he had to prepare the collection of his works for Gosizdat and then he would undertake a proper cure. It later transpired that he did no serious work at all upon this collection. And he can scarcely have believed in his own excuses. . ."

In July Esenin had produced a spate of poems (III, 159-170). Volf Erlikh comments on approximately this period:

> If he didn't write for a week, he started going mad with fear. Esenin, who at one time wrote nothing for two years, was afraid of a three-day silence. Esenin, who had possessed almost the gift of improvisation, now spent several hours on writing sixteen lines, a third of which could be found in his old poems. Esenin, who remembered by heart everything he had written in the course of ten years' work, recited his latest poems only with a manuscript. He didn't like these poems. . . One morning he says: "I have no rivals and that's why I can't work." At midday he complains: "I've lost the gift." At 4 p.m. he drinks a glass of rowanberry vodka and is put to bed unconscious. . .

In late July he suddenly left Moscow with Tolstaya, and headed once more for the south. On July 26 he added a pungent postscript to Tolstaya's card to Erlikh– Esenin wrote in pencil, in very shaky handwriting:

> Dear Vova
> Hallo there
> I don't lead a bad
> "life,"
> But if you've not married yet
> Then don't take a wife.

Arriving in Baku, he wrote a poem, "Gentle Wind. An Evening Blue and Gloomy" ("Tikhii veter. Vecher sine-khmuryi"), in which he candidly expressed an unidealistic view of love.[14]

In August Esenin and Tolstaya lived in a former khan's country house in Mardakyany outside Baku–an "illusion of Persia," remarks Chagin, with "a huge garden, fountains and all kinds of Oriental intricacy. . ." In the calm of Mardakyany Esenin was able to write several poems in August, including the closing works of the "Persian Motifs" cycle. In one poem he gave his definition of the agony of being a poet–it means: "... Leaving a scar upon one's tender skin,/ Caressing others' souls with the blood of one's feelings"; "... That is why a poet will not stop/ Drinking wine when he goes to his torments" (III, 113). "At this time," states Tolstaya, "Esenin felt very ill. It was again conjectured that he had tuberculosis. He coughed, became thinner, was sad and pensive. . ."

In Moscow, Ivan Evdokimov was becoming alarmed by the delay in preparing Esenin's collected works. He sent the poet a letter, and on August 31 Esenin telegraphed back: "I'm coming." This visit to the Caucasus was "far from healing" in its effects, observes Nasedkin, and Esenin returned to Moscow "even more exhausted." Nor can further derisive comments about his poetry have soothed his nerves—on August 25 and September 1 Gaik Adonts published an article declaring Esenin to be "all in the past," "alien to, and far from, the present times," uninteresting and unnecessary as a poet.

Early in September Esenin and Tolstaya left Baku—and Esenin could not resist drinking heavily in the train on the way from Baku to Moscow. On September 6 his refreshments apparently included at least one bottle of port—and an event occurred, which is never openly discussed by Soviet critics. The fullest published Soviet reference seems to be Nasedkin's brief comment: "Returning from his last trip to the Caucasus, Esenin when drunk insulted a certain official. The insulted person brought an action against him. Esenin was distressed and sought a way out. . ."

This threat of legal action hung heavily over the poet's head in the coming months, and he was afraid of being taken to court. Documents in a Moscow archive reveal the exact nature of this incident. Eyewitnesses in the train stated on September 6 that, at some point between Tula and Serpukhov, Esenin caused a scandal when passing from the restaurant car—he tried to break into the compartment of a diplomatic courier, A. M. Roga. On September 8 Roga lodged an official complaint that the poet had made several attempts to enter his compartment. When warned, Esenin "swore at me in extremely expressive words not used in decent society, and threatened to beat my face in. . . By all external appearances Esenin was completely intoxicated. . . On the journey the doctor Levin, a member of the Mossovet [Moscow

Soviet], agreed to examine Esenin's condition, but Esenin would not let the latter approach him and called him a dirty Yid *[obrugal zhidovskoi mordoi]. . ."* Investigation into this complaint was delayed because Roga then went abroad, but on October 24 Doctor Levit[15] ("nationality: Jewish") gave written testimony that Esenin had been drunk and unruly throughout the journey, and had called him a "dirty Yid" *(zhidovskaia morda).* On October 26, the diplomatic courier, Adolf Martynovich Roga, aged 49, gave evidence that "the behaviour of citizen Esenin was outrageous. All the passengers were filled with indignation at his behaviour and drew up a statement. . ." Finally, on October 29, Esenin himself, describing his nationality as "Great Russian" *(velikoross),* wrote out the following remarks in his usual neat handwriting:

> On September 6, according to the statement of the Diplomatic Courier Roga, I on my passage from Baku (Serpukhov-Moscow) allegedly insulted him in abusive language. On that day I was drunk. This citizen made a number of caustic comments about me and pointed out to me that I was drunk. I answered him in similar caustic vein. I did not see citizen Levit at all and consider that his evidence does not concern me. An agent of the G.P.U. saw me and asked me not to go to the restaurant car. I gave my word and did not go. I do not believe in God and have never said "for God's sake" since the age of about 14.[16] I went into no one else's compartment, as I had a compartment of my own. As for the rest I can say nothing. My wife who was sober was travelling with me. People could have talked with her. Citizen Levit made no attempt to examine my condition. This can be testified by the representative of Azerbaijan travelling from the [oil] fields to a Trades' Union conference. I will find out his surname and will tell it by November 4 to the head of the 48th local militia office. Sergei Esenin. 29/X 1925.

After this A. Lunacharsky wrote to the People's Judge, Comrade Lipkin, interceding on behalf of the poet: ". . . Esenin is in this respect a sick person. He drinks, and when drunk ceases to be responsible for his actions. Of course, people close to him will take care to see that such incidents do not recur. But I think that it is not worth causing the scandalous trial of a major Soviet writer because of his bad language when drunk, of which he now very much repents. I would therefore ask you to stop proceedings, if this is possible." On November 12 Ilya Vardin, Esenin's friend and a high-ranking Soviet literary official, added his word on behalf of Esenin:

> To the people's judge Comrade Lipkin. Dear Comrade! In addition to what Comrade A. V. Lunacharsky has said I inform you that the poet Esenin is at present under the observation of the Kremlin hospital. The other day he was examined by a group of doctors from the hospital. In the next few days Esenin will be put into one of the hospitals. I subscribe completely to the opinion of A. V. Lunacharsky, and for my part stress that anti-Soviet circles, above all in emigration, will use to the utmost any trial of Esenin to serve their own political ends. . .

The matter remained unresolved during Esenin's lifetime.

Esenin, 1925. (?)

Chapter Fourteen: "Goodbye, My Friend, Goodbye..."

When he returned to Moscow on September 6, Esenin continued to live with Sofya Tolstaya, although his attitude to her was extremely variable. He was without doubt a sick man, but he refused to submit to treatment in a sanatorium, and persistently drank, usually in the company of chance acquaintances and hangers-on. He still wrote prolifically, but the themes of his poetry became increasingly narrow. The awareness of all he had lost and would never regain permeates these short poems, in which the accordion plays and the poet asks: "Where are you, my joy? Where are you, my fate?" (III, 180). On September 13 he dictated four nostalgic poems dedicated to his sister Shura (Alexandra). Esenin was very proud of his fourteen-year-old sister, and he admitted in one poem that he hoped she would "repeat" his "youth" (III, 181). These poems, which tell of his naive delight at the abundance of cats in Moscow and his love for his native land, with its folk songs and birch trees, are disarmingly simple. Indeed, Nasedkin recalls: ". . . In his last months Esenin was exceptionally simple. He spoke little and in kinds of scraps of sentences. He used to muse for hours on end. . . Throughout 1925, and especially now, he was strongly attracted by simplicity in his relations with people, by simplicity of speech and clothes, just as in his poetry. . ."

This same simplicity may have underlain the quiet registration of his marriage to Sofya Tolstaya on September 18. Alexandra Esenina states that, apart from Tolstaya, Esenin, Ekaterina and herself, only Nasedkin and their cousin Ilya Esenin were present. On the evening of September 18 they drank a little wine and then began to play a game of *bouts rimés.*[1] Alexandra writes that they soon stopped playing, whereupon Tolstaya, as was her wont, tidily gathered up the pieces of paper and stored them away. As a result, part of this game may be seen today in the State Literary Museum in Moscow.

The next day, Esenin wrote the poem "Oh You Sledge! And Horses, Horses!" ("Ekh vy, sani! A koni, koni!," III, 187-

188), which–as Tolstaya notes–was the first of a whole series of short poems set in a winter landscape. Instead of autumnal fading, his mood was now echoed by wintry iciness–the snowstorm, sledge, and memories of lost youth. He seemed unwilling, perhaps even afraid, to write about his present mood; instead, he sought refuge in remembering his childhood years. In "Blue Mist. Snowy Expanses" ("Sinii tuman. Snegovoe razdol'e," III, 191-192) he again returned–in his memories, and apparently also literally–to the place of his birth,[2] and recalled, not only his grandfather and grandmother, but also the snow in the cemetery, where "we all shall be." At his last public recital, he burst into tears when declaiming this poem, and could finish the last eight funereal lines only after a great effort.

Esenin's preparations for his collected works continued to be haphazard and disorderly; he arrived at Evdokimov's office drunk, complaining of people's insults and leaving after a short stay. It was obvious to Evdokimov that Esenin had only a vague idea about the correct dates of several poems, but together with Tolstaya they managed to date them as well as they could and so compile the first volume. The poet showed a marked reluctance to correct the manuscripts thoroughly, but by the end of November all three volumes went to the printer. Evdokimov had noticed the mixture of coarse abuse and tenderness in Esenin's attitude to Tolstaya. "Living in her flat he felt dependent," claims Alexandra Esenina, "and this oppressed him."

Early in October Esenin composed many miniature poems, of four, six, eight, or ten lines. He himself was surprised at his productivity. "I can't stop. I'm like a machine that's been wound up," he said to Nasedkin. On the night from October 4-5 he dictated no fewer than seven such poems to Tolstaya (III, 195-201), a sum total, however, of only forty-four lines. In these poems there is lost youth, lost love, lost happiness, the moon and the snowstorm. His life continued its downward path. On October 16 he complained of financial hardship to Anna Berzin: "My position is worse than that of a pig being fattened for slaughter. . . I haven't a coin. Not even to buy a ticket for the cinema, or for Shurka to travel by tram. . . Half my life for 100 roubles. . . Your S. Esenin. P.S. Don't you use alcoholic drinks. They do terrible harm to one's health and prosperity. I have always known this, and thus I preach it. S.E."

Although he might joke about the evils of alcohol, his condition gave serious grounds for concern. A Moscow archive contains a copy of a letter from the poet's father, Alexander Nikitich Esenin, to his son, written on October 18: ". . . Dear Seryozha spare yourself for us and your sisters, all our hope resides in you alone, you are still very young in years, you ought to live for a long time yet on earth, you have brains and a famous talent. . . There is nothing you lack. Why are you killing yourself, what is it you miss. . . Dear Seryozha! I tearfully beg you to abandon this evil drink. . ." Mariengof comments:

> In the last months of his terrible existence Esenin was a human being for no more than one hour in the day, and sometimes even less. His consciousness already began to darken after the first morning glassful. And yet after the first glass there inevitably followed—a second, then a third, fourth, fifth. . . And so from day to day, from night to night. . . He wrote his remarkable poems of 1925 in that one single hour when he was a human being. He wrote them with almost no crossings-out, and yet nonetheless they were immaculate even in form.

When Esenin told Nasedkin: "I am seeking my perdition... I am tired of it all," Nasedkin's reaction was: "It seemed to me then that Esenin was losing faith in himself. Trying to encourage him, I advised him to stop writing for a while, to take a medical cure against his bouts of hard drinking, to look about him, to find new themes etc. etc. Esenin remained silent." After the end of September he "began to have hallucinations. His persecution-mania intensified." Nasedkin, Ekaterina Esenina and Anna Berzin started to "plot" a forced cure for the sick poet, and invited Voronsky to join their "plot"—but "as yet Esenin would not hear of any treatment." In October, the poet when drunk protested to Evdokimov: "Evdokimych, I don't want to go abroad! They want to send me off to the Germans for treatment! It's disgusting! I don't want to! Why the devil should I! Those Germans!... Everyone is trying to persuade me to go abroad for a cure—including Berzin and Voronsky. They don't understand—I would be worse off there... Oh, Evdokimych, if only you knew how I love Russia!. . ."

Nasedkin, observing Esenin from close-at-hand, noted: "His week was divided into two halves, the sober and the drunk." When intoxicated, Esenin insulted people:

> Sometimes he remembered insults he had suffered two or three years earlier. His old acquaintances kept away from him, and as a replacement bohemia flowed up, beggarly and avid for a booze-up at someone else's expense. At first glance, Esenin when sober hardly resembled a sick man. Only by looking at him more keenly did I notice that he was very tired. His nerves became frayed as a result of trivial things, his hands shook, his eyelids were highly inflamed. Although there were days too when these signs of overstrain and inner ailment diminished. . .

When sober, Esenin read, wrote, and received no guests: "99% of his meetings with them [his friends] took place on his days of hard drinking, in restaurants, pubs, in other people's flats and any chance place, only never in normal human surroundings. In his relations with people one thing was beyond doubt: he befriended and maintained contact only with manifest admirers of his poetic talent. Hence it is so difficult to judge what Esenin really thought of one or other of his companions. . ." "Esenin's drunken raging could not delude one," states Ivan Evdokimov, "it could not appear fortuitous–beneath it people sadly saw an excruciating spiritual drama, whose secret we do not know. . . And he confided his secret to no one, no one. . ."

Esenin wrote a brief autobiography in October 1925 for inclusion in his *Collected Works* (V, 20-22), but, like all his autobiographies, it is fragmentary and at times misleading. He himself evidently felt this–he told Evdokimov in December: "There should be a biography in the first volume. Bung out what I myself wrote there! *It's all lies, all lies!...* I've loved, kissed, boozed... no, that's not it... that's not it... that's not it... I'm bored, Evdokimych, I'm bored!" Whilst it is an exaggeration to say that the autobiography is "all lies," it is certainly true that most of it is a verbatim repetition of parts of his 1922 Berlin autobiography, omitting many of the more provocative details of that former work. Now that he had completely broken with Imaginism, he could proclaim its death: "In 1919 I and a number of companions published the Manifesto of Imaginism. Imaginism was a formal school which we wanted to establish. But this school did not have any ground beneath it and it died of its own accord, leaving the truth with the organic image" (V, 22). He also declared: "I would gladly renounce my many short and long religious poems, but they are highly significant as a poet's path before the Revolution... In the sense of formal development I am now drawn more and more towards Pushkin. . ." (V, 22). Esenin did not end this, his last autobiography, with the same words as in June 1924. Then he had written: "My life and my works lie yet ahead" (V, 19). He can scarcely have believed this now, although Nasedkin notes that "he tried not to surrender the banner of first poet until the end of his days."

Despite the recollection of the Futurist poet N. Aseev that, in late 1925, Esenin "spoke of his good feelings towards us, and wanted to meet Mayakovsky," Esenin and Mayakovsky never became close friends or allies during the years 1923-25. Nevertheless, their relationship was much more subdued in these last years than it had been before 1922, and no doubt this was partly as a result of Esenin's general loss of buoyancy and exuberance after his foreign travels. He now realised that his life had taken the wrong path, and that the future of Russian poetry did not lie with Imaginistic eccentricity. Mayakovsky himself comments on his last meetings with Esenin:

> . . . Then Esenin went off to America and some other places and returned with a clear inclination towards what was new. . . During this period I met Esenin several times, our meetings were elegiac, without the slightest discord. I looked with pleasure upon Esenin's evolution: from Imaginism towards VAPP [the All-Russian Association of Proletarian Writers]. Esenin spoke with interest about other people's poems. There was one new trait in the most self-loving Esenin: he showed a certain envy in his attitude to all those poets who had united organically with the Revolution and with their class, and who saw before them a wide and optimistic path. In this, I think, lay the root of Esenin's poetic nervousness and his self-dissatisfaction, which was strained by wine and the callous, clumsy attitude of those who

> surrounded him. Latterly Esenin even showed a certain unmistakable sympathy towards us (the *Lef*-poets):[3] he called on Aseev, rang me up on the telephone, sometimes simply tried to come across us. . .

Early in November Esenin spent a few days in Leningrad. One dank autumnal night he walked hatless beside the river Neva, shivering from the cold. He explained why he did this: "I wanted to drown myself in the Neva." Then, one night when drunk, Esenin and Sakharov fell asleep on the same bed–and during the night Sakharov was awakened by the poet trying to strangle him: "Esenin was shaking, as in a fever, and kept on asking, as if to himself: –'Who are you? Who?' " Early the next morning Esenin smashed a mirror to pieces, weeping as he did so. He told the poet Sadofev, evidently with Tolstaya in mind: "I'm living with a person whom I hate"–but a few minutes later he added: "I would have been a corpse long ago but for the person with whom I am living... She is holding me back from death." Chernyavsky quotes Klyuev's words, after Esenin had visited him in November: "It is terrible to look at him, nothing remains of the man but his skin. . ."

Back in Moscow, on November 12-13 Esenin wrote down the only extant version of his poem "The Black Man".[4] Towards the end of 1925 he became almost obsessed by this poem, which reflects his alcoholic hallucinations and insomnia. In Leningrad in early November he had recited the poem to Georgy Ustinov. At that time, recalls Ustinov, it "was not yet polished, he mumbled some passages to himself as if trying only to preserve the rhythm, and he said that he had been working on this poem for more than two years." At one of his last public recitals, in the Herzen House *(Dom Gertsena),* he broke down, unable to finish reciting "The Black Man."

The despairing awareness of imminent death now filled Esenin's mind. Hoarse-voiced and intense, he appeared at the Press House in about November–and he again broke down, this time upon reaching funereal lines in a lyric poem. "He was overcome by emotion," writes Ivan Gruzinov. "He could not pronounce a word. He was choking with tears. He stopped reciting. After a few moments he gained control of himself. With difficulty he finished declaiming the closing lines. This public recital was the last in Esenin's life. Esenin was saying his farewell to the stage." In this same month he asked Gruzinov to write an obituary for him, explaining his strange request thus: "I'll go into hiding. Devoted friends will arrange my funeral. Articles will be printed in the newspapers and journals. Then I'll reappear. I'll lie low for a week or two, so that the journals will have time to publish articles about me. And then I'll appear... We'll see how they write about me! We'll learn who is my friend, and who is my enemy!"

It was high time for the poet to rest and undergo medical treatment. Moreover, in hospital he would be safe from the immediate threat of legal proceedings, following the Roga affair.[5] Before subjecting himself to treatment, however, Esenin sought out various past acquaintances, including Avgusta Miklashevskaya. He gazed for a long while at the actress and her son, and then said: "That is all I need... I am going into hospital—come and visit me." Most significant of all, he became reconciled with Mariengof. Shershenevich writes: "Just before he entered the sanatorium Esenin called on Mariengof and said: 'I have come to make it up with you,' and observed somewhat specially, in a friendly way: 'Well, Tolya, when one day you write about me, do not write nastily.' Could one possibly have expected that Seryozha, with his stubbornness, would have been the first to ask for reconciliation, had this not been before his death?. . ."

On November 26 Esenin entered the Psychiatric Clinic of the First Moscow State University. Here, on December 5, a detailed Medical History of the poet was compiled, referring, among other things, to "Delirium Tremens and Hallucinations since November 1925." The Medical History seems to have discovered no active physical illness such as consumption. According to Oleg Leonidov, those who saw Esenin at this time were struck by his cheerfulness and desire to work, but also noted that he "spoke obsessively of death, of the patients surrounding him who dreamed of suicide, of girls trying to hang themselves on their own tresses, of those who stole 'Gillette' blades in order to cut their veins. . . And he said that he himself would soon die."

Esenin's suicide-impulse undoubtedly intensified towards the end of 1925. Mariengof writes: "Esenin's determination to 'depart' was maniacal. He tried to cut a vein with a fragment of glass, to throw himself out of the window, to stab himself with a carving-knife, he lay under the wheels of a suburban train. . ."

His physical condition appeared to improve, after enforced abstention from alcohol for several weeks, but this was not allowed to continue, for Esenin was too impatient to remain confined in the clinic. On December 7, only eleven days after beginning his cure, he sent a telegram to Volf Erlikh, who was in Leningrad: ". . . Immediately find two-three rooms. After the 20th am moving to live in Leningrad. Send me a wire. Esenin" (V, 173). Esenin was evidently planning to break with Tolstaya, for he wrote a note to his wife from the clinic in December: "Sonya. Transfer the room to your name. You know, I'm going away and therefore it's not expedient to pay excess money, especially at high rates. S." V. Nasedkin visited him in the clinic on December 20, and recalled that Esenin was not calm there:

> . . . One old acquaintance came to him several times with a message from Z. Raikh, asking for means for the upkeep of his daughter Tanya. He was threatened by a new trial, there was little money left in Gosizdat, his constant worries about his sisters and parents were a heavy burden on him. The cure seemed too protracted to him. And so Esenin decided to go to Leningrad. A new life lay ahead. He spoke about this most of all. In Leningrad he would perhaps marry, only a simple and pure girl. He would arrange his fortnightly journal via Ionov, he would edit and work. And in spring, perhaps, he ought to go abroad to see M. Gorky. . .

On December 21, upon discharging himself from the Psychiatric Clinic, Esenin again came to Ivan Evdokimov, as he had done briefly a few days before. He was "completely drunk" and in a bad temper, and once more demanded that his money from Gosizdat be given only to him. Accordingly, Evdokimov dictated an application to this effect, which the drowsy poet wrote out (V, 175).

The next day a doctor from the clinic tried in vain to find Esenin, and left his telephone number with Ivan Gruzinov, requesting that Esenin ring him without fail. Perhaps the doctor feared for his safety. In the evening of that day Gruzinov and Sakharov met the poet at the entrance of the Writers' Union Club. Esenin, who was with Klychkov, was drunk: "His lips for some reason were bright red, as if from cuts or bites." He rebuked both Gruzinov and Sakharov for not visiting him in hospital, and they put him on a divan in an empty room, where Gruzinov later saw him, "lying on his back on the carpet, between the table and divan." The poet Evgeny Sokol relates how he spent the night of December 22-23 in Esenin's company. Esenin had drunk a lot in the course of December 22 and had been ejected from the club in the Herzen House following a scandal. At about 11 o'clock that evening he drank some wine and complained: "It's not my fault. They deliberately provoke me into a scandal, they hound me... They're envious of me... The scum... I'm a writer. I'm an important poet, and who are they? What have they written? What have they created of their own? They live on my lines! They live on my blood, and they dare to censure me. . ." Sokol admits that many false friends envied Esenin and relished his scandals. That night Esenin complained bitterly of the neglect and disrespect shown towards Shiryaevets' grave, claiming that people trample on the grave, where "we all shall lie... Perhaps we shall be there soon. . ." He returned several times to this theme, and also recited the whole of "The Black Man." Sokol in turn recited a poem he had written on December 17 and dedicated to Esenin, which includes the line: "swinging in a noose..." Esenin was restless and nervous, and argued at length that only a person who feels pain is entitled to write poetry. He recited many of his poems, on the one theme of death, longing and pain. On the way home he talked of his future, saying that he would undertake a long journey—along the Volga to the Caspian, then to Baku, the Caucasus and the Crimea, returning in autumn to Leningrad. Of Tolstaya he said: "She is separate. She and I are now quite separate." He also said something about a divorce. He did not want to remain alone in the early hours of December 23, and when Sokol went away at about 6 a.m., Esenin awoke his sister and asked her to sit up with him.

The last day of his life in Moscow had begun. He can hardly have slept at all, for if Sokol left him at 6 a.m. on December 23, by 9 a.m. he was in the Gosizdat building, somewhat drunk and demanding money before his departure for Leningrad. Evdokimov saw him there at 10 a.m., and told him to return at 2 p.m. for the money. Esenin agreed: "You're right. I must go to say goodbye to Voronsky. I like Voronsky. And he likes me. I'll go to *Red Virgin Soil.* I need to collect money there too." He told Evdokimov to send the proofs of his *Collected Works* to Leningrad, for "I'm going there once and for all." He was wearing a black silk scarf with a design of red poppies: "It's a present from Isadora... Duncan... Ah, how that old woman loved me!... If I were to write to her now and summon her... she'd come tearing along to me from anywhere on earth... There are some fools... blast them... who say... Esenin is finished! But I shall write... I shall wri-ite! Curing me, feeding me... and so on! The devil take it!" Evdokimov looked at Esenin's face, which seemed fresher and calmer after his weeks undergoing a cure, and advised him to spend a further month in the clinic and get really strong. Esenin replied, rather enviously: "If only I had your health, Evdokimych!" He at last received his cheque at about 4 p.m.

Some two hours later Nasedkin saw him arrive at Sofya Tolstaya's. Esenin was drunk and unfriendly: "He said absurd things to Shura and the others. He was almost beside himself. His luggage was ready. All Esenin's belongings, down to the smallest things, were packed in suitcases. Before he left (saying goodbye to no one) Esenin gave me a Gosizdat cheque for 750 roubles,–he had not managed to call in at the bank that day and was travelling almost without any money. He asked me to send it on the next day. . ." Only a few hours remained before Esenin left Moscow. Sofya Tolstaya was to recall: "Our marital relations were severed four days before his death." He clearly intended to make a clean break with Moscow–hence he went to take his leave of Tanya and Kostya, the two children from his marriage with Zinaida Raikh. He seemed particularly fond of his fair-haired daughter Tanya. He had also gone to see Anna Izryadnova, the mother of his first child in distant Moscow days—Izryadnova remembers: "I saw him shortly before his death. He said he had come to say goodbye. In reply to my question: 'What? Why?,' he said: 'I'm clearing out, I'm going away, I feel bad, no doubt I'll die.' He asked me to look after, and not to spoil, our son."[6] In the evening of December 23 Esenin set out for the railway station with his cousin, Ilya. Snow was falling as his cases were loaded onto a sledge.

Opinions differ as to why Esenin abandoned Moscow and went to Leningrad. This move was essentially different from his recent restless wanderings to Konstantinovo and the Caucasus. When he left Moscow on December 23, he tried to break completely with his past: he said goodbye to his children, and took nearly all his manuscripts and papers with him. It was a bad omen that he began to drink immediately after leaving the clinic (and that he had cut short the proposed two-month cure there)—yet he did assure friends that he planned to work in Leningrad. Shershenevich comments: "We did not understand his path, we did not understand that the tragedy had already reached its finale. . . He went to that city [Leningrad] in order to end his life there where he had begun his poetic work, his poetic life, like an elephant which before its death returns to the lake of its birth. . ."

Esenin arrived in Leningrad on the morning of Thursday December 24, and it appears that he called first at Erlikh's lodgings. As Erlikh was out, Esenin left three suitcases in his room with a note: "Vova, I've gone to the restaurant, Mikhailov's is it, or Fyodorov's. I'll expect you there. Sergei." When Erlikh came home he found the note and went to the restaurant which was shut—but a cab awaited him to take him to the hotel Angleterre, where Esenin had gone to see his old friend, Georgy Ustinov. According to Elizaveta Ustinova, Georgy Ustinov's wife, Esenin almost "ran" into their hotel room at 10 or 11 a.m., and invited them to the room which he had booked (No. 5), to drink champagne to celebrate his arrival.[7] They went to his room, where Esenin told them that he had left Moscow for good, would begin a new life in Leningrad, and "would completely stop drinking wine. He had broken with his relatives once and for all, would not return to his wife–in short, he spoke of a complete renewal of his way of life. He was very elated. . ."

Esenin and the Ustinovs drank the champagne, and Georgy Ustinov prevented him buying any more by saying that he (Ustinov) had to go at once to the office of the *Red Newspaper (Krasnaia gazeta).* Volf Erlikh called at the hotel; Esenin went with Elizaveta Ustinova to purchase some things for the forthcoming holiday (it was Christmas Eve, and Esenin bought a goose, various foodstuffs, wine, cognac and champagne); and then, back in the hotel, he sat and talked with the Ustinovs, Ushakov (a friend of Georgy Ustinov), G. Kolobov and Erlikh. They conversed from 4 till 9 p.m., according to Erlikh; Elizaveta Ustinova declares that Esenin reminisced about the past and spoke of his immediate future. He wanted to share some lodgings with the Ustinovs, "assuring us that he would not drink, that he had come to Leningrad to work and to begin a new life." He also told E. Ustinova that "he no longer wrote poetry but was working a great deal on a large work in prose–a story or novel." (This was evidently a piece of mystification on his part). That evening, says Georgy Ustinov, Esenin drank little, was not drunk, but recited the finished version of "The Black Man" "about ten times," as if he wanted to "instil something in us, to underline something. . ."

From 9 till 11 p.m. the poet sat alone with Volf Erlikh. Esenin "philosophised on various themes: about how good it was that we were both alone again, and that at his age it was time he edited a journal; about the complete 'un-Russianness' of Anatole France and about Pushkin's letters. We talked of many things. . ." In the end they agreed to differ over the merits of two poems by Khodasevich, and fell asleep.

Early the next morning, on Friday December 25, Esenin suddenly decided to visit Nikolai Klyuev. At perhaps about 6 a.m. he woke up and suggested: "Listen, let's go to Klyuev!" According to Erlikh, they remained in the hotel room overlooking St. Isaac's Square until 9 a.m.–Esenin lay in bed gazing at the dawn sky, exclaiming happily: "Look, the dark blue light, the light is so blue!"[8] At perhaps about 9 Esenin and Erlikh set out, but called at several wrong addresses as Esenin could not remember where Klyuev lived. At last they found him. Erlikh writes:

> We got Klyuev out of bed. Whilst Klyuev was dressing, Esenin explained: "Do you understand? I like him! He is my teacher." A few minutes later he said: "Nikolai! Can I light my cigarette from your icon lamp?"—"What are you saying? Seryozhenka!... How can you! Look, here are some matches!..." We started smoking. Klyuev went to get washed. Sergei laughed.—"Let's play a trick on him!"—"How?"—"We'll extinguish the icon lamp. He won't notice. I swear to you, he won't notice!"

Erlikh continues that Klyuev indeed noticed nothing; the artist Mansurov arrived; they all went back to Esenin's hotel room; and Esenin recited some poems. Klyuev left at about 3:30 p.m., promising to return by 9—but he did not reappear.

Esenin had told Erlikh: "Klyuev and I quarrel every time we meet. We're different types of people. But I feel the need to see him. He was once my teacher, and he always will be. I like him." At this meeting on December 25, after Esenin had recited his latest verse, Klyuev commented caustically: "I think, Seryozhenka, that if you collected these poems into one little book, they would become the favourite reading material of all the girls and tender youths living in Russia." Upon hearing this, Esenin "became gloomy," states Erlikh; Mariengof even claims that "after these words, so I was told by a person who does not lie,—Esenin wept." The above episode took place in Esenin's room in the hotel Angleterre, where Esenin had introduced Klyuev to Elizaveta Ustinova with the remark: "This is my teacher, my elder brother." Unfortunately, E. Ustinova soon left the room, and learned only later that Esenin and Klyuev had argued but "parted agreeing to meet again the following day. The next day Esenin said that he had thrown Klyuev out. But that was not really accurate." Georgy Ustinov also denies that Esenin "threw Klyuev out": "Esenin parted with Klyuev in a restrained manner, but even invited him to come without fail in the evening. Klyuev promised, but did not come."

Olga Forsh describes a memorial recital after Esenin's death in which Klyuev spoke of this last meeting: "I am weeping over him. Why did he not listen to me? He would have been alive still! And yet I knew that he would end like this. When we met for the last time, I knew that this was the hour of farewell. I looked: he was all enveloped by blackness. . ." When people objected that Klyuev should not have left Esenin alone, Klyuev replied: "I used to remonstrate a lot with him earlier. . . But do you think he followed my advice? He swore. And once he was all black, then a wise man ought to walk away from him. Otherwise his blackness might have spread to me! When Judgment is being passed on a man, then one cannot intervene. I went home. I did not sleep, for–I was weeping."

Esenin drank little on December 25–indeed, both that and the following day seem to have elapsed without further incident. Erlikh recalls that they talked, drank tea, ate goose, then talked again. The shops were shut for the holiday, and Esenin was able to obtain only a limited amount of beer. He spoke of sharing a flat with the Ustinovs, and of asking I. Ionov (head of the Leningrad branch of Gosizdat) to give him a journal to edit. Ivan Pribludny came for a short while. One evening, before going to sleep–perhaps on December 25–Esenin said to Erlikh: "Do you understand? If I were a White Guard, it would be easier for me! The fact that I am here is not by chance. I am here, because I have to be here. My fate is decided not by me, but by my blood. Therefore I do not complain... I understand nothing of what is going on in this world! I am devoid of understanding!"

Saturday December 26 was spent quietly with the Ustinovs. It was subsequently reported that "during his whole stay in Leningrad Esenin led a secluded life, seeing almost no one except for N. Klyuev and a few other people close to him. The hall porter was instructed to admit no one to see him." Esenin explained this latter action to the Ustinovs as "necessary so that people from Moscow could not spy on him." Elizaveta Ustinova tried to make him feel at home–the samovar was always on the boil, and, when possible, his friends tried not to leave him alone. They had little wine and beer that day, and E. Ustinova (whom Esenin nicknamed "Auntie Liza") asked him why he usually drank. The following conversation ensued, with Esenin speaking first:

> "Ah, Auntie, if only you knew how I have lived these last years! I am so bored now!"
>
> "But your poetry?"
>
> "Boring poetry!" – He paused, smiling embarrassedly, almost guiltily.
>
> "Well, what about women? You have loved and know how to relax among women."
>
> "Huh, if only you knew how many I have loved and in what way, then you wouldn't believe it. Now I am incapable of love *(Teper' ia ves' izliubilsia).* I need no one and nothing–I don't want anything! Now, champagne makes one merry and cheerful. Then I love everybody... including myself! Life is a cheap but necessary thing. Breakfasts, dinners, children, worries, do you think all that is important? You know, I'm a 'God's pipe' *(Bozh'ia dudka)."*
>
> I asked him to explain what "God's pipe" meant. Esenin said:
>
> "It is when a person spends his treasures but does not replenish them. He has nothing to replenish them with and he is not interested in so doing. And I am just like that."
>
> He laughed, with a bitter crease around his lips.

On December 26 Georgy Ustinov arrived with Ushakov and the writer Izmailov; Erlikh also came. "Esenin recited his verse. He recited 'The Black Man' several times in its finished form, considerably shortened." Discussing Klyuev's critical comment of the previous day, Esenin spoke reproachfully about Klyuev, but "five minutes later," states E. Ustinova, "he said that he liked him. Recalling this today Esenin laughed." Perhaps on this same day Esenin said to Erlikh: " 'You know, I'll lose one arm!' He stretched out his left arm and tried to move his fingers. 'Do you see? They hardly move. I went to a doctor about it. He said my arm would serve another five or six years, perhaps more, but sooner or later it will wither. He said the tendons are broken, and so I've had it'."[9]

In the early hours of December 27 Esenin wrote in his own blood his last poem, "Goodbye, My Friend, Goodbye" ("Do svidan'ia, drug moi, do svidan'ia," III, 228). Later that morning, when washing himself, he complained that the water-heater in the bathroom might explode as there was much heat and no water—he even suspected that people were trying to blow him up. After shaving, he washed his wrist and said: " 'Auntie Liza, listen! It's scandalous! There's no ink in my room! Do you understand? I wanted to write a poem and there was no ink. I looked and looked, but could find none. See what I did!' He rolled up his sleeve and showed his arm: it was cut." Elizaveta Ustinova was angry at Esenin's action, but Esenin was unrepentant. Erlikh continues: "Sergei bent down towards the table, tore a sheet from a writing pad, and held it at a distance: it was a poem. Then he said, as he folded the sheet in four and put it in my coat pocket: 'This is for you. After all, I've never written anything for you? That's true... and nor have you dedicated anything to me!' Ustinova wanted to read it. So did I. I reached for my pocket. 'No, wait a while! Read it when you are alone. After all, there's no hurry!' "

By an unhappy coincidence, Erlikh forgot to read the poem that day—the remaining hours were taken up with the samovar, a few bottles of beer, giblets, and people: "Sergei spoke cheerfully and with animation." When the contents of the poem became known on December 28, it was already too late. If the poem had been read on December 27, Esenin's friends would no doubt not have left him alone that night—yet, as Georgy Ustinov says: "But what of the following nights? He wasn't a child to be accompanied importunately even to the lavatory. And he himself would not have permitted this. . ."

The literal text of Esenin's last poem was as follows:

Goodbye, my friend, goodbye.
My dear, you are in my heart.
Predestined separation
Promises a future meeting.

Goodbye, my friend, without handshake and words,
Do not grieve and sadden your brow,—
In this life there's nothing new in dying,
But nor, of course, is living any newer.[10]

There has been speculation about the identity of the "friend"

Esenin mentions in these lines. Volf Erlikh implies that the poem was dedicated to him, whilst N. Verzhbitsky now claims that there is "every reason" to think that it was "addressed to G. A. Benislavskaya, but V. Erlikh, to whom it was handed, did not convey the note to its rightful address." In the absence of conclusive proof, however, Trotsky's view seems the most plausible—that the poet died, "having said farewell to an unspecified friend—perhaps to all of us." Elsewhere in his poetry Esenin had invoked an unnamed "friend"[11]—this was a literary device which lends immediacy to his verse.

Georgy Ustinov writes: "Was not Esenin convinced that the note with his poem had been read by us all, but that we were not paying him any attention, and were allowing him every opportunity and liberty to do whatever he wanted with himself? This would have been a blow for the hypersensitive and suspicious Esenin:—That means no one here loves me! That means no one needs me!" Ustinov continues:

> The whole of Esenin's very last day was torturously painful for me. It was unbearable to stay alone with him, and yet somehow we could not leave him by himself in order not to offend him. I went into his room in the afternoon. Esenin was sleeping with drawn blinds. Upon seeing me, he got up from the couch and came and sat on my knees, like a little boy, and he remained sitting thus for a long time, with one arm around my neck. He complained about the unsuccessful way his life was unfolding. He was completely sober. Then people entered the room. Esenin moved to a chair and recited his verse,—and again—"The Black Man." The painful mood did not pass but somehow intensified, intensified to such an extent that it was difficult to bear... Under some pretext I retired to my room.

On December 28 Georgy Ustinov gave the following written evidence to the police:

> . . . Yesterday, December 27, my wife and I, and comrades Erlikh and Ushakov, who lives in this same hotel, sat with Esenin from about 2 p.m. till 5 or 6 p.m. Esenin was slightly tipsy, but subsequently sobered up almost completely. We talked of Moscow days, when he had lived with me, he reminisced about his first wife Z. Raikh, with

> whom he parted in 1919-20, and about his children who had remained with Raikh, he showed me a cloth document case—apparently a present from her to Esenin, and on the case, low down in small letters written in pencil, Raikh's inscription—something about longlasting love. Esenin considered one of Raikh's children not to be his own and he spoke indignantly about her treachery and falsehood. When we left (we left all four together) Esenin promised to call on me, but did not do so. In the evening I also was unable to call on him. . .

Erlikh remembers leaving Esenin at about 8 p.m., and then returning to collect his briefcase which he had forgotten. Esenin was alone, sitting quietly and looking through some old poems. They said goodbye a second time. "At about 9 p.m.," writes Georgy Ustinov, "Erlikh dropped in on him. Esenin was sitting fully-clothed: it was rather cold in the room. He had draped his overcoat round his shoulders. When Erlikh was departing, Esenin said to him: —'Go, Vova, and have a good sleep! I also shall have a good sleep, and tomorrow—we'll start working! Get us a flat with seven rooms. I'll take three for myself, and the Ustinovs can have the other four'. . ." E. Ustinova suggests that perhaps Esenin draped the overcoat round his shoulders in order to conceal a cut he had just made near his right elbow—this wound, discovered after his death, was shallow, from a Gillette razor. In saying goodbye to Georgy Ustinov, Esenin had asked: " 'Of course, you'll call in on me?'—'Of course.'—'Come without fail, only as soon as possible! Tell them to let me into your room in the mornings'. . ." In fact, Ustinov was visited by the writer Sergei Semyonov that evening from 9 p.m. till midnight, and decided to let Esenin sleep soundly that night.

At about 10 p.m. Esenin went to the hotel hall porter and requested that no one be allowed to come to his room. He allegedly told the hall porter that he made this request "as he was tired and wanted to rest." Voronsky observes: "He undoubtedly suffered from persecution-mania. He was afraid of loneliness. And another thing: people say—and this has been verified—that in the hotel Angleterre before his death he was afraid of remaining alone in his room. In the evenings and at night, before going to his room, he used to remain for a long time sitting alone in the entrance hall. But it is better not to think about this, for who knows what lay behind Esenin's persecution-mania and what kind of illness this was." After this possible hesitation, Esenin returned alone to his hotel room.

He was unaware that in Moscow that night the writer Boris Pilnyak was saying to Vsevolod Ivanov: "You know, Vsevolod, things are bad with Sergei, we shall have to stand in the guard of honour for him. . ." At much the same time, at the 14th Party Congress in Moscow, the Communist leader S. M. Kirov asked Pyotr Chagin about Esenin, and upon learning that the poet was in Leningrad, declared that they would soon continue their patronage of him—for both Kirov and Chagin were to be sent to work in Leningrad. Nor had Esenin read several encouraging reviews published in provincial newspapers only a few days before.

Alone in his hotel room Esenin prepared to meet his death. Several hours passed. In Moscow, early on December 28, at about 2 or 2:30 a.m., Kachalov, Mariengof and others drank a toast to the absent poet. At about 10:30 a.m. on December 28, Elizaveta Ustinova knocked on his door to call him for breakfast: "I knocked for a long time, Erlikh came—and we both knocked. Finally I asked the superintendent to open up the room with his master key. The superintendent opened the door and went away. I entered the room: the bed was not touched, I went to the couch—it was empty, to the divan—no one, I raised my eyes and saw him in a noose by the window. I went out quickly."

The manager of the hotel Angleterre, V. M. Nazarov, gave evidence that at about 10 or 10:30 a.m. E. Ustinova had come to him and asked for a key to Esenin's room: ". . . After opening the lock with a great effort, since the key was sticking in the lock inside the room, I went away. . ." A minute or two later E. Ustinova and Erlikh came rushing to him upon finding the dead poet. The police were summoned, and N. Gorbov, a divisional inspector, arrived at the hotel, where he promptly drew up an official report:

> . . . Arriving on the spot I discovered hanging from a pipe of the central heating system a man in the following state: his neck was not held tight in a loop, but only on the right side of the neck, his face was turned towards the pipe, and the wrist of the right hand had caught

> hold of the pipe. The corpse was hanging just beneath the ceiling, and the feet were about 1½ metres from the floor. Near the spot where the man was hanging there lay an overturned night table, and the candelabrum standing on it lay on the floor. When the corpse was taken from the rope and examined, a cut was found on the right arm above the elbow on the palm side, there were scratches on the wrist of the left arm, and a bruise beneath the left eye. He was dressed in grey trousers, a white. . . shirt, black socks and black patent-leather shoes.

Georgy Ustinov writes: "Esenin died in Ryazan fashion, as the yellow-haired youth I had known. . . Sergei Esenin wrapped twice round his neck the rope from a suitcase imported from Europe, kicked the night table from under his feet, and hung facing the blue night, looking out onto St. Isaac's Square."

Outside the window of his hotel room loomed the huge brooding hulk of St. Isaac's Cathedral. Esenin's suicide was "primitive"—unlike Mayakovsky's bullet in the heart, says Vsevolod Rozhdestvensky; "only women and village lads hang themselves," maintains Alexei Kruchyonykh.

The room in which Esenin killed himself was in a chaotic state—objects had been thrown about, and there were pieces of torn manuscripts. After the first brief announcement of his death in the Leningrad *Red Newspaper (Krasnaia gazeta)* on the evening of December 28, a flood of reports and tributes began to appear throughout the Soviet press. In many provincial newspapers it was alleged that before his death he had "attempted to write a note *(zapiska)* in his own blood." These reports may all have stemmed from the mistaken belief that Esenin's last poem, "Goodbye, My Friend, Goodbye," which was indeed written in the poet's blood though a day before his death, was in fact a "note" found in his room after his suicide. At all events, no "suicide note" has ever been revealed, and nor does there seem to be any convincing reference to such a note in any memoir, published or unpublished.

Certain non-Soviet works contain mystifying and unsubstantiated allusions to a "will" or "testament" written by Esenin before his death. Perhaps inevitably following such a suicide, there are other rumours too. The BBC television film *Isadora* (first seen in Britain in 1966) purported to show a note from Esenin addressed to Isadora Duncan shortly before his death. There seems to be no real evidence that there is, or ever was, a note of this kind.

Shershenevich tried to claim that the poet's suicide was "not the result of a well-considered desire to leave this life. No, it was a fateful error which conquered common sense. And this mistake was aided—by the lonely hotel room and alcohol." The position of Esenin's right arm—raised and bent—when he was found dead led some people to wonder whether, at the last moment, he had tried to save himself. Moreover, the rough-and-ready way in which he had wound the rope round his neck suggested to some that he may have been merely "playing" with death. Georgy Ustinov writes:

> The corpse was holding with one hand on to the central heating pipe. Esenin had not made a noose, he had wound the rope around his neck just like a scarf. He could have jumped out at any moment. Why did he seize hold of the pipe? In order not to fall out—or in order to avoid the possibility of dying? People say that the autopsy established that his death was instantaneous, from a broken spine. Perhaps he miscalculated the force of his fall when he kicked the stool away from under him—and died by accident, wanting merely to play with death? All this is as yet an insoluble mystery... The doctor who carried out the autopsy said—in answer to my question whether autopsies can reveal anything about the last mental experiences...—"Science is powerless here. We can establish only the physical anomalies, but the psyche flies away together with the last breath. . ."

One memoirist, V. E. Ardov, quotes Klychkov as suggesting that Esenin made a fatal miscalculation: hearing footsteps outside his hotel room, he assumed it was Erlikh coming to see him, and put his neck in the noose intending that Erlikh should rescue him. In actual fact, the footsteps were those of a person returning at 3 a.m. to the neighbouring room in the hotel. Although Ardov quotes Klychkov as saying that he subsequently discovered the man who had returned to the next room at 3 a.m. on December 28, this version seems purely hypothetical. After all, Esenin had written his farewell poem a day earlier, he had locked his room from the inside, and his poetry of 1925 is full of the expectation of imminent death. As Leonid Leonov says of Esenin's last poems: "He foretold his end in every theme, cried out about it in every line: one merely needed ears to hear him. But we were deaf. . ." Or, as Shershenevich remarks: "Everywhere in his verse the single theme began to appear–the theme of imminent death. . . We thought it was only a literary theme. We thought it was only a poetic device, and yet it turned out to be the terrible truth. . ."

Many memoirists expressed surprise at Esenin's suicide. Although for several years the poet's mood had been elegiac, people expected that he would struggle on, and suspected also that in "real life" he was not as depressed as the lyrical hero of his verse. On the other hand, many acquaintances felt that his suicide was inevitable and logical. As Voronsky observed: "It is somehow strange to answer idle questions as to why Sergei Esenin hanged himself. In his last poems the poet answers this 'why' publicly, with extreme directness, openness and sincerity, and warns about his end. . . Around the poet there are neither friends nor loved ones, he is a foreigner even in his native region. . . He thinks only of himself, individualism has reached extreme lengths. The poet is ill, he is on the edge of the grave. . ." Yury Olesha ponders: ". . . No, evidently it could only have happened as it did. He departed young, golden, with strands of hair drifting in the air." The critic P. S. Kogan writes: "It is not so much his death that is strange as the fact that he found the strength to live so long. After all, his whole life was an expectation of death. He did not live, but rushed about, sought oblivion, intoxication, but there was no life. . . He was the most honest of poets, for he awaited death and understood its inevitability." Ilya Sadofev claims: "In recent times all who knew him could not conceal their concern for his health and his life." Malvina Maryanova asserts: "He went towards his doom, and no support from his friends could have saved him." Alexei Chapygin comments: "Not wanting to ooze blood any longer in the vomitory of life, he proudly spat in life's face and departed."

On December 29 the official autopsy was carried out. The *Red Newspaper (Krasnaia gazeta)* reported the next day: "The autopsy established that Esenin died from suffocation, in addition to which the loss of blood resulting from the cuts in his veins might in its turn have contributed to a fainting condition. . . The autopsy also revealed that there were no abnormalities in Esenin's brain." "The experts concluded that Esenin's corpse remained hanging for about six or seven hours." Thus, as E. Ustinova discovered the body at about 10:30 a.m., Esenin's death may have taken place at about 3:30-4:30 a.m. on December 28. The artist Mansurov, who made a sketch of Esenin's corpse in the mortuary, later told Chapygin: "I saw him before he was cut open–his body was strong and beautiful, the body of a healthy man, and there were not even any signs that he was a drinker–he was not worn out."

After the autopsy, somewhat later than 5 p.m. on December 29, Esenin's body was moved to the premises of the Leningrad Section of the All-Russian Union of Writers (Fontanka, 50). Many wreaths were laid on the open coffin. A photograph shows Nikolai Klyuev, bearded and hatless, gazing sorrowfully at the dead poet.

Through the night from December 29-30 Esenin's body was taken to Moscow by train. A procession of several thousand people accompanied the catafalque from the station in Moscow to the Press House on Nikitsky Boulevard, where a large banner bore the words: "The body of the great Russian national poet Sergei Esenin lies here." The coffin was placed in the main hall of the Press House, and a large number of Esenin's friends stood in the guard of honour. A photograph depicts Zinaida Raikh, Ekaterina Esenina, Esenin's mother, and many others, beside the body of the poet in the now open coffin.

The public filed past all through the night from December 30-31. The funeral procession, followed by several thousand bare-headed mourners, left the Press House at 11 a.m. on December 31. After stopping at the Monument to Pushkin, the Herzen House, and the Kamerny Theatre, at about 2 p.m. it reached the Vagankovskoe Cemetery. People crowded everywhere–on the trees, on the fences round the graves, and on the high snowdrifts.

Sergei Gorodetsky is said to have recalled that, at the moment when the coffin was lowered into the grave, a woman's voice rang out amidst the silence: *"Proshchai, moia skazka..."*

("Farewell, my fairy tale...").[12]

Isadora Duncan telegraphed to the press of Paris: "The news of the tragic death of Essenine has caused me the deepest pain. He had youth, beauty, genius. Not content with all these gifts, his audacious spirit sought the unattainable, and he wished to lay low the Philistines. He has destroyed his young and splendid body, but his soul will live eternally in the soul of the Russian people and in the souls of those who love the poets... I weep his death with anguish and despair."

Esenin had declared: "In Russia nearly all the poets died without seeing a complete edition of their works. But I shall see my collected works. I shall see them!"

He was buried on December 31, 1925, and the first volume of his *Collected Works* appeared, after some delay, on March 31, 1926.

NOTES

Chapter One

1. Sergei Esenin, *Collected Works in Five Volumes (Sobranie sochinenii v piati tomakh)* (Moscow, 1968), V, 11. All further quotations from Esenin's works are taken from this edition (Moscow, 1966-68), unless otherwise stated. Henceforth references will be given thus: V, 11 (the Roman numeral denotes the volume, the Arabic indicates the page) and incorporated into the main text.

2. Thus the young Sergei Esenin grew up known as "Seryoga Monakh," although the name Esenin has a lyrical sound of its own. He himself rhymed his surname in his verse with *vesennii* (spring-like, I, 250) and *osennii* (autumnal, III, 215)—and several friends, upon first hearing his surname, mistook it for "Yasenin" (which is indeed an alternative form in the family) and linked the name with the ash tree *(iasen')* and clarity *(iasnost').*

There is no agreed transliteration of the poet's name in English. "Sergey Yesenin" is an alternative, but "Sergei Esenin" seems neater and hence preferable. The stress is on the second syllable in both names: Sergéi Esénin.

3. A document of December 1925 includes the information: "Mother's children 14; alive 4." This son, it seems, was called Alexander Ivanovich Razgulyaev.

4. A *verst* is about two-thirds of a mile.

5. The timetable also shows the long hours taught:

Monday:	9-11 a.m. Russian history; 11:30-12:30 p.m. Russian language; 1-3 Geography; 3-4 Geometry; 4:30-5 Scripture.
Tuesday:	9-10:30 Russian language; 10:30-12 Arithmetic; 1-2:30 Natural history; 2:30-3:30 Geometry; 3:30-4:30 Church Service.

Ten minutes break allowed between each subject.

Wednesday:	9-10 Natural history; 10-12 Arithmetic; 1-2 Geometry; 2:30-4 Russian history; 4-5 Scripture.
Thursday:	9-11 Geography; 11-12 Arithmetic; 1-3 Natural history; 3:30-4:30 Church Slavonic language; 4:30-6 Geometry.
Friday:	9-12 Russian language; 1-4 Russian history; 4-5:30 Geography; 5:30-6 Geometry; 6-7 Church Service.
Saturday:	9-12 Church Slavonic language; 1-2 Russian language; 2-3:30 Arithmetic; 4-5:30 Geometry; 5:30-6:30 Natural history.

Sunday: Scripture. Russian language and solutions of problems.

6. Esenin's medical history, compiled in December 1925, refers to measles at the age of three, scarlet-fever at nine, and diphtheria at eight (or perhaps five–the writing is poor). A little later he had typhus–when he was sixteen, according to the December 1925 report, in 1913 according to Sardanovsky. Early in 1914 he suffered from a severe nosebleed, which kept him off work and made him extremely anaemic for a while (V, 49). Sardanovsky recalls how, after swimming across the Oka in July 1914, "Sergei sat on the sand and blood came from his throat."

7. From his letters to a friend, M. Balzamova, it appears that Esenin attempted to break with Anna Sardanovskaya in 1912-13, soon after arriving in Moscow. Some letters exist from Esenin to Anna Sardanovskaya, and their publication is awaited.

Chapter Two

1. At about this time, Esenin wrote to M. Balzamova: "My mother died morally for me a long time ago, and I know that my father is on the point of death. . ."

2. In a letter to M. Balzamova, Esenin characterised a new friend, Isai Pavlov, as "similar in his convictions to us (Panfilov and me), a follower and ardent admirer of Tolstoy, also a vegetarian. . ."

3. Balzamova, incidentally, seems to have been the unwitting cause of the only sharp quarrel recorded between Esenin and Panfilov. In one letter to Grisha, Esenin wrote of Mariya Balzamova: "I've already put a stop to my nonsense with her... It all ended so well–tears when we met, and laughter and pride upon parting. Splendid! the end of a non-start romance!" Evidently Panfilov took offence in some way, and Esenin had to defend himself: "If your letter is demanding from me everything that is beautiful, pure, noble, delicate, but hypocritical then you should know that that is not sincerity... If anything in my letter touched the strings of your soul, then realise that I'm not an abstract idea of some kind or other, but a human being not devoid of feelings and shortcomings and weaknesses" (V, 36-37). In his next letter Esenin proposed that he and Grisha forget their past discord, and the note of friendly, frank self-expression was resumed. The poet also patched up this particular disagreement with Balzamova; his last known postcard to her is dated April 1915.

4. These words seem to be an expression of personal feeling, and not just a reflection of the content of his drama *The Prophet.*

Chapter Three

1. Perhaps some lines in *Chetyrnadtsatyi god* influenced Esenin's poem "Hail, My Native Russia" ("Goi ty, Rus', moia rodnaia," I, 116-117), which was first published on November 14, 1915. This poem is usually dated "1914," on the basis of Esenin's own pronouncement in 1925. The last lines strike a patriotic chord ("... I'll say: 'I don't need paradise,/ Give me my motherland'," I, 117 ["... Ia skazhu: 'Ne nado raia,/ Daite rodinu moiu'."]). Esenin's poem may not have been written until 1915, for these lines bear a marked resemblance to Gorodetsky's words in *Chetyrnadtsatyi god* ("... For if Adam were to have a paradise,/ Then it should be in Russia." ["... Ved' esli byt' Adama raiu,/ V Rossii nado byt' emu."]). Gorodetsky's book was published in Petrograd in 1915.

2. Esenin also befriended Leonid Kannegiser in 1915-16. It seems that Kannegiser visited Esenin in Konstantinovo in mid-1915. Marina Tsvetaeva characterises Esenin and "Lyonya" as "inseparable" friends in Petrograd in January 1916.

3. Lel' is the name of an ancient Russian god, rather like Cupid.

4. Klyuev's date of birth is usually given as 1887, but A. K. Gruntov refers to his birth-certificate, which indicates October 10, 1884 (in the journal *Russian Literature (Russkaia literatura)*, No. 1, Leningrad, 1973).

5. In his later memoirs, written in the 1960s, Ivnev unconvincingly retracted this view.

Chapter Four

1. A non-Soviet writer, V. Ozerov, quotes a note—which he admits may be a forgery—allegedly from Rasputin to Colonel Loman. In this note, Rasputin recommends two "lads" to Loman: ". . . They're fine fellows, especially this fair-haired one. I'm sure he'll go far." According to V. Ozerov, Colonel Loman then decided to introduce the two young men to the Empress. Ozerov is evidently mistaken in identifying the two as "Esenin and Kusikov"—Alexander Kusikov did not meet Esenin until at least late 1917.

2. See p. 39 above.

3. See p. 43 above.

Chapter Five

1. In fact, Oreshin claims that he first met Esenin in the late autumn of 1917 [G. M.].

2. Apparently Zinaida Raikh's mother was Orthodox, and her father renounced his Lutheran faith and became Orthodox upon marrying. Her

mother's mother was evidently Jewish.

3. Vladimir Chernyavsky claims to have been the godfather of their first child, and states that Andrei Bely was godfather to their second.

4. There is presumably no proof that Esenin denied paternity—see Konstantin Esenin's own words, quoted in Matvei Roizman, *Everything I Remember about Esenin (Vse, chto pomniu o Esenine)* (Moscow, 1973), p. 164.

5. See p. 67 above.

6. Seryozha—an affectionate diminutive of "Sergei," often used when addressing children.

7. Indeed, hardly any significant letters written by the poet between mid-1917 and mid-1920 are published.

Chapter Six

1. The Soviet critic P. Yushin has even made the controversial—though seemingly mistaken—claim that, in December 1917, Esenin took an oath of loyalty to the Tsar.

2. This manuscript is in the Central State Archive of Literature and Art, Moscow.

3. See p. 89 above.

4. *aggel* is a Church word meaning "the evil spirit," "the devil," "Satan."

5. In fact, Esenin used to go to the *Chairman* of the Moscow Soviet, Lev Kamenev [G. M.].

6. The title literally means "The Red Ringing," in which "red" may suggest the red of revolutionary Bolshevism. However, *krasnyi zvon* is also a traditional religious phrase, indicating the main peal of church bells, the "beautiful chimes."

7. He was to maintain this practice all his life, and hence recent Soviet editions of his verse, which print many religious words with small letters, are not complying with the poet's express wish.

8. The critic V. A. Vdovin queries this date, and suggests that the poem was composed no earlier than March 1919 (in the volume *Esenin and the Present Day [Esenin i sovremennost']* [Moscow, 1975], pp. 61-62).

Chapter Seven

1. In the Institute of World Literature, Moscow, a fragment written out by Esenin, headed "The Calf" ("Telets"), shows his work on these lines,

confirming that in 1918-19 he wrote obscenely and blasphemously on holy themes.

2. Such attacks intensified in 1920-21. In February 1920 V. Friche was incensed by Shershenevich's lines: "I remind myself of a sheet of paper / Thrown down a water-closet." Friche described Shershenevich as "the creator of tavern-venereal-gambling images," and asked: "Is it not time for the poets of the working democracy to think again? Is it not time they dissociated themselves decisively and irrevocably from Imaginism, which reminds one—I apologise for the expression, but it is not mine—of a sheet of paper thrown down a water-closet?"

In about July 1920 a critic, "Triemia," commented on Esenin's book of verse, *Treriadnitsa:* "The author has taste and ability, but he is hopelessly stuck in the mire of originality-at-all-costs." Reviewing *Treriadnitsa* and Mariengof's *Hands Like a Tie (Ruki galstukom),* "Triemia" observed: "Both books are carelessly published, the proofs have been corrected very badly, punctuation marks are almost totally absent. . . Their price is monstrously high. It is criminal to allow at the present time the publication of *such* nasty little books and at *such* prices!"

Later in 1920 a critic, "Keuk," wrote: "One must sincerely wish that Esenin will shake the dust of Imaginism from his feet as soon as possible and embark upon the right path. He is undoubtedly talented and it will be a pity if he wastes all his powers and abilities on poetic affectation."

V. Iretsky in 1920 attacked the Imaginists' excesses, and continued: "This is particularly annoying in the case of Sergei Esenin. Why does the talented poet summon the esteemed public with the aid of a buffoon's gestures?"

In the Berlin journal *Russian Book (Russkaia kniga)* in early 1921 A. Yashchenko asserted that the Imaginists have "souls full of worms."

Chapter Eight

1. Perhaps Shershenevich meant some of the Imaginist volumes which had no place mark indicated, or the books published under the imprint "Ordnas" (which is "Sandro" spelt backwards—the nickname of Alexander Kusikov).

2. The sixteen pages of *Zvezdnyi byk* contain only 101 lines of original verse by Esenin and Kusikov. Despite the paper shortage, the Imaginists were lavish with pages they left blank.

3. In December 1921 Esenin wrote an inscription to A. M. Kozhebatkin, "my colleague in cards, vodka, and all our daredevil life," and signed himself: "The Soviet Rasputin. S. Esenin."

4. See p. 89 above.

5. There is some doubt about the date of the two letters Esenin sent to Povitsky (the originals are undated). Povitsky himself, many years later, claimed: "They were written in 1920, very soon after his departure from Kharkov, where he was my guest in the early summer of 1920" (letter from Lev Povitsky to the author, Moscow, May 3, 1968). In contrast, some Soviet critics–perhaps correctly–suggest "1918-1919" as their date.

6. Esenin and Mariengof were given equine nicknames–they called Esenin "Vyatka." The titles of several Imaginist volumes are connected with horses–the two volumes of *The Cavalry of the Storms (Konnitsa bur',* 1920); Shershenevich's book *A Horse as a Horse (Loshad' kak loshad',* 1920); Esenin's unpublished volume *Rye-Horses (Rzhanye koni,* 1921); the anthology *The Horse Garden. All the Band (Konskii sad. Vsia banda,* 1922). Their cafe was named the Pegasus Stall (Stoilo Pegasa). Sergei Grigorev made the pun that to write understandingly about the Imaginists one needs to be a "connoisseur"–the French word sounds like the Russian words *kon'* (horse) and *SR* (Socialist Revolutionary). Ivan Gruzinov asserted that the horse is "the predominant image, the emblem of the Imaginists."

Horses figure also in the title of Esenin's poem, "The Mares' Ships" ("Kobyl'i korabli," II, 84-87), written perhaps towards the end of 1919 and first published in early 1920. In this extremely "Imaginistic" and powerful work, the violent images about the "torn bellies of the mares" are based in the grim reality of those days. Mariengof relates that he and Esenin saw the corpses of horses lying in a Moscow street, with crows picking at the eye-sockets. In "The Mares' Ships" Esenin voiced his growing disillusionment with the October Revolution–the reference in the poem to "malicious October" (II, 86) is not merely a lament for bad weather.

7. See p. 118 above.

8. The word "Sorokoust" means a church service to commemorate the dead; prayers for the dead, spoken for forty days after a person's death.

9. In this, Esenin was psychologically akin to Shershenevich, who frequently felt himself a clown, a buffoon, Harlequin. These lines, which Esenin wrote in 1922, echo two lines written by Shershenevich in 1919 and published in Vadim Shershenevich, *Co-operatives of Joy (Kooperativy vesel'ia),* "Imazhinisty," 1921: "What the devil is the use of these eccentricities,/ If I cannot carry them out" ("Na chorta li eti chudachestva,/ Esli vypolnit' ikh ne mogu").

Chapter Nine

1. According to Gorodetsky, Gruzinov and Startsev, Esenin did indulge in occasional "mechanical" experiments at writing verse during his Imaginist period, but this was only a brief phase–his desire to invent a

"machine of images" or "verse machine" was short-lived. None of his published verse seems to have been created by this random combining of nouns, adjectives and verbs originally written on separate pieces of paper.

2. In May 1921 Esenin began a long letter to Ivanov-Razumnik, which he never sent (V, 93-98). Here he sharply criticised Blok and Klyuev for their lack of poetic form and of feeling for metaphors, and Blok and Mayakovsky for their "un-Russian" quality. As in "The Keys of Mary" and "Life and Art" (IV, 205), he advocated images of "double vision" (V, 96-98)–that is, a poetic feeling for the world which was steeped in the ancient merging of heaven and earth, religion and daily life, the metaphorical and the literal. In fact, in mid-1921 he had deepened, but not substantially altered, his poetic outlook of late 1918. He wrote to Ivanov-Razumnik that "I calmly and gladly call myself and my companions 'Imaginists' " (V, 97). By the term "Imaginism" he evidently understood his own development of Scythianism–he longed for the "transfiguration of the world by means of these images" (V, 98), and felt that only Andrei Bely of the original Scythians really understood his attitude (V, 97).

On August 7, 1921 Alexander Blok died. Esenin is said to have resented bitterly the frivolous response of the other Imaginists to Blok's death–yet Esenin himself had passed many caustic judgments on Blok's poetry earlier in 1921 (V, 93-95), and was to attack Blok as a "home-bred Verlaine" in his joint *Manifesto* with Mariengof on September 12.

3. Klyuev was particularly attached to the legendary drowned city of Kitezh, which for him was a symbol of non-industrial, non-Soviet Russia.

4. Esenin seems to have been protesting too much about his lack of fear–in 1921 he also inscribed a book for Ilya Ehrenburg with the words: "... Tell Paris I'm not afraid of it..."

5. Now known as Ulitsa Moskvina ("Moskvin Street").

6. The date 1921 is confirmed by Ivan Gruzinov, one of those whose names appeared on the leaflet. Gruzinov writes: "1921. Esenin had just returned from Tashkent. . . Soon after his arrival the Imaginists conceived, as often happened, a further literary stunt. Late at night we stuck lots of proclamations on the streets of Moscow. . ." And then Gruzinov quotes the Mobilisation Order.

7. This formal division evidently did not coincide with personal friendship. Kusikov, working in the same bookshop as Shershenevich, was apparently more well-disposed towards Shershenevich than towards the two friends, Esenin and Mariengof.

8. Gorodetsky called *Pugachov* Esenin's "best work." Ivanov-Razumnik described it as a "powerful, strong work": "Esenin is very young and promises a great deal. 'Imaginism' is rubbish, dead weight, fetters on one's feet"–but Esenin is a real poet, whose path is still only beginning. Mariengof praised *Pugachov* as Esenin's "first completely mature work," the verse of

which is written "with real mastery and good taste." Ehrenburg called *Pugachov* a "wonderful book... This is a truly *singing* talent." Favourable opinions were also expressed by Mikhail Pavlov, P. S. Kogan, A. Vetlugin, V. Letnev and others. Trotsky, however, found the Imaginist Pugachov somewhat ridiculous, and the play as a whole a failure because of its Imaginistic method.

9. The frequency of Esenin's references to certain months of the year in his works of 1920-22 is revealing: August (II, 102, 103, 183), September (II, 94, 164, 167), October (II, 186, 190). Autumn is ever present (II, 89, 104, 105, 164, 167, 170, 186, 187, 191). Only in memories of childhood and youth could he recall April evenings (II, 100) or a May night (II, 192), or speak of the July rain (II, 168). In the following years, his predilection for autumn and August was to intensify—especially in his "A Hooligan's Love"("Liubov' khuligana") cycle of late 1923.

10. In May 1918 Esenin had published a four-line folk quatrain accusing Mayakovsky of stealing from Whitman.

11. No doubt it was galling also for Esenin, Mariengof and Shershenevich to be called "Futurists" by the critic Ya. E. Shapirshtein-Lers (in his book *The Social Meaning of Russian Literary Futurism [Obshchestvennyi smysl russkogo literaturnogo futurizma]* [Moscow, 1922]).

Chapter Ten

1. In fact, Esenin's height was 1.68 metres (about 5 feet 6 inches), according to a document of July 1923.

2. The word "wine" occurs once in an image in "The Hooligan's Confession": "the wine of my seething hair" (II, 102). There is an isolated prediction in a poem published in 1917: "... I know that as a drunkard and thief/ I shall live out my life" (II, 18).

3. That is, Ilya Ilich Shneider.

Chapter Eleven

1. Esenin wrote to Mariengof on July 9, 1922: "In Berlin I created, of course, a great deal of scandal and commotion. My top hat and opera cloak (sewn by a Berlin tailor) made everyone furious. They all think that I came on the Bolsheviks' money, as a Chekist [member of the secret police] or as an agitator. I found all that enjoyable and amusing. . ." (V, 111).

2. Esenin later claimed that he wrote this poem in "1915." Yet it was first published in February 1919, and Esenin would scarcely have waited four years before publishing such a talented work.

3. The Belgian poet Franz Hellens was at this time working with his

Russian wife on a French translation of Esenin's poems. *The Hooligan's Confession (La confession d'un voyou),* translated by Franz Hellens and Marie Miloslawsky, was duly published in Paris in 1922.

4. See note 1 of Chapter Ten.

5. At Mani-Leib's Esenin recited the conversation between Chekistov and Zamarashkin which opens *Strana negodiaev.* In the published text, the neutral word *evrei* (Jew) appears twice (II, 197). However, Esenin allegedly recited *zhid* (Yid)—and this is supported by Esenin's own manuscript, where he wrote "I know you're a real Yid" ("Ia znaiu chto ty nastoiashchii zhid") and "You called me a Yid!" ("Ty obozval menia zhidom!").

6. This is dubious: there seems to be no other testimony that Esenin's grandfather was ever an epileptic.

7. This reference to Poe and Musset would seem to suggest alcoholism or hallucinations, rather than epilepsy.

8. By the "bearded grandfather" Esenin evidently meant God. In the manuscript of *Zheleznyi Mirgorod,* the poet addressed religious-minded Russians thus: "Go to the devil with your God and your churches. It would be better to turn these churches into lavatories..."

9. This was the first time Desti had met Esenin—her earlier accounts about Esenin and Isadora in Moscow, Western Europe and America were all based on what she had heard from Isadora and others.

10. In the poem, Esenin constantly uses the words "chernyi chelovek" ("black man"). Presumably he did not mean a negro by this phrase, despite Walter Duranty's assertion *(I Write As I Please,* [London, 1935], p. 226) that the poem "described the feelings of a drunkard on the verge of delirium tremens, who was haunted by the face of a negro grinning at him. . . The negro face was that of Claude McKay, the coloured poet who had visited Moscow a year or so before and had been a friend of Essenin. . ." In fact, Claude McKay, whilst admiring Esenin's poetry, writes that he never met Esenin in person *(A Long Way From Home,* [New York, 1969], p. 188).

11. See p. 183 above.

12. See pp. 201-202 and 207 above. The poet's references to suicide in the past years, whether jokingly or in earnest, were now quite numerous. He had referred at least four times to hanging himself (I, 193; V, 109, 118, 122), and once to shooting himself (see p. 138 above). In 1921 he had told Professor Rozanov that "a lyric poet should not live long. Or he should stop writing at a certain age." In 1912 the adolescent Esenin had drunk some poison (see p. 48 above).

Chapter Twelve

1. Recent Soviet publications censor the opening of *Zheleznyi Mir-*

gorod, which in *Izvestiya* began thus: "I did not read L. D. Trotsky's article last year about contemporary art, as I was abroad. I have come across it only now, upon my return home. I read what he wrote about myself and smiled sadly. I like the genius of this man, but you know... you know... Nonetheless, he is remarkably right in saying I would return not the same as I was before. Yes, I have returned not the same. . ." (The five-volume edition merely begins with the words: "... Yes, I have returned not the same," IV, 158).

2. In his "Song of the Great Campaign" ("Pesn' o velikom pokhode") Esenin named Trotsky (and Zinovev) on two occasions, whilst in his poem "Homeless Rus" ("Rus' bespriiutnaia") he also referred to Trotsky. Describing homeless children, Esenin regretted the waste of their potential—they might have become fine poets, such as Pushkin, Lermontov, Koltsov, Nekrasov or Esenin himself. After the last line on III, 55 Esenin commented: ("In them are even Trotsky,/ Lenin and Bukharin..." ["V nikh dazhe Trotskii,/ Lenin i Bukharin..."]).

3. A *poputchik* (literally a fellow traveller) in Soviet literature at this time was a non-Party writer not primarily interested in, inspired by, or reflecting the aspirations of the proletarian Soviet state, but nevertheless not actively opposed to such aspirations.

4. Esenin himself declared in an unfinished article at about this time that the fellow travellers were the "only talented people, able to perceive the pulse beat of our age" (IV, 222), and he expressed admiration for the works of Pilnyak, Vsevolod Ivanov and Mikhail Zoshchenko (IV, 222-224). Vsevolod Ivanov appears to have been a good friend of Esenin.

5. Esenin is said to have met M. I. Kalinin in 1923, and S. M. Kirov in 1924 or 1925.

6. Both these poems—"Don't Curse. That's How Things Are!" ("Ne rugaites'. Takoe delo!," II, 115-116) and "I Shall Not Deceive Myself" ("Ia obmanyvat' sebia ne stanu," II, 117-118)—are provisionally dated "1922" because Esenin gave them this date in 1925. However, it seems more probable that they were written in 1923. After all, the poet did not publish them when he was abroad.

7. Phrases from Esenin's poem to Miklashevskaya, "Though You've Been Drained by Someone Else" ("Puskai ty vypita drugim," II, 135).

8. In the poems Miklashevskaya is shrouded in autumnal mist. Even her name, Avgusta, is reminiscent of the season. Apart from numerous direct references to autumn, other lines describing Miklashevskaya are also in a minor key: "your icon-like and stern face"; "your meek gaze"; "you kiss, but your lips are like tin." She is calm, static: "the golden-brown pool of your eyes," "gentle tread, slender waist."

9. Miklashevskaya married young, but left her husband because she fell in love with another man, by whom she had a son. She did not set up

house with the father of her child, and was "tired" because she had to act at the Kamerny Theatre and in cabarets, and also look after her child by herself.

10. The witnesses for the defence included Lvov-Rogachevsky, A. Efros, A. Sobol, Sakharov, and Vyacheslav Polonsky.

11. In fact, Esenin expressed his contempt for Sosnovsky ("a petty little journalist. . . bearing as close a relationship to literature as does a star in the sky to the sole of his boot. . .") in an article "Russians" ("Rossiiane"), not published during the poet's lifetime.

12. The arrangement of the sixteen poems in *Moscow of the Taverns (Moskva kabatskaia)* (1924) gives the book a profoundly elegiac tonality. The near-hysteria of tavern despair is largely negated by the following seven poems of "A Hooligan's Love," and the closing "I'm Not Regretting, Calling, or Weeping..." ("Ne zhaleiu, ne zovu, ne plachu...") Revealingly, the last lines in the book are: "May you everlastingly be blessed,/ That you came to blossom and to die" (II, 112).

13. According to an unproven rumour, Shiryaevets killed himself because of unrequited love, by drinking poison from a ring he wore.

14. One of the lines in the draft version of this poem is: "I will say a farewell thank you" ("Ia skazhu proshchal'noe spasibo").

In Tver on June 9, 1924 Esenin apparently took part in a recital of peasant poets, held in memory of Shiryaevets.

15. On August 3, 1922 the Esenins' hut had been burned down in a fire in Konstantinovo.

16. The Imaginists' letter was published bearing the signatures of R. Ivnev, A. Mariengof, M. Roizman, V. Shershenevich and N. Erdman. Matvei Roizman now claims that Ivnev, N. Erdman, and Roizman himself did *not* sign this letter *(Vse, chto pomniu o Esenine,* [Moscow, 1973], pp. 241-245).

17. The poem "The Son of a Bitch" ("Sukin syn") was first published on September 23, 1924. It is placed in the five-volume edition of Esenin's works as if it belonged to his Caucasus period, but this seems mistaken. A copy of the poem, not written out by Esenin, is dated "July 31, 1924" (Manuscript Department of the State Saltykov-Shchedrin Public Library, Leningrad, *f.* 474, Album 1). This copy of the poem contains two small corrections in Esenin's handwriting, and is signed by him.

Chapter Thirteen

1. Partly quoted on p. 94 above.

2. Her real name was Olga Kobtsova, according to V. Belousov *(Sergei Esenin. A Literary Chronicle [Sergei Esenin. Literaturnaia khronika]*, [Mos-

cow, 1970], Part 2, pp. 325-326). Belousov reproduces a photograph of Esenin and Kobtsova.

Esenin apparently derived the name "Ol-Ol" from Leonid Andreev's play, *Days of Our Life (Dni nashei zhizni).* In Andreev's play, Olga, a seventeen-year-old kept woman, is called "Ol-Ol."

3. A paraphrase of Pushkin (V, 309). In his more experimental, Imaginist period Esenin had protested against the use of verbs for rhymes (V, 95-96).

4. An allusion to Pushkin's productive period at Boldino in 1830.

5. Throughout the latter half of 1924, Esenin liked alluding to the contest between himself and Marx, although the two contestants never seem to have joined battle in earnest. He declared in June that he had never read Marx (III, 16); in October he referred to the boring wisdom of Marx (III, 46, 47); in December he felt he could not stomach five pages ("The Snowstorm" ["Metel' "], III, 90), and then he felt he *would* be able to understand *Das Kapital* ("Spring" ["Vesna"], III, 93).

6. Soviet critics often quote with satisfaction the narrator's (i.e., Esenin's) reply to the peasants' question, "Who is Lenin?": "He–is you" (III, 284). This was scarcely an original thought of Esenin's, however–the epigraph to an obituary article about Lenin in the journal *Red Virgin Soil (Krasnaia nov')* (1924, No. 1, p. 144) said: "Lenin–is we ourselves."

7. *Pereval* ("The defile," "The pass," "The divide") was a literary group, founded in 1923-24 and influenced by Voronsky's ideas.

8. Tolstaya has added an explanation to Esenin's manuscript: "The letter is to me. He was drunk. July 1925. S. E."

9. Telegram sent by Esenin to Tolstaya, from Konstantinovo, July 15 [?].

10. *Katso*–a Caucasian word meaning "friend," which Esenin often used after his return from the Caucasus.

11. The title comes from one of Esenin's poems (II, 111).

12. Pyotr Chagin's surname was a pseudonym–his real surname was Boldovkin (according to N. P. Stor, Moscow, February 15, 1975).

13. One line of Esenin's "Persian Motifs" derives from Fitzgerald's *Rubaiyat of Omar Khayyam.* The line: "And sold my Reputation for a Song" appears in a Russian translation of 1922 as: "A chest' moia za pesniu prodana" (Edward Fitzgerald, *Omar Khayam: Rubai,* translated into Russian by O. Rumer, [Moscow, 1922], p. 36)–and in one of Esenin's "Persian Motifs": "Chest' moia za pesniu prodana" (III, 122).

14. V, 201 and other recent Soviet publications contain a misprint in the second word, which should be *veter* (wind), not *vecher* (evening). It seems unconvincing to regard this poem as one of the "Persian Motifs."

15. Roga quotes the doctor's name as Levin, but according to other documents it was Levit.

16. A. Roga had claimed that, when eventually confined to his compartment, Esenin had begged the policeman guarding him "to let him go to the restaurant car 'for God's sake' ('radi boga')." Esenin is somewhat facetiously refuting this piece of evidence.

Chapter Fourteen

1. In this game of *bouts rimés* the participants were set two pairs of rhyming words, and had to compose four-line stanzas using these rhymes at the ends of the lines.

2. The first version of this poem is dated September 22, 1925 (III, 355). It appears that Esenin visited his native region for a day or two at this time, returning to Moscow on September 23.

3. *Lef*–the Left Front of Art, a group headed by Mayakovsky.

4. See p. 210 above.

5. See pp. 269-271. On October 25, 1925 F. E. Dzerzhinsky, head of the Cheka (secret police), gave instructions that Esenin should be cared for (according to Matvei Roizman, *Vse, chto pomniu o Esenine* [Moscow, 1973], p. 62).

6. This son, Yury, perished in the late 1930s, during the Stalin era.

7. This seems to have been the same room (No. 5) in which Esenin had stayed with Isadora Duncan in February 1922.

8. Words from the poem "The Hooligan's Confession" (II, 101).

9. Presumably Esenin expressed this fear as a result of the injury to his left hand in early 1924 (see pp. 238-239 above).

10. See p. 148 above.

11. See, for example, II, 125-126 (where Kusikov is probably meant); III, 43; and, above all, "The Black Man" ("Chernyi chelovek," III, 301, 304), where Esenin called out: "My friend, my friend,/ I'm ill, I'm so very ill..."

12. Zinaida Raikh used to refer to Esenin as "moia skazka" ("my fairy tale")–see Matvei Roizman, *Vse, chto pomniu o Esenine* (Moscow, 1973), p. 162.

SOURCE NOTES AND BIBLIOGRAPHY

The source notes for each chapter, and the general bibliography, are intended as a selected guide rather than an exhaustive list. Fuller documentation may be found in the footnotes to my D. Phil. thesis, "The Life and Works of Sergei Esenin (1895-1925)," of which there is a copy in the Bodleian Library, Oxford.

The transliteration system in the Source Notes and Bibliography differs slightly from that used elsewhere in the book.

SOURCE NOTES

Introduction

The Dylan Thomas article, written in the early 1930s, is quoted in Constantine Fitzgibbon, *The Life of Dylan Thomas* (London, 1965), p. 72.

I

Sources on Esenin's childhood and schooldays:

Atiunin, I. G., "Riazanskii muzhik, poet lirik—Sergei Esenin." Biographical sketch, 1926. Institute of World Literature, Moscow, *fond* 32, *opis'* 3, no. 4.

Esenin, K. S., "Ob otse," in *Esenin i russkaia poeziia* (Leningrad, 1967).

Esenina, A. A., Memoirs about Esenin [1960]. State Literary Museum, Moscow, OF 4563/1-2.

Esenina, Alexandra, "Eto vse mne rodnoe i blizkoe... (O Sergee Esenine)," in *Molodaia Gvardiia*, No. 7 and No. 8 (Moscow, 1960).

Esenina, Ekaterina, "V Konstantinove," in the almanac *Literaturnaia Riazan',* Book 2 (Riazan', 1957).

Khitrov, E. M., "Moi vospominaniia o Sergee Esenine," *Spas-Klepikovskii Rabotnik Prosveshcheniia,* No. 1 (Spas-Klepiki, February 1924), [copy in the State Literary Museum, Moscow, OF 477/1-4].

Khitrov, E. M., "V Spas-Klepikovskoi shkole," in *Vospominaniia o Sergee Esenine* (Moscow, 1965).

Prokushev, Iu., *Iunost' Esenina* (Moscow, 1963).

Rozanov, Ivan, *Esenin o sebe i drugikh* (Moscow, 1926).

Sardanovsky, N. A., Memoirs about Esenin, 1926. Institute of World Literature, Moscow, *fond* 32, *opis'* 3, no. 36.

Smirnov, I. E., Notebook containing timetable of Spas-Klepiki school. State Literary Museum, Moscow, OF 475.

Solzhenitsyn, Alexander, "Na rodine Esenina," *Sochineniia* (Frankfurt a.M., 1966)[comments about Konstantinovo].

Titov, Nikolai Ivanovich, "Detstvo Esenina," Memoirs, 1957-62. Institute of World Literature, Moscow.

Vorontsov, Klavdy, Memoirs about Esenin [1926]. Institute of World Literature, Moscow, *fond* 32, *opis'* 3, no. 8.

The manuscript memoirs of Sardanovsky and Vorontsov are particularly valuable, as is Atiunin's biographical sketch. The often published memoirs of Esenin's sisters are sentimental but interesting. N. I. Titov's unsophisticated memoirs, although written many years after the events, have a certain candour, and should not be dismissed out of hand. Iury Prokushev's book is informative, but frequently gives a misleading emphasis in its interpretation of the facts: at all costs, Prokushev seeks to demonstrate the "democratic" and "realistic" bases of Esenin's life and work.

II

Sources on Esenin's Moscow years (1912-15):

Deev-Khomiakovsky, G., "Pravda o Esenine," *Na literaturnom postu,* No. 4 (Moscow, 1926).

Esenin, S. A., Letters to Mariia Bal'zamova ("Neizvestnye pis'ma Sergeia Esenina k M. P. Bal'zamovoi," foreword by D. A. Konovalov, preparation of the text and notes by V. V. Bazanov), in *Esenin i sovremennost'* (Moscow, 1975).

Esenin, S. A., Letter to Lidiia Mitskevich. Institute of World Literature, Moscow, *fond* 32, *opis'* 2, no. 12.

Fomin, Semen, "Iz vospominanii," in *Pamiati Esenina* (Moscow, 1926).

Gorshkov, V., "Odna iz vstrech s Eseninym (Otryvok iz dnevnika)," Memoirs written in February 1926. State Literary Museum, Moscow, *N-v* 116/ 1-2.

Izriadnova, A. R., Memoirs, in *Vospominaniia o Sergee Esenine* (Moscow, 1965).

Kleinbort, L. M., "Vstrechi. Sergei Esenin" [1926]. State Literary Museum, Moscow, *N-v* 11.

Konovalov, D., in the newspaper *Priokskaia Pravda* (Riazan', August 18, 1967).

Panfilov, A. F., Letter to S. A. Esenin, March 2, 1914. Manuscript Department of the State Lenin Library, Moscow.

Prokushev, Iu., *Iunost' Esenina* (Moscow, 1963).

For information about Shaniavsky University, see the book *Moskovskii Gorodskoi Narodnyi Universitet imeni A. L. Shaniavskogo* (Moscow, 1914).

There is some doubt about Deev-Khomiakovsky's accuracy of detail—writing in 1926, he may have exaggerated Esenin's political activity, and the revolutionary spirit of the Surikov Society in general.

III

Sources on Esenin's first months in Petrograd (1915-16):

Arensky, Roman [Zinaida Gippius], "Zemlia i kamen'," *Golos zhizni,* No. 17 (Petrograd, April 22, 1915).

Azadovsky, K. M., "Esenin i Kliuev v 1915 godu (Nachalo znakomstva)," in *Esenin i sovremennost'* (Moscow, 1975) [texts of Kliuev's letters to Esenin].

Babenchikov, M., "Esenin," in the volume *Sergei Alexandrovich Esenin* (Moscow-Leningrad, 1926).

Bazanov, V. V., "Literaturnaia khronika 'Sergei Esenin,'" *Russkaia literatura,* No. 4 (Leningrad, 1971).

Bazanov, V. V., "Materialy k tvorcheskoi biografii Sergeia Esenina," *Russkaia literatura,* No. 1 (Leningrad, 1972).

Bazanov, V. V., "Materialy k biografii S. A. Esenina," in *Esenin i sovremennost',* (Moscow, 1975) ["itinerary" of Esenin's whole life].

Cherniavsky, Vl., "Tri epokhi vstrech (K biograficheskim materialam o Sergee Esenine)," (May 1926). State Literary Museum, Moscow, *N-v* 10/1-2.

Ch[erniav]sky, Vl., "Pervye shagi," *Zvezda,* No. 4. (Moscow-Leningrad, 1926).

Cherniavsky, V. S., "Vstrechi s Eseninym," *Novyi mir,* No. 10 (Moscow, 1965).

Filipoff [Filippov], Boris, "Nikolai Kliuev. Materialy k biografii," in Nikolai Kliuev, *Polnoe sobranie sochinenii,* Volume 1 (New York, 1954), and "Nikolai Kliuev. Materialy dlia biografii," in Nikolai Kliuev, *Sochineniia,* Volume 1 (Germany, 1969).

Gippius, Zinaida–see Arensky, Roman.

Gorodetsky, Sergei, "O Sergee Esenine," *Novyi mir,* No. 2 (Moscow, 1926).

Gorodetsky, Sergei, "Pamiati S. Esenina," in the volume *Esenin. Zhizn', lichnost', tvorchestvo* (Moscow, 1926).

Ivanov, Georgy, *Peterburgskie zimy* (Paris, 1928); revised edition (New York, 1952).

Ivanov, Georgy, Introductory article in Sergei Esenin, *Stikhotvoreniia 1910-1925* (Paris, [1950/1951]).

Ivnev, Riurik, "Ob Esenine," in the volume *Sergei Alexandrovich Esenin* (Moscow-Leningrad, 1926).

Ivnev, Riurik, Memoirs [1926]. Institute of World Literature, Moscow, *fond* 32, *opis'* 3, no. 16 and no. 17.

Ivnev, Riurik, "On ostavalsia samim soboi," in the weekly *Literaturnaia Rossiia,* No. 40 (144), October 1 (Moscow, 1965).

Khodasevich, Vladislav, "Esenin," *Sovremennye zapiski,* No. XXVII (Paris, 1926).

Loman, A. P. and Zemskov, V. F., "Darstvennye nadpisi S. A. Esenina

(Inskripty)," *Russkaia literatura,* No. 3 (Leningrad, 1970).
McVay, Gordon, "Nikolai Klyuev. Some biographical materials," in Nikolai Kliuev, *Sochineniia,* Volume 1 (Germany, 1969).
McVay, Gordon, "Black and Gold: the Poetry of Ryurik Ivnev," *Oxford Slavonic Papers,* Volume IV (Oxford, 1971), New Series.
McVay, Gordon, "Esenin's First Steps to Fame: Petrograd, 1915-16," *Journal of Russian Studies,* No. 25 (England, 1973).
Murashov, Mikhail, "Sergei Esenin v Petrograde," in *Sergei Alexandrovich Esenin* (Moscow-Leningrad, 1926).
Rozhdestvensky, Vsevolod, "Sergei Esenin," *Zvezda,* No. 1 (1946).
Rozhdestvensky, Vsevolod, *Stranitsy zhizni* (Moscow-Leningrad, 1962); second edition (Moscow, 1974).
Sadovsky [Sadovskoy], B. A., "Vstrecha s Eseninym (Iz vospominanii)." State Literary Museum, Moscow, *N-v* 130.
Sakulin, P., "Narodnyi zlatotsvet," *Vestnik Evropy,* No. 5 (Petrograd, May 1916).
Shklovsky, Viktor, *O Maiakovskom* (Moscow, 1940).
Tsvetaeva, Marina, "Nezdeshnii vecher," *Sovremennye zapiski,* No. LXI (Paris, 1936); also in Marina Tsvetaeva, *Proza* (New York, 1953).
Vdovin, V. A., "Nekotorye zamechaniia o vstuplenii Sergeia Esenina v literaturu," *Nauchnye doklady vysshei shkoly, Filologicheskie nauki,* No. 2 (Moscow, 1965).
Vdovin, V., "Materialy k biografii Esenina," *Voprosy literatury,* No. 7 (Moscow, July, 1970).

The quotation from Thomas Mann's *Doctor Faustus* is from the translation of H. T. Lowe-Porter (London, 1949).

G. Ivanov and V. Khodasevich both published their memoirs when emigres.

IV

Sources on 1916 - early 1917:

Gippius, Z., *Siniaia kniga. Peterburgskii dnevnik. 1914-1918* (Belgrade, 1929).
I.A., Prof., "Vstrechi s Sergeem Eseninym," *Grani,* No. 3 (Frankfurt a.M., 1947).
Iushin, P., *Poeziia Sergeia Esenina 1910-1923 godov* (Moscow, 1966).
Iushin, P. F., *Sergei Esenin. Ideino-tvorcheskaia evoliutsiia* (Moscow, 1969).
Ivanov, Georgy, in Sergei Esenin, *Stikhotvoreniia 1910-1925* (Paris, [1950/1951]).
Khodasevich, Vladislav, *Sovremennye zapiski,* No. XXVII (Paris, 1926).
Murashov, Mikhail, in the volume *Sergei Alexandrovich Esenin* (Moscow-

Leningrad, 1926).

Murashov, M. P., "Sergei Esenin," written in 1957, in the volume *Vospominaniia o Sergee Esenine* (Moscow, 1965).

Ozerov, V., "Sergei Esenin (Biograficheskaia spravka)," in Sergei Esenin, *Izbrannye stikhotvoreniia,* Volume 2 (Regensburg, 1946).

Rozhdestvensky, Vsevolod, *Zvezda,* No. 1 (1946).

Rozhdestvensky, Vsevolod, *Stranitsy zhizni* (Moscow-Leningrad, 1962); second edition (Moscow, 1974).

Vdovin, V. A., "Sergei Esenin na voennoi sluzhbe ," *Nauchnye doklady vysshei shkoly, Filologicheskie nauki,* No. 1 (Moscow, 1964).

Vdovin, V., "Dva avtografa Esenina," *Voprosy literatury,* No. 4 (Moscow, 1968).

Vdovin, V., "Materialy k biografii Esenina," *Voprosy literatury,* No. 7 (Moscow, 1970).

Vdovin, V., "Materialy k tvorcheskoi biografii S. Esenina," *Voprosy literatury,* No. 10 (Moscow, 1975).

Zaborova, R. B., "Iz arkhivnykh razyskanii o Sergee Esenine," *Russkaia literatura,* No. 2 (Leningrad, 1970).

V. Vdovin's article in *Voprosy literatury* (Moscow, 1970, No. 7) is the best and fullest about Esenin's war-service. Vdovin has been extremely productive concerning the years 1915-17 in Esenin's life, and has published many valuable articles.

V

Sources on 1917:

Chapygin, A. P., Memoirs about Esenin. Institute of World Literature, Moscow, *fond* 32, *opis'* 3, no. 46. Written in 1926.

Esenina, T. S., "Zinaida Nikolaevna Raikh," in the volume *Esenin i sovremennost'* (Moscow, 1975).

Ivnev, Riurik, in the volume *Sergei Alexandrovich Esenin* (Moscow-Leningrad, 1926).

Levin, Veniamin, "Esenin v Amerike," in the newspaper *Novoe Russkoe Slovo* (New York, August 10, 1953).

Mariengof, Anatoly, "Moi vek, moia molodost', moi druz'ia i podrugi," Memoirs written in 1953-55. Manuscript Department of the State Lenin Library, Moscow.

Oreshin, Petr, "Moe znakomstvo s Sergeem Eseninym," *Krasnaia niva,* No. 52 (Moscow, 1926).

Shabunin, A., "Esenin edet na Sever...," *Sever,* No. 1 (Petrozavodsk, 1969).

Vinogradskaia, Sof'ia, *Kak zhil Sergei Esenin* (Moscow, 1926).

Also the volumes *Skify,* Volume 1 (St. Petersburg, 1917) and Volume 2 (St. Petersburg, 1918).

VI

Sources on the period October 1917 - early 1919:

Bazanov, V. V., "Sergei Esenin i knigoizdatel'stvo 'Moskovskaia Trudovaia Artel' Khudozhnikov Slova'," in the volume *Esenin i sovremennost'* (Moscow, 1975).

Bunin, I. A., *Vospominaniia* (Paris, 1950), p. 16.

Chagall, Marc, *My Life* (London, 1965), translated by Dorothy Williams.

Ehrenburg, Ilya, *Liudi, gody, zhizn'*, Books 1-2 (Moscow, 1961).

Iushin, P., *Poeziia Sergeia Esenina 1910-1923 godov* (Moscow, 1966) [p. 227–concerning Esenin's alleged pro-Tsarist "oath" in December 1917].

Ivanov-Razumnik, R., *Pisatel'skie sud'by* (New York, 1951).

Ivanov-Razumnik, R. V., *Tiur'my i ssylki* (New York, 1953).

Lundberg, E., *Zapiski pisatelia 1917-1920* (Berlin, 1922).

Povitsky, L. O., "Sergei Esenin," Memoirs written in the 1940s-1950s. Manuscript Department of the State Lenin Library, Moscow.

Semenovsky, D., "Esenin. Vospominaniia," in the anthology *Teplyi veter* (Ivanovo, 1958).

Ustinov, Georgy, in the newspaper *Krasnaia gazeta* (Leningrad, December 29, 1925), evening edition.

Ustinov, Georgy, "Moi vospominaniia ob Esenine," in the volume *Sergei Alexandrovich Esenin* (Moscow-Leningrad, 1926).

Ustinov, Georgy, "Gody voskhoda i zakata (Vospominaniia o Sergee Esenine)," in the volume *Pamiati Esenina* (Moscow, 1926).

Vdovin, V., "Dokumenty sleduet analizirovat'," *Voprosy literatury,* No. 7 (Moscow, 1967) [refuting Iushin's allegation about Esenin's pro-Tsarist "oath" in "December 1917"].

Zuev-Insarov, D. M., "O chem govoril pocherk Esenina." State Literary Museum, Moscow, *N-v* 29.

VII

Sources on 1919:

Farber, L. M., *Sovetskaia literatura pervykh let revoliutsii 1917-1920 gg.* (Moscow, 1966).

Furmanov, Dm., *Iz dnevnika pisatelia* (Moscow, 1934).

Gorodetsky, Sergei, *Novyi mir,* No. 2 (Moscow, 1926).

Gorodetsky, Sergei, in the volume *Esenin. Zhizn', lichnost', tvorchestvo* (Moscow, 1926).

Ivanov, V., *Formirovanie ideinogo edinstva sovetskoi literatury 1917-1932* (Moscow, 1960).

Ivnev, Riurik, *Chetyre vystrela v Esenina, Kusikova, Mariengofa, Shershene-*

vicha (Moscow, 1921).

Ivnev, Riurik, "Vospominaniia o Esenine," Typescript written in 1964-66, lent by Ivnev.

Ivnev, Riurik, "Pravda i mify o Sergee Esenine," *Volga*, No. 5 (Saratov, 1967).

Ivnev, Riurik, *U podnozhiia Mtatsmindy* (Moscow, 1973).

Kirillov, V., "Vstrechi s Eseninym," in the volume *Sergei Alexandrovich Esenin* (Moscow-Leningrad, 1926).

Mariengof, Anatoly, *Vospominaniia o Esenine* (Moscow, 1926).

Mariengof, Anatoly, First draft of *Roman bez vran'ia,* 1927. Institute of Russian Literature, Leningrad, R. 1. op. 7, N. 54.

Mariengof, Anatoly, *Roman bez vran'ia* (Leningrad, 1928), second edition.

Mariengof, Anatoly, Memoirs, 1953-55. Manuscript Department of the State Lenin Library, Moscow.

Mariengof, Anatoly, Extracts from memoirs, *Russkaia literatura,* No. 4 (Leningrad, 1964).

Mariengof, Anatoly, "Roman s druz'iami," *Oktiabr',* No. 10 and No. 11 (Moscow, 1965).

Mar'ianova, M. M., Memoirs about Esenin, written in 1955. Institute of World Literature, Moscow, *fond* 32, *opis'* 3, no. 23a.

McVay, Gordon, "Alexei Kruchenykh: The Bogeyman of Russian Literature," *Russian Literature Triquarterly,* No. 13 (Ann Arbor Mich., USA, 1976).

Men'shutin, A., and Siniavsky, A., *Poeziia pervykh let revoliutsii 1917-1920* (Moscow, 1964).

Poletaev, N., "Esenin za vosem' let," in the volume *Sergei Alexandrovich Esenin* (Moscow-Leningrad, 1926).

Shershenevich, Vadim, "Pamiati Sergeia Esenina," *Sovetskoe iskusstvo,* No. 1 (Moscow-Leningrad, 1926).

Shershenevich, Vadim, "O druge," in the volume *Esenin. Zhizn', lichnost', tvorchestvo* (Moscow, 1926).

Siniavsky, A.—see Men'shutin, A.

Startsev, Ivan, "Moi vstrechi s Eseninym," in the volume *Sergei Alexandrovich Esenin* (Moscow-Leningrad, 1926).

Vasilevsky, L., "Kafe snobov (Pis'mo iz Moskvy)," *Vestnik Literatury,* No. 7 (Petrograd, 1919).

Vygodsky, David, Notes about Esenin. Manuscript Department of the State Saltykov-Shchedrin Public Library, Leningrad, *f.* 276, *op.* 1, *ed. khr.* 5.

See also the leading article, "Nezhelatel'nye vystupleniia," in the journal *Vestnik Literatury,* No. 10 (Petrograd, 1919); and the article by "Staryi pisatel'," entitled "Novoe poeticheskoe stoilo," in *Vestnik Literatury,* No. 11 (Petrograd, 1919).

Several of the above memoirists (notably Mariengof and Shershenevich) offer information covering the following years also.

VIII

Sources on 1920:

Annenkov, Iury, "Vokrug Esenina," *Opyty*, No. 3 (New York, 1954).

Annenkov, Iury, *Dnevnik moikh vstrech. Tsikl tragedii,* Volume 1 (New York, 1966).

Aseev, N., "Tri vstrechi s Eseninym," in the volume *Sergei Alexandrovich Esenin* (Moscow-Leningrad, 1926).

Chapygin, A. P., Memoirs about Esenin. Institute of World Literature, Moscow, *fond* 32, *opis'* 3, no. 46.

Esenin, S. A., Letters to L. O. Povitsky [not included in the five-volume editions of Esenin's works]. Institute of World Literature, Moscow, *fond* 32, *opis'* 2, no. 14.

German, Emmanuil, "Serezha," in the newspaper *Vecherniaia Moskva* (Moscow, December 31, 1925).

Grigor'ev, Sergei, *Obraz Konenkova* (Moscow, 1921).

Markov, V., "Legenda o Esenine," *Grani,* No. 25 (Frankfurt a.M., 1955).

McVay, Gordon, "Sergei Esenin and Lev Povitsky," *Russian Literature Triquarterly,* No. 4 (Michigan, U.S.A., 1972) [extracts from Povitsky's memoirs; texts and photocopies of Esenin's letters to Povitsky].

Povitsky, L. O., Memoirs written in the 1940s-1950s. Manuscript Department of the State Lenin Library, Moscow [partly published in *Neva,* No. 5 (Leningrad, 1969)].

Samobytnik, A., poem entitled "Mashinnyi rai," *Griadushchee,* No. 1-2 (Petrograd, 1920).

Vol'pin, Valentin, "O Sergee Esenine," in the volume *Sergei Alexandrovich Esenin* (Moscow-Leningrad, 1926).

Works of Imaginist theory include:

Avraamov, Arseny, *Voploshchenie. Esenin-Mariengof* (Moscow, 1921).

Grigor'ev, Sergei, *Proroki i predtechi poslednego zaveta. Imazhinisty. Esenin, Kusikov, Mariengof* (SAAV, 1921).

Gruzinov, Ivan, *Imazhinizma osnovnoe* (Moscow, 1921) [written in June 1920].

Mariengof, Anatoly, *Buian-ostrov. Imazhinizm* (Moscow, 1920).

Shershenevich, Vadim, "Slovogranil'nia (Ob Imazhinizme)," *Znamia,* No. 3-4 (5-6) (May-June, 1920).

Shershenevich, Vadim, *2 x 2 = 5. Listy imazhinista* (Moscow, 1920).

Sokolov, Ippolit, *Imazhinistika* (Ordnas, 1921).

For an exposition of some of these theoretical works, see C. V. Ponomareff, "The Image Seekers: An Analysis of Imaginist Poetic Theory, 1919-1924," in *The Slavic and East European Journal,* published by the University of Wisconsin Press, Fall 1968, Volume XII, No. 3.

IX

Sources on 1921 - May 1922:

Abramovich, N. Ia., *Sovremennaia lirika* (Moscow, 1921).

Ehrenburg, Ilya, *Liudi, gody, zhizn',* Books 1-2 (Moscow, 1961).

Esenin, S., and Mariengof, A., *Manifesto* of September 12, 1921, in the projected book *Epokha Esenina i Mariengofa* (incomplete copy of the book in the State Literary Museum, Moscow, OF 5008). Published by V. Belousov, *Sergei Esenin. Literaturnaia khronika,* Part 2 (Moscow, 1970), pp. 244-245.

Gruzinov, Ivan, *Imazhinizma osnovnoe* (Moscow, 1921).

Gruzinov, Ivan, "Esenin," in the volume *Sergei Alexandrovich Esenin* (Moscow-Leningrad, 1926).

Iashchenko, A., "Russkaia poeziia za poslednie tri goda," *Russkaia kniga,* No. 3 (Berlin, March, 1921).

Iretsky, V., "Plavil'nia slov," *Vestnik Literatury,* No. 9 (21) (1920).

Lunacharsky, A., "Svoboda knigi i revoliutsiia," *Pechat' i revoliutsiia,* No. 1 (Moscow, 1921), May-July.

L'vov-Rogachevsky, V., *Imazhinizm i ego obrazonostsy. Esenin, Kusikov, Mariengof, Shershenevich* (Ordnas, 1921).

Mariengof, Anatoly, Manuscript of *Roman bez vran'ia,* 1927. Institute of Russian Literature, Leningrad, R. 1, op. 7, N. 54 [containing *chastushki* of Esenin].

Shershenevich, Vadim, *Komu ia zhmu ruku* [1921; also entitled *Shershenevich zhmet ruku komu]*.

Shershenevich, V., "Rul' napravo!," *Teatral'naia Moskva,* No. 31 (Moscow, March 14, 1922).

Shershenevich, Vadim, "Poety dlia teatra," *Teatral'naia Moskva*, No. 34 (Moscow, April 4, 1922).

Shiriaevets, A. V., *Kamenno-zheleznoe chudishche ("O gorode. Gorod, gorozhanin i poselianin v poezii poslednego vremeni"),* written in October 1920. Institute of World Literature, Moscow, *fond* 29, *opis'* 1, no. 280.

Surma, Iu., *Slovo v boiu (Estetika Maiakovskogo i literaturnaia bor'ba 20-kh godov)* (Leningrad, 1963).

Vol'pin, Valentin, in the volume *Sergei Alexandrovich Esenin* (Moscow-Leningrad, 1926).

X

Sources on Esenin and Isadora Duncan in 1921-22:

Babenchikov, M., in the volume *Sergei Alexandrovich Esenin* (Moscow-Leningrad, 1926).

Benislavskaia, G., Memoirs. Quoted in V. Belousov, *Sergei Esenin. Literaturnaia khronika,* Part 2 (Moscow, 1970), p. 91.

Desti, Mary, *Isadora Duncan's End* (London, 1929).

Duncan, Irma, and Macdougall, Allan Ross, *Isadora Duncan's Russian Days and Her Last Years in France* (London, 1929).

Duncan, Isadora, *My Life* (London, 1928) (and many reprintings).

Gal'perin, Iu., *Literaturnye vechera* (Moscow, 1974) [the section "Nasha Eseniniana" reproduces the spoken memoirs of Avgusta Miklashevskaia and Anna Nikritina].

Hurok, Sol, *Impresario.* A memoir, in collaboration with Ruth Goode (London, 1947).

Lunacharsky, A., Memoirs about Isadora Duncan, in the volume *Gul zemli* (Leningrad, 1928).

McVay, Gordon, "Sergei Esenin and Isadora Duncan," *Slavic and East-European Studies,* Volume XVI (Quebec, 1971) (published 1972).

Nikritina, A. B., "Esenin i Mariengof," in the volume *Esenin i sovremennost'* (Moscow, 1975).

Sabaneev, L., "Moi vstrechi: Isadora Duncan," in the newspaper *Novoe Russkoe Slovo* (New York, February 15, 1953).

Seroff, Victor, *The Real Isadora* (New York, 1971); (London, 1972).

Shneider, Il'ia, *Vstrechi s Eseninym* (Moscow, 1965); expanded edition, (Moscow, 1974) [weak memoirs].

Shneider, Il'ia [here transliterated as Ilya Ilyich Schneider], *Isadora Duncan. The Russian Years,* translated by David Magarshack (London, 1968) [weak memoirs].

Vdovin, V., "Zarubezhnaia poezdka Esenina," *Voprosy literatury,* No. 10 (Moscow, 1966).

The Dylan Thomas letter of 1935 is quoted in Constantine Fitzgibbon, *The Life of Dylan Thomas* (London, 1965), pp. 192-193.

The books of Irma Duncan and Allan Ross Macdougall, Mary Desti, Sol Hurok, Victor Seroff and Il'ia Shneider (none of them wholly reliable) also offer much information about Esenin's foreign travels in 1922-23.

XI

Sources on Esenin's foreign travels in 1922-23:

Belousov, V., "Sergei Esenin za granitsei," *Oktiabr',* No. 5 (Moscow, 1958).

Gor'ky, M., Letter to E. K. Ferrari, October 10, 1922. Quoted in the volume *Vladimir Maiakovskii,* Volume 1 (Moscow-Leningrad, 1940), p. 87, edited by A. L. Dymshits and O. V. Tsekhnovitser; and in the volume *Gor'kii i sovetskie pisateli. Neizdannaia perepiska,* Volume 70 (Moscow, 1963),

"Literaturnoe nasledstvo," p. 568.

Gor'ky, M., "Sergei Esenin" (first published in 1927), in M. Gor'ky, *Sobranie sochinenii v tridtsati tomakh,* Volume 17 (Moscow, 1952).

Gul' [Goul], Roman, *Zhizn' na fuksa* (Moscow-Leningrad, 1927).

Huddleston, Sisley, *Bohemian Literary and Social Life in Paris* (London, 1928).

Kinel, Lola, *Under Five Eagles. My Life in Russia, Poland, Austria, Germany and America, 1916-1936* (London, 1937).

Levin, Veniamin, "Esenin v Amerike," in the newspaper *Novoe Russkoe Slovo* (New York, August 11, 12, and 13, 1953).

Lundberg, E., *Zapiski pisatelia 1920-1924,* Volume 2 (Leningrad, 1930).

McVay, G., "An Unpublished Letter by Sergey Yesenin," *The Slavonic and East European Review,* Volume XLVI, No. 107 (London, July 1968) [letter to Alexander Kusikov, dated February 7, 1923]. Republished by R. Goul (Gul'), in *Novyi zhurnal,* No. 95 (New York, 1969).

McVay, Gordon, "Sergey Esenin in America," *Oxford Slavonic Papers,* Volume VI (Oxford, 1973), New Series.

Merkur'ev, I. (Finkel'shtein, I.), letter in the literary supplement No. 7 to the newspaper *Nakanune* (Berlin, June 11, 1922).

Shershenevich, Vadim, "Ne slova, a fakty," *Teatral'naia Moskva,* No. 43 (Moscow, June 7-11, 1922).

Shklovsky, Viktor, *O Maiakovskom* (Moscow, 1940).

Stokes, Sewell, *Isadora Duncan. An Intimate Portrait* (London, 1928).

Tolstaia-Krandievskaia, N. V., "Sergei Esenin i Isadora Duncan. Vstrechi," in the volume *Vospominaniia o Sergee Esenine* (Moscow, 1965).

Vasil'evsky, I. (Ne-Bukva), in the literary supplement No. 11 to the newspaper *Nakanune* (Berlin, July 30, 1922).

Vdovin, V., "Napisano rukoi Esenina...," *Voprosy literatury,* No. 7 (Moscow, 1968) [pp. 252-254—concerning the manuscript of *Zheleznyi Mirgorod*].

Vetlugin, A., "Nezhnaia bolezn'," in the literary supplement No. 6 to the newspaper *Nakanune* (Berlin, June 4, 1922).

Yarmolinsky, A., "Esenin v N'iu-Iorke," *Novyi zhurnal,* No. 51 (New York, 1957) [including the full text of Esenin's letter to Mani-Leib].

The Russian language Berlin newspaper *Nakanune* in May-June 1922 contains numerous references to Esenin. The arrival of Esenin and Isadora in New York on October 1, 1922, and their departure on February 3, 1923, are described in detail in newspapers of the following day, October 2, 1922 and February 4, 1923—e.g., the *New York Herald, New York Times* and *New York Tribune.*

XII

Sources on the period late 1923 - late 1924:

Benislavskaia, G., Memoirs. Quoted in V. Belousov, *Sergei Esenin. Literaturnaia khronika,* Part 2 (Moscow, 1970), p. 94.

Berzin', A. A., Letters to S. A. Esenin [1924]. State Literary Museum, Moscow, 25/1-5.

Blagoi, D., "Materialy k kharakteristike Sergeia Esenina," *Krasnaia nov',* No. 2 (1926).

Borisov, S., "K biografii Sergeia Esenina," *Krasnaia niva,* No. 2 (Moscow, January 10, 1926).

Cherniavsky, Vl., Memoirs. State Literary Museum, Moscow, *N-v* 10/1-2.

D'or, O. L., "Sergei Esenin v Amerike," in the newspaper *Pravda* (Moscow, August 28, 1923) [parody of *Zheleznyi Mirgorod]*.

Efimov, Bor., cartoon in *Krokodil,* No. 1 (Moscow, January 13, 1924), (80).

Esenin, S. A., Manuscript of poem about Lenin [1924]. Manuscript Department of the State Lenin Library, Moscow.

Esenin, S. A., Photocopy of a letter to G. Benislavskaia, after April 28, 1924. Institute of World Literature, Moscow, *fond* 32, *opis'* 5, no. 9.

Esenin, S. A., Manuscript of his Autobiography, June 20, 1924. Institute of World Literature, Moscow, *fond* 32, *opis'* 2, no. 1.

Evdokimov, Ivan, Typescript of memoirs. Institute of World Literature, Moscow, *fond* 32, *opis'* 3, no. 12.

Fomin, Semen, in the volume *Pamiati Esenina* (Moscow, 1926).

Ivanov-Razumnik, R., *Pisatel'skie sud'by* (New York, 1951).

Ivnev, R., Mariengof, A., Roizman, M., Shershenevich, V., Erdman, N., Letter to the editors, published in *Novyi zritel',* No. 35 (Moscow, September 9, 1924).

Leonidov, Oleg, "Zhivoi Esenin," in the newspaper *Krasnaia gazeta,* No. 20 (Leningrad, January 21, 1926), evening edition.

Liakhovets, D., "Moe interv'iu (Vmesto fel'etona)," in the newspaper *Vechernie Izvestiia* (Moscow, May 12, 1924) [mock interview with Esenin, alluding to the poet's drunkenness, debauchery, and anti-Semitism] .

L'vov-Rogachevsky, V., Introductory article in the book A. Shiriaevets, *Volzhskie pesni* (Moscow, 1928).

Miklashevskaia, Avgusta, "Vospominaniia o Esenine," written in 1958. State Literary Museum, Moscow, *N-v* 269.

Miklashevskaia, Avgusta, "Sergei Esenin," *Don,* No. 2 (Rostov-on-Don, 1963).

Naumov, E. I., "K istorii odnoi druzhby (S. Esenin i G. Benislavskaia)," *Russkaia literatura,* No. 3 (Leningrad, 1970).

Nazarova, A., Memoirs. State Literary Museum, Moscow, *N-v* 120.

Nikritina, A. B., Letter to the author (Leningrad, February 4, 1968).

Oksenov, Innokenty, "O sud'be Esenina." Institute of World Literature, Moscow, *fond* 32, *opis'* 3, no. 27.

Oksenov, Innokenty, "Iz vospominanii o Sergee Esenine," in the volume *Pamiati Esenina* (Moscow, 1926).

Polonsky, Viach., "Pamiati Esenina," *Novyi mir,* No. 1 (Moscow, 1926).

Roizman, M., " 'Vol'nodumets' Esenina," in the volume *Vospominaniia o Sergee Esenine* (Moscow, 1965).

Shershenevich, V., Letter to A. Kusikov, January 23, 1924. In the possession of A. Kusikov, Paris.

Trotsky, L., *Literatura i revoliutsiia* (Moscow, 1923) [Trotsky had discussed Esenin in the newspaper *Pravda,* Moscow, October 5, 1922].

Tynianov, Iu., "Promezhutok," *Russkii Sovremennik,* No. 4 (Moscow-Leningrad, 1924).

Volin, Boris, editor, *Krasnyi Perets,* No. 16 (Moscow, December 1923).

Voronsky, A., "O proletarskom iskusstve i o khudozhestvennoi politike nashei partii," *Krasnaia nov',* No. 7 (17) (Moscow, December 1923).

Voronsky, A., "Literaturnye siluety: Sergei Esenin," *Krasnaia nov',* No. 1 (Moscow, 1924).

Voronsky, A., *Krasnaia nov',* No. 5 (22) (Moscow, August-September 1924).

Voronsky, A., "Pamiati o Esenine," *Krasnaia nov',* No. 2 (Moscow, 1926).

Voronsky, A., "Ob otoshedshem," in Sergei Esenin, *Sobranie stikhotvorenii,* Volume 1 (Moscow-Leningrad, 1926).

Zakharov-Mensky, N., "Tol'ko neskol'ko slov" [1926]. State Literary Museum, Moscow, *N-v* 152.

Zamiatin, Evg., *Russkii Sovremennik,* No. 2 (Moscow-Leningrad, 1924).

Zoshchenko, Mikh., "Pered voskhodom solntsa," *Oktiabr',* No. 6-7 (1943).

XIII

Sources on the period September 1924 - late 1925:

Adonts, Gaik, "O poezii Esenina," *Zhizn' iskusstva,* No. 34, August 25, and No. 35, September 1 (Leningrad-Moscow, 1925).

Bebutov, G., *Otrazheniia* (Tbilisi, 1973).

Belousov, V., *Sergei Esenin* (Moscow, 1965), pp. 7-50 [Belousov has written numerous articles about Shagane, grossly exaggerating her importance in Esenin's life].

Chagin, P., Foreword to Esenin's volume *Rus' sovetskaia* (Baku, 1925).

Chagin, Petr, "Sergei Esenin v Baku," in the weekly *Literaturnaia Rossiia,* No. 40 (Moscow, 1965).

Erlikh, Vol'f, *Pravo na pesn'* (Leningrad, 1930).

Esenin, S. A., Typewritten copy of his letter to his sister Ekaterina, September 17, 1924. State Literary Museum, Moscow, 430/1-2.

Esenin, S. A., Notes to Sof'ia Tolstaia. State Literary Museum, Moscow,

374/2, 374/3, 374/7.

Esenin, S. A., Declaration to the police, October 29, 1925. Institute of World Literature, Moscow, *fond* 32, *opis'* 2, no. 33 [Documents concerning the incident of September 6, 1925 are found in the Institute of World Literature, Moscow, *fond* 32, *opis'* 2, nos. 28-36].

Esenina, Ekaterina, Letter to S. A. Esenin, December 30, 1924. State Literary Museum, Moscow, 38.

Evdokimov, Ivan, "Sergei Alexandrovich Esenin," in the volume *Sergei Alexandrovich Esenin* (Moscow-Leningrad, 1926).

Fainshtein, Lev, "Sergei Esenin v Baku," in the volume *Sergei Alexandrovich Esenin* (Moscow-Leningrad, 1926).

Kachalov, V. I., "Vstrechi s Eseninym," *Krasnaia niva,* No. 2 (Moscow, 1928).

Leonidze, Georgy, "Ia vizhu etogo cheloveka," *Literaturnaia Gruziia,* No. 5 (Tbilisi, 1967).

Lezhnev, A., Review of Esenin's volume *Strana sovetskaia,* in the newspaper *Pravda* (Moscow, March 15, 1925).

Libedinsky, Iu., *Sovremenniki* (Moscow, 1961).

Lunacharsky, A., Letter to the People's Judge, Comrade Lipkin [November 1925]. Institute of World Literature, Moscow, *fond* 32, *opis'* 2, no. 34.

Manuilov, V., "O Sergee Esenine," *Zvezda,* No. 2 (Leningrad, 1972).

Mar, S., in the newspaper *Novaia vecherniaia gazeta* (Leningrad, December 29, 1925) [seen in a file of cuttings, State Literary Museum, Moscow, *N-v* 44].

McVay, G., "Pis'ma i zapiski S. Esenina," *Novyi zhurnal,* No. 109 (New York, 1972) [including copies of Esenin's letters to his sister, Ekaterina, September 17, 1924, and to his father, August 20, 1925, and materials on the incident of September 6, 1925; also Esenin's notes to Sof'ia Tolstaia, 1925].

Narin'iani, Sem., "Strochka nonpareli," *Ogonek,* No. 1 (Moscow, 1959).

Nasedkin, V., Letter to S. A. Esenin [August 1925]. State Literary Museum, Moscow, 385.

Nasedkin, V., *Poslednii god Esenina* (Moscow, 1927).

Selikhanovich, Alexander, in the newspaper *Bakinskii rabochii* (Baku, September 25, 1924).

Shipov, Andrei [the pseudonym of Ivan Rozanov], Review of Esenin's volume *Stikhi (1920-1924)* in *Narodnyi Uchitel',* No. 2 (Moscow, February, 1925).

Shveitser, Vladimir, "Etiudy k portretam," *Moskva,* No. 2 (Moscow, 1964).

Sokolov, K. A., Letters to S. A. Esenin, December 1924. State Literary Museum, Moscow, 59/1-2.

Stor, Nikolai, "Sergei Esenin," in the newspaper *Zaria Vostoka* (Tiflis, December 30, 1925).

Tabidze, N. A., "Zolotaia moneta," in the volume *Vospominaniia o Sergee*

Esenine (Moscow, 1965).
Tolstaia, S. A., Notes to Sergei Esenin. State Literary Museum, Moscow, 389/1, 389/2, 389/4.
Tolstaia, S. A., Commentary on Esenin's poems, State Literary Museum, Moscow, 439/1.
Vardin, Il'ia, Letter to the People's Judge, Comrade Lipkin, November 12, 1925. Institute of World Literature, Moscow, *fond* 32, *opis'* 2, no. 35.
Verzhbitsky, Nikolai, Letters to S. A. Esenin [1924-25]. State Literary Museum, Moscow, 29/1-5.
Verzhbitsky, Nikolai, *Vstrechi s Eseninym* (Tbilisi, 1961) [unreliable memoirs].
Vinogradskaia, Sof'ia, *Kak zhil Sergei Esenin* (Moscow, 1926).
Voronsky, A., "Literaturnye zametki," *Prozhektor,* No. 5 (Moscow, March 15, 1925).

XIV

Sources on late 1925, and since:

Ardov, V. E., "Dva slova o Esenine," Memoirs. Institute of World Literature, Moscow, *fond* 32, *opis'* 3, no. 3.
Aseev, N., in the volume *Sergei Alexandrovich Esenin* (Moscow-Leningrad, 1926).
Berzin', Anna, "Poslednie dni Esenina," *Kuban',* No. 7 (Krasnodar, 1970).
Erlikh, Vol'f, "Chetyre dnia," in the volume *Pamiati Esenina* (Moscow, 1926).
Erlikh, Vol'f, *Pravo na pesn'* (Leningrad, 1930).
Esenin, Alexander Nikitich, Letter to his son, S. A. Esenin, October 18, 1925. Copy (not the original) in the State Literary Museum, Moscow, 434/1-6.
Esenin, S. A., Letter to Anna Berzin', October 16, 1925, in the weekly *Literaturnaia Rossiia,* No. 40 (Moscow, 1965).
Forsh, Ol'ga, *Sumasshedshii korabl'* (Leningrad, 1931) [In this book, Kliuev appears under the pseudonym "Mikula"].
Leonidov, Oleg, in the newspaper *Krasnaia gazeta* (Leningrad, January 21, 1926), evening edition.
Leonov, Leonid, "Umer poet," *30 dnei,* No. 2 (Moscow, 1926).
McVay, Gordon, "The Last Days of Esenin," *Canadian Slavonic Papers,* Volume XIV, No. 3 (Ottawa, 1972) [tells of the last month of Esenin's life, and the factors contributing to his death].
McVay, Gordon, "Yesenin's Posthumous Fame, and the Fate of his Friends," *Modern Language Review,* Volume 67, No. 3 (Britain, July 1972) [This article tells of the changing fortunes of Esenin's official popularity in the Soviet Union since 1925, and the fate of his friends during

those years. The peasant poets Kliuev, Klychkov, Oreshin and Nasedkin perished during the Stalin era. Several of the women in Esenin's life died unnaturally: Galina Benislavskaia shot herself by Esenin's grave in December 1926; Isadora Duncan was killed in a car accident in Nice in September 1927; Zinaida Raikh was brutally murdered in 1939].

McVay, G., "Soviet Poets Discuss Sergey Yesenin," *The Slavonic and East European Review,* Volume XLVIII, No. 113 (London, October 1970) [The views of present-day Soviet poets about Esenin].

McVay, Gordon, "Sovetskie poety o Sergee Esenine," *Novyi zhurnal,* No. 100 (New York, 1970) [Extracts from letters of present-day Soviet poets discussing Esenin, in Russian].

McVay, Gordon, "Sergei Esenin (1895-1925): A Gallery of Rare and Unpublished Photographs," *Russian Literature Triquarterly,* No. 8 (Michigan, U.S.A., 1974) [forty-two photographs, annotated].

McVay, Gordon, "Manuscripts of Sergei Esenin," *Russian Literature Triquarterly,* No. 8 (Michigan, U.S.A., 1974) [including little-known extracts from *Strana negodiaev* and *Lenin*; and *bouts rimés* composed in 1925].

Olesha, Iury, *Ni dnia bez strochki* (Moscow, 1965).

Pil'niak, Bor., "O Sergee Esenine," *Zhurnalist,* No. 1 (Moscow, 1926).

Sadof'ev, Il'ia, "Zvonkogolosyi gost' " [1926]. Institute of World Literature, Moscow, *fond* 32, *opis'* 3, no. 34.

Sokol, Evgeny, "Odna noch' (Iz vospominanii o S. Esenine)," in the volume *Pamiati Esenina* (Moscow, 1926).

Trotsky, L., "Pamiati Sergeia Esenina," published, for example, in the volumes *Esenin. Zhizn', lichnost', tvorchestvo* (Moscow, 1926), and *Pamiati Esenina* (Moscow, 1926).

Ustinov, G., Written testimony on December 28, 1925. Institute of World Literature, Moscow, *fond* 32, *opis'* 2, no. 41.

Ustinov, G., in the newspaper *Krasnaia gazeta* (Leningrad, December 29, 1925), evening edition.

Ustinov, G., in the volume *Sergei Alexandrovich Esenin* (Moscow-Leningrad, 1926).

Ustinova, E., Typescript of memoirs. Institute of World Literature, Moscow, *fond* 32, *opis'* 3, no. 41a.

Ustinova, E., "Chetyre dnia Sergeia Alexandrovicha Esenina," in the volume *Sergei Alexandrovich Esenin* (Moscow-Leningrad, 1926).

Vol'pin, V. I. (compiler), *Pamiatka o Sergee Esenine* (Moscow, 1926) [materials about Esenin's death and funeral].

BIBLIOGRAPHY

In this selected bibliography, an asterisk indicates works not yet read by the author of this book.

Bibliographical Works

Detailed bibliographies about Sergei Esenin include:

Mordovchenko, N., *K bibliografii S. A. Esenina* (Riazan', 1927).

Vol'pin, V., and Zakharov-Mensky, N. (compilers), in the book Sergei Esenin, *Stikhi i proza,* Volume 4 (Moscow-Leningrad, 1927).

Khovriakov, N., *Sergei Alexandrovich Esenin (1895-1925). Pamiatka chitateliu* (Karaganda, 1958).

Serebriakov, V. B. (compiler), *Sergei Alexandrovich Esenin (1895-1925). Ukazatel' literatury* (Riazan', 1965).

Karpov, E. L., *S. A. Esenin. Bibliograficheskii spravochnik* (Moscow, 1966); second edition, expanded and revised (Moscow, 1972).

Iushin, P. F., *Sergei Esenin. Ideino-tvorcheskaia evoliutsiia* (Moscow, 1969), pp. 407-468.

For a survey of some of the memoirs, critical works and verse translations which have appeared in England and North America over the past half-century, see McVay, Gordon, "S. A. Esenin in England and North America. A Review Article," in *Russian Literature Triquarterly,* No. 8 (Michigan, U.S.A., 1974).

Main Editions of Esenin's Works

Sergei Esenin, *Sobranie stikhotvorenii,* in four volumes (Moscow-Leningrad, 1926-27).

Sergei Esenin, *Sobranie sochinenii,* in five volumes (Moscow, 1961-62).

Sergei Esenin, *Sobranie sochinenii,* in five volumes (Moscow, 1966-68).

Volumes

Esenin. Zhizn', lichnost', tvorchestvo (Moscow, 1926), [Articles and memoirs by E. Nikitina, S. Gorodetsky, V. Shershenevich, M. Murashov, I. Rozanov, L. Trotsky, A. Il'ina (Seferiants), F. Lutskaia, B. Rozenfel'd, B. Brainina, E. Kheraskova, L. Gorshkova; poems dedicated to Esenin and by Esenin; short bibliography].

Pamiati Esenina (Moscow, 1926), [Articles and memoirs by L. Trotsky, I. Rozanov, E. Sokol, G. Ustinov, V. Erlikh, I. Gruzinov, N. Tikhonov, I. Oksenov, M. Roizman, S. Fomin, V. Rozhdestvensky, I. Belousov,

V. Dynnik; numerous poems dedicated to Esenin; photographs].
Sergei Alexandrovich Esenin. Vospominaniia (Moscow-Leningrad, 1926), [Edited by I. Evdokimov. Memoirs by R. Ivnev, M. Babenchikov, M. Murashov, I. Startsev, N. Poletaev, V. Vol'pin, L. Fainshtein, I. Gruzinov, G. Ustinov, V. Kirillov, N. Aseev, I. Evdokimov, E. Ustinova].
* *Literaturnyi Rostov–pamiati Sergeia Esenina* (Rostov-on-Don, 1926), [Edited by P. Kofanov. Articles and memoirs by I. Berezark, L. Trotsky, Iu. Iuzovsky, N. Gratsianskaia, V. Rozhdestvensky; poems].
* *Protiv upadochnichestva, protiv eseninshchiny* (Moscow, 1926), [Contributors include G. Bergman, A. Bezymensky, G. Lelevich, Ts. Fel'dman, K. Radek, N. Semashko, I. Bobryshev].
Upadochnoe nastroenie sredi molodezhi. Eseninshchina (Moscow, 1927), [Major speech by A. Lunacharsky; shorter speeches by, among others, L. Sosnovsky, V. Polonsky, V. Maiakovsky, V. Friche, L. Leonov, K. Radek].
Vospominaniia o Sergee Esenine (Moscow, 1965), [Edited by Iu. Prokushev. Numerous memoirs, largely first published in 1926 or later; edited now with cuts].
Esenin i russkaia poeziia (Leningrad, 1967), [Valuable volume, including articles by I. Eventov, I. Pravdina, V. Zemskov, V. Vdovin; memoirs by K. Esenin and I. Markov; bibliography].
Sergei Esenin. Issledovaniia, memuary, vystupleniia (Moscow, 1967), [Mediocre volume, edited by Iu. Prokushev. Various, mostly weak, articles; poets' tributes to Esenin; memoirs].
Esenin i sovremennost' (Moscow, 1975), [Valuable publications by V. V. Bazanov and K. M. Azadovsky; memoirs by T. S. Esenina and A. B. Nikritina; various articles].

Books and Booklets

Andreev, A., *Esenin. Legenda* (Moscow, 1973).
Astakhov, V. I., *Strana berezovogo sittsa. Po eseninskim mestam Riazanshchiny* (Moscow, 1970), [illustrated booklet].
Astakhov, V.; Fral'tsov, B., *Eseninskoe Konstantinovo* (Moscow, 1974), [guide book].
Barabash, S.; Kassin, E.; Red'kin, M., *Ia bolee vsego vesnu liubliu* (Moscow, 1972), [Photographs and poems].
Beliaev, I., *Podlinnyi Esenin. Sotsial'no-psikhologicheskii etiud* (Voronezh, 1927).
Belousov, V., *Sergei Esenin* (Moscow, 1965).
Belousov, V., *Persidskie motivy* (Moscow, 1968).
Belousov, V., *Sergei Esenin. Literaturnaia khronika*, Part 1 (Moscow, 1969); Part 2 (Moscow, 1970).

Druzin, V., *Sergei Esenin* (Leningrad, 1927).
Dynnik, V., *Liricheskii roman Esenina* (Moscow, 1926), [as in the volume *Pamiati Esenina]*.
Erlikh, V., *Pravo na pesn'* (Leningrad, 1930).
Esenina, A., *Rodnoe i blizkoe. Vospominaniia* (Moscow, 1968).
Esenina, E. (compiler), *Sergei Esenin* (Moscow, 1928), [album of photographs].
Eventov, I., *Sergei Esenin* (Leningrad, 1957).
Galkina-Fedoruk, E. M., *O stile poezii Sergeia Esenina* (Moscow, 1965).
Gruzinov, I., *Esenin razgovarivaet o literature i iskusstve* (Moscow, 1927), (1926).
Kirshon, V., *Sergei Esenin* (Leningrad, 1926).
Kliuev, N., and Medvedev, P. N., *Sergei Esenin* (Leningrad, 1927), [Kliuev's poem "Plach o Sergee Esenine," and Medvedev's article "Puti i pereput'ia Sergeia Esenina"].
Konstantinov, F. D., *Sergei Esenin. Graviury* (Leningrad, 1971), [folder of eleven loose-leaf engravings].
Korzhan, V., *Esenin i narodnaia poeziia* (Leningrad, 1969).
Koshechkin, S. (compiler), *Sergei Esenin. Otchee slovo* (Moscow, 1968).
Koshechkin, S., *Sergei Esenin. Razdum'ia o poete* (Moscow, 1974).
Kravchenko, A., *Poeziia Sergeia Esenina. Material k lektsii* (Moscow, 1957).
Kruchenykh, A., *Drama Esenina,* Production No. 134 (Moscow, 1926).
Kruchenykh, A., *Gibel' Esenina (Kak Esenin prishel k samoubiistvu),* Production No. 134a and No. 134b (Moscow, 1926).
Kruchenykh, A., *Esenin i Moskva Kabatskaia,* Production No. 135a and No. 135b (Moscow, 1926).
Kruchenykh, A., *Chornaia taina Esenina,* Production No. 136 (Moscow, 1926).
Kruchenykh, A., *Liki Esenina ot kheruvima do khuligana,* Production No. 137 (Moscow, 1926).
Kruchenykh, A., *Novyi Esenin,* Production No. 138 (Moscow, 1926).
Kruchenykh, A., *Na bor'bu s khuliganstvom v literature,* Production No. 140 (Moscow, 1926), [includes section on "Prodelki esenistov"].
Kruchenykh, A., *Prodelki esenistov,* Production No. 140a (Moscow, 1926).
Kruchenykh, A., *Khuligan Esenin,* Production No. 141 (Moscow, 1926).
Kulinich, A., *Sergei Esenin* (Kiev, 1959).
Lelevich, G., *Sergei Esenin. Ego tvorcheskii put'* (Gomel', 1926).
Marchenko, A., *Poeticheskii mir Esenina* (Moscow, 1972).
Mariengof, A., *O Sergee Esenine. Vospominaniia* (Moscow, 1926), [also known as *Vospominaniia o Esenine]*.
Mariengof, A., *Roman bez vran'ia* (Leningrad, 1927) and (Leningrad, 1928).
Medvedev, P. N.–see Kliuev, N.
Nasedkin, V., *Poslednii god Esenina* (Moscow, 1927).
Naumov, E., *Sergei Esenin. Zhizn' i tvorchestvo* (Leningrad, 1960); second

edition (Moscow-Leningrad, 1965).
Naumov, E., *Sergei Esenin. Lichnost', tvorchestvo, epokha* (Leningrad, 1969); second edition (Leningrad, 1973).
Pokrovsky, G., *Esenin–eseninshchina–religiia* (Moscow, 1929) and (Moscow, 1930).
Pokrovsky, V., *Tri rechi protiv* (Leningrad, 1927).
Prokushev, Iu. L., *Sergei Esenin* (Moscow, 1958) and (Moscow, 1959).
Prokushev, Iu., *Sergei Esenin. Literaturnye zametki o detstve i iunosti poeta* (Moscow, 1960).
Prokushev, Iu., *Iunost' Esenina* (Moscow, 1963).
* Prokushev, Iu., *Sergei Esenin (Poiski, nakhodki)* (Moscow, 1968).
Prokushev, Iu. (editor), *Na rodine Esenina* (Moscow, 1969).
Prokushev, Iu., *Sergei Esenin* (Moscow, 1971).
Prokushev, Iu. L., *Sergei Esenin. Poet. Chelovek* (Moscow, 1973).
Prokushev, Iu. L., *Sergei Esenin. Obraz, stikhi, epokha* (Moscow, 1975).
Reviakin, A., *Chei poet Sergei Esenin?* (Moscow, 1926).
Roizman, M., *Vse, chto pomniu o Esenine* (Moscow, 1973).
Rozanov, I., *Esenin o sebe i drugikh* (Moscow, 1926).
Shneider, I., *Vstrechi s Eseninym. Vospominaniia* (Moscow, 1965); also (Moscow, 1974).
Vasil'kovsky, A. T., *Sergei Esenin. Ocherk tvorchestva* (Elabuga, 1960).
Verzhbitsky, N., *Vstrechi s Eseninym. Vospominaniia* (Tbilisi, 1961).
Vinogradskaia, S., *Kak zhil Sergei Esenin* (Moscow, 1926).
Vol'pin, V. I. (compiler), *Pamiatka o Sergee Esenine* (Moscow, 1926).
Yudkevich, L. G., *Liricheskii geroi Esenina* (Kazan', 1971).
Yushin, P., *Poeziia Sergeia Esenina 1910-1923 godov* (Moscow, 1966).
Yushin, P. F., *Sergei Esenin. Ideino-tvorcheskaia evoliutsiia* (Moscow, 1969).

Non-Soviet Critical Works

Auras, Christiane, *Sergej Esenin. Bilder- und Symbolwelt* (Munich, 1965).
de Graaff, Francisca, *Serge Ésénine (1895-1925). Sa vie et son oeuvre* (Leyden, 1933).
de Graaff, Frances, *Sergej Esenin. A Biographical Sketch* (The Hague, 1966).
Laffitte, Sophie, *Serge Essénine. (Une étude)* (Paris, 1959).
* Palin Crisanaz, Maria Pia, *Favola e mito nella poesia di Sergej Esenin* (Florence, 1971).
* Peshich, M. M., *Sergej Jesenin. Zhivot i delo* (Belgrade, 1957).
Varese, Marina F. Rossi, *Sergej Esenin* (Florence, 1974).
Veyrenc, Jacques, *La forme poëtique de Serge Esenin. Les rythmes* (The Hague/Paris, 1968).
* Watala, Elwira; Woroszylski, Wiktor, *Życie Sergiusza Jesienina* (Warsaw, 1973).

Film and Recordings

A piece of motion picture film survives showing Esenin on November 3, 1918, at the unveiling of a statue to the poet Kol'tsov in Moscow.

Esenin's voice may be heard on certain Soviet gramophone records, reciting, for instance, Khlopusha's monologue from *Pugachov* (II, 174) and parts of his poems "I Have Left My Native Home" ("Ia pokinul rodimyi dom," II, 70) and "The Hooligan's Confession" ("Ispoved' khuligana," II, 99-100). These recordings were made, it seems, in Moscow in January 1922, under the supervision of S. I. Bernshtein.

INDEX TO WORKS BY ESENIN DISCUSSED, MENTIONED, OR IMPLIED IN THE TEXT

The following index consists of three parts: (1) a list of the English translations used repeatedly in the text, together with the Russian original; (2) a list of Esenin's works–excluding separately published books–arranged in alphabetical order according to their Russian titles; (3) an alphabetical list of Esenin's separately published books–which includes some projected volumes.

1. ENGLISH TITLES AND THE RUSSIAN ORIGINALS

Autobiography (May 1922) – see Sergei Esenin (1922)
Autobiography (1923) – see Avtobiografiia (1923)
Autobiography (June 1924) – see Avtobiografiia (1924)
Autobiography (October 1925) – see O sebe
"Black Man, The" – Chernyi chelovek
"Celestial Drummer, The" – Nebesnyi barabanshchik
Collected Works (1926-27) – *Sobranie stikhotvorenie* (1926-27)
"Hooligan, The" – Khuligan
"Hooligan's Confession, The" (poem) – *Ispoved' khuligana*
Hooligan's Confession, The (book) – *Ispoved' khuligana*
"Hooligan's Love, A" (cycle) – Liubov' khuligana
"I'm not regretting, calling, or weeping" – Ne zhaleiu, ne zovu, ne plachu...
"I'm the Last Poet of the Village" – "Ia poslednii poet derevni..."
"Iron Mirgorod, The" – Zheleznyi Mirgorod
"I shall not caress..." – see "Ne stanu nikakuiu..."
"Jackdaws, The" (undiscovered poem) –Galki
"Keys of Mary, The" – Kliuchi Marii
"Land of Scoundrels, The" – Strana negodiaev
"Life and Art" – Byt i iskusstvo
"Moscow of the Taverns" (cycle) – Moskva kabatskaia
Moscow of the Taverns (book) – Moskva kabatskaia
"My Life" – Moi put'
"My soul yearns for the heavens" – "Dusha grustit o nebesakh..."
"Mysterious World, My Ancient World" – "Mir tainstvennyi, mir moi drevnii..."
"Persian Motifs" (cycle) – Persidskie motivy
Persian Motifs (book) – see *Persidskie motivy*
"Play, Accordion. Boredom... Boredom..." – see "Syp', garmonika. Skuka... Skuka"
"Prophet, The" (inextant drama) – Prorok
"Return Home" – see "Vozvrashchenie na rodinu"
"Sister, sing me the song that old mother..." – "Ty zapoi mne tu pesniu, chto..."
"Song of the Great Campaign" – Pesn' o velikom pokhode
"Soviet Rus' " (poem) – Rus' sovetskaia
Soviet Rus' (book) – *Rus' sovetskaia*
Transfiguration (book) – *Preobrazhenie*
Village Prayer Book, A (book) – *Sel'skii chasoslov*

2. WORKS IN ALPHABETICAL ORDER BY THEIR RUSSIAN TITLES

BOOKS ARRANGED IN ALPHABETICAL ORDER BY RUSSIAN TITLES

SUBJECT INDEX